Christopher A. deVargas
6658 Youree Dr. Ste. 180 PMB 345
Shreveport, LA  71105

MW01025763

# JUSTICE DENIED

How the Federal Court System
Failed Former Louisiana Insurance
Commissioner Jim Brown

## James H. Brown, Jr.

The Lisburn Press
www.LisburnPress.com

PUBLISHED IN THE UNITED STATES OF AMERICA

Visit our website at LisburnPress.com

First edition published September 2004

*Cover design by Sarah Powell*

**Library of Congress Cataloging-in-Publication Data is available.**

ISBN: 1-4184-1801-3 (e)
ISBN: 1-4184-1800-5 (sc)
ISBN: 1-4184-1799-8 (dj)

For information regarding special discounts for bulk purchases, please
contact The Lisburn Press Special Sales at info@LisburnPress.com.

*Printed in Canada*

*This book is printed on acid-free paper.*

Photo Credits: Unless otherwise credited, all photos are from the author's
collection, the Louisiana Department of Insurance, and the Louisiana
Secretary of State's Office.

Special acknowledgement to those people who assisted in editing and formation of this book. They include Helen Smith, Rannah Gray, Ruth Laney, Sharon Paul and Kim Springfield.

TO MY FATHER:

<u>JAMES H. BROWN, SR.</u>
He was the most decent man I've ever known,
and was always my strongest supporter.

# Preface

The diary entries in the pages that follow are my account of the six-year struggle I faced in opposing the federal government's effort to unjustly convict me of false criminal charges. But the book tells much more, including stories about my public and political life over the past forty years. This is neither an autobiography nor a comprehensive history of my public life. It is more of a personal narrative; thoughts I recorded each day as events unfolded. I talk about how my family and I responded to the pressures of the false charges; how an incumbent public official could be reelected after he was blindsided by a 56-count indictment just a few weeks before the election; what I went through in building the Louisiana Insurance Department virtually from scratch, and why insurance companies worldwide have been attracted to Louisiana. I also talk about the trial itself, and the devastating effect it had on my family and me. I discuss the aftermath of the trial, including the appeals process, and the massive commitment of time and money I made, trying to keep from going to jail while hoping to win my appeal.

I believe that experience—mistakes made and lessons learned—sets the foundation for future decisions. I have always felt that one can learn a lot from past events. That's why, for many years, I have kept a diary of my daily activities. My notations were originally intended for my own reference and remembrance, with no thought of publication. I reread random sections of my journal from time to time, reinforcing past decisions or sometimes second-guessing them. It has just made good sense for me to look back, with an eye to the future. As Santayana said, "Those who cannot remember the past are condemned to repeat it." My journal has been an invaluable aid in remembering the events that transpired over the past seven years. (Seven years! Who could have imagined that a fairly routine insurance decision would have consumed me for so long a period of time).

This is my first book, but I have always enjoyed putting words to paper. One of my University of North Carolina roommates, Jonathan Yardley, was the editor of the student newspaper *The Daily Tarheel.*[1]

---

[1] Jonathan has for many years been book editor of the *Washington Post*.

He talked me into writing a weekly column on university life; that was my first published work.

For years I have jotted down anecdotes and observations of political life in Louisiana. In the late 1980s, I turned this material into a series of lectures on twentieth-century Louisiana political history, and I taught courses at both Tulane University in New Orleans and Louisiana State University in Baton Rouge. Some of that history is included in this book as background.

But in the end, this book is my personal narrative of what my family and I went through as I warded off the unjust, false charges brought against me.

I am a survivor!

I can only hope that few other American citizens have to go through what I endured during the past seven years.

# Introduction

"When did you first decide that you wanted to be involved in public life?"

I've been asked that question hundreds of times.

Some people know early on that they want a career in public office, but I had already finished college by the time the first seeds of interest were sown. Events that were happening halfway around the world played a significant role in my coming to politics—or should I say that politics came to me.

In 1962, as I was finishing my senior year at the University of North Carolina in Chapel Hill, I wasn't sure what I wanted to do with my life. One of my mentors was Dr. Sam Hill, the head of the religion department, upon whom I often called for counsel. Having attended Cambridge University in England, Dr. Hill suggested that I consider a one-year sabbatical in Great Britain, which would give me more time to decide about the future.

I had attended Carolina on an athletic scholarship, recruited by the now legendary basketball coach Dean Smith. I had received scholarship offers in both track and basketball from schools throughout the country, including the University of Southern California, the University of Virginia, and Southern Methodist University.

Dean Smith had just been hired away from the Air Force Academy to be an assistant to Carolina head coach Frank McGuire. It was common knowledge that Smith was being groomed to be McGuire's successor.

In the spring of 1958, I was finishing up my senior year at Ladue High School in the suburbs of St. Louis, Missouri. I was called to the principal's office and told that a Mr. Dean Smith was there to see me. While his family waited in an older-model Chevrolet with a U-haul trailer hooked to the back, Coach Smith told me that he was on his way to Chapel Hill to begin his new coaching career. He had been asked by the coaching staff at Carolina to stop by and recruit me. And in his mild mannered but persuasive way, it didn't take him long to convince me that Chapel Hill should be my new home

I did go to Chapel Hill, but I ended up being a much better sprinter and hurdler than a basketball player. But even though my premier sport was track, I can legitimately lay claim to being the first basketball recruit Dean Smith ever brought to Carolina. He went on to become the winningest coach in the history of college basketball. We still cross paths every year or so, and I never fail to remind him that his two most important recruits were his first (me) and some other fellow who came along years later named Michael Jordan.

While I was at Carolina, track allowed me to travel throughout the country. I was fortunate to be the Atlantic Coast Conference champion in both the high and low hurdles, and I also ran on numerous winning relay teams at major meets throughout the country. I suppose my biggest college victory was at the Carolinas A.A.U. national track meet in 1963, where I beat world record holder Ellis Gilbert in the low hurdles and just missed setting a world record myself.

My application to attend Cambridge University was accepted, and I was also invited to join the U.S. track team that was touring Europe during the summer and fall of 1962. I headed to England on Icelandic Airlines (the cheapest way to get to Europe) with my track shoes, about four hundred dollars in cash, and a bundle of enthusiasm for what I hoped would be an enjoyable year abroad.

The highlight of the summer for me was being the leadoff runner on the American 400-meter relay team, where I handed off the baton to the world's fastest human, "Bullet Bob" Hayes. He was the world record holder in the 100-yard dash. Our relay team also included Ralph Boston who was the world record holder in the broad jump and Paul Warfield who went on to have a successful professional football career with the Philadelphia Eagles. We competed several times a week in major cities throughout Europe, and we never lost a race.

Strangely enough, my track career led to the first significant political crisis I ever faced. We had a two-week break in the schedule, and the American team was going to vacation in various parts of Europe, then regroup in Bremerhaven, Germany, for our next official competition.

A meet promoter approached me to run in East Berlin during the break. The promoter assured me that I would receive full expenses and appropriate prizes. There was no professional track in the 1960s, but the better runners could negotiate for their prize – a clock radio, a T.V. set, maybe a refrigerator, all of which could be cashed in after the meet.

I had never been to East Germany, and I figured if the promoter was willing to cover the expenses of a struggling student runner, why not go for it.

I had the honor of being a member of the U.S. Track team in 1962, competing against countries throughout Europe.

The Berlin Wall was still standing, and America did not recognize East Germany as a legitimate country. It was considered a Russian puppet state, and the U.S. maintained no diplomatic relations with the country. Once you crossed to the other side of the wall, you were on your own.

On the afternoon of the track meet, I crossed the border from West Berlin at Checkpoint Charlie, along with the agent who had arranged for me to run in the meet. (He also served as my interpreter.) It was an evening meet, and I was scheduled to compete in the high hurdles against an East German who was world ranked. The East Germans had built up the competition as a grudge match between our two countries and made it a point of honor for their national pride.

Our team had been competing several times a week, but the break had given me a lengthy rest from the grind of competition. I felt extra spring in my legs and anticipated a good run and victory over the East German.

The 100-meter dash was about to begin when my agent brought over an American who wanted to talk to me. He did not fully identify himself, but he said he was with the American Embassy in West Germany. He told me in strong terms that it would be completely unacceptable for me to run the high-hurdles race that was about to start. As a member of the American team, he argued, I was a representative of my government. Since America did not recognize

East Germany, I would be giving tacit recognition to a country that the United States felt was illegitimate. He implied that by competing I could start an international incident; if I had any patriotism, I would get my gear and head back across the border to West Berlin immediately.

What a dilemma for a twenty-one-year-old who was simply enjoying the opportunity to travel and had no real understanding of the international consequences supposedly at stake. I wanted to run, but I certainly was not going to go against the wishes of my country. So I gathered my warm-ups and had the interpreter tell the meet promoter that I was not going to run.

As the announcement was being made that I would not compete, I headed for the locker rooms, which were located at the other end of the stadium, diagonally across the infield. Thousands of people in the stadium stood up and whistled loudly, which was their way of booing. I learned later that the announcer had told the crowd the American was afraid to compete against the East German. I was angry and disappointed, but I had enough common sense to change my clothes and get back across the border.

Many years later, I would look back on this controversy as my first political act. I guess the possibility of starting an international incident certainly qualifies as a baptism in politics.

After finishing up my European tour with the American team, I headed back to England to start the fall semester at Cambridge. I read (the British term for studying or majoring in) English literature and attended lectures by such British authors as Kingsley Amis, C.P. Snow, T.E. White, and many other writers whose works I had read at Carolina. From breakfast seminars to daytime lectures to afternoon readings to evening tutorials, I was immersed in English literature. Politics was the furthest thing from my mind—that is, until the Cuban missile crisis.

I had rented a room in the house of an English family who lived a few blocks from the Cambridge campus. Mrs. Davenport, the lady of the house, awakened me at 2:00 A.M. on October 22, 1962. She said a neighbor had just called and told her to turn on the radio to hear a major press conference by President John F. Kennedy.

It was an extremely cold morning, and there was no central heating in the house, so I grabbed a blanket off my bed, threw it around me, and went downstairs to the living room. A fire was going in the fireplace, and the Davenport family had gathered around the radio. President Kennedy was just beginning his remarks.

*Good evening, my fellow citizens. This government, as promised, has maintained the closest surveillance of the Soviet military buildup on the island of Cuba. Within the past week, unmistakable evidence has established the fact that a series of offensive missile sites is now in preparation on that imprisoned island. The purpose of these bases can be none other than to provide a nuclear strike capability against the Western hemisphere.*

Picking up the milkman's daily delivery outside of the home where I rented a room during my stay at Cambridge University in 1962.

The President then announced a naval blockade of Cuba, which he called a "quarantine." He made it clear that any ship bound for Cuba that was carrying offensive missiles, or any other military hardware, would be stopped and turned back. He continued:

*It shall be the policy of this nation to regard any nuclear missile launched from Cuba against any nation in the Western Hemisphere as an attack by the Soviet Union on the United States, requiring a full retaliatory response on the Soviet Union. And any hostile move by the Russians anywhere in the world against the safety and freedom of peoples to whom we are committed, including in particular the brave people of West Berlin, would be met with action.*[2]

[2] John F. Kennedy, *Public Papers of the Presidents of the United States*. (Washington: U.S. Government Printing Office 1960-63).

As he ended his speech, the neighbors from next door joined us in the living room. I was not sure how serious the matter was, but there was no doubt in the minds of my British hosts, who had lived the day-in, day-out horror of two world wars; they believed that we were on the brink of another world war, and they were devastated. The women in the room were crying. Eventually, everyone turned to me and asked why the President would want to start such hostility over a minor island south of Florida. I had no idea how to respond.

The next day several members of the Cambridge Union, the local debating society, approached me. They had sought me out because I was one of very few Americans at Cambridge. They wanted to have a full airing of America's position on the Cuban crisis, and they requested that I speak on behalf of the United States. I protested that I wasn't well versed in American foreign policy, and that they really should find someone else. But they said no one else was available and they hoped I would have the courage to stand up for my country.

I knew I was in over my head, and I needed help. The only place I could think of was the American Embassy in London; maybe someone there could give me some background information about why the blockade was necessary. After a ninety-minute train ride, I was in London by mid-day.

It was about forty degrees, much colder than usual for October in London, as I made my way on foot up Grosvenor Square toward the Embassy. I was surprised to see several thousand protesters outside the diplomatic compound, and hundreds of British policemen surrounding the Embassy. Chants of "Get out of Cuba!" and "American imperialism!" reverberated through the crowd.

I pushed my way to the gates of the Embassy and identified myself to the military guard as an American citizen. I was asked for my passport, which I did not have with me, but my Louisiana driver's license was proof enough, and I was allowed to go through the gates.

At the information desk inside, an Embassy official asked my business. "I really could use some help," I said, explaining that I was an American studying English literature at Cambridge University. "I've been challenged to debate some Brits at the Cambridge Union this evening, and defend America's position of blockading Cuba. Quite frankly, I am not that well versed in our foreign policy, and I'm really in over my head. Can you help me?"

An Embassy staffer gave me a verbal briefing and a little background information. It is an understatement to say that I was lost in the forest of international conflict.

When I spoke up for the American position and tried to defend my country that evening, I was hissed and booed by an overwhelming majority of the crowd. The Russians had stated that the only missiles in Cuba were "defensive," and that America was the villain. Try as I might, I could not convince the Brits any differently. I was up against several other speakers who rattled off numerous dates, events, and consequences of World War II and the Cold War. They were well versed in the politics of the day, and I was obviously less than qualified to be my country's sole defending voice.

For the second time in just a few months, I was put down in my attempt to support or defend the United States. I was getting quite a baptism in international politics, but these difficult experiences were not enough to keep me from political life in the years to come.

Over the next 40 years, numerous other confrontations would shape my political life, which encompassed a country law practice in northeast Louisiana, eight years as a state senator, two terms as secretary of state, a futile run for governor (against incumbent Edwin Edwards in 1997), and finally the role of commissioner of insurance, the public office that seemed to best suit my strengths and abilities.

This was a position that let me thrive, where I could build a major state department almost from scratch, directly affect the lives of every Louisiana citizen, and have an impact on financial decisions that affected companies worldwide.

Commissioner of Insurance seemed like the natural spot for me. When I took office in 1991, I never imagined the roller coaster of highs and lows that would eventually lead me into the singular major crisis of my life. Simply put, I was convicted of a crime I did not commit.

As I have read over my diary entries from that time, two precepts stayed with me. First, I accept the fact that most of us face major stumbling blocks in our lifetimes, and that bad things often happen to good people. President Kennedy said it bluntly in a 1962 news conference when asked about army reservists who were opposed to being recalled to active duty: "There is always inequity in life. Some men are killed in War and some men are wounded, and some men never leave the country. Life is unfair. "[3]

I'm sure we all agree with that conclusion. The question for me was how to handle the unfairness, the adversity.

Prophets, philosophers and political leaders through the ages have told us that we should not accept life's unfairness, the dictates of fate, but should object to any injustice, particularly false accusation. In *The First Dissident*, William Safire writes of an innocent and angry sufferer:

> *There's no justice on earth guaranteed from on high. But there is a morality that we work out, as best we can, for ourselves and each other. That morality begins with the obligation to hold fast to our integrity—in Job's phrase, "to maintain my ways"—by protesting injustice against all the odds, no matter how distant and remote its source may seem.*[4]

The message I've tried to convey in this book is that I did not accept the dictates of fate but objected to the injustice thrown at me. I never hesitated to express my moral outrage and opposition to the overwhelming power of the federal prosecutors.

I've had a sign on the wall of my office since this ordeal began: Illegitimus non-carborundum. (Don't let the bastards grind you down.)[5]

Do not hesitate to defy the powers that be when you are being abused and know you have done nothing wrong. This is my story of how I survived the biggest single crisis I am sure I will ever face. But I wanted to do more than just survive; in Faulkner's words, I wanted to not merely endure but to prevail.[6]

My effort to "prevail" is still under way.

---

[3] Ibid.

[4] Safire, William. *The First Dissident: The Book of Job in Today's Politics*, Random House, NY 1992.

[5] The phrase apparently originated with British Army Intelligence early in World War II. It was popularized when U.S. General Joseph W. "Vinegar Joe" Sidwell (1883-1946) adopted it as his motto.

[6] William Faulkner, Nobel Prize Speech, Stockholm, Sweden, December 10, 1950.

# The Charges

*Someone must have slandered Joseph K., for without having done*
*anything wrong he was arrested one fine morning.*
                                        Franz Kafka, *The Trial*

## Friday, September 24, 1999
## Baton Rouge. Louisiana

The call came in around 10:30 A.M. from Brad Myers, a contract attorney for the insurance department.

"Jim, I'm over at the federal courthouse, and I have bad news. You were just indicted. Fifty-six counts."

I sat there stunned, in my office chair staring blankly at the wall. At first, the full impact didn't register. Then it started to sink in.

"Tell me what you know, Brad. What am I charged with?"

He quickly summarized a series of allegations that included conspiracy, insurance fraud, witness tampering, and making false statements to federal officials, all related to Cascade Insurance Company.

"You've got to be kidding!" I protested. "The biggest crook in America doesn't get 56 counts. What on earth are they trying to do to me?"

"I'm getting a copy of the charges now," Brad said. "It's massive, 47 pages. I'll try to have it over to you in the next hour."

The election date for insurance commissioner was only a month away. Brad is a former federal prosecutor, so I felt he would know.

"Have you ever heard of a statewide elected official being charged like this right before an election?" I asked.

"Never," said Brad. "It just doesn't happen. I'm sorry."

I hung up the phone and resumed staring at the wall. I was so shaken by the bad news, I hadn't even asked who else was charged.

Allan Pursnell, one of my deputy commissioners, walked in with additional news. "I just got a call from the Associated Press. They found out about the charges and want your reaction." Allan told me that five other people had been indicted with me— former governor Edwin Edwards, former district judge Foxy Sanders, Shreveport attorney Ron Weems, receiverships director Bob Bourgeois, and

1

David Disiere of Shreveport, an insurance executive and owner of Cascade Insurance Company.

I told Allan I needed some time before talking to the AP. I wanted to call my wife Gladys. And I wasn't about to give a statement until I could collect my wits, think it through, and try to make some sense of what had just happened to me.

I had just been indicted!

# 1996

**Louisiana State Capitol**

**Tuesday, May 28, 1996**
**Baton Rouge, Louisiana**

Ron Weems had called my office earlier in the week and asked for a meeting to discuss a Louisiana insurance company called Cascade. I had very little firsthand information about the company, but I vaguely remembered that there was some relationship with an Oregon company. Several years earlier, an Oregon insurance regulator had visited with me briefly at a national meeting of insurance commissioners. Apparently, there were problems to be resolved between the two companies, and I told him my staff would be in touch. That was the last I remember hearing about the company until Ron Weems asked to see me.

Ron was a Shreveport attorney who had supported me politically in past elections, going back to the time I served as secretary of state. He was in my office from time to time representing various insurance clients that had regulatory issues before the insurance department. He had a reputation as one of the top business attorneys in the state.

Cascade had not been selling insurance in Louisiana for a good while. In fact, at the time of Ron's call, the company was under the control of the insurance department. When any insurance company fails to pay its claims, or does not have enough capital and surplus (money in the bank or other assets) to meet minimum state requirements, then by law, the company is taken over by my regulatory office. Like every other state in the country, Louisiana's insurance department has a receiverships section that oversees troubled insurance companies. Cascade had been under the control of the receiverships section since 1992.

Cascade had previously been located in Texas and was originally taken over by the Texas insurance department. But it had sold automobile insurance policies in Louisiana, and more than two thousand Louisiana policyholders had claims against Cascade in 1992. Under Texas law at that time, these Louisiana citizens would not receive one penny, since any moneys held by Texas would go to pay only Texas citizens.

To solve the problem, my staff suggested that we allow the company to be "re-domesticated" or moved from Texas to Louisiana by joint agreement of both states. That way, Louisiana law would apply, and these Louisiana citizens would get their claims paid. It just made good sense to protect Louisiana policyholders.

The insurance departments of Texas and Louisiana jointly agreed to send Cascade back to Louisiana, and a Baton Rouge district-court judge approved the transaction. Our department then began the orderly process of gathering various assets of the company, and reviewing numerous claims so that Louisiana citizens could get paid.

At the time the company was taken over by Texas in the early 1990s, a Shreveport insurance executive named David Disiere was running it. I did not know Disiere at the time, and our paths would not cross until several years later.

Cascade was not the only insurance company that was being closed down by the receiverships division. In the mid-1990s, my office had taken over and shut down more than 80 insurance companies. In fact, during my first 18 months in office as commissioner of insurance, the department shut down the largest number of insurance companies in our state's history. To understand why so many companies were shut down, a little history will help.

I had won a hotly contested election for the state's top insurance post in the 1991 regular statewide election, in which Edwin Edwards was elected to his fourth term as governor. The newly elected attorney general was a Lake Charles district attorney named Richard Ieyoub. Both would later play prominent roles in the Cascade controversy.

I had defeated a number of challengers, including former insurance commissioner Sherman Bernard. He had held the office for 16 years until 1997, when newcomer Doug Green, who had run as a reformer, defeated him.

Green's stay in office was short-lived. He was indicted halfway through his term for taking kickbacks from the principals in one of the largest insurance debacles in state history, Champion Insurance Company. Green was sentenced to 25 years in jail and is still serving his sentence in a federal prison in Florida.

Sherman Bernard was later convicted of insurance fraud for federal crimes involving giving insurance licenses in return for campaign contributions during his last term in office in the 1980s. After pleading guilty in 1993, he served more than two years in a federal prison in Montgomery, Alabama.

Since Green was already in jail, there was no elected insurance commissioner in office in 1991. Statewide officials normally take the oath of office in January for a four-year term. Because of the vacancy created by Green, I was sworn in as Louisiana's insurance commissioner a month early, on December 3, 1991. It is an understatement to say that I was unprepared for the mess I found when I walked in the door. In short, I faced a disaster.

Insurance companies, quite simply, were not being regulated. Thousands of claims owed to policyholders were unpaid. A number of insurance companies were broke and should have been shut down years earlier.

The insurance department was woefully understaffed, and, with some exceptions, numerous employees were untrained for the jobs they were doing. Although there were approximately two thousand insurance companies operating in Louisiana, only one certified financial examiner was working for the insurance department to keep tabs on these companies. And he was an unindicted coconspirator in a major insurance-fraud case!

It was obvious I was going to have to rebuild the department from scratch, do extensive training, beef up the staff, and undertake a major audit of every insurance company operating in the state.

On top of the corruption and incompetence, I found that many legitimate insurance companies throughout the country were shying away from Louisiana. They just did not want to do business in a state where the insurance department had such a bad reputation.

Other forces were at work that was causing major complications for Louisiana's business community. The cost of workman's compensation insurance was increasing at a dramatic rate—almost 20 percent per year. There were no companies wanting to sell insurance that would protect Louisiana workers. The day I took office, there was only one private company selling workman's-compensation insurance in the state.

Smaller Louisiana companies,[7] many of which were not paying claims filed by Louisiana policyholders were selling auto insurance. Literally hundreds of complaints were coming in weekly against a number of small Louisiana auto insurers. The pattern of complaints

---

[7] Small Louisiana insurance companies that specialize in auto insurance are referred to as "non-standard" insurers. In the past, these companies were allowed to start up a new business with as little as $300,000 in assets. Under new rules I instituted, no group wanting to start a new auto insurance company would be given consideration without having on hand at least $5 million in capital and surplus.

told me at once that many of these companies were in serious financial difficulty.

Under Louisiana law, each insurance company was required to file an annual financial statement as well as quarterly reports on its financial condition. I found that many companies were not filing anything. Reports that were filed often went unchecked. In fact, during my first complete tour of the insurance department building, I opened a closet door to find hundreds of unopened financial statements still in their envelopes. A financial examiner with the department had reviewed not one of these financial reports. In short, there was no way of knowing the financial condition of many of the insurance companies doing business in Louisiana.

I tried to identify the few competent people in the office, and I brought in a number of new young employees, many just out of college. I brought in experts from throughout the country to institute crash-training programs in the area of financial solvency and other regulatory fields.

Mississippi Insurance Commissioner George Dale (left) was always there
to lend assistance to our office from the very beginning.

Insurance is the only financial industry that is regulated on a state-by-state basis. The Office of the Comptroller of the Currency regulates banks in Washington, D.C. The Securities and Exchange Commission regulates stocks, bonds, and other securities.

The National Association of Insurance Commissioners (NAIC) coordinates insurance activities nationally. Fortunately, this association was able to identify key regulators who would be willing to come to Louisiana, and quickly train my staff in the more sophisticated areas of insurance regulation.

I was grateful to have a number of commissioners volunteer to help, both by sending key employees into our State and by coming themselves. Commissioner George Dale of Mississippi, the longest-serving insurance commissioner in the country, was particularly helpful. He and his staff made numerous trips to Baton Rouge and offered advice, training, and regular encouragement. A number of other commissioners from the southeastern states were available on short notice to help me train the new employees we were bringing on board.

The results came quickly. About the time I took office, the NAIC put a new program into place, requiring a complete audit and review of every insurance department in the county. A certification process was instituted wherein a team of examiners reviewed the regulatory operations of each state. Thanks to a concentrated effort on the part of a recommitted and retrained staff, Louisiana became one of the first states certified under the new program. Virtually everyone involved in the regulatory process—the insurance industry, other state regulators, and all of us in the department—were pleasantly surprised that we could improve so quickly and become certified.

Our work really began after a whole new series of procedures was put into place. We started a systematic review of every insurance company doing business in Louisiana. First came the auto companies, because most of the complaints we received were against them. The initial news was not good. In the first year and a half I was in office, the department shut down 32 companies that sold auto insurance. They simply did not have enough money in reserve to pay the numerous claims coming in. These companies were bringing in new premiums every day from current policyholders. But the test we applied was simple: if a company was using today's premium income to pay yesterday's claims, they were broke and in violation of the law. I had no choice but to shut them down.

My staff at the Insurance Department is pictured with me receiving an award for being one of the top Insurance Departments in the country. The National Association of Insurance Commissioners presented this award at their annual meeting in 1992.

A number of insurance companies aggressively fought our efforts to take them over, even though it was obvious that they didn't have the money to pay the numerous claims coming in. Often the companies hired high-priced law firms to fight the insurance department every step of the way. Charges were often levied in court that I was overly aggressive, and that there was no justification for allowing the department to step in and shut down the company. Some of these legal challenges were pursued all the way up to the Louisiana Supreme Court, but our actions were always upheld.

Sometimes the challenges went beyond the legal system.

I had appointed a team of investigators and accountants to go to New Orleans with a "cease and desist" order on one company that my staff had concluded was broke and could no longer stay in business. The team was to gather all the financial records and make an internal evaluation of the status of the company. When we arrived, the company's doors were locked. We identified ourselves as being from the Department of Insurance; from behind the locked door an employee said they would have to find an officer of the company to let us in. After 30 minutes of waiting, I directed my staff to knock down the door and begin their work. We had called in backup—some Louisiana State Troopers— to be sure the law was followed.

When my staff entered the offices, they found employees back in the kitchen putting various computer tapes in the microwave oven to melt them down. There was obviously a major effort under way to destroy key financial records.

When a search was made of the office, a stack of tapes was found that contained recordings of several meetings involving principals and consultants of the company. The tapes revealed plans for a lot more than assembling a legal team to oppose our efforts. The following transcribed conversation was delivered to me shortly after the company was seized.

*Then you are going out of business.*

*Let me see if they think it is so unpleasureable to come in and liquidate our company. I will put four million dollars in the bank trust account for our defense. In other words, smart aleck, you want to liquidate the company, let me see you liquidate it. We are going to fight you. We have got a trust account with four million dollars. The quicker you want to resolve this thing, the quicker this four million dollars goes back in the company that is solid.*

*It turns into World War Nine, but the objective is not to have them say, "Let's see what we can do at this basic level." My motto has always been "You kill my cat, I kill yours." I prefer not to do that if I don't have to. You know that is a fine welcome to my world if you want to do it that way. That is my pleasure.*

*We want to let them know, if push comes to shove we want to let them know that we will not tolerate it. This is no [expletive]fairy tale.*

*You give me a blank check and let me go kill somebody. We are going to bury them. If they try to hurt us, our families, and our employees, we are going to bury them. You see I am not hasty. You see I am not jumpy. I will go where we have to go, I will be calm. We will shut our mouths, we will use our pros and then we will [expletive] with you.*

10

Was this a direct threat on my life and the lives of my staff? I don't know. The tapes were turned over to federal and state law enforcement, and the principals of this company all ended up going to jail.

It was satisfying to see the bad guys punished, and it was also good to see that our efforts to rebuild the department and crack down on insurance fraud was recognized in the media.

The *Ville Platte Gazette* wrote:

> *"Brown has shut down 36 fly-by-night insurance companies, sent many dirty (insurance) dealers to jail, sued a host of people and continues to shake up the once notorious Louisiana insurance industry."*[8]

The *Shreveport Times* said:

> *"Brown has ordered teams of Insurance Department examiners to conduct annual audits of all Louisiana-based insurance companies. The goal: locate unhealthy firms before they become yet another high-priced statistic on taxpayers' rate cards."*[9]

The *Journal of Commerce* noted:

> *"Louisiana's new insurance commissioner is making good on his promise to clean house. Rather than take on a few problem companies with shaky finances, Jim Brown last week ordered a special team of examiners to do solvency audits on each and every insurance company domiciled in Louisiana."*[10]

The *Caldwell Watchman* wrote:

---

[8] *The Ville Platte Gazette,* August 18, 1994.
[9] *The Shreveport Times,* June 13, 1992.
[10] *The Journal of Commerce,* March 10, 1992.

11

*"Brown inherited an office, which was riddled with years of prior corruption. Brown has taken an aggressive stand with the insurance companies that do business here. Brown's actions have shown those companies that if they don't have the strength, the honesty, or the ability to do business here, they need to leave or they will be closed down."*[11]

The *Baton Rouge Advocate* said:

*"Brown's changes have helped turn Louisiana from a state with a tarnished image to one that appears to be headed in the right direction, said insurance industry representatives."*[12]

And finally, these comments ran in *Best's Review,* a respected national insurance magazine:

*"There is an integrity and respectability about Louisiana's insurance department that wasn't there before Brown," says Dennis Jay of the Coalition Against Insurance Fraud, Washington, D.C. Tom Oglesby, executive vice president of the Independent Insurance Agents of Louisiana, calls Brown's work "forthright and courageous." He says Brown "didn't just rebuild the insurance department, he built the department."*[13]

In short, my office had made significant progress in my first two years on the job. I hoped to have a calmer regulatory environment in the years to come.

When Ron Weems called me in May 1996, Cascade Insurance Company had been shut down and was under the direct control of the receiverships division of the insurance department. Ron told me that he represented David Disiere, the owner of Cascade. Both Ron and Disiere knew that even though the insurance department had taken

---

[11] *The Caldwell Watchman,* July 28, 1993.
[12] *The Advocate,* January 24, 1993.
[13] *Best's Review,* October 1994, p. 26.

over Cascade, Disiere still had a financial obligation under Louisiana law to be sure that every policyholder was paid and that all debts owed by the company were satisfied; otherwise, my office could sue Disiere for whatever money he owed.

The purpose of Ron's visit was to complain about the lack of information and cooperation he and Disiere were getting from the receiverships division. According to Ron, Disiere had continually stated that there was enough money and other assets available in Cascade to pay off all debts.

Unfortunately, the insurance department did not have direct control over the receiverships division. Virtually, all final decisions made by the Receiverships division had to be approved by a Baton Rouge judge in the 19th Judicial District Court. The judge in charge of the Cascade estate was A. Foster "Foxy" Sanders, who was finishing his final year of a six-year term in office.

Former United States Attorney Stan Bardwell (left) was my pick to head up the division in the Department of Insurance that shut down financially troubled insurance companies.

Previously, settlements and other financial decisions had been worked out in negotiations among the receiverships division of the insurance department, the attorney general's office, and the various other parties involved. Documents would be drawn up and presented for approval to a specific judge of the 19th Judicial

13

District Court. But this was not the way Foxy Sanders operated.

Sanders became involved and enmeshed in every detail of the receiverships division. No one was hired or fired without his approval. He became a part of virtually every decision made. For all practical purposes, he ran the receiverships division, which was contrary to Louisiana law.

In 1995, I had selected to head the receiverships division a former United States Attorney for the Middle District of Louisiana, Stanford O. Bardwell. In shutting down insurance companies and suing insurance executives, my office, by its nature, excited a great deal of controversy. I wanted to send out a strong signal that the office would be run fairly, efficiently, and without favoritism. I felt that Stan Bardwell was the man to help me send this message. He was a Republican, but that made no difference to me. There was no questioning his competence and integrity. By hiring Stan, I was signaling the insurance industry that there was a level playing field where companies would be treated fairly and strict standards would be upheld. I told Stan to keep me posted, but I was not going to interfere with his daily operations. He would run the show.

Obviously, this conflicted with the "hands-on" approach of Foxy Sanders. These two strong-minded individuals clashed repeatedly, and Sanders began an effort to push Stan aside. Although Sanders had no legal authority to do so, he brought in his lifelong friend Bob Bourgeois to replace Stan Bardwell.

One of the purposes of Ron Weems' visit was to complain about Sanders' heavy-handedness. Weems hoped that the insurance department would confront Sanders and raise questions about how he regularly overstepped his authority.

I told Ron that I agreed that Sanders was obstinate and uncooperative, but he would be leaving the bench in a few months, and I hoped a more reasonable judge would replace him. That was really the only encouragement I could give Ron and David Disiere in May 1996.

## Monday, August 19, 1996
## Baton Rouge, Louisiana

In the late afternoon, I checked my phone messages and saw that Edwin Edwards had called. The former governor was now practicing law in Baton Rouge, with his office just a few buildings away from Semolina's Restaurant, one of a chain owned by my wife, Gladys and her twin sister Gloria Carter. Edwards goes to the restaurant sometimes with his new wife Candy, and I occasionally run into him on the block when I go to Semolina's for lunch. Even though he has retired from public life after four terms as Louisiana's governor, Edwards stays abreast of political activities on the state and local levels. He certainly has been the best source of political gossip in the state.

I returned his call, and he came right to the point. "Look, what can you tell me about Cascade Insurance Company?"

It was not unusual for former and current public officials to call me about various insurance matters. I've had calls from most of the former governors, including John McKeithen and Dave Treen. Former Lieutenant Governor Jimmy Fitzmorris calls from time to time. So do a host of legislators, former judges, and other public officials. If I can't answer their questions, I put them in touch with someone in my department, and we solve the problem if we can. I told the former governor that my knowledge was limited. I mentioned my meeting with Ron Weems several months earlier, and the fact that David Disiere was going to have to convince the receiverships division that all the claims and obligations of Cascade would get paid. Otherwise, he was going to have to financially stand behind anything that was owed. "But my office is really not in charge," I told him. "Foxy Sanders has taken direct, hands-on control of this and other companies in receivership, and he is calling the shots. He will have to sign off on any final agreement to bring this matter to an end for Disiere."

The governor told me he had been retained by David Disiere to work with Ron Weems and try to settle the matter. He obviously had little information himself and was trying to learn what problems Disiere faced.

"You know just about everything I know now," I said, after giving him what little background information I had. "A number of lawyers have told me that Sanders is being awfully hard to deal with. You supported him in his election, so maybe you can have a civil discussion with him. That's about all I can tell you. Good luck."

The governor told me he would keep me posted on any developments. We hung up, and I dismissed the matter, assuming I

15

would probably hear nothing more. It was not a problem for the insurance department, and perhaps Edwards would have some success in trying to reason with Sanders where others had failed.

I had known Judge Sanders for years, and he had supported me in several of my runs for office. Since the State Capitol and my office were in Baton Rouge, most of the insurance orders that required approval went to his court. Because my office had been shutting down so many troubled companies, the other judges in the Baton Rouge district routinely assigned one judge to be the "insurance-duty judge" on a rotating basis, and Sanders had held the position for the past year and a half. Whenever judicial approval was necessary in an insurance matter, Sanders was the judge who made the decision.

In the final months of his term, he became more and more immersed in virtually every legal decision, which was normally made by the attorney general's office or the legal staff of the insurance department. He began second-guessing and publicly criticizing business decisions made by the attorney general's office. The speculation around the courthouse and throughout the legal community was that Sanders wanted to be the next mayor of Baton Rouge. His comments often earned him headlines in the local newspaper, and it was obvious he enjoyed the attention. The average judge just doesn't make the news that often, but Sanders would announce he was investigating a particular insurance problem and get a story in the local press. His "investigations" generally went nowhere, but they kept his name before the public.

Knowing he would be leaving the bench in a matter of months, my staff and I did our best to keep our distance from him, confident that we would be dealing with a less ambitious and fairer judge in the near future.

**Wednesday, August 21, 1996**
**San Francisco, California**

I left Baton Rouge around noon, heading to San Francisco with a brief layover in Phoenix. The three-hour non-stop flight gave me time to review my mail, reading material, and staff memos that have been piling up.

My youngest daughter Meredith will meet me for supper at the Phoenix airport. She is attending nursing school at the University of

Arizona in Flagstaff and will make the two-hour drive down to Phoenix just so we can have a short visit.

I have often second-guessed the fact that I urged each of my three daughters to broaden their horizons and pick a college outside of Louisiana. I felt that the going to school in another part of the country would widen their perspective on the world. And that's just what happened.

Campbell, my oldest, has become a major news correspondent for NBC. I can turn on the evening news and see her regularly. But she often works seven days a week, including holidays, and it's hard for her to find time to come down to visit her dad. Gentry, my second daughter, has built a successful career as an advertising executive in Memphis. Her husband Michael is a stockbroker, and they are actively involved in the Memphis business and cultural community.

Meredith, my youngest daughter, wants to work in a medical facility on the West Coast.

All three found success after having traveled extensively and made their nests in other parts of the country. Although I am happy for them, I also miss seeing them. Perhaps if I had encouraged them to attend college in Louisiana, they would have settled closer to home.

I've been blessed with four wonderful children, and my daughters are extremely close to one another. Unfortunately, they live in far away places and a proud father doesn't see them nearly enough. From left to right, Campbell, Meredith, and Gentry.

My son James has expressed a desire to attend LSU in Baton Rouge. This time, I'm not going to interfere.

I will spend the next two days in San Francisco with several other insurance commissioners from throughout the country. Lloyd's of London will be a front-burner issue. A number of U.S. investors have filed lawsuits against Lloyd's of London, claiming that they were defrauded by business decisions made by Lloyd's executives. We will spend several days looking for ways to build in additional checks and balances to protect U.S. policyholders.

I started out this morning with a 6:00 A.M. television interview at one of the Baton Rouge stations. Several interviews with radio stations throughout the state followed. There was a great deal of press interest in my announcement on Monday that auto insurance rates throughout the state would be lowered.

After the press interviews, I met with Stan Bardwell, who was heading up the receiverships division. Stan complained at length about the tactics of Judge Sanders. He pointed out that the law gave me the authority to appoint a director of receiverships to run the day-to-day operations. Under this system Stan, as head of receiverships, would make the decisions then go to Judge Sanders for final approval. Sanders was becoming more and more involved in the internal workings of the receiverships office. He has ordered Stan to fire certain people and hire others. He is second-guessing Stan on a number of proper decisions he has made. Stan wondered what help I might be able to give in keeping Sanders from interfering in what was purely the authority of the receiverships office.

In the past, I have asked the attorney general's office to become more involved. Under the law, Attorney General Richard Ieyoub acts as our legal adviser, and I was hoping he and his staff would be more aggressive in dealing with Judge Sanders. Even though Sanders has final authority over decisions coming from the receiverships office, he still has an obligation to follow the law and not cross specific lines of authority drawn by the legislature. I told Stan I would convey our mutual concerns to the attorney general at my first opportunity.

After Stan left, I visited with my chief of staff Kip Wall. I told him of my call from Governor Edwards and his interest in Cascade Insurance Company. Kip had been in contact with Ron Weems over the summer, and he briefed me on the open warfare between Ron and David Disiere, and Judge Sanders.

18

According to Kip, Sanders had been conducting his own investigation into the activities of Cascade and Disiere. He had directed an internal review that raised questions about how Disiere had run the company years ago and what Disiere might now owe to the insurance department. The report had become public, and Disiere had filed a lawsuit against Sanders and a lawyer Sanders had hired named Ed Gonzales. In the lawsuit, filed in federal court, Disiere had charged that Sanders and the others involved had violated his constitutional rights, and that Sanders was on a witch hunt against Disiere. When Disiere's lawyer Ron Weems tried to take a statement from one of the parties involved, Sanders had moved to have Ron held in contempt of court. Weems, with some justification, felt that Sanders would try to put him in jail for contempt.

Ron had kept Kip posted on these developments over the summer months. Both Kip and I felt the lawsuit was probably one of the reasons Edwin Edwards was becoming involved. We speculated that Disiere had hired Edwards in an effort to make peace and settle the controversy.

In any event, there was really little our office could do, since Sanders had made it clear he was calling the shots within the receiverships division.

I knew Sanders was completely overstepping his bounds, but his term as judge would expire in a matter of months. A more fair-minded judge will assume oversight of the receiverships division, one who will follow the law and bring this controversy to an end.

## Friday, August 23, 1996
## San Francisco, California

After two full days of considering various proposals from my committee staff, other commissioners, and representatives of Lloyd's of London, it looks like we are close to developing a list of new rules that will significantly raise the financial obligation that Lloyd's will have to keep on deposit in the United States.

I reviewed the day's events over dinner with New York superintendent Ed Muhl[14] and Texas deputy commissioner Jose

---

[14] In New York, the insurance commissioner is referred to as superintendent.

Montemayor.[15] When the three of us returned to the hotel, representatives of Lloyd's were waiting with what they believed to be extremely bad news. Earlier in the day, a Virginia federal judge had issued a 141-page opinion that could open the door to numerous lawsuits against Lloyd's by U.S. investors.[16] The judge raised questions about whether Lloyd's was in violation of certain U.S. securities laws and gave the company a deadline to supply extensive information.

Lloyd's attorneys, with some justification, feared a domino effect might bring the world's largest insurance institution to its knees.

There are approximately three thousand American investors in Lloyd's, most of who were concerned about major financial losses over the past 10 years. Allegations have been made that Hurricane Andrew caused losses in 1992, by pollution liabilities, and even by outright greed and fraud on the part of certain Lloyd's managers. These American investors, however, had initially agreed to settle all their differences in British courts. The decision by the Virginia judge has opened up the possibility of thousands of lawsuits all over the

Meeting with Lloyd's of London Chairman David Roland (right) to raise the standards for Lloyd's to do business in the United States. With me (far left), is Ronnie Johnson, my executive assistant for the department and Baton Rouge attorney Bob Finet, who worked with us to settle the Lloyd's problem.

---

[15] Montemayor would be appointed Texas insurance commissioner by Governor George W. Bush the following year.

[16] The full 141-page opinion can be found in Westlaw citation 1966 WL 490177.

United States that would start a brush fire of potential legal liability for Lloyd's of London.[17]

As Insurance Commissioner for Louisiana, my concern was not so much the health of Lloyd's as it was the ability of this company to pay off any claims made by Louisiana businesses. If all these lawsuits, in effect, started a "run on the bank," legitimate claims from Louisiana might not get paid. My fellow commissioner from California, Chuck Quackenbush, joined us in discussing these concerns. We stayed up late considering whether we, as public officials, could intervene in the Virginia lawsuit.

The Lloyd's attorneys had the hotel manager call back the employees who ran the Marriott's business center, and they kept the fax machines and copy machines busy all night as they frantically prepared legal briefs and appeals to a higher U.S. Court.

I got to bed about 2:00 A.M. and was about to fall asleep when the phone rang. It was David Rowland, chairman of Lloyd's of London. It was almost noon in London, and Rowland was extremely apologetic for calling me in the middle of the night. He, too, was worried about the possible domino effect that might undermine the financial condition of Lloyd's. We agreed to have the lawyers review the 141-page legal decision and talk again early next week.

**Sunday, August 25, 1996**
**Chicago, Illinois**

This is my ninth Democratic National Convention. President Bill Clinton and Vice President Al Gore will obviously be re-nominated. My dad, Jim Brown, Sr., and my sister Madalyne join me as a delegate. Dad represents the Shreveport area, and Madalyne is always a top vote getter down in Plaquemines Parish. (It sure doesn't hurt that she is married to the local sheriff, Jiff Hingle.) The three of us have been delegates for the last two conventions. I'm not sure there is another family in America, in either party, who can make that boast.

The convention in Chicago this year was a far cry from what I witnessed 28 years ago in this city. The father of the current mayor, Richard J. Daley, held the same office then and became the lightening

---

[17] For a more complete analysis of Lloyd's of London and its problems over the past 15 years, see references in Bibliography.

rod for riots that ravaged the convention and the city. The turmoil of the 1968 convention certainly played a significant role in the defeat of Hubert Humphrey by Richard Nixon. This year, the Democrats have made an all-out effort to see that controversy does not erupt again.

The convention is being held at the United Center, which seats 23,000 people and is always sold out when Michael Jordan and the Chicago Bulls play basketball. A huge panel has been built behind the speaker's platform with 56 screens making up one giant image. VIPs host receptions each evening in the 216 hospitality skyboxes, and speakers expound from the podium from noon until late evening. Christopher Reeve, who was paralyzed in a riding accident, gave an emotionally charged speech in support of the disabled. Former Reagan press secretary Jim Brady and his wife Sarah continued the high emotional pitch as they spoke about banning assault weapons. (It has been 15 years since Brady was shot on March 3, 1981, during an attempt on President Reagan's life.) Senator Ted Kennedy, former New York Governor Mario Cuomo, and an array of other prominent Democrats spoke for hours.

The Democrats are obviously successful in putting up a strong show of unity and goodwill to try to erase the bad memories from 1968. The Republicans, who will meet in Los Angeles a few weeks from now, have their work cut out for them.

My first Democratic convention was in Atlantic City, in 1964. On summer break from Tulane Law School, I drove my twelve-year-old Volkswagen convertible up to New York City to visit relatives, and made a last minute decision to divert to Atlantic City. The Democrats were gathering in the old civic auditorium on the boardwalk, which for many years was the site of the Miss America pageant. I was able to park my car about half a block from the auditorium and walk right up to the front door. A guard asked me where I was going, and I said I wanted to join the Louisiana delegation.

"Are you supposed to be with them?" he asked.

"I sure am," I said. That wasn't exactly true, but I was still hoping to get in the door.

"Well, welcome to Atlantic City, and go right on in."

I stood about 50 feet away from the stage where President Lyndon Johnson kept the crowd in suspense until he announced that Hubert Humphrey would be his running mate. Johnson was a cinch to be reelected, and the Democrats pulled together as one big happy family.

What a contrast to what happened four years later.

In 1968, the Democratic convention was held in Chicago. I was living in Ferriday then with my first wife Dale and our two-month-old daughter Campbell. Dale had studied at the Chicago Art Institute and wanted to visit her college roommate. On short notice, we decided to pack up the car and head north.

The main party headquarters was at the Sheraton Hotel, which faces Lake Michigan in downtown Chicago. I spent my first day at the convention "people watching" in the lobby, and reading the scores of brochures being passed out by special-interest groups lobbying delegates at the convention.

Major opposition to the Vietnam War was building, and a large number of protesters had gathered in Grant Park across from the Sheraton. Confrontations were breaking out between protesters and police officers all around the hotel.

I ran into Ingersoll Jordan, an old friend from Tulane who was now working for Congressman Hale Boggs, and we made our way down the street to the Blackstone Hotel to have dinner. The restaurant at the Blackstone is in the basement. Just as we started our meal, I looked up to see white smoke seeping down the stairs into the dining room. My experience in the military told me immediately that it was tear gas, and I knew we had to get out quickly. The waiter had just put down my filet mignon. I grabbed the steak off the plate, slapped it over my nose and mouth, and dashed up the stairs through the tear gas, losing my friend in the confusion.

By the time I reached the street, riots were breaking out up and down Michigan Avenue and all over Grant Park. I knew I could get a better view from the top of the Sheraton, so I headed for the elevator in the lobby. When the doors opened there were three people inside: Governor John McKeithen, Senator Russell Long, and State Senator Mike O'Keefe. I had met O'Keefe in New Orleans a year or two earlier, and I immediately recognized McKeithen and Long. Rumors had been circulating around the convention that McKeithen was under consideration as a possible choice for Vice President on a Hubert Humphrey ticket.

Sticking out my hand, I introduced myself to John McKeithen. "Governor, I'm Jim Brown from Ferriday, Louisiana." McKeithen smiled, but he was visibly surprised at my introduction.

"Why, Jim, what are you doing here?" he asked.

"Governor," I said, "I came all the way up here to support you for vice-president."

McKeithen laughed, slapped me on the back, and told me he could not be more pleased.

Some months later, O'Keefe told me they had been on their way up to Vice-President Humphrey's suite to urge him to put McKeithen on the ticket. When he didn't get tapped for the job, the governor left in a huff and headed back to Louisiana.

## Monday, October 21, 1996
## Linville, North Carolina

Gladys and I flew up to Asheville a few days ago and then made the hour-and-a-half drive northeast to Grandfather Mountain. Our trip was a spur-of-the-moment idea after a hectic week, and both of us are looking forward to getting away for a long weekend. As a bonus, the leaves are changing into their fall colors, and the view is spectacular.

Gladys's parents have owned a home here for a number of years. It's on the grounds of the Grandfather Golf and County Club, and we have been skiing here in the winter and vacationing here in the summer for the past 15 years.

Coincidentally, my former in-laws, Alma and Dick Campbell, have a house within shouting distance directly across the seventeenth fairway. I consider this a blessing, because my three daughters from my first marriage, as well as numerous nieces, nephews, in-laws, and out-laws can regularly get together. There are always plenty of beds to go around.

My first stop on arriving at Grandfather Mountain is Faye's General Store in Linville. For the past 40 years, Faye's has been the early-morning hangout for anyone who wants to know where to find trout and the best flies to catch them.

I'm not the world's best fly-fisherman—not even close. My line gets tangled on every other cast, and I have a hard time tying the most basic knots. But that doesn't stop me from trying.

Now I do talk and look like a fly-fisherman. I certainly have all the right equipment. Over the years, I have gathered an assortment of fly rods and reels from Orvis, Loomis, Sage, House of Hardy, and other manufacturers here and abroad.

24

My favorite rod is an Orvis two-piece, two-weight, six-foot-long graphite that I borrowed from my New Orleans friend David Voelker more than 10 years ago. Every time I see David, I tell him I'm going to give the rod back. He laughs, and has obviously accepted the fact that he will never see it again.

What you need for the narrow, steep Carolina mountain streams are short, light rods. You can often get a back cast snagged on the low-hanging limbs that protrude over the water.

Faye's husband, Paul Hughes, ties flies about as good as anybody you can find in this part of the state. So I make a habit of going by the store for coffee (it's on Coffee Street in Linville), to pick up on the local gossip, and to buy a set of flies to get me through the week.

I don't know why, but governors always seem to know when I am drinking coffee at Faye's.

Earlier this year Gladys and I had drove up over Mardi Gras to catch the last of winter and let me try to catch my first trout of the season. I was at Faye's drinking coffee around 7:30 in the morning; it was an hour earlier in Louisiana. The phone rang. One of the locals picked it up and told me that Governor Mike Foster was calling me.

Now, remember, it's 6:30 A.M. in Louisiana, and it's Mardi Gras. I thought it was Gladys playing a joke on me.

"Jim, Mike Foster. Got a minute?"

"Morning, Governor. You sure know how to run a fellow down, don't you?"

"I called Gladys, and she told me you had gotten out early. I don't want to disturb your fishing, but I needed to talk to you a minute about the LWCC."

The Louisiana Workman's Compensation Corporation is the place of last resort to buy workman's-compensation insurance when no other company will offer it to businesses in Louisiana. It had been created by the legislature in the late 1980s to give businesses an additional option when very few private choices were available. The legislation was the brainchild of Mike Foster, who was then a state senator. Once he became governor, Foster had continued to keep a close eye on the non-profit corporation's operations. My office was doing a regular audit of the company, and the governor wanted to be sure there were no problems.

I assured the governor that he had no reason to be concerned, but I said I would check with my staff for an update. We talked fishing for a while (he's the state's number one spokesman for hunting and fishing), and I agreed to give him a report when I got back to Louisiana.

My coffee-drinking companions at Faye's had a hard time believing the governor would call me in the mountains at the crack of dawn on a state holiday to discuss insurance business.

On this October trip, I teamed up with a local retiree and was about to head out the door to try our luck on a mountain stream. Once again, the phone rang at Faye's, and once again it was for me. This time it was Gladys. "Governor Edwards just called," she said. "He said there's no rush, but could you call him sometime today." I told her I would return the call this afternoon, and I headed out to load up on trout.

Most local fly-fishermen will tell you that October is the best time of year to catch trout in the mountains. You can catch bigger trout in the summer, particularly when there is a full moon. But if you want numbers, late fall is the best time to be on the water.

We found a small stream coming off Grandfather Mountain and running into the Linville River. The water was cold and clear. We alternated between using a Stonefly and a G-Nell fly. I was sure I was doing all the right things. Because the water was so clear, I was using a nine-foot leader so as not to spook the trout. My leader's tippet was four-pound test, with a floating line and strike indicators. My presentation felt good, and I worked the banks in front of some large boulders, where I was convinced the fish would be.

Fly fishing in North Carolina

Several hours went by. After a few casts, my partner's rod bent and he landed a brook trout. Shortly after that, he hooked and landed a small brown trout. His fish seemed to sparkle in the sunlight that seeped through the overhead foliage. He caught a couple of more browns before landing his first rainbow.

When all was said and done, he had loaded up. I had caught one lousy, 12-inch brown trout that I immediately turned loose.

As I said, I am not the world's best fly-fisherman.

I returned Governor Edwards's call later that afternoon. At this point, I must leap forward in time to quote from the indictment that would eventually be filed against me. The prosecutors' accusation reads:

> *"On or about October 21, 1996, Brown, from North Carolina, called Edwards' home and had a conversation with Edwards wherein they discussed the quickest way to terminate Disiere's investigation and get a settlement which would be most favorable to Disiere."*[18]

Let me say that this statement is <u>hogwash</u>! The transcript of the conversation between Edwards and me shows absolutely no discussion of "the quickest way to terminate Disiere's investigation" nor is there any reference or talk of any kind about a "settlement, which would be most favorable to Disiere." This is just one of many examples I will point out of the prosecutors' propensity to file allegations that are completely untrue.

My conversation with Edwards on October 21 is the first illegally recorded conversation the prosecutors have on tape. I say illegally because there was no legal justification for recording the conversation in the first place.[19]

Edwards called that day to ask what I knew about some of the people working in the receiverships office and to ask my advice on how to structure a settlement that he hoped to propose at some point to Judge Sanders. I told Edwards that I had no authority to be part of any agreement because the office of receiverships was not under the control of the insurance department. The transcripts show me telling Edwards, "that comes under the receiverships, and I still don't have it back."[20]

---

[18] Indictment, *U.S.A. v. Brown, et al.,* C.D. 99-151-B-M2, p. 14, paragraph 16 (September 24, 1999).

[19] A full discussion as to why the prosecutors had no legal right to record this conversation can be found in the diary entry dated Thursday, July 8, 1999.

[20] *U.S.A. v. Brown, et al.,* C.D. 99-151-B-M2, Tr., No. (October 21, 1996).

I further told him I hoped that the receiverships authority would be returned to the insurance department, where it is supposed to be under Louisiana law.

There was also some discussion of the logistics of collecting some of the outstanding moneys from reinsurance[21] that might be available, and we talked about what the former governor could do to bring the controversy to a close.

From the beginning, I had made it clear to Governor Edwards, Ron Weems, and anyone else who asked that David Disiere was going to have to see that every claimant was satisfied and that all the bills were paid. I was convinced that, at some point in the future after Judge Sanders left the bench, the receiverships division would come back under my authority. Governor Edwards and Ron Weems both knew that a fair settlement was going to have to be reached. If that didn't happen, my office could open up an entire new investigation. I knew they didn't want this, so I expected we would eventually have a fair settlement in which everyone was paid.

Edwards said he would talk to me when I returned to Louisiana, and we concluded what I considered a routine call from a lawyer representing his client in the course of normal business.

Little did I know that my words would be twisted and distorted, and that years later I would have to explain virtually every part of this and other subsequent conversations with Edwin Edwards.

## Thursday, October 31, 1996
## Baton Rouge, Louisiana

It's Halloween! Most of my employees came to work in appropriate attire, and I had to pick the best costume. I have always tried to avoid being a judge in costume contests or beauty pageants, because you end up making one person happy and disappointing everyone else. But this time I rose to the challenge and picked a truly ugly Halloween witch.

In the afternoon, I talked to Governor Edwards. He told me he had talked to Judge Sanders and it was obvious that the judge was up to

---

[21] Reinsurance is often purchased by an insurance company to spread its risk in the event that a major claim is made. The insurance company gives part of the customer's premium to the reinsurer, and the reinsurer assumes a percentage of the risk. Most insurance companies purchase some type of reinsurance.

his old tricks of playing one side against the other. I had previously told Edwards that Sanders should get out of the day-to-day operations of the receiverships office and return the authority to me, where the law says it belongs. Today Edwards told me, "And what Sanders wants to do is for you to call and ask for a luncheon meeting to discuss this situation."[22]

Sanders realized his time is running out. He only has two months left to serve as judge. I assume he has concluded that other judges would leave the receiverships office alone, and let my office run it, as the law requires. But he apparently wants to remove Stan Bardwell and replace him with Sanders' longtime friend Bob Bourgeois.

I joked with Edwards that Sanders was obviously playing some games but said that I would have lunch with him and Bourgeois. But Edwards told me that Sanders was also hoping that, after he left the bench, my office would allow Ed Gonzales to continue doing legal work for the receiverships division.

Gonzales is a former assistant U.S. Attorney working out of the Middle District of Louisiana in Baton Rouge. Sanders hired him as a "special master" to review receivership activities. To our knowledge at the insurance department, there had never been a "special master" (whatever that was supposed to be) hired by an insurance commissioner anywhere in America. This seemed to be little more than a way for Sanders to give Gonzales a job. The general opinion of those working in the receiverships office was that Gonzales got his job from Sanders as a political favor to Gonzales' brother, Judge Doug Gonzales, who sat on the Second Circuit Court of Appeals in Baton Rouge. Once Sanders left the bench, he wouldn't be able to protect Ed Gonzales any more, so he was apparently trying to ensure that Gonzales could continue working.

Gonzales' job is secure until December 31, when Sanders leaves the bench. If the receiverships office comes back under my control, Gonzales' work will be evaluated just like that of any other employee. Edwards and I agreed that if anything significant came out of my lunch with the judge and Bob Bourgeois, I would let him know.

---

[22] *U.S.A. v. Brown, et al.*, C.D. 99-151-B-M2, Tr. No., p. 16 (October 31, 1996).

## Saturday, November 2, 1996
## New Orleans, Louisiana

The presidential election is only three days away, and President Clinton made one final swing through Louisiana this evening. I received a call from his campaign committee yesterday to see if I would be available to speak at a large outdoor rally in Woldenburg Park on the Mississippi River in downtown New Orleans.

Whatever one thinks of the president, even his strongest critics acknowledge that he is probably the best politician there is at relating to people. Clinton looks you in the eye and makes you think there is no one else for miles around. It is a gift, but he also works hard at it.

The first time I talked to him one-on-one was in 1991, the night I was elected insurance commissioner. My staff had arranged a victory party at a Baton Rouge restaurant, and we wound up the celebration around midnight. Gladys and I were leaving; my six-year-old son James was sound asleep on my shoulder. Just then Gus Piazza, the owner of the restaurant, called out that I had a telephone call. I assumed it was a news reporter wanting a comment about my victory. But then Gus said, "It's the Governor of Arkansas, Jim. He wants to talk to you." I took the phone and had my first conversation with Bill Clinton.

"I just heard the news of your victory as commissioner of insurance, Jim. I wanted to call and offer my congratulations," said the governor.

I assumed that someone from Louisiana had given him my name and election-night phone number. I am sure I was only one of many successful Democratic candidates whom Bill Clinton called that evening. And I bet he did it night after night throughout the country. That focus, that tenacity, is certainly one of the reasons he has been so successful throughout his public life.

Tonight the president seems to be well on his way to a landslide victory over Bob Dole. I joined Senator John Breaux, senatorial candidate Mary Landrieu, and several other state officials on the platform to "warm up the crowd" before the president was to speak.

A crowd of 2,000 people in the French Quarter on Saturday night doesn't need much warming up. I gave a typical stump speech to rally the troops. I'm not sure how much of my ten-minute talk was heard, but there was lots of cheering .

Clinton was at his best, obviously thriving on the enthusiasm he had generated in New Orleans. He knew he was going to win big, and he was certainly enjoying the moment.

After his speech, public officials and other campaign staff members congregated in a small tent set up as a holding area for the president before he headed for the airport. He continually worked the crowd in the tent, stopping twice to make small talk with me.

Making small talk with the President.

Frankly, I was anxious for him to leave so that I could get back home to Baton Rouge. Gladys and I were hosting a dinner party that had been in the planning stages for months; we had several out-of-town guests coming in. I had assured her I would be home early enough for at least part of the meal. As the president drifted among the crowd, I kept looking at my watch. I wanted to leave, but protocol would not let me go before the president.

I was standing next to my long-time friend, former state senator Tommy Hudson, who was a coordinator of the Clinton campaign in Louisiana. The president came by for the third time and continued to make small talk. "Fellows, is there anything else you think I should do in the short time I have left?"

31

I couldn't resist. "Mr. President, you would do me a great personal favor by getting in your motorcade and leaving. I'm in big trouble at home for being late to a dinner party. The best thing you can do for me is to get on out of here."

The president laughed and headed for the door. I wonder if anyone else has ever looked Bill Clinton in the eye and told him to "get out of town."

## Thursday, November 14, 1996
## London

My fifth day in London. I have been coming here for the past several years in November to keep an eye on a number of London based insurance companies doing business in the United States. From Baton Rouge, I flew to Atlanta, changed planes, and traveled all night, landing at Gatwick Airport around 6:00 A.M. Delta Airlines has facilities in the airport where you can shower and change clothes. Assuming you can sleep on the plane (which I can), you can arrive fairly fresh and put in a full day of work in London.

I always take the train from the airport to downtown London, which takes about 30 minutes. There are no major highways, so a cab ride often takes an hour and a half. The train ride gives me time for a cup of tea, a quick scan of the London newspapers, and a picturesque view of the English countryside.

Sunday, I took a cab from Victoria Station to my hotel, dropped off my bags, and had the driver take me to St. Paul's Cathedral. Sunday was Remembrance Day, which is similar to Veterans' Day in the U.S., but the British are more personally involved. It seems as if everyone in the city is wearing a poppy to commemorate the huge British losses during World War I. More than 59,000 British soldiers are buried among the poppies in Flanders Fields in Belgium. Every school child learns of Major John McCrae, a Canadian doctor who tended to the dying on the battlefield and wrote the memorable war poem "In Flanders Fields."

*In Flanders fields the poppies blow*
*Between the crosses, row on row,*
*That mark our place; and in the sky*
*The larks, still bravely singing, fly*

32

*Scarce heard amid the guns below.*
*We are the Dead. Short days ago*
*We lived, felt dawn, saw sunset glow,*
*Loved and were loved, and now we lie*
*In Flanders fields.*[23]

Churches are packed throughout Britain on Remembrance Day. Over the past few years, I have made it a habit to be in London on that day and attend services at St. Paul's Cathedral. The Lord Mayor of London is in attendance, along with numerous other public officials. Following a traditional ceremony full of pomp and circumstance, a parade winds through the business district; most of those who attend the service join in. A large contingent of World War I veterans make their way through the streets of London. It's a moving sight to see.

When I arrived at St. Paul's for the 10:00 A.M. service, the church was already full. People milled around outside the church, hoping to find a place to sit. An elderly female usher pointed at me and told me it would be very difficult to find a seat. I was dressed in a British-cut suit and needed a haircut, so perhaps she mistook me for a Londoner. She asked if by chance I was a member of the St. Paul's Society.

The society has a building fund to maintain the church. Last year I had made a ten-pound donation (about sixteen dollars) to join the society. When I confirmed that I was a member, she led me down the center aisle to the front pews and sat me right behind the Lord Mayor. That was certainly one of the best donations I ever made, and I vowed to renew my membership every year. I hope I have the chance to be in St. Paul's on Remembrance Day for many years to come.

Tuesday evening, I was the guest of honor at a reception at the East India Club, sponsored by my Baton Rouge neighbor Bob Fenet. Bob's wife Sally is English, and Bob has been active in the British insurance industry for many years. He asked representatives of many of the international insurance companies in London to join us and learn more about Louisiana. I have always felt the more that companies do business in Louisiana, the greater the competition, which results in lower prices. So I certainly wanted to encourage these companies to open offices in our state.

---

[23] Origin of "In Flanders Fields," National Archives of Canada, MG30 EI33, Vol. 4.

Thursday evening, while packing for my early-morning flight to Baton Rouge, I called my office for messages. Since it is seven hours earlier in Louisiana, I returned several calls, including one to Governor Edwards. We had what I believed to be a routine conversation; he continues to urge me to meet with Judge Sanders. The judge is pushing his friend Bob Bourgeois to take an active role in the receivership activities. He no doubt wants Bourgeois to stay on in some capacity after the judge leaves the bench.

From what I know of Bourgeois, he's a capable fellow with a background in finance and insurance. I told the governor I would try to meet with the judge and Bourgeois next week. We shared some political gossip, and I ended what I thought to be a normal business conversation. I would learn years later that the prosecutors felt otherwise.

## Friday, November 15, 1996
## New Orleans, Louisiana

I arrived back in Louisiana in time to attend the 75<sup>th</sup> birthday celebration of former lieutenant governor Jimmy Fitzmorris in New Orleans. Fitz is a lifelong friend of my dad's; they started working for the Kansas City Southern Railroad back in the 1930s. If you live in New Orleans and have attended any civic gathering in the past 50 years, you have

Jimmy Fitzmorris (next to me) has been my mentor and friend for the past 40 years. We are pictured with Governor Edwards signing a new law I had authored as a State Senator. Also with us is former House Speaker and long-time friend, Bubba Henry (right).

probably crossed paths with Jimmy Fitzmorris. He is indefatigable, and he seems to genuinely enjoy attending the numerous gatherings required of a public servant.

In 1965, when I returned to Tulane for my final year of law school, a barn-burner of a mayor's race was taking place. Fitzmorris, who was on the New Orleans city council, was challenging incumbent Mayor Victor Schiro. Fitz had been endorsed by the *Times-Picayune* and looked to be on his way to a solid victory.

I had spent the summer in upstate New York as director of an athletic camp and returned to New Orleans by train in early September. The train rolled in to the New Orleans station on Friday morning, September 10, 1965; Hurricane Betsy had just devastated the city.

Fifty people had died and thousands of homes were destroyed. I walked from the downtown train station all the way up St. Charles Avenue, crawling over trees and telephone poles that had been knocked down and were blocking the street.

Mayor Schiro was all over television and radio, showing up all over town to lend a hand and calm people's fears. Anyone who suffered any type of hurricane loss received a personal letter from the mayor offering assistance. The storm gave Schiro's campaign a tremendous boost and cost Fitzmorris the election. In talking to me about his defeat, Fitzmorris was stoic; he was the same way when quoted in the local press:

> *"To everyone who was watching the television news—and that was everyone who got his television set to work, it was (President) Lyndon Johnson and Vic Schiro, in charge of Hurricane Relief. Jimmy Fitzmorris, 'the challenger,' was nowhere to be seen. "But such is politics, and after it's over, you learn to laugh it off, which I did" said Fitz.*[24]

At his birthday party this evening, his energy was as boundless as ever. His hair is grayer, but a lot of us, including yours truly, can say that now.

---

[24] James E. Fitzmorris, Jr., and Kenneth D. Myers, *Frankly Fitz!* (Gretna, La.: Pelican Publishing Co. 1992) 172.

**November 18, 1996**
**Baton Rouge, Louisiana**

I had lunch today with Judge Sanders and Bob Bourgeois. Sanders is obviously trying to give me a comfort level with Bourgeois. He repeatedly told me that Bourgeois would work with the insurance department to shut down troubled estates, and that we could count on him not to pursue his own agenda. I took this as a subtle admission that Sanders did have his own agenda, since he was ignoring the law and making major decisions involving companies in receivership. Most of the parties involved in reviewing the Disiere matter had felt that Disiere was going to have to eventually come up with two million dollars or more. Then Sanders brought up Ed Gonzales and said Gonzales had concluded that Disiere might well owe anywhere from five to ten million. I attributed this to Gonzales creating controversy to run up his legal bills.

I told Sanders emphatically, "If Ed Gonzales can go get ten million dollars then he should go ahead and do so. Whatever Disiere owes, he should pay to make this estate whole, and see that every policyholder is paid. He shouldn't be given any slack whatsoever. Tell Gonzales to go get the ten million."[25]

Sanders became a little defensive. He said he was sure that all sides—the court (Sanders), the receiverships department, and Disiere wanted to settle this matter.

Sanders further stated he had told Governor Edwards that he (Sanders) had hopes of settling this matter, and that Disiere and his lawyer should make an offer in the two-million-dollar range.

I told Sanders that none of this was really my problem since he was running the receiverships office. He said that he wanted to return authority to the insurance department before he left the bench, and that he wanted to settle all the controversy. I told him I appreciated that and hoped all these problems could be resolved.

The judge and I agreed that Disiere should be given no special preferences. Whatever the final figure was, every claim had to be paid.

---

[25] *U.S.A. v. Brown, et al.* C.D. 99-151-B-M2, Tr. No. 32 (November 18, 1996) p. 2.

After lunch, I called Governor Edwards and told him about my conversation with Sanders, including his comment that Ed Gonzales says he can get ten million. Edwards and I agreed that if Gonzales thought he had a legitimate claim of ten million against Disiere, or any amount above what was being negotiated, he should go ahead and make the claim.

I suggested that Edwards try to get everyone representing the Disiere interests, including Ron Weems, to meet with Bob Bourgeois and other key people from the receiverships office, in an effort to resolve this entire problem.

Up until now, there has been no communication between the two sides. Ron Weems is calling Edwards, Edwards is calling me. Judge Sanders is urging me to meet with Bob Bourgeois, and any serious negotiations are stalemated. Perhaps a meeting in the next few days can move this matter off center.

## Tuesday, November 19, 1996
## Baton Rouge, Louisiana

For the first time since all these discussions began, both sides in the Cascade controversy sat down at a table at the insurance department. Ron Weems came down from Shreveport along with Joe Cage to represent Cascade and David Disiere. Cage was the in-house lawyer for Cascade, and had formerly served as the United States Attorney for the Western District of Louisiana (all of north and most of south Louisiana).

There were no negotiations, merely a "feeling out" of each side. Judge Sanders had Bob Bourgeois there representing the receiverships office. Sanders basically moved Stan Bardwell out of the process. Stan apparently is handling a few minor estates but has very little authority. This is unfortunate, because Stan was thorough in his work and helped demonstrate that we were serious about shutting down troubled estates and cleaning up the mess that had been created. Bourgeois was capable, but there was just no legitimate reason for Sanders to remove Stan Bardwell.

Governor Edwards had asked me to call him after the meeting, and I reported that both sides, including Bob Bourgeois, seemed to be acting in good faith. Bourgeois is asking for more information; I hope all sides will meet again soon.

It is obvious that Edwards's role is to bring all sides together, but I also feel that everyone is using me to do their job. Sanders regularly asks me to give messages to the other people involved, and Edwards asks me to set up meetings. I don't mind doing all this, but I don't have the authority to make any final decisions. The law says the buck stops with me, but it obviously doesn't. But it is the right thing to do, trying to get all these sides talking. With Sanders leaving the bench in a matter of weeks, hopefully things will get back to normal.

## Monday, December 2, 1996
## Baton Rouge, Louisiana

Governor Edwards called again to see if I could help set up a meeting with the Disiere group headed up by Ron Weems and Bob Bourgeois. Ron is apparently having trouble getting Bourgeois to return his phone calls. Edwards said they would like to get Bourgeois to the bargaining table so that the information Bourgeois had requested could be passed along.

I agreed to call Bourgeois and encourage both sides to meet. I looked on the call as a routine conversation with no particular significance. Again, I would later learn that the prosecutors saw it differently. Either through ignorance, or a direct effort to color the truth, the prosecutors would later twist this conversation into much more than it was.

## Tuesday, December 10, 1996
## Baton Rouge, Louisiana

Edwards called to tell me that Ed Gonzales had prepared a RICO lawsuit against Disiere asking for twenty-seven million dollars. RICO stands for Racketeer Influenced and Corrupt Organizations. Filing a lawsuit against someone under RICO implies criminal activity, and under federal and state law the parties suing can ask for triple damages. Gonzales was taking this little-used procedure to, in effect, blackmail Disiere and his representatives into settling. No reasonable person with any time to review this matter could ever conclude that Disiere owed anything close to twenty-seven million. Gonzales would probably end up destroying Disiere's company in Louisiana.

I told Edwards I understood that Gonzales was working on some type of report, but I had no idea he was going to threaten a twenty-seven-million-dollar lawsuit.

Edwards concluded that Gonzales was doing this as a way of perpetuating his income, and keeping a job. I told Edwards I was sure I would be hearing from Bob Bourgeois about this latest turn of events. Edwards and I both feel that Gonzales is a misguided missile, capable of making wild allegations just to embarrass the insurance department and me. Edwards promised to keep me advised in the days to come.

## Thursday, December 12, 1996
## Baton Rouge, Louisiana

Rumors have been spreading through the political grapevine that Senator John Breaux is talking with President Clinton about a possible appointment as U.S. Ambassador to France. Pamela Harriman, who held the post for several years, has just resigned, and this is certainly one of the choice political appointments one could receive in Washington.

The *New York Times* even commented on Breaux's interest in becoming ambassador:

> *There is, of course, another dream job for the Cajun, whose father spoke French before he spoke English: Ambassador to France. "I asked Clinton one time, 'Do you think I could handle France?'" Mr. Breaux says slyly. "He said, 'The question is whether France could handle you.'"* [26]

I had run into Jim Nickel, Breaux's long-time assistant and right arm in Louisiana, and we discussed the senator's possible future. One consideration is certainly who would replace Breaux. Under Louisiana law, Republican Governor Mike Foster would make the appointment. Nickel and I agreed that the president would be reluctant to give Breaux this prestigious position and let him resign from the U.S. Senate. There were too many close votes, and Clinton would

---

[26] *New York Times*, June 28, 1999.

obviously need some assurance from Governor Foster that a Democrat would take Breaux's place. There's a chance I could be that Democrat.

This is not the first time I've expressed an interest in becoming a U.S. Senator. In 1986, Russell Long retired as Louisiana's senior senator. There was a scramble to be the front-runner, involving a number of potential candidates. Included in the list were then Congressman John Breaux, Republican Congressman Henson Moore, and the president of the Louisiana Senate, Sammy Nunez. All three of these officials were long-time friends. I served for a number of years in the State Senate with Sammy Nunez, and held him in high regard. Henson Moore was a former law partner of mine. John Breaux had replaced Governor Edwards in Congress, and we had been friends since I entered public life.

Political pollster Dick Morris, who had been doing political work for then Governor Bill Clinton, contacted me. Morris had heard of my interest in being elected to the Senate and convinced me to hire him to do a poll to evaluate my chances. (Yes, it's the same notorious Dick Morris who handled Clinton's presidential election, and who

Senator John Breaux is pictured with me as a guest on my statewide TV show I hosted for some 15 years.

continues to create controversy on many national talk-show programs.)

I was serving as secretary of state at the time and had much more name recognition than the congressmen, each of whom represented only one district. Morris's poll showed that I was well in the lead, and he urged me to go ahead and run.

Money was a consideration. Breaux, a Democrat, and Moore, a Republican, both were Washington insiders who had better relationships with their national parties. They were going to be able to generate significant contributions from throughout the country. And besides, I had a much stronger interest in the governor's race the following year. In any event, I chose not to run and John Breaux went on to build a highly successful Senate career.

I told Jim Nickel I felt I had a good working relationship with Mike Foster and just might be able to sell him on the idea of appointing me to take Breaux's place. Nickel said he would visit with Breaux about the idea. The senator called a few days later.

Breaux and I had a pleasant conversation, and he told me he was dead serious in pushing for ambassadorship. He said that his wife Lois agreed that this would top off his career in public life. Ambassador to France is certainly a plum, and I'm sure John feels he could build business relationships that could help him significantly once he retires from public life.

I told him I would check the law and see how the appointment process applied. There would no doubt be a special election several years down the line, and it would take the cooperation of Governor Foster for the whole idea to work. Breaux thinks Clinton will have to receive strong verbal assurance from Foster that a Democrat would be appointed, and he feels I would be acceptable to the president. He said he would certainly push for such support. I told him I would check the law, put out some feelers, and call him soon.

**Friday, December 13, 1996**
**Baton Rouge, Louisiana**

I had several calls from Senator Breaux today, and I told him about my research of the law.

If he resigns from the Senate to become ambassador to France, the governor would appoint his replacement. The appointment would last for two years, until the fall election of 1998. John asked me to fax him a copy of the law, and he urged me to talk to Governor Foster, who would certainly be a critical part of the process. John said the president had made it clear to him that no appointment could be made unless Foster would appoint me or some other acceptable Democrat. I assured John I would meet with Foster early next week and let him know the results.

Tonight was my first Christmas party of the season. Democratic patrons (those who contribute a thousand dollars a year to the party) held their annual gathering at the home of Baton Rouge attorney Lewis Unglesby and his wife Gail. Jim Nickel was there and again confirmed the serious interest Senator Breaux had in being ambassador to France. He encouraged me to see Governor Foster, and he felt there was an excellent chance that some understanding could be reached between the president and Senator Breaux.

On the drive home, Gladys and I had our first serious conversation about the possibility of moving to Washington. Our son James seems stable and happy at University High School on the LSU campus. Both of us have strong family ties to the state, and that would make the move hard. Gladys would find it particularly difficult to leave her twin sister Gloria. They are almost inseparable; they meet each morning at Coffee Call and usually end the day talking on the phone. We wondered how a move would affect us as a family.

## Monday, December 16, 1996
## Atlanta, Georgia

I have spent the last two days at the National Association of Insurance Commissioners meeting in Atlanta. My fellow regulators and I meet quarterly to coordinate regulatory activities throughout the country.

Of particular interest is the fact that our surplus lines committee has worked out new requirements with Lloyd's of London and other international insurers that will place more money in trust in the United States to protect American policyholders. We still have a few months to go to finalize the new regulations, but we have come a long way in strengthening the overall regulatory system of insurance companies throughout the world.

An early reception and dinner with all the commissioners is traditional; we do general socializing, not business. I chatted briefly—for no more than two minutes—with Oregon Insurance Commissioner Kerry Barnett. He mentioned a shared interest in an Oregon company owned by David Disiere and suggested that we talk about the company after the first of year. I agreed. This seemingly innocuous conversation was of little importance to me. But it would have major consequences later because it was either misinterpreted or purposely slanted by overzealous prosecutors.

## Tuesday, December 17, 1996
## Baton Rouge, Louisiana

My secretary had made an appointment for me to see Governor Foster at 11:30 A.M. My plan was to talk to him about appointing me to the U.S. Senate. On the spur of the moment, I decided to drop by Governor Edwards's office and ask his thoughts on the senate appointment and his suggestions on how to approach Foster. I called to confirm that he would be in the office and he agreed to see me at 10:00 A.M. Before I could say a word about the senate race, Edwards brought up the controversy involving Sanders, Disiere, and Ed Gonzales. I told him I had met with Sanders the previous week and outlined his plan to bring the whole matter to a close. Sanders was now upping the ante; he wanted Disiere to pay four million dollars over a period of time. If Disiere refused, Sanders said that Gonzales would file his RICO lawsuit. Sanders was set on raising the stakes considerably.

I told Edwards that Sanders had put Gonzales on a contingency, or percentage, basis. In other words, he would make a percentage of what he collected. The more he sued for, the more he would financially profit.

I told Edwards that Sanders wanted the matter settled in the four-million-dollar range and had asked me to call Ron Weems and share this information with him. Edwards repeated that the lawsuit would have dire effects. "This RICO suit will kill Disiere," he said. "I mean that's going to just devastate him in the market."[27]

---

[27] *U.S.A. v. Brown, et al.* C.D. 99-151-B-M2, Tr. No. 55, December 17, 1996.

I told Edwards about my brief visit with the Oregon commissioner the night before, and we discussed the fact that Disiere had problems in both Louisiana and Oregon. Finally, I brought the conversation around to the senate race, which was my purpose for going to see Edwards in the first place.

After I outlined the plan Breaux and I had discussed, Edwards said he felt it was doable, but he wasn't sure President Clinton would be willing to appoint Breaux ambassador. But he encouraged me to talk to Governor Foster in case the president did make a final commitment to the senator.

Edwards thought that Breaux should consider other options. "What John ought to do—and of course he doesn't ask me for advice any more—what he ought to do, I think, is try to get himself aligned with [Vice President] Gore, and be the vice-presidential nominee in 2000, because I think Gore has got a pretty clear shot at it, and he and Clinton are good friends. The only difference is they both are from the South. But I think John would have an outside chance of being the nominee," Edwards said.[28]

I thanked the former governor for his advice, and told him I would stay in touch.

Mike Foster was cordial and listened intently when we met in his office on the fourth floor of the State Capitol. I outlined Senator Breaux's proposal, and gave him a number of reasons why he should consider appointing me. "First of all, Governor," I said, "you will certainly get a large share of the credit for John Breaux's becoming ambassador to France. With the French ties in South Louisiana, his appointment will hopefully have some economic benefit to Louisiana, and the credit will be yours. Secondly, I think you can tell Republican supporters that you made it easier to get a Republican in the U.S. Senate two years from now. Any newly appointed Democratic senator—hopefully me—would certainly have a more difficult time being reelected than Senator Breaux. Finally, you will be considered a consensus builder, having reached out to both parties. Democrats would appreciate your bipartisanship, and I think it would enhance your own political standing at election time. I think all these reasons make sense, and I hope you will consider appointing me if the president calls you."

---

[28] Ibid.

Foster told me he wanted to think about it, but he was favorable to the idea. "If I am called by the president, and it's outlined as you've stated, I could appoint you, Jim. We've worked together on a number of insurance issues, and I agree it would help Louisiana for Breaux to be ambassador to France. Pass that on to the senator."

I left Foster's office elated and called Gladys to pass on the good news. "We shouldn't start packing yet, but there is an excellent chance we could end up in Washington," I said.

I called John Breaux and outlined the favorable response I had received from Governor Foster. He told me he would try to reach President Clinton in the next day or two and be back in touch. I sensed that he was confident of receiving the president's blessing and that the whole plan could work out well for both of us.

### Thursday, December 19, 1996
### Baton Rouge, Louisiana

John Breaux called from Washington this morning to tell me he would meet with the president tomorrow. We both plan to be in New Orleans Saturday to attend the swearing in of newly elected Senator Mary Landrieu at noon. We agreed to meet at the Praline Connection, a cafe in the Warehouse District, before the swearing in. John hopes by then to have a green light from the president.

### Saturday, December 21, 1996
### New Orleans, Louisiana

I arrived at the Praline Connection at 10:00 A.M. for my meeting with the senator. He showed up around 10:30 and headed to my table with what I perceived to be a long face. He didn't look encouraging. "Bad news," he told me. "The president won't make the appointment." He explained that Clinton had some concerns about legislation before Congress, and that several controversies were brewing involving the president's personal activities. Clinton felt he needed Breaux in the senate too much and couldn't let him leave. The timing just wasn't right.

Although I understood, I was disappointed that it did not work out for both of us. John speaks French, is extremely personable, and would have made an outstanding ambassador. And I no doubt missed

45

the opportunity of a lifetime—to finish my political and public career in the U.S. Senate.

(As I would find out in the years to come, I never would have been part of the Cascade mess if the president had appointed John Breaux ambassador to France. The president's personal problems that required Breaux to stay in the senate would end up drastically affecting my life.)

## Friday, December 27, 1996
## Baton Rouge, Louisiana

As the year draws to a close, I've been wrapping by returning a few phone calls and meeting with key staff members. Kip Wall, my first assistant, updated me on what we were able to finish up at year's end. He had received a call from Ron Weems, Disiere's lawyer, and had been told by Weems that Disiere had finally settled his obligations with Bob Bourgeois and the receiverships office. Weems asked that the insurance department sign off on the final settlement agreement. Kip and I agreed this would not be appropriate. Our office had not been part of the final negotiations and we were not privy to the details of the settlement. Although Weems assured us it was a good settlement, and that every single policyholder would be paid, we had not had the time to do our own due diligence. Kip had been told that all parties to the negotiations were in agreement, including Ed Gonzales. Gonzales was stating publicly that the settlement was "a good business decision."

In spite of the unanimous support of all the parties involved, Kip and I did not want to endorse the settlement. We had not seen the draft of the RICO lawsuit and were not familiar with the various allegations.

But we agreed that, since all the other parties thought the settlement was satisfactory, we would not take a public position against it. I suggested that Kip say just that—the insurance department would not endorse the settlement, but we had no grounds to object to it. Kip agreed to go to court and express our position.

I was anxious to shut down as many of these troubled estates as possible. A number of insurance companies in receivership had stayed under court-ordered supervision for years. It was nice to know that Cascade would no longer be a problem, that all policyholders would be paid, and that Sanders would finally be leaving his position as judge.

I suggested to Kip that he get a copy of the RICO petition prepared by Gonzales and have the various allegations analyzed. Disiere still had an Oregon company he wanted to bring back to Louisiana. My instruction to Kip was to take no action on Disiere's request until every allegation made by Gonzales had been evaluated. Kip agreed to have one of our contract lawyers start working on a complete review of Cascade and Disiere's activities. But at least the Louisiana problems with Cascade were over. Or so I thought.

# 1997

The Department of Insurance building located across
the street from the State Capitol; it was torn down
to make room for a parking lot in 2003.

**April 10, 1997**
**Hamilton, Bermuda**

Beaches, palm trees, beautiful weather, colorful flowers, excellent food—and I'm heading for the airport back to Baton Rouge.

I arrived last night and will stay in Bermuda less than 24 hours. This morning I made a speech to the National Association of Defense Counsel. Baton Rouge attorney O'Neal Walsh had asked me to speak to this major organization of defense lawyers about my involvement in setting new rules for international insurance companies.

A large number of the 7,000 foreign companies in Bermuda are insurance and investment firms. In fact, Bermuda has become one of the world's leading insurance centers, and I would have liked to stay for several days. But Gladys was ill at home, and the legislature was beginning a busy new session. It was not the right time for me to enjoy the Bermuda beaches.

But it was a worthwhile trip, because representatives of several international companies talked to me about business opportunities in Louisiana. More companies selling insurance in our state means more competition, which means lower insurance rates. That would be a plus for businesses throughout the state, so I spent a lot of time last night and this morning talking up Louisiana as a good place to do business.

(As the Cascade investigation unfolded, the prosecutors would eventually quiz numerous members of my staff about this trip to Bermuda. They could not believe that I would fly all the way to Bermuda and spend less than 24 hours there. The implication was that I must be laundering money or doing some other evil deed. Their questions became a joke around the office as they continued to pursue this wild goose chase. It was just one more of many ridiculous theories the U.S. Attorney's office in New Orleans would pursue at a tremendous cost to the taxpayers of the state and of this country. My efforts to convince insurance executives from all over the world to do business in Louisiana were viewed by these narrow-minded prosecutors as possibly having criminal overtones. How absolutely absurd!

**April 28, 1997**
**Baton Rouge, Louisiana**

Today the state is buzzing with talk of how a bunch of FBI agents broke into Edwin Edwards's home and office in Baton Rouge, seizing documents and a large amount of cash. The search warrant used to enter the former governor's home and office was being faxed all over the state, and it is obvious that the investigation is widespread.

According to news reports, approximately $60,000 in cash was seized from Edwards's home safe, and an additional $400,000 in cash was taken from a safe-deposit box rented by the former governor's nephew-in-law Sam Roby, but which Edwards says is his.

Judging by the search warrants, the investigation includes various land purchases by Edwards; his possible involvement in Indian and other casinos; his paying $258,000 for a yacht in Gulf Shores, Alabama; state prison cattle purchases; the failed effort to bring the NBA's Minnesota Timberwolves to New Orleans; and his activities involving Cascade Insurance Company. The Cascade matter certainly caught my eye.

> *Specifically, the search warrant calls for the seizure of any documents that were part of litigation, involving Cascade Insurance Company, Deep South Surplus, and Southern National Management, including a total of $100,000 paid by attorney Joe Cage. Agents also asked for a $20,000 payment to Edwards from Cage on November 7, 1996, "related to David Disiere."*

Joe Cage was a former United States Attorney who had been part of the legal team representing David Disiere during the settlement of Cascade. He had been general counsel to Disiere's companies when Edwards was hired to also work on the settlement. Part of the legal fee paid by Disiere came through Joe Cage's legal account. Although lawyers who share fees often do this, I assume that this had caught the eye of the FBI and they were looking at the fee arrangement to see if anything improper took place. I thought an investigation of Cascade would go nowhere because I was not aware of anything improper having happened.

It was obvious that the FBI was throwing a "wide net" at Edwards in hopes of catching him with something. This is certainly a fishing expedition, and the investigation will no doubt go on for a long period of time. Since Cascade Insurance Company is involved, I expect my office will be asked to supply any records we have. It should be no different from the hundred similar investigations by federal agents on insurance matters for which we have supplied documents.

**May 5, 1997**
**Baton Rouge, Louisiana**

A lot happened today. I testified before two legislative committees, conducted several radio interviews, met with several lobbying groups about current legislative proposals, and had dinner with the other statewide elected officials. Oh, and one other thing. The FBI came to see me.

When I returned from the State Capitol around mid-morning, two agents were waiting in my conference room on the seventh floor of the insurance department. One agent, Harry Burton, had been involved in a few insurance investigations. I had never met his partner, David Lyons. But I had no reason to be particularly concerned about their visit.

This was not my first encounter with the FBI. In fact, in the past five years my office had made more than a hundred criminal referrals to the FBI and other law-enforcement agencies. Some sixty-three persons in Baton Rouge and New Orleans alone have been convicted of insurance fraud in federal court based on criminal referrals made by my office.

In the past, when my staff went into an insurance company to shut it down, we did a full overview and financial evaluation of the company's books and records. Whenever there was any indication of criminal wrongdoing, I instructed investigators to write up a detailed report identifying possible crimes and send it to the appropriate prosecutors. Sometimes the referrals went to the attorney general or to local district attorneys. But most of them went to the FBI and the Justice Department.

I had made criminal referrals throughout the country, including in New Jersey and California. Our referrals were well documented and generally led to convictions. My office has been praised by many law-enforcement agencies for cracking down on criminal activity in the insurance industry.

Former U.S. Attorney Bob Boitman, who still works in the U.S. Attorney's office in New Orleans, has praised our antifraud efforts on several occasions. He has spoken with me at seminars in Washington and Orlando and has acknowledged that the Louisiana insurance department has put together cases that led to criminal convictions. In October 1994, the nation's leading insurance journal *Best Magazine* did a major profile on my activities as commissioner, in which Boitman was quoted as saying, "A big part of our success in getting convictions of insurance executives is that we have been given cases that are eminently take-able. Jim Brown's office gives us cases we can get convictions on"[29]

This is the kind of praise we were receiving throughout the country. When any law-enforcement officer wanted to talk about any insurance-related problem, I always made myself available. In this case, it would prove to be one of the biggest mistakes of my life.

Fortunately, I had asked Brad Myers, one of the department's contract attorneys, to sit in on the meeting. Brad himself was a former Assistant U.S. Attorney who gave my office advice on legal matters. I assumed the FBI wanted us to produce documents on some case they were investigating, and I thought Brad would be a good point man to gather the documents and work with the agents in the months to come.

After a few pleasantries, Burton got right to the point. He asked what I knew about David Disiere and his operation of Cascade Insurance Company.

For a split second, I wondered if the FBI might have taped the conversations I had had with Governor Edwards. There were stories in yesterday and today's newspapers about rumors that the FBI had tapped Edwards's telephone as part of the riverboat-gaming investigation. But I really didn't give it a second thought, because I knew the conversations I had had with Edwards were above–board; there were certainly no improprieties involved, so I felt no cause for alarm.

---

[29] John Covaleski, "Stamping Out Insurance Fraud," *Best's Review*, (October, 1994) p. 24.

I told Harry Burton that I didn't know much about Disiere's operation of Cascade but would share whatever I knew.

This was certainly a correct response to Burton's question, whether he was asking about Cascade or any other insurance company. The insurance department had more than 80 companies in various stages of being shut down. Besides those companies in receivership, there were some 2,000 other active insurance companies doing business in Louisiana. I did not have a great deal of knowledge about any of these companies. It would be impossible for me, or any other insurance commissioner in the country, to have the time for an in-depth study of any one company. That's why I had developed a competent staff of examiners and financial experts, so that we could review companies through a team effort. My answer to Burton would be the same if he asked me about any active ongoing insurance company in Louisiana today.

But Burton's question was about the operation of Cascade by David Disiere. Disiere had not operated Cascade since 1991. I was not even serving as insurance commissioner when the state of Texas took over Cascade and removed Disiere from control. I would have had to go to Texas and spend months studying Cascade, going through thousands of records, to get up to speed on Disiere's operation of Cascade.

If my staff and I *had* gone to Texas, we would have discovered that before Disiere owned it Cascade was known as KM Insurance and owned by the K-Mart Corporation. Formed in 1981, the company had insurance operations in a number of states besides Louisiana and Texas, including Arizona, Arkansas, Florida, Georgia, Missouri, and New Mexico. There were numerous holding companies and trusts involved in the ownership of the stock of Cascade.

None of this really mattered to the Louisiana insurance department when the company was transferred back to Louisiana. Our concern was to get Louisiana policyholders the money they were owed and to see that Disiere paid all the outstanding bills.

In short, I could not have given Burton a more truthful and forthright answer.

Burton, who took extensive notes, asked a number of additional questions about Cascade during our thirty-minute interview. My responses were fairly routine. Several times, I told him I would have to check with my staff for specific information.

At the conclusion of our meeting, Burton pulled out of his pocket a subpoena requiring me to appear before a federal grand jury in New Orleans on June 4. That's when I became immediately suspicious of his motives. I had cooperated in answering his questions and made it clear that I would provide whatever additional information he needed. There was absolutely no reason to issue me a subpoena. I wondered if I was being set up by Burton. (The other agent, David Lyons, said nothing throughout the interview.) I was cordial, but the minute the door shut behind them I asked Brad Myers his opinion of Burton's motive. He didn't hesitate. "He could be setting you up," Brad said. "There just was no reason to hand you a subpoena when you were being so cooperative."

Even with the subpoena, I wasn't really worried. To the best of my knowledge, the Cascade matter had been settled fairly, and all the policyholders had been paid. I wondered if this visit by the FBI could be related to the fact that Edwin Edwards was involved. Perhaps he or others involved in Cascade had made statements that were taped by the FBI, leading to an investigation. But as I mentally replayed my conversations with Edwards, I could not point to anything that would cause me concern or suggest that any impropriety had taken place.

Brad Myers felt that, despite the grand-jury subpoena, I had no reason to worry about the interview. He agreed to check his sources at the U.S. Attorney's office to see if he could pick up any gossip as to what the FBI might be investigating. Meanwhile, I had a full agenda for the rest of the day and for the week to come. I plunged ahead, hoping the Cascade matter would soon be put to rest.

**May 10 1997**
**Mansura, Louisiana**

More than 20,000 people converged on the small Avoyelles Parish community of Mansura today for the annual Cochon de Lait Festival. Even non-French-speaking Louisianans know that a cochon de lait means great tasting roast suckling pig cooked over an open fire. Mansura is one of the older communities in central Louisiana, chartered in 1860 and named for Mansura, Egypt, by the son of one of Napoleon's soldiers. Every year numerous public officials participate in the annual parade, and this year is no exception.

A local banker named A.J. Roy, a member of a prominent Avoyelles Parish family that had been active in politics for many years, coordinated my participation. A.J.'s late father Sookie was a strong supporter of mine in a number of statewide races. A.J. agreed to send a plane down to pick me up along with several other public officials. State treasurer Ken Duncan made the trip, along with Governor Edwards. Ken and I were anxious to hear his reaction to the recent search warrants and seizures.

The former governor characterized it as a fishing expedition; no specific allegations had been made, at least for now. "The feds are looking at everything I've ever done in hopes of tripping me up on something," Edwards said. "They're still mad over not convicting me in 1985, and I have resigned myself to the fact that they are going to keep investigating me until the day I die."[30]

He was quite angry over the seizure of his personal funds. "They went to my bank in Baton Rouge, and were going to drill through the safe-deposit box to break it open. Can you believe that? I was in Gulf Shores at my condo, and Marion [his brother] called to tell me what was happening. I told him to tell them, 'Man, don't drill through the safe-deposit box. We'll give you the key. What you're doing is crazy.'"

Edwards seemed puzzled about why the FBI wanted records involving Cascade. He, too, felt that there was nothing to investigate and that this part of the investigation was particularly bizarre.

"This whole thing, particularly the insurance matter, is going to prove to be a wild goose chase for them," he said. "They really have crossed the line with what they are doing to me and my family."

We landed in Marksville and "passed a good time" at the festival. Edwards joined the pilot in the front of the plane on the return trip home, and the flight was smooth with no weather problems. I had flown with Edwards on numerous occasions when he was governor, and he often took the controls of the airplane. He had been a navy pilot in World War II and had flown both with a copilot and alone during his public career.

---

[30] In 1985, Governor Edwards was twice tried by the U.S. Attorney's Office in New Orleans for fraudulently granting hospital permits. The first trial resulted in a hung jury, and he was acquitted in the second trial.

Edwards traveled Louisiana more than any other governor in the state's history. When I was a state senator and later secretary of state, I would often check his schedule. If he were flying into my district or anywhere else I needed to go, I would ask to fly with him. He was usually accommodating, and a plane trip was a great opportunity to have a private audience with the governor for several hours.

I have probably flown on private planes a thousand times, but the only truly harrowing experiences I ever had were when Edwin Edwards was flying the plane.

I once flew up to Newellton, Louisiana, with the governor to dedicate a new hospital in my senatorial district. Congressman Otto Passman joined us on the flight from Baton Rouge and brought along his executive assistant, Jack Hill.

On several previous occasions, I had heard Passman introduce Jack Hill as Jack Gates. Jack Gates was his close friend the editor of the *Monroe Morning World,* and Passman often got the names confused. He did it again in Newellton. As he made his remarks to the crowd, Passman turned to the local dignitaries and said, "I want to introduce my executive assistant, Jack Gates."

Red-faced, Hill leaned up on the edge of his chair and whispered, "It's Jack *Hill*, Otto." Passman corrected himself, and we all had a good laugh at his mistake.

When we left the Newellton airport, the governor was at the controls. We had ascended to about one thousand feet when the door of the plane actually fell open and flipped downward. It was hanging by one hinge.

I was sitting by the door next to Jack Hill, who had forgotten to fasten his seat belt. For a few frightening seconds, he slid toward the door and almost fell out of the plane. Just as I grabbed Hill to pull him back in, Passman screamed, "Somebody grab Jack Gates!"

Hill had nearly fallen out of the plane but he hollered, "Otto, it's Jack *Hill*!

Somehow we managed to pull the door back into position, and I hung on to it by the chain until Edwards could get the plane back on the ground.

Very little got past Edwin Edwards, and he had a memory like an elephant. In the late 1970s, I flew with him to a joint speaking engagement in Shreveport. On the long flight home, he asked me to put up a little money and join him in a game of bourée. Knowing the governor could outplay me at any card game any day of the week, I politely declined. In an attempt at humor, I quoted one of my favorite authors, T. E. White, who wrote the wonderful book about King Arthur *The Once and Future King*. "I don't pass time, I use my time," I said. Edwards rolled his eyes and obviously was not amused.

Some 18 years later, I was flying home with the governor from Lake Charles. Someone suggested a card game, and Edwards didn't miss a beat. He looked at me and said, "Don't include Brown. He doesn't pass time, he uses his time." After all those years, he still hadn't forgotten my dig.

I ran against Edwards in the 1987 governor's race, and we often

Governor Edwards and I debated each other on a number of occasions when I ran against him in the 1987 Governor's race.

showed up at the same event, trying to get votes away from one another. On a Saturday morning in June I planned to attend the Peach Festival in Ruston. A private plane was to pick me up at the Lakefront Airport, because I had attended a campaign event in New Orleans the night before.

When I arrived at the local flying service, my pilot told me the weather was too bad to fly a single-engine plane up to Ruston. I had given up on going to the Peach Festival when Edwards walked in the door. He was going to Ruston, too, but he his pilot was flying a twin-engine plane with fully equipped radar. Edwards graciously invited me to come along on his plane. I appreciated the offer, particularly considering that I was campaigning against him.

We were halfway to Ruston when the weather got worse, and his pilot informed him that we had to return to New Orleans. When we landed, the governor told me he had several hours to kill before an afternoon campaign event. To return his favor, I suggested he join me at the home of my in-laws, Doris Solomon and T.G. Solomon. I had called ahead and knew that my mother-in-law was cooking a big Lebanese breakfast. The governor agreed to join us.

After breakfast, several of my wife's relatives showed up to play bridge. The governor jumped right in and joined the ladies, playing cards for several hours. (When my mother-in-law asked me to join them, I said, "Look, I'm trying to get elected governor. You all keep the present governor busy at the card table while I get on the phone and try to raise some money."

I experienced the worst thunderstorm of my life in a small plane with the governor at the controls. We had both attended a reception in my hometown of Ferriday in the mid-1980s when I was secretary of state. When we took off there were rain clouds in the area, but the governor indicated that we could easily fly around them.

Halfway to Baton Rouge, the plane started pitching violently, and the sky was bright with lightening. What should have been a thirty-minute flight ended up taking us two-and-a-half hours. When we finally got out of the plane, I lost my supper and everything else I had put in my stomach that day, but the governor acted as if nothing unusual had happened. The other pilot of the plane told me a few weeks later that he had never been more frightened in his life.

Our flight home from the Cochon de Lait Festival was much less eventful. Edwards again assured us that the investigation of him was going nowhere. Whatever happened on the other issues, I was convinced the Cascade investigation was certainly a fishing expedition by the FBI that would lead to nothing. How wrong I was!

## June 4, 1997
## New Orleans, Louisiana

Today I appeared before a federal grand jury in New Orleans. The subpoena the FBI agents had given me in May called for me to report with a variety of documents involving Cascade Insurance Company. The case is apparently being jointly handled by the U.S. Attorney's office in both Shreveport and New Orleans. I'm not sure why, but the Baton Rouge office has been left out of the loop. This seems strange, since virtually everything involving Cascade took place in Baton Rouge. The subpoena called for me to report at 1:00 P.M. to a meeting room on the fourth floor of the U.S. District Court building in downtown New Orleans. Brad Myers drove down to New Orleans with me. Since Brad was a former prosecutor and had been present at my FBI interview last month, I thought he could help clear up questions or gather support documents the grand jury might need in months to come.

We arrived promptly at 1:00 and were told by a security guard to wait in a small holding room. There we sat for more than three hours. Finally an assistant federal prosecutor, Steve Irwin, came into the room to talk with us.

Irwin had a reputation in Baton Rouge of being a hard-nosed prosecutor and was not generally liked by most of the state officials he dealt with. But my case was different. Our office had helped Irwin make a number of high-profile convictions of insurance executives. He had repeatedly praised the support he received from my staff.

When he came into the office, I asked him, "Steve, what's this all about? Can you at least assure me that the Cascade investigation is not focused on me?"

Steve hesitated and seemed a bit embarrassed. "Look, Commissioner, I have told these folks that you and your office have been extremely cooperative on every investigation we have undertaken. There are apparently some unanswered questions, but I hope we can get this all cleared up. I think if you can clarify a few things, you can put this all to rest, at least as far as you are concerned."

But Brad was skeptical. When Irwin left the room, Brad suggested I merely drop off the documents that had been subpoenaed and leave the grand-jury room. "These fellows can really play some games with you if you're not careful," he said. "They can trip you up over little or nothing. You haven't reviewed all this information, and obviously, they have. I would advise you to say nothing, give them the documents they want, and tell them you will consider coming back at a later date after you have reviewed the materials involved."

The assistant U.S. Attorney handling the Cascade investigation before the grand jury was William J. Flanagan from the Shreveport office of the Justice Department. He had a reputation of being a straight shooter who was fair in his dealings. His father-in-law is former state senator J.B. Davis of Shreveport. I served in the senate with Davis in the 1970s; in fact, we sat right next to each other. I had the highest regard for him, and although I did not know Flanagan, I believed he would be fair with me.

Brad made it clear that without specific assurances that I was not being investigated; it would be a mistake to start giving information without reviewing the details. I agreed. We dropped off the several boxes of Cascade materials that had been subpoenaed. Then we drove back to Baton Rouge, a little more puzzled and a lot more concerned.

We tried to come up with some idea of what the prosecutors were investigating. Cascade was a troubled insurance company that needed to be shut down. All claims had been paid, and the Louisiana taxpayers had not lost a penny. Was it because Edwin Edwards was involved? Was there something we didn't know about Judge Foxy Sanders? Where could they be coming from?

Brad and I raised lots of questions, but by the time we got back to the State Capitol we still had no answers.

**October 21, 1997**
**Baton Rouge, Louisiana**

Former Vice-President Al Gore and I share a personal moment on one of his numerous visits to Louisiana. Looking on is U.S. Senator Mary Landrieu, future Federal Judge Jim Brady, and Agriculture Commissioner Bob Odom (far left).

Today I joined other Democratic elected officials to greet Vice President Al Gore who was here to dedicate a new law center at Southern University. A few of us met privately with him for about half an hour before his noon speech. Although no specifics were discussed, he made it obvious he was laying plans for the 2000 presidential race.

Five thousand people attended the outdoor dedication. The vice president acknowledged my presence and made reference to a positive *New York Times* story that described me as one of the toughest insurance regulators in America. (As I was to learn in the years to come, the U.S. Attorney in New Orleans, who had been appointed by the Clinton-Gore administration, chose to ignore the aggressive and tough reputation I had developed.)

### Friday, November 13, 1997
### Baton Rouge, Louisiana

Several members of my staff helped me take additional documents to the federal grand jury in Baton Rouge today. Some employees were questioned about meetings in our office that might have been recorded.

The federal prosecutors are operating under the misconception that we had a sophisticated taping system in our conference room and in my office, and that conversations had been recorded.

Of course, there was no such sophisticated equipment, and no conversations were taped. I keep going back to my interview with Harry Burton and the other FBI agent last May. The prosecutors may think that I have a recording of the interview and want to get it from me. They may be worried that Burton's version of the conversation isn't correct and that I have conflicting information.

Frankly, I'm beginning to wish that I *had* taped the conversation. Burton took extensive notes, but there is always the possibility that he could change what he wrote down. Basically, it's his word against mine. I was fortunate to have Brad Myers as a witness, but not sure how many details he will remember.

At any rate, it was a big waste of time to take several employees to the grand jury to talk about a sophisticated recording system that did not exist. I was ordered to be at the federal courthouse at 9:00 A.M. and sat there for the entire morning. The grand jury took a break for lunch, and I was back again at 1:00. Finally, around 3:00 the prosecutors took me before the grand jury to quiz me about the taping system.

This seems to be nothing but harassment. It would certainly have been much more efficient to schedule me for a specific time. It is becoming more and more apparent that the New Orleans prosecutors are playing games and not acting in good faith.

Several days ago, the *Baton Rouge Business Report* ran a lengthy article on the Cascade matter, commenting at length about local lawyer Ed Gonzales. He has benefited more than anybody else in the Cascade settlement because of all the money he was paid. The *Business Report* commented:

> *Gonzales may receive more than $1 million from Cascade's assets from different interests in the investigation. Gonzales received $70,000 over the course of six months, during which he conducted the investigation into Disiere's companies in Louisiana, Texas and the Northeast. That was the total Gonzales pocketed as part of a $90-an-hour fee arrangement Sanders ordered paid out of the Cascade estate.*

> *Court documents show Sanders canceled his previous order giving Gonzales $70 an hour at 9:40 A.M. on Dec. 12, 1996.*

> *It is unusual for a court order to include times: most legal documents are dated, not timed. Gonzales then turned into a special contract attorney for the Office of Receivership officially representing the Cascade estate. That contract will pay him 20 percent of the settlement, which totals at least $5 million according to Disiere.*

> *Last summer, Gonzales, who is a friend of the FBI agent investigating the case, said he had been talking to the FBI about insurance matters and said he is not under investigation.*

*Brown said recently that the Insurance Department could not get access to much of the Cascade investigation, because Sanders ordered all of Gonzales' billing records under the $90-an-hour contract sealed. Few other billing records—from the previous private law firms and the attorney general's office—were sealed when those attorneys were handling the case.[31]*

The FBI agent who is a "friend" of Ed Gonzales is none other than Harry Burton. Gonzales obviously is upset with me for raising concerns about the questionable sums of money he received for his work in the Cascade matter and for refusing to allow Gonzales and his partner, Wade Shows, to reap large legal fees with another contingency-fee contract. So I am certainly suspicious when I hear that he is talking to his "friend" Harry Burton.

I talked yesterday to my longtime friend and adviser, attorney Camille Gravel of Alexandria. In recent months I have been calling Camille regularly to update him on this investigation. At this stage, we both still feel that it won't lead to anything, but Camille is advising me to talk to an out-of-state attorney about representing me as the Cascade matter continues to heat up. He says that anytime someone makes more than one trip to the grand jury, for an abundance of caution they certainly should hire an attorney.

Camille suggested that I talk to Washington, D.C., attorney Bill Jeffress, who has had extensive experience representing clients in Louisiana. Jeffress has a reputation as one of the top criminal lawyers in the country. First of all, I will need someone of Jeffress' caliber if the investigation turns more in my direction. Secondly, there are too many investigations going on in Louisiana, which could mean that someone else will call on Jeffress for his services. If I wait too long and let him get hired by someone else in another Edwards' investigation, he would not be able to represent me later. There is always the possibility that Edwards himself may want to hire Jeffress if indictments come down in the riverboat-gambling case. Rumors are rampant that Edwards and others could be indicted before the first of

---

[31] *Baton Rouge Business Report,* John Hill, November 11, 1997:

the year. Edwards knows Jeffress' reputation, and I know they talk from time to time.

I called Jeffress in Washington, and he told me he had kept up with my case in the papers and in regular phone conversations with Camille Gravel. He is available to represent me. We agreed to meet before the first of the year. Meanwhile, I am putting together documents, news clippings, and correspondence to forward to Jeffress for his review.

Both Camille Gravel and Brad Myers will stay on in an advisory capacity—possibly more, depending upon what happens. Hopefully, the entire Cascade investigation will soon reach a dead end. I remain as puzzled today as I was months ago, but I guess the mystery won't be solved any time soon. With the Christmas holidays coming up, I doubt I'll hear much more until after the first of the year.

# 1998

**Hot air balloons land on the grounds of the State Capitol beside the statue of Huey Long. His gravesite overlooks the State Capitol and the Insurance Department.**

**Friday, March 13, 1998**
**Baton Rouge, Louisiana**

Word of the Cascade federal grand jury surfaces from time to time, but there seems to be little focus or direction. The prosecutors from the New Orleans U.S. Attorney's office continue to be on a fishing expedition.

News stories appear in the press almost daily, speculating about where the entire Edwards investigation is heading. Several articles indicate that his involvement in obtaining riverboat-casino licenses is being reviewed in detail. Last month the FBI was ordered by a federal judge to give back $450,000 seized from Edwards's safe last year. It apparently relates to San Francisco 49ers owner Eddie DeBartolo, who hired Edwards to help him get a casino license. But the governor was out of office at the time, so there is a question as to whether that was illegal. Associated Press columnist Guy Coates summed it up pretty well in a recent column:

> *"The problem with this whole thing is that we hear nothing but rumors. We know nothing. We hear everything. Everything the Feds have is sealed. There are people, who, just for kicks, start new rumors everyday."*[32]

A rather bizarre incident happened this week. Judge Foxy Sanders was called before a grand jury at the federal courthouse in Baton Rouge. On his way out of the building, he met with reporters and announced that he would be a candidate for mayor next year. Bob Bourgeois, who is still overseeing the receiverships office, said he would manage Sanders' campaign. When asked about taped conversations with Governor Edwards, Bourgeois had this to say: "I believe those tapes not only elect him Mayor of Baton Rouge, they may elect him Governor of the state from what I know about it."[33]

Apparently the grand jury is focusing on a property sale involving Sanders that has nothing to do with Cascade. This is one more reason why this looks like a fishing expedition. But even if that's all it is,

---

[32] Guy Coates, *The Advocate*, February 16, 1998.
[33] *The Advocate*, March 30, 1998.

fishing expeditions can be dangerous. Innocent people often get caught in the crossfire. It seems clear that the "fishing" relates to Edwin Edwards. I am convinced that if he had not been Disiere's lawyer there would be no Cascade investigation. I'm trying not to worry about it. Good lawyers are monitoring the grand jury's activities, and so far nothing worrisome has surfaced relative to my office. Still, I will be glad when they shut the entire matter down.

## May 20, 1998
## New Orleans, Louisiana

It was standing room only in the chambers of the Louisiana Supreme Court building on Loyola Avenue in downtown New Orleans. I squared off against State Senator Cleo Fields from Baton Rouge in arguing before the state's high court the issue of impounding automobiles that are uninsured.

I had proposed a law in last year's legislative session that would allow a police officer to impound and tow any car whose driver could not produce proof of basic liability insurance. Louisiana continues to have one of the highest numbers of uninsured motorists in the country. The legislature strongly supported my proposal, and the new law took effect on the first of this year.

Baton Rouge District Judge Bob Downing ruled that the impoundment law was unconstitutional, saying it was an unlawful seizure of personal property to impound an uninsured automobile. The attorney general's office had represented the state in pushing to uphold the law before Judge Downing. When the case went to the Supreme Court, I wanted to personally represent the state, both as insurance commissioner and as a lawyer.

For the first time in the court's history, television cameras were allowed in the courtroom. Live coverage of our arguments was broadcast throughout the state, and a large number of state and national reporters were there. Senator Fields is an astute politician and certainly one of the major African-American leaders in the state. He brought chuckles from the judges when he candidly admitted that this was his first oral argument, since he was recently licensed to practice law. It was also my first appearance before the state's highest court.

Our oratory skills aren't going to make that much difference. The issue is too big; it affects every driver in the state. It comes down to how the public interest is best served. Can someone's property, his automobile, be impounded and taken off the streets when the driver does not meet the legal requirement of having valid insurance? Is it an infringement on his personal rights to tie certain obligations to those rights?

I argued before the high court that driving is a privilege, not a right. With that privilege comes responsibility. A driver must have a valid driver's license; that is required by law, and there are no exceptions. The car must be safe to drive; it must have brakes that work, lights can be turned on at night, and other basic safety features. If those requirements are not met, the car can be removed from the road. I told the court that the legislature was merely adding one more requirement: a driver must have proof of insurance to use the public highways. There is no insurance required if one wants only to drive around on his own land. But when a driver uses a public highway, he assumes additional responsibilities.

Senator Fields made a good argument in favor of the individual's basic property rights. But public opinion is on my side. I have seen polls in which more than 85 percent of the population supports impoundment if the driver of the car does not have valid insurance. To the average citizen, the issue is one of fairness. Why should the law-abiding driver have to buy car insurance when someone else can ignore the law, fail to buy insurance, yet still be allowed to drive? It just isn't fair. The Supreme Court will certainly apply the law, but I think the judges cannot help but be affected by public opinion. I am confident they will render a decision that the impoundment law is legal and constitutional.

Senator Fields and I both recognize the tremendous amount of public interest in the impoundment law. We agreed to travel the state together in the coming weeks and debate the issue in a number of cities.

**Friday, September 4, 1998**
**Prague**

Uncollected insurance claims owed to Louisiana holocaust victims or their heirs are what bring me to Prague.

I am one of seven insurance commissioners who serve on the International Holocaust Commission. Last year a team of

70

commissioners began investigating complaints by holocaust survivors that hundreds of millions of dollars could be owed in insurance claims that were never paid by the Nazis just before and during World War II. Insurance was just as important to German and other eastern European citizens then as it is to us today. In the late 1930s, the German government stripped Jewish residents in Germany and surrounding countries of all their insurance benefits. The Nazi regime ordered insurance companies to pay all proceeds from life, property and casualty, and other claims directly to the German government. This systematic seizing of insurance benefits continued throughout Eastern Europe as the Nazi takeover spread. A number of major insurance companies, active throughout the world today, either paid these claims to the German government or held on to money that might be owed to beneficiaries.

It's a complicated issue. Some companies say they had no choice but to pay the German government and they have no further obligation. Policyholders who bought the insurance say that a contract was signed and that those insurance companies should pay up. Many of the original companies no longer exist, but conglomerates that are operating throughout the world today bought others. Some companies that could have liability include Generali of Italy, the Winterthur Group of Switzerland, and several German companies, including the Girling Group, Munich Re, and the Allianz Insurance Group.

We have been meeting at one of the government judicial buildings in Prague for several days. Six other insurance commissioners have joined me, along with representatives of many of the major insurance companies that were either directly insuring these policyholders in the late 1930s or of the conglomerates that bought companies that were operating then. We wear earphones so that we can understand the interpreters who are covering our meetings in English, French, German, Italian, and Czechoslovakian. It would be an understatement to say that the meetings are moving slowly; we have a long way to go to make any significant progress.

Prague is a dynamic industrial city that leads Eastern Europe in overall growth. The city's main thoroughfare, Wenceslas Square, reminds me of the Champs Elysée in Paris. The Vltava River splits Prague. The government buildings where we meet are on the west bank, along with Prague Castle and St. Vitus Cathedral. You can

71

cross to the east bank on the Charles Bridge (Krluv Most), which is lined with statues has towers at either end.

Just a block from the hotel is the old Jewish quarter, where a lengthy wall was built surrounding the pink synagogue. The Jewish cemetery is the second oldest in Europe, established in the fifteenth century. There are some 12,000 tombstones jammed together and leaning on one another, with as many as 12 people buried horizontally by each tombstone, one on top of the other. The walls around the Jewish quarter are inscribed with the names of some 80,000 holocaust victims murdered by the Nazis. We are certainly in an appropriate location to be talking about reparations to the survivors and their heirs.

I learned a lot about Prague and Czechoslovakia from my oldest daughter Campbell, who spent a year here in 1991. Democracy was pushing Communism aside, and Czechoslovakia had a new president, Vaclav Havel. Campbell had the unique opportunity of teaching English to members of Havel's cabinet. Her letters and phone calls were full of tales about standing on the conference table in the cabinet room, blaring out English slang, giving high-fives to cabinet members, and putting an American spin on the words they were learning.

I leave tomorrow for Monte Carlo, where I will speak on Sunday to an international reinsurance conference. Reinsurers from throughout the world will be in attendance, and I'll continue to sell Louisiana as a good place to do business. The conference should be productive for the state, and I certainly won't object to spending a few days on the French Riviera.

**November 4, 1998**
**Baton Rouge, Louisiana**

There was little doubt during the past few weeks that Edwin Edwards was on the verge of being indicted. Rumors have been circulating for some time that the Edwards investigation, unrelated to Cascade, was centered on riverboat-casino licenses. Other rumors abound. Pay-offs involving a prison in Jena, Louisiana, and the Timberwolves basketball franchise were other projects being investigated. Pieces of the puzzle started falling into place, and a clearer picture emerged during the past three weeks.

On October 6, the owner of the San Francisco 49ers, Eddie DeBartolo Jr., pled guilty for failure to report a crime—that Edwards had extorted more than $400,000 from him in exchange for Edwards's help in securing a riverboat license. All this allegedly took place after the former governor had left office.

Three days later, the best friend of the governor's son Stephen pled guilty. Ricky Shetler admitted to giving Stephen Edwards more than $500,000 in cash and goods in return for Stephen's help in getting a casino license in Lake Charles.

On October 16, one of the governor's closest friends, Bobby Guidry, pled guilty. Guidry also received a riverboat license. In return, he said, he paid $100,000 per month to the governor, his son Stephen, and the governor's aide Andrew Martin. The governor had stood in Guidry's wedding; they had vacationed together and hunted together regularly. Guidry is now saying that he was a victim of extortion. Whatever the case, all these events certainly were leading toward the indictment of Governor Edwards himself.

Today it finally happened.

Besides Edwards, those indicted were his son Stephen, Andrew Martin, Eunice businessman Cecil Brown, Senator Greg Tarver, and Baton Rouge businessman Bobby Johnson. All of the indictments center on efforts to extort money involving riverboat casinos. There was no mention of criminal activity involving any other matter, including the Cascade Insurance Company.

I heard the news on the radio as I drove to T.J. Ribs' restaurant for lunch. Somebody from my office also called me on my cell phone to give me the news.

Once a month, I convene a meeting of property and casualty insurance companies and body-shop owners. There is always a great deal of controversy as to what insurance companies will pay and what body-shop owners say they need to repair damaged vehicles. We had met earlier this morning so that both sides could discuss their complaints and concerns. Several members of the group had asked me to join them for lunch at T.J. Ribs. As I left the restaurant around 1:30, the governor and his family were on their way in. In spite of the catastrophic news he had received an hour earlier, Edwards was still keeping a public persona, heading for one of the busiest restaurants in town.

73

He motioned me over to a quiet corner and, with everybody in the entire restaurant watching, we talked quietly for several minutes.

"I just want to tell you, in spite of what happened to me today, I don't anticipate a thing happening on the insurance matter," he told me. "I've done nothing wrong. I don't know of anything that anyone did wrong, particularly in your case. And no matter what they promise me in return, I will never, ever, do anything but tell the truth in the Cascade matter—that you were above-board in all your dealings, that you did absolutely nothing wrong, and that it would be a huge miscarriage of justice for any charges to be brought, especially against you. Far from investigating, the feds ought to be congratulating us for bringing to an end this controversy. Not one penny was lost by the state or anyone else, and it's wrong for there to be any inference that you, I, or anyone else did anything wrong."

I told him I appreciated his thoughts, particularly at this difficult stage in his life. "Governor, I certainly feel bad for you and your family. But we are both survivors, and I'm sure this thing will work out for both of us."

Edwards's wife Candy came over to give me a hug. We expressed our mutual concern, and then the Edwards family went their way and I went mine.

## Tuesday, November 10, 1998
## Baton Rouge, Louisiana

> *There can be no such thing as public liberty*
> *without freedom of speech.*
> Benjamin Franklin[34]

It's disturbing! Already the secrecy begins. District Judge Frank Polozola has imposed a gag order on Governor Edwards and everyone else involved in the riverboat-licensing case. His order prohibits Edwards and the other defendants, along with the attorneys involved, from talking to the media "from now until the final verdict."

Of course, this is exactly what the prosecutors want. It is a tremendous advantage for the prosecution when a defendant cannot defend himself in public. Although he is no longer in office, Edwards

---

[34] This quotation is inscribed on the wall of Cox Corridor II, a first-floor House corridor at the Capitol in Washington, D.C.

is still a public figure. Senator Greg Tarver is in office now and certainly needs to defend himself to his constituents. There is a lot of talk about a quick trial, but that is just not going to happen. It will be well over a year before this case goes to trial. Thus Edwards, Tarver, and the other defendants will have their hands tied for many months to come. Unfortunately, I think this will be a trend.

Polozola is known not just for his brashness and his dictatorial attitude in his courtroom but as a "prosecutor's judge." I fully expect him to insist on an anonymous jury as part of his continuing effort to shroud this case in secrecy. This flies in the face of a democracy's guarantee of a fair and open trial, but that's Polozola's style. Whether a person is guilty or innocent, fair rules should be enforced. This gag order is a sign that the Edwards defendants will be climbing up hill in their case to defend themselves.

## Friday, December 24, 1998
## Baton Rouge, Louisiana

The federal grand jury that indicted Governor Edwards and five others last month met again today. The prosecutors are apparently still interested in the Cascade matter. I remain puzzled about what crime they think has been committed.

Attorney General Richard Ieyoub and several of his staff members were called before the grand jury, apparently to outline their involvement in contracts with Ed Gonzales and some of the other lawyers in the case. There seems to be questions being raised as to how Gonzales received his contract, and why he went from being paid on an hourly basis to a percentage of what was recovered in Cascade. And no one has any idea as to what crime was supposed to have taken place.

Rumors abound, but the consensus seems to be that the prosecutors don't know how strong the casino-licensing charges are and want to find more on Governor Edwards, if there is anything to find.

So the fishing expedition continues. I can't see how this affects anyone in my office or me. I wasn't part of any final decision, involving Cascade, and all the policyholders got paid. But I distrust the intentions and motives of the prosecutors from the U.S. Attorney's office in New Orleans. Their reputation precedes them. They don't play by the rules, and they apparently have a "gotcha" mentality. In short, anyone involved in Cascade, myself included, should keep his guard up. I still see no major danger signals for now, and I'm glad the holiday season is here.

# 1999

The Louisiana State Capitol is reflected in the
windows of the Department of Insurance.

**Tuesday, April 20, 1999**
**Baton Rouge, Louisiana**

Four months into the New Year and the office is running well. I returned yesterday from a quick trip to London, where I spoke at a regulatory conference. Louisiana's progressive reputation as a solid insurance market continues to grow. New companies are coming to our state, which should result in lower prices. The office is receiving good press throughout the country. There was national news coverage of the fact that the National Association of Insurance Commissioners has re-accredited our department. The statement from the national organization said:

The Louisiana Department of Insurance is re-accredited as one of the nation's top insurance departments in 1999 for the second time under my watch. Presenting the accreditation award is Glenn Pomeroy, President of the National Association of Insurance Commissioners.

*The Louisiana Department of Insurance has been re-accredited by the National Association of Insurance Commissioners five years after breaking with the past in the most intense modernization effort since insurance regulation first began in Louisiana.*

*The recognition certifies that the Department has maintained or exceeded the NAIC's stringent financial regulation standards since Louisiana won accreditation in 1993, the first Deep South state to do so. What this means to consumers and taxpayers is that the Louisiana Department of Insurance, operating entirely from self-generated funds, has the expertise and resources to spot financially troubled insurance companies in the early stages to minimize and prevent losses.*

*Accreditation came after an NAIC team of experts performed a thorough onsite examination of the Louisiana Department in Baton Rouge to determine if the NAIC's standards were met.*

*NAIC President, Glen Pomeroy, congratulated Commissioner of Insurance Jim Brown and the Louisiana Department. "You have attained a significant achievement. You have raised the degree of professionalism of your department to a new level," said Pomeroy.*[35]

The *Shreveport Times* gave a strong endorsement last month to our children's health-insurance plan, headlined "Brown's Proposal Makes Sense." The impoundment law continues to receive solid support from newspapers throughout the state. The *Times* editorialized, "There is, after all, some good news in Louisiana that indicates progress is being made. Insurance rates are dropping on vehicles. Jim Brown should be proud. The legislation that was pushed by Insurance Commissioner Jim Brown has proved to benefit the public as well."[36]

The *Lake Charles American Press* ran an editorial headlined "Louisiana's teen driving law is a model other states are following," commenting on my proposal, now law, that raises the driving age and puts more restrictions on younger drivers.[37]

---

[35] Press Release, National Association of Insurance Commissioners, Kansas City, MO, January 5, 1999.

[36] *Shreveport Times,* February 28, 1999.

[37] *Lake Charles American Press*, March 22, 1999.

The *Baton Rouge Sunday Advocate* ran a lengthy story on our efforts to lower workman's compensation rates in the state, and a number of national publications also did features on the insurance department.[38]

We still hear occasional rumblings about Cascade. The grand jury meets from time to time, but there seems to be no focus as to what is being investigated. With the statewide election less than six months away, I am optimistic that the prosecutors' investigation will soon reach a dead end. At this stage, there is no mention of any opposition to my re-election. Hopefully, all this good news will continue.

**June 6, 1999**
**Columbia, Louisiana**

Cars were lined up for blocks on either side of the road along Highway 165 through downtown Columbia. Hundreds of people had come to pay their last respects to former governor John J. McKeithen. Earlier in the day, I had gone to his home, Hogan Plantation, to visit with his family and friends who had stopped by before the funeral. His son Fox had succeeded me as secretary of state, and I had represented Columbia and Caldwell Parish when I served in the state senate. It was a day for greeting old friends and sharing memories of the former governor. He led the state during my time in law school and my early years practicing law in Ferriday. So he was the first governor whose activities I followed on a regular basis. His accomplishments included building the Superdome, pushing the adoption of a state code of ethics, and working hard to bring new industry into the state, particularly along the Mississippi River.

McKeithen and Edwin Edwards did not maintain much of a relationship during Edwards' first term as governor.

McKeithen had actively supported Edwards for an open congressional seat in 1966. But there had been little contact between the two once Edwards replaced McKeithen as governor.

I was sworn in as a state senator the same day that Edwards took office as governor. It was McKeithen's last day in office; after the ceremonies were over, the former governor drove home to Columbia. Close friends of McKeithen later told me that the former governor

---

[38] *Baton Rouge Sunday Advocate*, July 11, 1999.

expected the new governor to offer the use of the state plane to fly the McKeithen family back to Columbia. But no offer was made.

I asked Edwards about this later, and he said all McKeithen had to do was let him know that he wanted the plane to take him home. McKeithen expected the offer, but Edwards was too overwhelmed with taking office to notice. McKeithen felt slighted, resulting in an unfortunate misunderstanding.

Adding insult to injury, I think McKeithen felt that Edwards should have called from time to time to ask his advice during Edwards' first term or invite McKeithen to the Governor's Mansion. But Edwards was just too busy with day-to-day activities to think about calling the former governor. If McKeithen had called him, I'm sure Edwards would have returned the call immediately. For whatever reason, it was not a good relationship. There was not much communication between them, and McKeithen was miffed at the lack of attention.

As the 1975 statewide races approached, McKeithen hinted that he would consider running for governor again against Edwards. "I'd be glad to come back," he told the Baton Rouge Press Club in December 1974. "I am not overly busy in Columbia. I have seen about all you can see in two years. I would enjoy being governor again."

McKeithen said he was checking out his support for the race. "If I sense the majority of the people want me to come back and finish what I started, I will run," he said, adding that if he did run against Edwards he would "offer my record of accomplishment against his record of no accomplishment."[39]

In January 1995, Edwards asked me to come by the Governor's Mansion. "You're John McKeithen's senator, and you've known him for a long time," he told me. "I'd like for you to go talk to him and help me evaluate whether he is going to run against me."

If I was the best representative Edwards could find for this mission, it was obvious he had not stayed in contact with the former governor during his first term. I considered myself a friend of McKeithen, but I was certainly no confidant.

---

[39] Baton Rouge *State Times*, December 10, 1974.

I was one of the youngest members of the legislature, and I felt that I was in it over my head to try to serve as a liaison between two major political figures. Also, I had learned over the years that you did not go "talk" to John McKeithen. You went to visit, and you mostly listened. Still, I agreed to make the trip.

Governor John McKeithen actively supported me in my first race for State Senator in 1971.

I phoned McKeithen, and he graciously invited me up to Columbia. Several days later, on a cold day in January, I made the four-hour drive and met him at his office. We sat in front of the fireplace and talked for several hours. John McKeithen was a master of oral history. You could toss out just about any subject related to the state and he always had a number of stories and anecdotes that he related with gusto.

But he was less chatty when I brought up the upcoming governor's race. He was short on specifics; I felt that if he were serious about running, he would have already put together a detailed game plan. If he planned to be a candidate, he was keeping it close to his vest, and that just wasn't McKeithen's style. After several hours, I accepted his offer for a cup of coffee for the road. He handed me a plastic mug with his name on it, and I headed back to Baton Rouge.

The next day, I told Edwards that I did not think McKeithen would run against him in the fall. I also suggested that Edwards initiate more contact with McKeithen—phone calls and, especially, an open invitation to the Governor's Mansion on LSU-football weekends.

John McKeithen played an important role in my early political development. He openly supported me every time I was on the ballot. I join many others who will greatly miss him.

**Tuesday, July 6, 1999**
**Baton Rouge, Louisiana**

> *Of all the officers of the Government, those of the Department of Justice should be kept most free from any suspicion of improper action on partisan or factual grounds.*
> Theodore Roosevelt[40]

Thirty-six newspapers around the state, all members of the Moody chain, ran editorials this week under the headline, "What are the true intentions of the Justice Department?" The comments condemn the efforts of the U.S. Attorney's office to directly affect elections in Louisiana.

*A review of the actions of the United States Justice Department over the last few years raises the question of whether the U.S. Attorney's Office and the U.S. Department of Justice is really interested in fighting political crime in Louisiana, or whether its real focus is to shape the course of Louisiana politics.*

*The Justice Department's investigations into political crime in Louisiana follow a pattern of questionable timing which has, in fact, actually shaped the Louisiana political process, but usually accomplishes little or nothing other than needlessly tarnishing reputations, ruining careers, and ensuring certain apparent political objectives.*

---

[40] Letter to Attorney General William H. Moody, August 9, 1904, in Homer S. Cummings, *Federal Justice* (Cambridge, Mass.: Da Capo Press, 1937), 500.

*Even as we write, we have information that yet another sitting state official has become the target of a long-running investigation going back to the year 1996. We suspect that news of this investigation and a possible indictment will be leaked this summer suspiciously near the time for qualifying for reelection.*[41]

The lengthy editorial goes on to mention a number of state officials who have been abused by the U.S. Attorney's office, including Governor Mike Foster and Attorney General Richard Ieyoub. I have received numerous copies of the Moody editorial from friends and from average citizens who share its concern over the tactics of the U.S. Attorney. I have decided to go public in denying the rumors and spurious allegations that are appearing more frequently in the press. Qualifying for statewide elections, and my reelection effort, are a little more than a month away. Some of the recent news stories were obviously based on leaks from the U.S. Attorney's office in New Orleans. Maybe the prosecutors, fearing they don't have a strong case against me, can encourage my opponents and get me defeated in the election.

According to neutral observers, however, no one can figure out what I am supposed to have done. There has been no allegation that I benefited financially or in any other way. The receiverships office was not under the jurisdiction of my office, so I had no legal authority to take any action that would help Cascade, David Disiere, Governor Edwards, or anyone else. Many people are asking what I could possibly be guilty of. Perhaps that's the prosecutors' tactic. Leak unfounded but damaging allegations to the press, stir up opponents who think I might face future charges, and get me defeated. Then perhaps, in desperation, I will come to them with some criminal scenario involving Edwin Edwards.

My lawyer Bill Jeffress has told the prosecutors that if I knew of any criminal wrongdoing I would gladly tell them. I've done it many times in the past. The cooperation of my office has led to the conviction of numerous people for insurance fraud. But I have no knowledge of any crime committed in the Cascade case.

---

[41] *Crowley Post-Signal*, July 6, 1999.

On the other hand, I'm not sure that's relevant to the U.S. Attorney's office. The prosecutors apparently feel that if they have to make something up, so be it – anything to get Edwards. It's hard to believe that this is a tactic used by the government, but sadly it's looking more and more as if that is the case.

**Thursday, July 8, 1999**
**Baton Rouge, Louisiana**

Reaction to the Moody editorial has been swift and strong. I have received letters from all over the state expressing outrage over the U.S. Attorney's office trying to influence the election process. Numerous letters to the editor have expressed the same sentiment. This is from the *Crowley Post-Signal:*

> *Since your editorial, the U.S. Attorney has done it again. This time they have insinuated that Insurance Commissioner Jim Brown is somehow in trouble in connection with the Edwards case. All vague, of course, which leaves Brown to twist slowly in the wind as his election comes up this fall. This is clear political meddling, pure and simple. With all the nastiness in Washington, the Department of Justice needs to stay home and clean up its own house.*[42]

From the *Lake Arthur Sun-Times:*

> *How right you were about the U.S. Attorney trying to affect Louisiana elections by timing of their legal action. Right after you ran your editorial about that issue, it got "leaked" that Insurance Commissioner Jim Brown may be involved in a U.S. Attorney investigation. His election is only a few months away. How coincidental?*[43]

From the *Gueydan Journal:*

---

[42] *Crowley Post-Signal*, June 27, 1999.
[43] *Lake Arthur Sun-Times*, July 1, 1999.

*You have opened up a curious can of worms with your editorial about Department of Justice interference with Louisiana elections.*[44]

From the *Abbeville Meridional:*

*Thank you for your editorial about the U.S. Attorney trying to affect Louisiana elections. No investigation like this should take nine years, with rumor and innuendo ruining reputations along the way. How would U.S. Attorney Eddie Jordan like it if he was the victim of such rumors?*[45]

From the *Church Point News:*

*You were right about the U.S. Attorney's office playing politics. We need more media coverage of this issue to expose exactly what you editorialized about: Federal meddling in Louisiana elections.*[46]

The *New Orleans Times-Picayune* also ran a lengthy article over the weekend on the entire Cascade matter.[47] It was basically a rehash of the allegations about David Disiere and Governor Edwards, with few comments about me, but it is obvious the U.S. Attorney's office is continuing to push this investigation. Rumors abound, and I hear daily some outrageous allegation with no basis in fact. Some of it even appears in print. One rumor appeared in the June 24 edition of the *Louisiana Political Fax Weekly*, an insider's newsletter on Louisiana politics published by John Maginnis. The story stated: "Sources say that Brown's exposure comes from alleged personal use by him and his family of assets of Cascade Insurance Company, including a vehicle and a condo in Colorado."[48]

It would be an understatement to say that I was outraged. On no occasion had I used any car or condo belonging to Cascade or any

---

[44] *Gueydan Journal*, July 1, 1999.
[45] *Abbeville Meridional*, July 1, 1999.
[46] *Church Point News*, July 1, 1999.
[47] New Orleans *Times-Picayune*, July 4, 1999.
[48] *Louisiana Political Fax Weekly*, June 24, 1999.

other insurance company. The story was completely false and obviously damaging to me.

I immediately called John Maginnis. He admitted a mistake had been made and that I deserved a correction. Unfortunately, his weekly publication was about to take a two-week break. I told John that I felt the story was so damaging he should make an immediate correction. To his credit, he did just that. The next morning, a three-sentence fax went out to all *Fax Weekly* subscribers: "The June 24 story on the details of the federal investigation involving Insurance Commissioner Jim Brown is incorrect. I relied on unsubstantiated information from a source. The *Fax Weekly* retracts the story and regrets any problems it has caused to the Brown family."[49]

It is a rare thing for someone in the media to admit a mistake. John showed professionalism and class in his prompt correction of false information about me.[50]

In yesterday's *Times-Picayune*, James Gill wrote a column that obviously concerns me regarding the motives of the U.S. Attorney's office. "There is no doubt that the feds regard as their principal target [Governor Edwin Edwards]. The insurance commissioner will merely be lagniappe."[51]

James Gill is saying exactly what I feel is happening. Eddie Jordan and his crew in New Orleans are uneasy about their riverboat-licensing case against Edwards. To build up the pressure, they may feel they need additional indictments to push Edwards further out on the edge. Unfortunately, I may be caught in the crossfire. It is unfair, but it's also obvious. The U.S. Attorney's office has little concern for anybody who gets in the way as it tries to run down Edwin Edwards at any cost.

Numerous newspaper stories this week, raised questions about the legal authority for the FBI to obtain wiretaps of Edwards' home and office. It is common knowledge now that the FBI put electronic listening devices in Edwards' home, his office, and his son's office.

---

[49] Ibid., June 25, 1999.

[50] John Maginnis has written two important books on recent Louisiana political history. *The Last Hayride,* published in 1984, tells about Edwin Edwards's efforts to regain the Governor's Mansion in a campaign against incumbent Dave Treen. In 1992, Maginnis published *Cross to Bear,* covering the historic "race from hell" in which Edwards defeated David Duke in an election followed throughout the country.

[51] New Orleans *Times-Picayune,* July 7, 1999.

They also put a video camera in Edwards' office. Under federal law, a judge has to sign an order authorizing such wiretaps, and the order must be based on specific sworn facts presented to the judge by the FBI.

One of the codefendants in Edwards' riverboat-gambling case is Andrew Martin, who was executive assistant to the governor for years. Besides being indicted in the riverboat-gambling case, Martin was charged with income-tax evasion in federal court last March. These charges also relate to income Martin supposedly received through his riverboat-gambling activities.

My attorney Bill Jeffress called several months ago to see if I had any objection to Martin's hiring Bill's firm to file a lengthy motion claiming the FBI improperly and illegally obtained court authorization for wiretaps and electronic surveillance against Edwards and another codefendant, Cecil Brown. Bill said that his filing the motion would help me if charges were later filed against me in the Cascade case. Both the casino-gambling investigation and the Cascade investigation are based on information obtained from these wiretaps. If Bill Jeffress, representing Andrew Martin, could show the court that the FBI had given false information in asking for approval of the wiretaps, I would certainly benefit. No illegally obtained conversations between Edwards and me could be used against me. So I gave Bill the go-ahead to represent Andrew Martin.

Bill filed a detailed 105-page brief that alleged that federal prosecutors had based the wiretap application on uncorroborated claims by convicted swindler Patrick Graham of Houston. These claims included statements by Graham that he had paid Edwards and Cecil Brown almost $250,000 to help get a state contract to build a private prison in Jena, Louisiana. Conveniently, the application by the FBI failed to tell federal judge Don Walter of Shreveport that the tapes Graham made of conversations with Cecil Brown contained direct denials by Brown of any money paid to Edwards. Jeffress also wrote that a bankruptcy judge in Houston had later established that Graham really gave the money not to Brown but to Graham's brother for legal fees. The Houston judge called the Grahams "the most manipulative con men probably on the face of the world."

Bill Jeffress further stated in the brief that the FBI had told Judge Walter that the Graham brothers had never been known to give them false information. Bill's motion states that the FBI "deliberately misconstrued and creatively paraphrased" conversations between Graham and Brown "to suggest criminality that did not exist."

The Jeffress motion also charges that the FBI did not provide the judge with proof that the electronic surveillance was turning up evidence that could not be obtained any other way, as required by federal law. In short, Jeffress' brief on behalf of Andrew Martin says that the FBI gave false information to Judge Walter and that there was no justification to obtain the wiretaps in the first place.[52]

Bill Jeffress would not put something like this in a motion unless he strongly believed in what he was writing. His principles are just too high. That's why I hired him in the first place.

Most of us believe that a crime is a crime and that no one should get off on "technicalities." But I also think any fair-minded person believes there is a limit to how far the government should go. How would you feel if you discovered that, unbeknownst to you, every telephone conversation you've had in your home and office for the past few years had been taped? Think of the things you say in personal conversations with spouse or family, the things you say in jest, the things you say in anger. Would you want them all played back to you? Wiretaps certainly can be helpful and should be permitted, but only when there is direct evidence of a crime.

The FBI should not be allowed to go on a "fishing expedition," and listen in on someone they have "suspicions about" or someone they "just don't like." The full facts have yet to come out, but it is troubling that our government can target someone and then go listen to his conversations for months to see if they can possibly stumble upon a crime. That's more than troubling—it's downright scary.

**Wednesday, July 28, 1999**
**Baton Rouge, Louisiana**

News articles throughout the state continue to express puzzlement as to why I'm involved in the Cascade investigation. Political columnist John Maginnis wrote in his weekly statewide column:

---

[52] U.S. v. Martin, et al. U.S.D.C. Eastern District of La., Criminal Docket No. 99-069, Sect. G (M5-Motion to Suppress Wire Interceptions, P. 18, Exh. 5-B (p. 9).

*Not even an indictment, should that occur, may be enough to deny re-election to Insurance Commissioner Jim Brown. Prosecutors still seem to be struggling, if not fishing, to develop plausible criminal charges to attach to Brown's dealings with Edwards and the owner of a failed insurance company. Insurance agency owner Allen Boudreaux, a Metairie Republican, is thinking about running, but probably not without a timely assist from the Justice Department. Yet the closer the election draws near, the less likely the feds will act soon, lest they be accused of political interference.*[53]

I certainly have to prepare for a number of challengers and consider the worst scenario that could happen to me. It is time to gear up my campaign staff and bring in the group of professionals who helped me in my last two successful elections. I have instructed pollster Jim Kitchens to gear up for a lengthy poll right after qualifications conclude next month. I want to see who is actually going to challenge me and then do a detailed analysis of the candidates and the issues. Jim is preparing a "baseline" poll that will cover the positives and negatives about me, questions about the Cascade investigation, and the strengths and weaknesses of my opponents. The poll will also help me prioritize the issues I want to discuss during the campaign. Polls alone should not be the deciding factor in what issues I bring before the public. But when you have to convey a message in a thirty-second TV spot, it's a question of priorities. What's more important to the public, getting uninsured vehicles off the road to lower insurance rates, or pushing legislation to enforce building codes for better hurricane protection? How high a priority are healthcare issues? Again, only so much can be said in a television commercial. So polling is important to help set priorities.

I also called George Kennedy this week. George is a local media guru; the best I have ever dealt with in making the message look good on the screen. In the past George has often worked all night to create a television spot to be aired the next day.

And, of course, I have alerted Rannah Gray. She is my dear friend, has outstanding writing ability, and has been the mainstay of

---

[53] *Louisiana Political Fax Weekly,* July 9, 1999.

virtually every campaign I have run going back to the 1980s. Rannah was my executive assistant when I was secretary of state. She has

George Kennedy and Rannah Gray work with me on television production.

been working as assistant athletic director at LSU for several years. But when campaign time rolls around, Rannah gives her evenings (which often run into the early morning hours) to working with George to produce very effective television commercials for me. She has never turned me down, and it looks like this time I'm really going to need her. In fact, if the worst happens—I face numerous opponents and I do get indicted—I will certainly be facing the biggest political and personal struggle of my life.

**Friday, August 13, 1999**
**New Orleans, Louisiana**

It is always nice to be warmly received by old friends, and that was the case this morning when I spoke to the annual meeting of the Louisiana Municipal Association in Baton Rouge. Among the mayors and aldermen in attendance were many whom I have known since the 1970s, when I was a state senator. I took the time to reminisce about how far we have come in providing public services over the last thirty years.

It was a great reception by a friendly group who seemed to have no concern over the rumors about Cascade. When I left, I drove to my New Orleans office to attend several afternoon meetings. While there, I received a fax that a federal jury in New Orleans had convicted former Arkansas State Representative Doug Wood on multiple counts of mail fraud involving Southshore Holding Company. Policyholders, investors, and bondholders lost more than two hundred million dollars when Southshore collapsed before I became commissioner back in February of 1991.

91

Southshore became my number-one priority when I took office, as reported by a major insurance publication, the *National Underwriter,* in 1992.

> *Newly-elected Insurance Commissioner Jim Brown also hit the ground running, asking within 24 hours of taking office in December for legislative approval of emergency budget revisions to fund the immediate examination of dozens of domestic companies—many of which haven't been looked at by Louisiana's Department of Insurance for more than three years. Southshore's operation is the centerpiece of criminal and civil investigations by state and federal authorities in Louisiana and several other states.*[54]

The insurance department provided information that has led to the conviction of seven defendants, so far, in the Southshore case. Former U.S. Attorney for New Orleans Bob Boitman, who now serves as one of the top assistants to present U.S. Attorney Eddie Jordan, has repeatedly acknowledged how effective my office has been in making cases for the New Orleans office.

Boitman had called in July 1994 to ask me to join a task force of Department of Justice investigators, FBI agents, and several other insurance commissioners to discuss better ways to work together on insurance-fraud cases. At Boitman's suggestion, I invited four other commissioners, and we met with his group at the Department of Justice on the morning of Tuesday, September 13, 1994. At that meeting, Bob Boitman told the group in no uncertain terms, "Jim Brown and the Department of Insurance have been a tremendous help to the U.S. Attorney's office in New Orleans. Quite frankly, we could not make many of the cases we prosecute without his full cooperation."

It's extremely disappointing that the U.S. Attorney's office, which has for years relied on my office and my staff to help put their cases together, is now investigating me for questionable reasons. I don't know where U.S. Attorney Eddie Jordan is coming from, but it's unfair and it's wrong. But I'm just going have to live with it as qualification time for my reelection rapidly approaches.

---

[54] *National Underwriter*, January 13, 1992.

## Tuesday, August 19, 1999
## Baton Rouge, Louisiana

Despite the rumors that are circulating about the Cascade investigation, my office continues to receive good press coverage on insurance issues throughout the state. Today, the *Shreveport Times* ran a lead editorial praising our office for recommendations that have been adopted by the legislature to raise the driving age to sixteen, increase penalties for drunk drivers, and impound cars that are not insured. It was nice to see the strong headline *"Brown Fights for Consumers."*[55]

The *National Underwriter* also wrote a front-page story this week praising Louisiana for "thwarting efforts by missing financier Martin Frankel" to do business in Louisiana. Frankel had bilked millions of dollars from a number of states; when he tried to get a license in Louisiana, we promptly turned him down.[56]

There was some press attention this week to the Edwards riverboat-gambling case and the fact that the U.S. Attorney's office in New Orleans wants the federal judge in charge, Frank Polozola, to impanel an anonymous jury. In other words, no one would know anything about the jurors, including their names. The *Times-Picayune*'s story about the prosecutors' request said, "Anonymous juries are rare and most commonly associated with organized crime activities."[57] There are no drug dealers or mafia figures involved in this case. It is troubling that the U.S. Attorney's office wants to put a veil of secrecy over the proceedings. No one—the defendants, the public, or the system—benefits from this secrecy, except the prosecutors who imply that there is strong criminal activity. This is wrong, and I hope Judge Polozola does not grant such a motion. There is no justification for an anonymous jury in the riverboat-gambling case or in any other case related to public officials in Louisiana.

---

[55] *Shreveport Times*, August 19, 1999.
[56] *National Underwriter*, July 13, 1999.
[57] *Times-Picayune*, July 13, 1999.

**August 19, 1999**
**Baton Rouge, Louisiana**

Today I talked to both of my lawyers, Bill Jeffress in Washington and Camille Gravel in Alexandria, trying to anticipate both legal and political events in the weeks to come. Qualifying for the fall election is September 8, and there has been much speculation throughout the state on various "what if" scenarios.

John Maginnis, in his weekly *"Louisiana Politics"* column that appears in newspapers throughout the state, summed up my dilemma fairly well:

> *A cloud has been hanging over Jim Brown since 1997 when a federal grand jury began investigating his dealings with former Governor Edwin Edwards and the owner of a failed insurance company. Yet the probe has been rather cloudy itself. Defense attorneys are puzzled how federal prosecutors will fit the known facts into a criminal theory, but they can be very creative.*
>
> *Brown has filled up his war chest for a third-term bid. As a result, possible opponents have stood back, waiting to see if he will be the third consecutive Louisiana insurance commissioner to be indicted. If the feds don't move against him in the next two weeks, he walks back in. Even if he were indicted, it would take a clear-cut case, not a dense paper chase to render Brown vulnerable.*[58]

Bill Jeffress has recommended that we take our case directly to the Justice Department in Washington. Today he sent a lengthy letter with numerous attachments to James Robinson, an assistant attorney general in Washington who heads up the criminal division of the Justice Department.

Bill is asking for a meeting of high-level Justice Department officials to review this entire matter. He is trying to set up a meeting with the prosecutors and our legal team to make our plea that there is

---

[58] John Maginnis, *"Louisiana Politics"* (weekly column), August 17, 1999.

no justification for any criminal charges. I have some concern over our ability to explain our side of this very complicated case. With hundreds of thousands of documents, it will take a major effort by someone unfamiliar with the case to weed through all that has happened over several years and draw a fair conclusion.

One of the biggest problems I face in getting a fair hearing from the Justice Department is the fact that Edwin Edwards is involved. Bill Jeffress summed it up well in his letter to Robinson:

*There are those who would say that if the name of this lawyer had been anything other than Edwin Edwards, the matter would not have been made the subject of a federal criminal investigation, much less a proposed indictment. We respectfully submit that return of an indictment would add fuel to doubts by many thoughtful people in Louisiana that ordinary principles of federal prosecution are applied when it comes to Edwin Edwards or, for that matter, other elected Louisiana officials. For that reason and others, the indictment would hurt, not help, the pending prosecution of Edwards and others in the riverboat-gambling case.*

*The proposed indictment of Commissioner of Insurance Jim Brown is especially puzzling, as it lacks virtually all of the elements on which federal prosecutions of state officials are commonly based. We understand that the government has a theory, discussed later in this letter, that Judge A. Foster Sanders sought, and Edwin Edwards provided, some corrupt inducement in connection with the matter. Whatever may be the evidence to support that theory, Jim Brown had no involvement in any such thing. He neither sought nor received any money or personal benefits. He had no financial interest, secret or otherwise. He had no official power over the settlement. He made no false public reports or statements; in fact, we know of no false public statements or reports by any person. Mr. Brown disclosed no confidential information of the Department of Insurance. And he took no official act that can fairly be characterized as detrimental to the interests of the State, its citizens, or the Department heads.*

Jeffress also raised the question of how unfair it would be to bring charges in the middle of a Louisiana election:

> *It is an understatement to say that an indictment of Jim Brown on the evidence in this matter would be a stretch. The timing of the prosecution, however, adds a further element of fundamental unfairness. The proposed indictment would come less than 60 days before this year's election in which Jim Brown is the incumbent. He would have no practical possibility of being tried and exonerated before Election Day. If there has ever been a case brought by the Department of Justice against an elected official so unfairly timed, we have no knowledge of it.*

In his lengthy (78 pages) presentation on the Cascade controversy, Bill made an eloquent case for how unfair it would be to bring any indictments at all, particularly in the coming months. But the Edwards factor continues to trouble me. Many observers believe, and I share their view, that the New Orleans prosecutors are worried about how strong their riverboat-gambling charges are against Edwards. They may well feel that an indictment of Edwards and others in the Cascade case will build public opinion against the former governor and make it look like there is a pattern of wrongdoing on his part. I would be caught in the crossfire, but it's obvious the prosecutors care little about fairness or who may get hurt in the process. I just hope I can get through the qualification period without anything else happening in this case. It is inconceivable that any charges will be brought once the election is underway.

## August 20, 1999
## Baton Rouge, Louisiana

Another state official, Elections Commissioner Jerry Fowler, was indicted yesterday by a state grand jury on multiple counts of malfeasance in office, money laundering, and conspiracy. Even though Fowler's problems do not touch my office in any way, his charges help fuel rumors about what may happen in the Cascade case.

The *Louisiana Political Review* ran a lengthy story about Fowler's indictments and then analyzed my situation:

> *Despite a federal investigation swirling around him and his department, Brown enters the election season with an enviable poll and financial numbers. An early August poll shows Brown's approval/disapproval rating at 57-16 percent. According to the latest campaign finance report, Brown had $600,000 in his war chest.*
>
> *The next couple of weeks could be critical for Brown. Next Tuesday, attorneys for him, Edwin Edwards, and others are meeting with Justice Department officials in Washington to talk over the federal investigation into the dealings of Cascade Insurance Company. The pro-forma meeting gives attorneys the opportunity to try to dissuade prosecutors from proceeding with indictments.[59]*

I was also quoted in the *Shreveport Times* today about the Washington meeting next week:

> *"This is one of a series of meetings to clear up any concerns the Justice Department has about this issue. I'm confident that no one in the Department of Insurance has any legal problems. We are obviously anxious to have this matter brought to an end."[60]*

That last comment is an understatement. Qualification for my reelection is a little more than a week away. It's hard to imagine that any indictments would come down in the Cascade case so close to the election season. But I certainly am not overly confident.

One of my best friends in high school was Jewish. When things seemed to be going a little too well for us, he would tell me, "I come from Russian Jews. My grandfather used to tell me that whenever

---

[59] *Louisiana Political Review*, August 19, 1999.
[60] *Shreveport Times,* August 20, 1999.

things were going along well, perhaps too well, he and his family would hear hoof beats. The Cossacks."[61]

I just pray I don't hear hoof beats in the coming weeks.

**Friday, September 10, 1999**
**Baton Rouge, Louisiana**

"You are my sunshine, my only sunshine." More than 1,000 friends of former governor Jimmie Davis to mark his 100th birthday sang the Louisiana state song. Davis looked frail and had to be helped up to the podium but he was all smiles and didn't miss a note of the song he wrote, which is known worldwide.

Very few people know that the governor had a horse named Sunshine. Sunshine was a palomino that Davis rode up the steps of the state capitol back in the 1961. He told the press that he just wanted Sunshine to see his office. Sunshine is buried in my old senatorial district in Tensas Parish. If you drive up Highway 61 following the Mississippi River to Natchez, through my old hometown of Ferriday, and head north toward the Arkansas border, you will pass through the town of Newellton. A right turn onto the main street of Newellton will take you to Highway 608, which curves around Lake St. Joseph. The Davis family farm is there; run by the governor's son Jimmie Davis, Jr. Right off the highway is a bronze plaque that marks the grave of Sunshine.

I had visited Governor Davis earlier that week at the house he built directly behind the present governor's mansion – although he was in bed and obviously weak, his mind was sharp. He reminded me about the first time we had met back in 1971, when I was running for the state senate. He had served two terms as governor, from 1944 to 1948 and from 1960 to 1964. In his earlier terms, he had been known as the "peace and harmony" governor; his accomplishments included an extensive highway-paving program, starting the retirement system for state employees, and requiring everyone to have a driver's license. (His own license is still Number One.)

---

[61] The Cossacks were generally peasant soldiers, often frontiersmen from southern Russia organized as cavalry. They were used to quell strikes and other disturbances, and attack villages in any way opposed to the Czar. Russian "shtetl" (isolated settlements of Russian Jews) was often their target.

But he was best known for his singing. In 1931, he went to Chicago and recorded "You Are My Sunshine," a classic that would become known throughout the world. But he wasn't satisfied with the recording, and he waited another eight years before he re-recorded and finally released it. The governor wrote more than 400 songs and recorded 50 albums. While most candidates would give a standard stump speech at campaign rallies, Jimmie Davis would entertain with such ditties as "High-Geared Mama" and "The Red Nightgown Blues."

When I met him in 1971, Davis was seventy-one years old. He decided to run for governor one more time. Most of the major candidates used television to make their political pitch, but Davis campaigned the way he always had. He got his band together, climbed aboard the Jimmie Davis bus, and went from town to town singing "You Are My Sunshine" and asking for votes.

At a stop in my hometown of Ferriday, one of the locals asked Davis about a proposed law requiring farmers to keep their cattle fenced—a controversial issue in rural parishes. Without missing a beat, Davis turned to his band, requested an "A" chord, and belted out the popular western tune "Don't Fence Me In."

I checked his schedule and noted that he was about to begin a three-day swing through every sizeable community in my senatorial district. Whether people would vote for Jimmie Davis or not, I knew they wanted to hear him sing. I quickly covered the entire area with signs that said: "Jim Brown invites you to a rally to elect him the next state senator from the 32nd district. Special guests: Governor Jimmie Davis and his band."

At his first rally, I asked the governor if I could say a word or two following his address, and he could not have been more gracious. At stop after stop, he gave me a rousing introduction. I worked the crowds that he had gathered, and just about everyone left with a Jim Brown card in his pocket.

Every time I have been on the ballot, Governor Davis has supported me. I know his time is running out, and it's a wonderful tribute to see so many friends gathered for what may be a farewell tribute to a beloved Louisianan.[62]

---

[62] Governor Davis died a year later, on November 6, 2000, at 101 years old. I had the pleasure of visiting with him on several occasions in the months before he passed away.

**September 15, 1999**
**Baton Rouge, Louisiana**

The official campaign has begun. Neither of my two opponents is well known in the state, but both have the potential to throw bombs and spend money.

It was no surprise that Allen Boudreaux qualified against me. An insurance lawyer from the New Orleans area, he runs a company that owns several small insurance agencies throughout the state. Allen has supported me for years and has attended most of my fundraisers. He has said he will spend a million dollars of his own money, so he certainly has to be taken seriously.

Announcing for re-election in 1999.

Allen has told a number of my friends that he sees an opportunity. He probably thinks that, if I do get indicted, I will pull out of the election, and he just might be in the right place at the right time. He said little about me in his announcement last week. I think he will sit back and see what transpires in the weeks to come. I doubt he will spend much of his own money under the present circumstances.

My other opponent is something of a surprise, but I suppose his candidacy is understandable. Winston Riddick has run for several statewide offices, including insurance commissioner back in the 1970's and attorney general in 1991. He served as my first assistant the first four years I was in office. In 1995, for a variety of reasons, I had asked Winston to leave the department. I tried to do it in a professional way, and I offered to help him explore other opportunities. He asked me to call the chancellor at the Southern University Law School and recommend him for a teaching position, which I did; he subsequently became a professor. In addition, I went before the Board of Ethics to testify on his behalf when he sought approval to represent clients before the insurance department. To this day, his wife remains general counsel to the insurance department.

But Winston apparently continues to feel ill will because I did not keep him at the department. And, like Boudreaux, he no doubt feels there is an opportunity. If I am going to face charges in the weeks to come, he probably wants to be "lying in the gap," with visions of taking over my job.

I really can't resent either man for qualifying. Anyone has the right to run for this job, and they are just positioning themselves in case the worst happens to me. Such is politics, and after thirty years in public life I certainly know the rules of the game. On the other hand, I assume that they also understand the rules. Whatever happens, I can handle the pressure and can stand toe to toe with any opponent. I'm certainly not going to be on the defensive. They will probably blame me for everything under the sun that ever went wrong at the insurance department. But they have also been involved in insurance activities. We will all be defending our records. Frankly, I look forward to the debates in the weeks to come.

The qualifying of Boudreaux and Riddick stirred very little interest in the press. In New Orleans *Gambit Weekly* observed:

> *Here is another race that could not be a race but for the aid of the Federal Bureau of Investigation. Republican challenger Allen Boudreaux can use all the help he can get from the feds, as Brown starts the race with only 16 percent disapproval rating and $600,000 in his campaign account.*
>
> *Boudreaux, a large insurance agency owner, is faced with having to underwrite his own campaign, due to the insurance industry's overall satisfaction with Brown. The*

*Metairie Republican was even denied his own party's endorsement.*"[63]

Riddick was dismissed by most press reports as running for reasons of "sour grapes," to get even for losing his job at the department. A number of articles throughout the state have downplayed the controversy in my reelection efforts and haven't even mentioned my opponents by name. The *Concordia Sentinel* commented:

> *Commissioner of Insurance Jim Brown has two opponents. Brown has more experience in campaigning than any candidate on the entire ballot. He has run successfully for the state Senate, Secretary of State, unsuccessfully for governor, and successfully twice for Commissioner of Insurance.*
>
> *Brown is the dean of the state scene, although it seems as though it was only yesterday when he arrived in Ferriday as a young lawyer burning alive with political ambition.*
> *He pre-dates all of them, going all the way back to Edwin Edwards' first term as governor, Brown's first as a Senator.*
>
> *And who knows? Four years from now, in the year 2003, Jim Brown may run for governor again in hopes of becoming the first governor elected in the 21$^{st}$ century.*[64]

I'm flattered that there is speculation about my future political plans. At this juncture, I'll settle for no indictments, and an easy reelection victory.

A number of former prosecutors and lawyers, by the way, are weighing in on the propriety of bringing indictments at election time. Former Baton Rouge U.S. Attorney Ray Lamonica was quoted last week as saying:

---

[63] *Gambit Weekly*, September 21, 1999.
[64] *Concordia Sentinel*, September 15, 1999.

*"My view was always that as a policy matter, the U.S. Attorney should not interfere with elections if he can avoid it. If you have the opportunity, you should do it before qualifying to make sure you're not having an impact on the election."*[65]

Similar comments were expressed by John Pavia, a law professor at Quinnipiac School of Law in Connecticut: "Every prosecutor who has responsibility for investigating alleged wrongdoing involving elected officials has a responsibility to wrap up their investigation and get the information out there in a way that has the least amount of impact on the election."[66]

Baton Rouge defense lawyer, Karl Koch, agrees: "The government has come forward with unsavory allegations about Louisiana politicians at the most sensitive times. Looking at the track record, it certainly looks as if the government is attempting to influence state political decisions, and that's not right. It's another example of how the federal government is trying to occupy the state of Louisiana."[67]

I still think the whole controversy is academic. It's not just a question of the timing in my case; it's the fact that there is no justification for any charges. From my perspective, we did nothing wrong. How on earth can the prosecutors make innuendoes about my department's handling of Cascade when every single policyholder was paid and the state did not lose one penny? It just doesn't make sense.

## Tuesday, September 21, 1999
## Baton Rouge, Louisiana

Jim Kitchens delivered my first poll results this morning. He ran a "baseline poll" to look at the strengths and weaknesses of my opponents and to evaluate my own situation. The numbers look good.

If the race were held today, I would win handily with 59 percent of the vote. Allen Boudreaux, the Republican, finished second with 11

---

[65] *Times-Picayune,* September 4, 1999.
[66] Ibid.
[67] Ibid.

percent, and Winston Riddick was way back with 4 percent. That leaves 26 percent of the voters undecided.

Not only are my favorable numbers high, the issues that I have been pushing for the last few years have strong public support. On some questions, my numbers went through the roof. For instance, there was this question: "If people refuse to buy the required insurance for their car, do you agree that it is only fair that the police should hold their car until they have the insurance required by law?"

Eighty-two percent of those polled agree with my seizure plan. My proposals on health insurance, particularly to help senior citizens, also polled extremely high. If I keep hammering these two major issues, which have been a cornerstone of my platform for several years, I should maintain a large lead and even increase it.

The poll also presented some negative issues. One question: "Jim Brown is being investigated by a grand jury. This just goes to show that he is a typical Louisiana politician, and someone new should be elected."

Forty percent of the voters agreed with that statement, but fifty percent disagreed. So at this stage the Cascade investigation really is not doing any significant damage to my reelection efforts.

Jim also polled a number of issues involving my opponents. I hope not to have to run a negative campaign, but if Boudreaux or Riddick attacks me, I will need background on key issues to properly respond.

The fact that Boudreaux was in the insurance business was enough to build a strong negative against him. The poll asked the following question: "Allen Boudreaux is a self-made businessman and owns a number of insurance agencies. Would this make you more likely or less likely to vote for him?"

Twenty-four percent said it would make them more likely but forty-three percent said it would make them less likely to vote for Boudreaux. When the poll asked about certain employees and associates of Allen Boudreaux who had faced legal problems, his negatives increased dramatically.

Winston Riddick has been involved in Louisiana politics for years and has faced his share of controversy. The mere fact that he is presently a law-school professor was enough to give him sizable negatives. Twenty-three percent of the voters felt favorably toward

Riddick when told he was a law professor, but thirty-four percent looked on this as a negative.

Both opponents will be hurt by the fact that they are relatively unknown. If they use their financial resources to do nothing more than attack me, they won't be giving the voters an alternative. They are going to have to build their own images first, and this is going to cost them a significant amount of money. Whatever my negatives, I have a positive image with the public. I'm not overconfident, but I feel good about the results of my first poll. As the campaign gets closer, Jim Kitchens will do significant additional work for me.

**Friday, September 24, 1999**
**Baton Rouge, Louisiana**

I just got indicted! Short of hearing that you have a life-threatening disease, it's hard to imagine getting worse news. You stare at the wall and stare some more as thoughts bounce around in your mind. *How could this be? How could they do this to me? Why now? How do I respond? Who do I call? What do I say? When do I say it? I should call Gladys! I need to call my children! What do I tell them? What do I say publicly? Do I start taking the flood of calls that will inevitably be coming in? What do I say to the press?* Over and over you ask yourself that question: *What should I do?*

After I got the news, I asked the phone desk to hold all my calls and give me time to pull my thoughts together. Then I made my first call, to Gladys. "I just received word I was indicted. Fifty-six counts."

She sounded shocked. "Now? In the middle of the election? Over nothing? How could they do that to you? It's so unfair." Then she asked the same question I had been asking myself: "What are you going to do now?"

"Obviously, I want to come home, shut the door, and tune out everything. But I can't. I need to get my thoughts together and make some kind of a statement. Probably call a press conference in a few hours. This whole thing is outrageous! I've been wronged! I need to forthrightly say this. If I say nothing, the perception will build that I have something to hide. And I don't. Let me think about it all for a while. I'll come home for lunch, and we can talk about it some more."

I asked my executive assistant Helen Smith to assemble the department heads and other key staff members in my conference room. They needed to hear from me what had happened and what my reaction would be.

"I'm shocked, angry, and extremely disappointed," I told them. "But we need to diminish the effect this is going to have on the office. I need each of you to help me keep the office moving forward. I know what happened, and I firmly believe the public will be sympathetic. A number of you worked on the Cascade case, and you know that our work was a major success. Not one penny was lost for the state. The policyholders got their money. It was probably the most successful receivership we have ever handled. There is absolutely no basis for these charges, and any reasonable person should understand this if we take the time to explain our position. That's my job, and I obviously will be doing it every day in the weeks to come. I need each of you to carry out your duties in a professional manner. When questions come up, tell anyone who asks that I am going to fight these charges aggressively, that I plan on being solidly reelected, and that I'm not going to let this tarnish or diminish the first-rate job our department has done in recent years."

My staff members were shaken but supportive. After they left, I sat down and wrote a short statement about how unfair the charges were, and how I plan to fight them. Allan Pursnell, who coordinates the department's media activities, agreed to set up a press conference.

"What are you going to say to the press?" he asked.

"I really don't know. I'm going to hand out a short statement, express publicly how wrong I feel I have been treated, and let it go from there. But I have to say *something*. I'm not going to keep silent or hide. The public wants to hear from me. They want my assurance that I've done nothing wrong. Notify the press that I will be in our main hearing room on the first floor at 1:30 this afternoon."

After a quick lunch with Gladys at home, I returned to the office and called both Bill Jeffress and Camille Gravel. They agreed I should hold a press conference and come out swinging. My brother Jack Brown and I talked briefly, and he agreed to go see my mother and explain what had happened. I didn't know how she would react; I will have a long talk with her later this evening. There are so many people to call—my four children, the relatives, in-laws, and a host of close friends—but first I need to speak to the press.

At 1:30 I took the elevator down to the main hearing room on the first floor of the insurance department. It holds around a hundred people, and the room was packed; people were spilling out of the room and into the hallway. I was expecting the local television stations, and the capitol press corps to put the news out on the wire service. It seemed that every daily newspaper in the state was there, and I counted eleven television cameras. Normally, I'd banter with various members of the press until the conference actually began. Not today. When I walked in, the room fell silent.

Members of my staff handed out copies of the statement I had quickly drafted at my desk this morning. It came right to the point, as I read it out loud:

*At the outset, let me say — and you'll be hearing this again – I am innocent. I did nothing wrong.*

*The investigation into this matter has been going on for three years. The prosecutors have chosen to bring this indictment just a few weeks before my election, knowing full well that I would not have time to defend or exonerate myself before Election Day.*

*I hope the people of Louisiana will recognize the gross unfairness of this action, and I hope the U.S. Attorney's Office isn't attempting to influence the election process in our state.*

*As this case unfolds, it will become apparent that I have had the misfortune of being an innocent bystander, who happened to be in the vicinity when a fight broke out between the federal government and Edwin Edwards. I want to assure the people of Louisiana that I have not violated the public's trust.*

*The government, in its zeal to pursue the former governor, has chosen to interpret actions of others, over whom I had no control, as part of a scheme involving me. I have had an extraordinary record of restoring the reputation of the Department of Insurance, and if the government believes otherwise it has been misled. I plan to show overwhelmingly that I have not wavered from the oath office I took in 1991, when the public first elected me as their Insurance Commissioner. In fact, I have built the Department of Insurance into one of the leading regulatory bodies in the country.*

*In this case, I exercised no authority, gave no advantage, nor sought any. At the time in question, I did not even have authority to act in the Cascade case, that authority being assumed by the 19<sup>th</sup> Judicial District Court.*

*I am not accused of receiving any monetary gain, any special favors, or any benefits. I am only charged with trying to restore the integrity of my office, and bringing back a portion that was taken away. It is outrageous for the prosecutors to interpret this as any crime. I was only doing what would have been expected of any public official.*

*To put it in perspective, this seems to me like the political equivalent of a drive-by shooting, because I was in the wrong place at the wrong time.*

*I have served the people of this state for the last 28 years in public office.*

*I have done nothing wrong!*

*I am innocent of these charges!*

*And I am confident of being solidly reelected as Insurance Commissioner.*

I answered questions for about 30 minutes, but it was obvious the press did not know a lot about the case. Many of them seemed as puzzled about the charges as I was. I repeatedly raised the issue of the timing of the indictment.

"You're going to have a hard time finding any instance in the history of this country where a statewide elected official was charged by a federal prosecutor so close to the election. It just isn't done. It's looked on as grossly unfair and completely improper. This investigation has been going on for three years. Why are these charges brought now, just weeks before the election? What are the real motives? This is a blatant effort to directly affect the election process in Louisiana, and I hope every Louisiana citizen is outraged over the actions of the U.S. Attorney's office in New Orleans."

I have held hundreds of press conferences during my political career. This was certainly the most difficult of my life.

When the press conference ended, several reporters who had covered my activities for many years came up to express their sorrow and wish me well.

I headed back up to my office on the seventh floor, where I fielded a series of phone calls. It was time to talk to family members and close friends, to prepare them for what would certainly be the lead story on the evening news. I was able to reach most of my family, including my four children, my mother, my brother Jack, and my sister Madalyne. All are supportive and eager to help in any way they can.

About an hour after the press conference, I received a copy of an order signed by U.S. District Judge Frank Polozola, who placed a gag order on anyone involved in the Cascade trial, preventing defendants like me, as well as potential witnesses, from discussing the charges. To say I was shocked is an understatement. The prosecutors have made outrageous charges, full of bald-faced lies that led to 56 criminal counts against me. I am in the middle of a major reelection campaign, with election only weeks away. But Polozola's order prevents me from declaring my innocence and explaining what I know about the case. I can't speak out and defend myself? Such a gag order flies in the face of any constitutional process. It enables the prosecutors to make charges to which I cannot respond. It is unfair, and it is wrong. I cannot and will not stand by and let this judge shackle me this way. Now I see why lawyers who deal with him in his court refer to him as Ayatollah Polozola.

I immediately placed a call to Bill Jeffress and asked him to prepare a motion to file Monday morning overturning the gag order. Bill agrees with me that what Polozola has done is unconstitutional, and he will have a strong motion prepared to file.

This evening I returned calls from family members and friends who wanted to express their condolences and to offer their help. Thank God tomorrow is Saturday. I'll have the weekend to think through my options and prepare for the weeks to come.

Whatever plans I make, I can't change or ignore one terrible fact:

I just got indicted!

## Saturday, September 25, 1999
## Baton Rouge, Louisiana

As I expected, the charges against Governor Edwards, Ron Weems, Judge Foxy Sanders, Bob Bourgeois, David Disiere, and me dominated the news all last night and throughout the day today. Most of the daily papers carried my picture on the front page in color. The state's largest paper, the New Orleans *Times-Picayune*, headlined the story "INSURANCE INDICTMENT SNAGS BROWN, EDWARDS." Photographs of me, in full color, were larger than any I can remember seeing in the *Picayune* over the past thirty years. Gladys commented that, actually, they were good pictures. They were taken at my news conference, where I defended myself aggressively. Television and radio did in-depth stories and analyses of the charges throughout the day.[68]

I would like to just "ride out the storm" and deal with this major crisis in my life in a leisurely fashion. But Election Day is a little over a month away. This will certainly be a referendum on how the citizens of Louisiana feel about the charges against me.

---

[68] *Times-Picayune,* September 26, 1999.

John Hill, bureau chief for the *Shreveport Times* and *Monroe News-Star*, called and wanted to interview me for the Sunday papers. Normally, Gladys is quite protective of our time at home and doesn't want reporters interfering in our family life. But she likes John and feels he has been not only fair but extremely thorough in his stories on this case over the past few years. John came to the house, and we talked at length about my weekend plans. He wrote a balanced story for his weekend deadline.

*The phones and doorbells rang constantly Saturday at the Baton Rouge home of state Insurance Commissioner Jim Brown, who was overwhelmed by the out-pouring of support from friends and political allies.*

*"It leads me to believe that the people of Louisiana will judge me on my record and not on unsubstantiated allegations that just aren't true," Brown said.*

*Dressed in shorts and a knit shirt, he looked unworried as he joked with his wife, Gladys, about whether she wanted to be seen with him at the movie Double Jeopardy on Saturday evening, the day after he was indicted on conspiracy and fraud charges. He told her he would "wear dark glasses."*

*An army of attorneys from around the state called Brown to say they felt the charges were unfair and thin–easily defensible.*

*Among them was Jack Martzell, the New Orleans lawyer who is one of Louisiana's leading defense attorneys, the lawyer who successfully defended Muhammad Ali on defamation charges.*

*"I haven't heard the evidence, but its convoluted and hard to grasp," Martzell said. "It's difficult to understand the crime."*

Brown, confident he will be exonerated in U.S. Judge Frank Polozola's court of law, first must defend himself in the court of public opinion in the Oct. 23 primary election in which he faces two opponents, neither of whom is well funded.

He must find a way to do that and stay within Polozola's gag order that prevents defendants and witnesses from talking to the press, other than to explain what is on the public record.

"Within the limits of the gag order, I'm going to make it clear that I'm not accused of benefiting in any way," Brown said.

"I think the public will be very skeptical and suspicious that these prosecutors may be trying to influence our state elections," Brown said.

He noted that Governor Mike Foster on Thursday raised the issue by questioning why the U.S. Attorney's Office in New Orleans had subpoenaed the financial records of his 1995–96 post-election, preinaugural transition office. Foster suggested prosecutors were playing politics with the governor's re-election bid.

"Governor Foster has raised questions about this disturbing trend," Brown said.

Brown begins fighting back Monday, when he will speak to the Baton Rouge Press Club. On Tuesday, he starts a statewide television media campaign that will emphasize his eight-year record in helping lower auto insurance rates, improving healthcare policies and enacting the law that lets police impound uninsured autos.

"I'm going to be positive about my record," Brown said. "I am confident voters will give me the benefit of the doubt, realize the unfairness of the timing of these charges and *look at my record as insurance commissioner. And when they do, I feel I'll be strongly re-elected."*

*Meantime, Brown will continue going out to the movies with his wife—without dark glasses.*[69]

We did go to the movies tonight, to see *Double Jeopardy*, about a woman (Ashley Judd) who goes to prison for a crime she didn't commit. After a major effort, she is vindicated and set free. I hope that was a good omen for me.

## Sunday, September 26, 1999
## Baton Rouge, Louisiana

*Never give in, never give in never, never, never, never—in nothing great or small, large or petty, never give in except to convictions of honor and good sense.*
Winston Churchill[70]

It's 3:30 A.M. and I still haven't slept. Friends were coming by and calling until after 11:00 P.M. tonight. I wish I had the luxury of taking several days off to put this whole nightmare in perspective. But I have some big decisions to make.

Realistically, I should consider whether or not to continue this race. I obviously have a Mount Everest of a challenge ahead of me. With only a month to go, I will no doubt be spending every waking hour refuting the charges against me. Both of my opponents have significant financial resources, so I can anticipate a continual pounding on television. I have to ask myself; can I get through to the voters? Will they hear my story? Will they give me the benefit of the doubt?

I have more than $600,000 in my campaign fund, which can be used for legal expenses. Hopefully, that will take care of my legal costs. So one possibility would be to withdraw from the race, use the

---

[69] *The Times,* Sunday, September 27, 1999.

[70] Prime Minister Winston Churchill in a speech at the Harrow School, Harrow, England, October 29, 1941. Robert Rhodes James, ed., *Winston S. Churchill: His Complete Speeches, 1897–1963* (London: Chelsea House, 1974), Vol. 6, p. 6499.

campaign funds to pay my legal fees, and spend all my time and effort defending myself against these false charges.

But I can point to three reasons why I should stay in this race. First, based on the response I have received from throughout the state over the last several days, there seems to be a strong public feeling that what happened to me is grossly unfair. Many people who are less informed will just hear the word "indictment" and think the worst. I really believe the more fair-minded citizens will listen to what I have to say and base their decision in the voting booth on the job I've done so far as insurance commissioner.

Second, reelection will certainly help my defense. The fact that I can overcome these charges and be reelected will give me momentum as I move toward the trial next year. And I think my winning will be a huge plus psychologically for my family, friends, and supporters, an important first step in my being found innocent.

Third, I am not a quitter. I cannot see myself being bullied into withdrawing from this election and giving in to the selfish agenda of the prosecutors. I did nothing wrong and the election will give me the forum to point to an out-of-control U.S. Attorney's Office in New Orleans that is obviously playing politics and trying to convict me to further individual careers. I have too much pride in the job I've done as insurance commissioner, and I would feel humiliated if I stepped aside.

Tom Petty and the Heartbreakers said it well:

> *Well I won't back down; no I won't back down,*
> *You can stand me up at the gates of hell,*
> *But I won't back down,*
> *Gonna stand my ground, won't be turned around,*
> *And I'll keep this world from draggin' me down,*
> *Gonna stand my ground and I won't back down.*[71]

This will no doubt be the hardest election I will ever face. I'm going to have to travel constantly to defend myself in every corner in the state. It's going to be expensive. If I can get the public to focus on the

---

[71] Tom Petty, "I Won't Back Down," *Tom Petty and the Heartbreakers Greatest Hits*, MCA Records, Inc., 1993.

issues of insurance and the job I have done during the past eight years, I can win this race. So, after weighing my options into the early morning hours, I have decided to aggressively continue my reelection campaign. And I won't back down.

**Monday, September 27, 1999**
**Baton Rouge, Louisiana**

I've jumped right into the fire with little time to prepare. I had agreed several weeks ago to debate my two opponents at the Baton Rouge Press Club at noon today. When I accepted, I anticipated a lively debate on insurance issues. The office continues to receive excellent state and local press — insurance rates are dropping, and we have pushed a number of national initiatives on healthcare, flood protection, and other important issues. I can stand head and shoulders over both Boudreaux and Riddick on any regulatory matter. But today, as I expected, insurance issues were secondary.

I spent a good deal of my allotted time talking about the unfairness of the gag order by Judge Polozola and pointing out how hard it was to answer specifics from my opponents. The press coverage of our debate really wasn't that bad, with emphasis on my comments about how the gag order would stifle serious debate on the issues. I have vowed to have my lawyers file — by tomorrow, hopefully — documents to set aside the gag order. It's hard to believe that the Fifth Circuit Court of Appeals would prevent a candidate for public office, just weeks away from an election, from defending himself and answering the charges in the indictment.

The prosecutors can make outrageous claims in writing that are circulated by the news media across the entire state, but my hands are tied and I cannot respond. The Gestapo would be proud, but I am hopeful that this gagging will not be allowed in America.

**Tuesday, September 28, 1999**
**Baton Rouge, Louisiana**

*Free speech concerning public affairs is more than self-expression; it is the essence of self-government.*
Justice William J. Brennan Jr.[73]

115

The papers this morning were full of criticism of the gag order placed on me. My comments to the Baton Rouge Press Club yesterday, where I strongly criticized the unfairness of the gag order, were prominently reported throughout the state. The headline in the *Baton Rouge Morning Advocate* read: "GAG ORDER STIFLING." The article went on to say that I planned to challenge the legality of the order in court this week.[74]

Many news stories quoted New York attorney Floyd Abrams, who has argued numerous free-speech cases before the Supreme Court. "It seems to me deeply disturbing to limit the nature and breadth of public debate about the fitness of an individual for public office," Abrams said. "That is the inevitable effect of this gag order."[75]

The gag order was also strongly criticized by the *Morning Advocate*, which said in an editorial:

*We believe the First Amendment gets short shrift in many cases when gag orders are issued.*

*When candidates involved in an election are placed under a gag order, the situation becomes critical. The candidates have a right—indeed a duty—to explain their actions to the voters. In all fairness, they should also be able to defend themselves in public.*[76]

Former New Orleans U.S. Attorney Harry Rosenberg also raised questions about the unfairness of the gag order:

*Jim Brown cannot be in a re-election campaign, and abide by a gag order every time a reporter asks him about the case," Rosenburg said. "That would be a kamikaze run."*[77]

---

[73] *Garrison v. Louisiana*, 379 U.S. 74 (1964). The unanimous opinion of the Supreme Court was that District Attorney Jim Garrison had not libeled criminal-court judges by saying that the withholding of investigation funds indicated the protection of Canal Street clip joints.

[74] *The Advocate*, September 28, 1999.

[75] *The Advocate*, September 29, 1999.

[76] Ibid.

[77] *Times-Picayune*, September 26, 1999.

The bombardment of criticism obviously got to Judge Polozola. Late today, he canceled his gag order *"to protect the free speech rights of candidates in the Insurance race."*[78] If he feels that way today, why didn't he feel the same way a few days ago, before he was so heavily criticized?

Most legal observers I talked to about the issue concluded that Polozola's order would not hold up. The Fifth Circuit Court of Appeals would have overturned it, and he knew it. So to quiet the mounting criticism, he tried to seize the high road by letting me speak out on these charges. My lawyers had already prepared a motion to set the gag order aside, so Polozola's action not only tied my hands for four days, it cost me significant attorneys' fees. Still, I'm glad he finally saw the light and rescinded the order.

## Friday, October 1, 1999
## Baton Rouge, Louisiana

There was a media blitz today, as I drove all over the state to meet with newspaper editors in Lafayette, Shreveport, and Alexandria. Endorsements will be made in the coming weeks, and I think I still have a good chance of being supported by most of the state's papers. The indictments aside, I have a solid record as insurance commissioner, and both of my opponents have their share of baggage that will keep them on the defensive.

My office called late this afternoon to tell me that Judge Foxy Sanders had pled guilty to being part of a conspiracy to commit mail fraud and to witness tampering in the Cascade case. None of us on the defense side was really surprised. All the lawyers in the case, as well as the others charged, were aware of a separate investigation of Sanders' approval of the sale of a piece of property in a different insurance estate. He had appeared before the grand jury in March 1998. News articles then raised questions about the propriety of the sale to a close friend of Sanders.

*The Arist liquidation case was complicated by a 1995 dispute about the sale of the company's assets.*

---

[78] *Times-Picayune,* September 28, 1999

*Vernon Ellerbe, a Baton Rouge construction company owner who bid on Arist assets, has been subpoenaed to appear before the grand jury today to answer questions about the Arist liquidation, sources familiar with the transactions said.*

*Ellerbe was a high bidder in 1995 for a New Orleans shopping center owned by Arist. But he lost the right to buy the shopping center after a disgruntled bidder complained that Ellerbe might have close business and personal ties to Sanders, who oversaw the receivership office before retiring in 1996, lawyers involved in the transaction said.*

*Arist was controlled by Frances Pecora, a former state insurance rating commission member whose husband, Nofio Pecora, was identified by the FBI as a key player in the Marcello crime family in the 1960s.*[79]

The lawyers who reviewed the Cascade matter for me always thought that Sanders had possible criminal exposure because of the Arist property sale. Apparently, Sanders thinks he can walk away from the entire matter with his guilty plea.

When someone pleads guilty in a case like this, the prosecutors will often file a factual basis, which is supposed to outline what the guilty party will say at a future trial. In his factual basis,[80] Sanders acknowledged that he was being investigated for possible bid rigging in the Arist case and that he had asked for Edwards's help in contacting the U.S. Attorney's office. Besides that admission, Sanders did little more than rehash the allegations made by the prosecutors in the indictment. There is really no new information that could be construed as any more damaging than the indictment itself. Even more surprising, Sanders did not specifically say that the settlement was a "sham," nor did he state that the policyholders had lost any money. It was obvious he was cutting the best deal he could for

---

[79] *Times-Picayune*, March 6, 1999.
[80] *U.S. v. Brown et al.* USDC 99-151-B-M2, Motion of Factual Basis by Alfred Foster Sanders III, USA Docket Entry No. 11, 10/01/99.

himself, and he did nothing more than parrot the charges of the prosecutors.

The headlines in tomorrow's papers will be a lot more damaging than what Sanders actually said. He did not accuse me of receiving any benefits, and he acknowledged that I was not in control of the receiverships office and therefore had no authority to settle anything. Thus, as best I can tell, his guilty plea does not undermine my assertion that I did nothing wrong.

In the original charges, Sanders was facing 230 years in jail and $15 million in fines. By willingly agreeing to say what the prosecutors want him to say, he faces either no jail time, or little more than six months in a halfway house, and a small fine. Since he had major exposure in the Arist investigation, he no doubt has decided to cut his losses. However, in spite of the headlines and news stories his guilty plea will create, I don't believe his testimony will be that damaging to me or anyone else.

## Tuesday, October 5, 1999
## Baton Rouge, Louisiana

I've never been inside a courtroom in the federal courthouse before. Gladys and her twin sister Gloria were with me when I showed up at 10:00 this morning for my arraignment. My son James wanted to come, but I want to keep him out of the spotlight as much as possible. In the months to come, he will have ample opportunity to attend court activities, and I'm sure he will receive his share of publicity, which I regret.

Numerous television cameras were on the courthouse steps, along with a large group of reporters from throughout the state. I waved hello but begged off making a statement until after the arraignment.

In the courtroom, Ron Weems and his wife Rose greeted us. They were both devastated by the indictment. I tried to reassure Ron that he has by far the strongest case to be made for his innocence. He was merely a lawyer doing his job, and there was no reason to charge him. He is obviously a victim of the "big net" approach of the prosecutors — scoop as many people as possible into the net, hoping that a few will agree to say whatever is necessary to get themselves loose.

I leaned over to Ron and whispered, "Point out David Disiere to me. I'm not sure what he looks like."

Gladys, twin sister Gloria, and I enter the Federal Courthouse on my way to arraignment.

Photo by Bill Feig
*The Advocate*

About that time, a tall, slender, well-dressed fellow headed our way, and Ron nodded in his direction. As the *Times-Picayune* reported the next day, "Brown greeted Disiere with a pat on the back, and said 'Good to see you,' and introduced Disiere to his wife, Gladys."[81]

I was supposed to be conspiring with Disiere to fix an insurance settlement, and I had to have his lawyer point him out to me. Some conspiracy!

Bob Bourgeois was next to enter the courtroom, followed by Governor Edwards and his wife Candy. In a brief procedure, all of us pled not guilty before magistrate Christine Noland, and we were released without having to put up any bond and with no travel restrictions placed on us. As Judge Noland told Edwards, "You've hung around for two trials; I think you are going to hang around for another one." She was referring to previous charges against the former governor involving hospital licenses, which resulted in a hung jury in 1985 and an acquittal in 1986.

I do share the concern of my lawyers, Bill Jeffress and Camille Gravel, about Edwards' statement that he will represent himself in the

---

[81] *Times-Picayune,* October 5, 1999.

upcoming trial. He talked at length to reporters, and there are numerous stories about it. The *Times-Picayune* reported:

> *Edwards represented himself during the arraignment and said he also will handle legal arguments during trial. His self-representation plans provided a few moments of levity during an otherwise mundane hearing in a cramped second-floor federal magistrate's courtroom. Asked by Magistrate Christine Noland whether he had experience in criminal cases, Edwards quipped: "As a defendant."*
>
> *Later, when Noland corrected Edwards for mistakenly stating the wrong date for the arraignment, the former governor said: "Oh, maybe I do need a lawyer."*
>
> *After the arraignment, Edwards said he hasn't handled a criminal defense since the 1960's when he practiced law in Crowley and defended a man accused of "shooting ducks too early in the morning."*
>
> *"I proved that his watch was not working properly, and we won the case," he said.*[82]

Although his statements were amusing, the defense team is concerned that the former governor may not fully grasp the complications of the Cascade case and the massive preparation that will be necessary in the months to come. The prosecutors have thrown a variety of charges, hoping something will stick. They have seized more than 800,000 documents that should be reviewed. There are numerous witnesses to be interviewed and statements taken.

But although I am worried about his decision, this is not the time to discuss it with Edwards. The trial is many months off, and I have an election to win first. But some time in the future, the defense team needs to have a candid discussion with the governor about the dangers

---

[82] Ibid.

he faces in representing himself. As the saying goes, "One who represents himself in court has only a fool for a client."[83]

## Tuesday, October 12, 1999
## Baton Rouge, Louisiana

Good news and bad news. I got first major newspaper endorsement today, from *Alexandria Daily Town Talk*, the voice of central Louisiana. The paper acknowledged that it was a tough call because of the indictment, but pointed out that: "Such indictments are unheard of actions since they came after the qualifying had ended." The paper went on to say:

> *Brown has transformed the office beset by myriad problems associated with legal problems that sent his two predecessors to prison. He has attacked with courage such problems as lack of health insurance among so many Louisianans, lack of vehicle insurance among many Louisianans and improving the climate for worker's compensation insurance.*[84]

This is a great shot in the arm, and I hope it will be the first of a number of endorsements. Not only does the editorial have strong impact throughout the central part of the state, but I can also use it in TV spots during the last week of the campaign. I hope that the momentum has begun to build.

There was also bad news from Jim Kitchens' first poll since the indictments. I dropped 19 points to 40 percent, with Boudreaux second at 15 percent, followed by Riddick with 6 percent. The undecided segment has grown significantly, as my weaker supporters have moved into the uncertain column. But it helps that they have not moved over to Boudreaux or Riddick. Both of my opponents are attacking me on television; the word "indictment" is being played

---

[83] *Faretta v. California*, dissenting opinion in a 6-3 ruling that allowed a defendant to refuse counsel, written by Associate Justice Harry A. Blackmun, U. S. Supreme Court, June 30, 1975. His actual words were "If there is any truth in the old proverb that 'one who is his own lawyer has a fool for a client,' the Court...now bestows a *constitutional* right on one to make a fool of himself."

[84] *Alexandria Daily Town Talk,* October 12, 1999.

over and over. I had expected this, but I'm surprised at the amount of money they seem to be spending. Both are well financed, and I anticipate a continuing barrage of television spots until Election Day.

Jim Kitchens says there's light at the end of the long tunnel I face. It's true I've dropped 19 points, which shouldn't be a surprise considering the indictments. But those votes haven't gone anywhere else. I hope to recoup them in the next few weeks. Jim also thinks that Boudreaux and Riddick are making a mistake in going negative with their message. It is no secret that I've been indicted. It's been front-page news for weeks. Negative attacks alone are not going to beat me. Neither candidate has "defined" himself, nor developed a rapport with the voters.

Kitchens started a "tracking poll" today and will give me daily numbers from now until Election Day. Pollsters generally agree that you need a six-hundred-vote sample to get a good indication of how voters feel and what the trends are. The Kitchens Group will do a two-hundred-vote survey each evening. They will throw away the earlier figures from four days ago and pick up the new numbers each day. I will have what is called a "moving window poll," showing me each day a six-hundred-vote sampling of how voters feel. I can gauge the response to my latest television advertising, and see how the negative spots used against me affect voters. I can also watch the movement of Boudreaux or Riddick, as Election Day gets closer.

I don't know of any other candidate who does a daily statewide tracking poll as the election progresses. But when a candidate is facing the all-out war I'm dealing with, daily numbers are a crucial part of my election strategy.

Tracking polls are nothing new in my campaigns. The Kitchens Group has run them for me for in the last three elections. Most candidates want to skimp on polls and spend their money on media buys, primarily television. But you can scattershot too many messages. I believe in finding one or two messages that work and pounding them home. And I think it's more effective to evaluate your message with daily information about how the public is responding to it.

Four years ago, when I ran for re-election against Republican Sally Nungesser, we were also tracking the governor's race. Governor Mike Foster was then a relatively unknown state senator, and few political observers felt he could break away from the pack to make the runoff in the final two weeks of the campaign. He was running as a basic, down-home Louisianan with traditional values. In his TV spots, he often wore hunting gear or a welder's cap.

With less than two weeks to go in the campaign, Jim Kitchens told me he saw some interesting trends in the governor's race. There was definite movement by Mike Foster, and Kitchens thought that, with a final push on television, Foster could make the runoff.

Governor Mike Foster joins me at a press conference to discuss my proposals that would lower the cost of automobile insurance in Louisiana.

I had worked with Mike when he was in the senate on revamping our worker's compensations laws in the state. In the early 1990s, worker's compensation rates were increasing by as much as 20 percent per year, and few companies wanted to do business in Louisiana. Being a businessman by profession (in construction), Mike was sensitive to the high cost of worker's compensation, and we talked about ways to solve the problem. Mike proposed legislation that would create a non-profit corporation to be the company of last resort when a business could not find insurance from any other company. His legislation helped put an end to our high insurance rates; and gradually, other companies started to come back to the Louisiana market. Today we have one of the better worker's compensation insurance climates in the country.

I appreciated Mike's help on that issue, and I liked him personally. A month earlier, I had agreed that he had little chance of emerging from the crowded field of candidates. But the Kitchens poll was showing otherwise just days before the election.

I called Mike and offered to share the poll information with him. He talked at length with Jim Kitchens and, based on our information, spent a considerable sum of money on television spots in the final week of the campaign. He made the runoff with State Senator Cleo Fields and went on to win a resounding victory in the general election a month later.

Following the election, Mike called to thank me. He told me that the tracking numbers had played a significant role in his making the runoff. Once again, the value of tracking polls had been proven to me.

## Wednesday, October 13, 1999
## Baton Rouge, Louisiana

Now that the public has had a chance to evaluate the charges against me, newspaper columnists throughout the state have been analyzing what happened to me and handicapping my chances of being reelected. So far, I have little reason to complain. The press coverage has been favorable. *Times-Picayune* columnist Jack Wardlaw wrote today:

> *As one might expect, Brown feels he's been treated unfairly by the U.S. Attorney's office because it sprang the indictment in the middle of a re-election campaign. Even if he is ultimately found innocent, Brown's political career could be irreparably damaged.*

> *This column does not comment on the outcome of pending criminal cases, but a reading of the indictments suggests that a member of the jury might reasonably demand that the government come up with a more credible motive for wrongdoing on Brown's part than it has so far. The suggestion that he would break the law to preserve his political patronage and curry political favor with Edwards seems a little thin from the standpoint of a political observer.*

> *Whatever the ultimate outcome, I do find it disturbing that the federal government has the power to influence the*

125

*outcome of a state election before it ever goes to court to prove its case.*[85]

The *Alexandria Daily Town Talk*'s Jim Leggett came up with the same conclusions:

*Insurance Commissioner Jim Brown, who seemed to have a lock on re-election until being indicted week before last, still could have that lock.*

*He said he is baffled by the indictments because he is not accused of doing anything for personal benefit. Lawyers and political observers around the state seem to agree and are likewise baffled.*

*It is strange that Brown was indicted after qualifying, something that is unheard of in federal circles.*[86]

In New Orleans, *Gambit Weekly*'s Clancy Dubos concluded:

*When this case is over, a bigger issue will remain—the one Brown raised at the outset; the fundamental unfairness of the feds indicting a candidate for major office in the middle of a campaign.*[87]

The *Franklin Sun's* publisher Sam Hanna analyzed my situation in his column, which appears in several Louisiana papers.

*On the plus side for Brown, he has been building political fences for many years and should be able to depend on his friends to act in his behalf at election time.*
*He's also a good talker, perhaps too fast, but still good on his feet. He's got to hammer home the point that he's not guilty.*[88]

---

[85] *Times-Picayune*, October 13, 1999.
[86] *Alexandria Daily Town Talk*, October 13, 1999.
[87] *Gambit Weekly*, September 28, 1999.
[88] *Franklin Sun*, September 29, 1999.

Just a few days after the indictments, the *Shreveport Times* expressed regret over the implications for the state. The paper went on to say:

> *To his credit, Brown has helped the state's political image during his term as Insurance Commissioner. While his department has not been without controversy, Brown has garnered national attention for making sweeping reforms in the agency and has been dedicated to keeping professionalism above politics in the regulation of the insurance industry. Sadly, his prosecutors are charging him with doing just the opposite.*[89]

Most of the columns conclude that I was pulled into this mess because of an effort to get Edwin Edwards. As John Maginnis said in his *"Louisiana Politics"* statewide column:

> *Jim Brown may have a point when he says he is the victim of a "political drive-by shooting." But then again, he was hanging out on a dangerous street corner.*[90]

Governor Mike Foster has joined me in criticizing U.S. Attorney Eddie Jordan and his office in New Orleans. Jordan has recently subpoenaed bank records of the governor's small transition fund, even though the governor had volunteered to give the prosecutors any information they wanted.

The Associated Press ran a statewide column by Guy Coates in which the governor is quoted as saying, "It smacks of a conspiracy."[91]

*Shreveport Times* bureau chief John Hill also wrote at length about the governor's questioning the motives of Eddie Jordan. His column went into some detail about the governor's anger at his records having been subpoenaed right in the middle of his reelection campaign.[92]

Another Associated Press column by Alan Sayre stated, "Governor Foster suggested a few weeks back that U.S. Attorney

---

[89] *Shreveport Times*, September 30, 1999.
[90] *"Louisiana Politics"* weekly column, September 27, 1999.
[91] *Baton Rouge Morning Advocate*, October 4, 1999.
[92] *The Times,* September 30, 1999.

Eddie Jordan was cooking up a scheme to embarrass him before the primary."[93]

Today Jordan took a cheap shot at me and the other defendants by saying the timing of his indictments was delayed by our actions. I continue to criticize Jordan and his office for bringing these charges right in the middle of a campaign.

Jordan, in a public statement, said he would have brought the indictments earlier, but all the defendants had asked for a meeting in Washington, D.C., to talk to the Justice Department about the lack of any justification to bring charges in the Cascade case. My lawyer Bill Jeffress, and other attorneys in the case, had asked repeatedly to meet with Justice Department officials. But the delay was caused by the Justice Department, not by any of us.

Bill Jeffress had set up an initial meeting in July, but the Justice Department canceled the meeting and waited more than thirty days before rescheduling it, so any delay was caused by Eddie Jordan's office, not by any of the defendants. His statement that our side delayed the meetings is completely false.

## Friday, October 15, 1999
## Baton Rouge, Louisiana

Another good news, bad news day.

Actually the bad news really isn't all that bad. Bob Bourgeois, who has been running the receiverships office at the direction of Judge Sanders, pled guilty to one count of conspiracy to commit mail fraud and witness tampering. Surprisingly, the lawyer who has represented him for the past two years said Bourgeois' plea was a mistake. The New Orleans *Times-Picayune* quoted attorney John DiGiulio as saying that he believes Bourgeois was pressured into the plea agreement by federal prosecutors. "I would not have participated in, and I guess my client knew I would not have participated in a sham plea agreement to a sham indictment," said DiGiulio.[94]

I read over the factual basis filed by the government supposedly saying how Bourgeois will testify. Surprisingly, my name is rarely mentioned. And just as surprising, I cannot see what crime Bourgeois

---

[93] *Associated Press*, October 19, 1999.
[94] *Times-Picayune,* October 14, 1999.

or anyone else committed. He does not admit there were any losses to policyholders, and he doesn't specifically say anyone did anything wrong.

One thing the prosecutors have not learned is the best timing for their public-relations effort. The fact that both Sanders and Bourgeois pled guilty on a Friday diminishes the effect the prosecutors are trying to create. Obviously, their primary goal at this stage is for me to be defeated for reelection. But Friday is the worst day to release negative news. Friday-night television news is not well watched, and the Saturday-morning paper is the least read paper of the week. Throughout the state, people's weekend plans overshadow their interest in the news. I've learned never to call a press conference for a major announcement on Friday. I'm glad the U.S. Attorney's office is so naïve when it comes to maximizing the effect of their announcements.

There was more good news today. I was endorsed by the *Shreveport Journal,* which slashed away at the prosecutors. Northwest Louisiana is an important part of the state for me, and the editorial will help build momentum for my campaign by casting doubt on the validity of the charges.

> *Jim Brown, by everything we know and by anything anyone has proved, has done an outstanding job of reforming and reshaping the State's Department of Insurance.*
>
> *Our own view is that the indictments against him are politically motivated hooey—and even if they weren't we hold fast to a standard of American justice: Innocent until proven otherwise. To the best of our knowledge, operations of the department under Mr. Brown's supervision have been the fairest, most honest and most efficient in memory. He has worked to lower premiums for the State's people, to increase healthcare coverage for children, to lower the number of uninsured motorists; in short, he has worked for the people. We strongly believe he should be re-elected to continue that work.*[95]

---

[95] *The Journalpage,* October 15, 1999.

**Wednesday, October 20, 1999**
**Baton Rouge, Louisiana**

The Kitchens daily tracking poll shows me "stuck" in the 40-percent range; undecided voters have widespread concerns about the indictment. My campaign has been running television spots for the past two weeks about my efforts to lower insurance rates and protect consumers. But many voters are obviously concerned about the charges. We have to find some way to move these voters off dead center, give them a reason to take a second look and give me the benefit of the doubt. It's time to approach the indictment issue head on.

My media team discussed the problem at length, considering different ways to tell voters how unfair the charges are. Should I have voiceovers do it over photographs of newspaper headlines supporting me? Testimonials from citizens throughout the state? How do you talk to voters about something so controversial? Finally, I made the decision. "There is only one way. Look the voters right in the eye, and tell them I am innocent and that I have been wronged. That's how it needs to be done."

Talking straight on to the voters.

I made some rough notes for a television spot in which I look directly at the camera. Rannah Gray helped me fine-tune the wording and scheduled the TV crew. We decided to tape the spot from my living room. To my knowledge, no other candidate in this country has ever bought TV time to tell voters he's been indicted. But that's exactly what I did. I looked at the camera, and with no introduction, talked directly to the viewers.

*I have a problem and I need your help. Out-of-control prosecutors are playing politics with our election. They are even investigating Governor Foster, and that's ridiculous.*

*I have not been accused of taking any money from anyone or benefiting in any way as Insurance Commissioner.*

*One former prosecutor said he could not understand why I was even indicted.*
*I have done nothing wrong, and I would like to ask for your support. I have given my best, and would like to keep working for you as Insurance Commissioner.*

To many political observers, I no doubt seem to have a death wish. They would argue one should not take thirty seconds of TV time, and spend thousands of dollars, to discuss the major disaster I face. A candidate just does not tell voters that he has been indicted! But that's exactly what I did. Did I make a major mistake?

We quickly received our answer, and the public response was overwhelming. Just a few hours after the spot ran, my campaign headquarters began receiving phone calls, e-mails and faxes agreeing that I had been wrongly treated. The consensus was that what was happening to me was unfair and that I should "hang in there" in the final week of the campaign. It didn't take long for us to conclude that we had made the right decision. By confronting the indictment head-on, I stopped my slide in the polls.

Sometimes you just have to go with your gut feeling. I believe that Louisiana voters will be fair. I think the majority of them will agree with what most of the newspapers have been saying—that I should be presumed innocent until proven guilty. A large majority of voters also seem to think it is improper for me to be charged in the middle of a campaign.

As the election approaches, we can feel the momentum moving in my direction. Boudreaux and Riddick are now attacking each other, and my 40-percent lead should start moving up. For the first time in the past month, I am confident that I will be the strong leader in the first primary and possibility even win in the primary.

## Friday, October 21, 1999
## Baton Rouge, Louisiana

Good news came in bundles today from a number of different directions. South, southwest and central Louisiana were flooded with

131

editorials from 41 newspapers, all part of the Moody publication chain, endorsing my reelection. Although one company owns the papers, individual editors determine whom to endorse. The decision to endorse me was unanimous, and there were front-page editorials on newsstands throughout the state. Most of the editorials reviewed the job I had done in the past eight years to lower insurance rates and protect consumers and then turned to the questionable motives of the New Orleans U.S. Attorney's office.

*Until a month ago, Jim Brown was a shoo-in to get reelected. Voters around the state were appreciative of the work he has done as State Insurance Commissioner and satisfied with the results.*

*Unfortunately, in the final few weeks before the election, federal charges have been brought against him by the U.S. Attorney in New Orleans that are puzzling.*

*First, the timing is questionable. After 3½ years of investigations, why would such charges be brought just a few weeks before the election? We know of no other example in the country where charges were brought against any statewide elected official so close to statewide election dates.*

*Lawyers reviewing the charges are wondering why Brown, who received no gain and had no authority to make decisions in the matter, was included in the charges. One lawyer stated publicly that "This is a sham indictment," while others have expressed the belief that the case will never go to trial. The general consensus is that the federal government pulled this trick out the bag in their all-out effort to get former governor Edwin Edwards at any cost.*

*Voters can review the record of Jim Brown and make their own determination as to his right to be re-elected without interference from the federal government. He has a big job ahead in taking on the agenda that he has set and we are*

*confident that he can get the job done: a job that will*
*improve the quality of life of all people here in Louisiana.*[96]

Copies of the editorials are coming in by fax from supporters all over the state. The endorsements are a tremendous shot in the arm. They will be a morale booster for my staff, and will help build momentum for my campaign. Right now, more than 95 percent of the papers that have endorsed anyone are supporting my candidacy.

The judges of the 19th Judicial District Court also gave me a vote of confidence today by signing off on my new appointee to head up the receiverships office. Bob Bourgeois stepped down last week once he pled guilty in the Cascade case, so a new director of receiverships had to be appointed. I selected a career civil servant to run the office in a businesslike manner, and the judges agreed. If there had been any concern about my ability to run the receiverships office in a fair, competent, and honest way, the judges certainly would not have approved my recommendation. I see this as vindication and acknowledgment by the judges that Judge Sanders should never have run roughshod over the office and should not have been allowed to instigate his illegal takeover.

Other good news comes from the camps of my two opponents. Both Boudreaux and Riddick are hoping to get into a run-off with me, and they are running about even in the polls. I'm no longer the focus of their attacks; instead, they are feeding on each other. They debated the issues on radio station WJBO today, moderated by longtime radio and television personality Ed Buggs. The Baton Rouge *Advocate* reported:

> *The mud is flying fast and furious in the race for Insurance Commissioner. Challengers Allen Boudreaux, R-Metairie, and Winston Riddick, D-Baton Rouge, are taking shots in commercials and in public at each other.*
>
> *"I'm wearing mud-proof clothing," Baton Rouge radio talk show host Ed Buggs joked with Boudreaux and Riddick before they appeared on Buggs' program.*

---

[96] *Crowley Post-Signal* and 40 other Moody newspapers, October 20, 1999.

*Riddick's ads claim Boudreaux was involved in criminal dealings with failed insurance companies. A Riddick radio spot linking Boudreaux to jailed former Insurance Commissioner Doug Green ran twice during the Buggs show.*

*Earlier in the day, Boudreaux held a news conference at the State Capitol where he called Riddick, a former deputy insurance commissioner, a 'political hack' who has been part of the problem for many years.*

*[Jim] Brown was in Kenner on Wednesday speaking to the Louisiana Surplus Lines Association, an insurance group, and couldn't participate in Buggs' show, said Allan Pursnell, Brown's spokesman.*[97]

The mutual attacks by Boudreaux and Riddick were exactly what my consultants had hoped for when we discussed the situation several weeks ago. What more can you say about me? I've been indicted. It's been said over and over, and you can only beat this issue so much. The problem facing both Boudreaux and Riddick is that they have to give the voters an alternative. Something positive has to be presented, but their mutual attacks undermine any chance of either one's building a favorable image .

In a poll released today by the Mason-Dixon Polling and Research firm in Washington, D.C., I was leading by 39 percent, Boudreaux was second with 18 percent, and Riddick was trailing with 7 percent. That means that 37 percent of the voters are undecided. The Baton Rouge *Advocate* concluded, "Political observers suggest the high number of undecided voters is due to all the mud-slinging and confusion over Brown's indictment. Secretary of State Fox McKeithen said it's unusual to have such a large number of undecided voters so close to an election day."[98]

If so many voters are still undecided after all the negative press I've gotten, that's good news for my campaign. I'll know soon. The election is only two days away.

---

[97] *The Advocate,* October 22, 1999.
[98] Ibid.

## Saturday, October 23, 1999
## Baton Rouge, Louisiana

Election Day is always a little frustrating. It's the calm before the storm. There is only so much you can do in the few hours until the polls close, particularly in a statewide race. This is the twelfth time my name has appeared on a Louisiana ballot. You always wonder what you can do to maximize your time in the final hours. The answer is, not a lot, but you can't stop worrying about it.

Gladys and I got up early and headed for Coffee Call, a New Orleans style hangout close to our home. Gladys and her friends start their day there seven days a week. We had a quick cup of café au lait while many of the regulars came up to the table to wish me luck.

Our son James joined us there, and we headed out to vote at 9:00 A.M. We were met at the polling place by a number of TV reporters. It's kind of a ritual that statewide candidates are photographed before and after they cast their vote. At home, after a quick workout, I took a number of phone calls from well wishers and did several afternoon media interviews. I did phone interviews with radio stations throughout the state, and several New Orleans TV stations sent crews to the house for interviews.

Election-night headquarters was Jumelle's Restaurant, which is owned by and named for Gladys and her twin sister Gloria. (Jumelle

Gladys, James, and me on our way to our election night celebration.

means twin in French.) TV crews started setting up their cameras and satellites in the late afternoon. I changed into a coat and tie and started doing live stand-up interviews on the hour beginning at 5:00. Most of the statewide races,

135

including the governor's race, have been rather dull, so the controversy surrounding my race has made it a major media story.

I was hoping for an outright victory with more than 50 percent of the vote, but realistically knew that would be tough to get. Both Boudreaux and Riddick have spent big money - Boudreaux is reporting almost $1 million dollars and Riddick more than five hundred thousand. Most of it was spent attacking me. I just hoped for a big lead that would give me strong momentum to move into the run-off election only thirty days away.

My vote total stayed in the 45-percent range through the early evening and slowly climbed in small increments. By the time the final count had come in around 10:30 P.M., I had 47 percent, Boudreaux was far back at 30 percent, and Riddick finished with 23 percent.

I held a 17-point lead over Boudreaux, and much of Riddick's support had come from Democrats who would normally have supported me. So I feel well positioned for the run-off. But basically, we are going back to square one. I know Boudreaux has significant financial resources to plow into the run-off campaign. The other statewide run-off involves two Republicans, so I will be the only Democrat on the statewide ballot. Voter turnout will be much lighter in the run-off, and it will take some analysis to determine just who will go vote. After a good night's sleep, I'll get up tomorrow and start working. We all know I have a major effort ahead in the next four weeks.

## Sunday, October 24, 1999
## Baton Rouge, Louisiana

I got some rest today, but also took some time to plan strategy with my campaign team.

I started off the day with a 45-minute bike ride. My workouts have been sporadic in the last few months, and my body is telling me it needs movement. The joints need lubricating, and I have a lot of frustrations to sweat out. After biking, I went for I a short swim, and I could feel a slight physical and great psychological improvement right away. I also take lots of vitamins, and I am convinced the exercise and nutrition program makes a difference, particularly at my age.

A St. Tammany Parish newspaper, the *News Banner*, had a front-page profile of me last week reviewing my athletic background, and talking about my commitment to physical fitness. I regularly receive inquiries about vitamins and workouts from throughout the state. When the campaign is over, I would like to update my exercise and nutrition ideas and have them printed up to send to friends who share my interest. Needless to say, with the election and the coming trial, this will not be at the top of my priority list, but I would like to get it done.

This afternoon, the campaign team gathered via conference call to talk about the weeks ahead. With my large lead, the ball is in Allen Boudreaux's court. Riddick strongly attacked Boudreaux in the last 10 days of the first primary, and kept him on the defensive. Boudreaux has yet to define himself. He has done nothing more than to keep up a negative attacks on me, and he still has not offered the voters an alternative. My media team all agree that Boudreaux should immediately start a positive campaign, talk about protecting the public, lowering insurance rates, and moving the department into the 21$^{st}$ century. Riddick's supporters are in the undecided category now, and an aggressive, positive pitch by Boudreaux would bring many of those voters over to him. But we all feel that he will continue his attacks. A lot of the undecided voters will probably either not vote at all or, as Rannah Gray surmised, "hold their noses" and vote for me. Either way, I should win.

I wish campaigns were not run this way. I have a strong record on insurance issues and would like to talk about reforms we should undertake in the future. I would much prefer to stay positive, but it is obvious this is just not going to happen. In most state races, incumbents come under attack. That's the nature of campaigns. Polls reveal that voters say negative campaigning turns them off. But the fact is, negative advertising works. If an elected official is known by the public and has a fairly strong positive record, and both sides run negative campaigns, the incumbent generally wins.

In my case, Boudreaux's advisers are apparently telling him they have me on the ropes. *Brown's indicted! No statewide official has ever been elected under indictment. You have him on the defensive. Attack! Attack! Attack!* It's bad advice, but I hope he follows it.

Our group analyzed the results for more than an hour. Jim Kitchens will start polling in about 10 days, once we have a better feel for Boudreaux's approach. George Kennedy and Rannah Gray are brainstorming ideas for TV spots in the final week. They plan on using some of my newspaper endorsements, and they want to finish on a positive note.

My campaign team says I should keep traveling throughout the state. They argue that voters respond well to my message that I have been wronged and that it is unfair to bring these charges in the middle of an election campaign.

We agree that I should do a statewide tour Wednesday, Thursday, and Friday, holding a series of press conferences and appearing on local morning talk shows. My message will be simple: I'm way ahead in this election and I'm going to win handily. There is no basis for the charges against me, particularly considering that I did not benefit it any way. And the timing of these charges is outrageous. Finally, I've done a good job as insurance commissioner, and my record should be acknowledged. The voters should give me a chance to clear my name and continue to serve them as I have in the past. We all agree that my spending three 20-hour days in the car will pay strong media dividends.

## Saturday, October 30, 1999
## Baton Rouge, Louisiana

The rain was pouring down in torrents, but that didn't keep die-hard fans away from Tiger Stadium, where the LSU Tigers took on traditional rival Ole Miss. It was on Halloween night 41 years ago that Billy Cannon made his famous 89-yard run and LSU beat Ole Miss 7-3.

Although he was convicted of counterfeiting in 1983, Dr. Billy Cannon (he is a dentist) is still a local hero. Before last year's Ole Miss game, there was a reunion of LSU's 1958 national championship team. Cannon got a 10-minute standing ovation.

I was one of the first to know about Cannon's counterfeiting activities. While serving as secretary of state in 1983, I was visited by special agents from the Treasury Department. Someone had come to my office to file incorporation papers and paid the 87-dollar filing fee with a counterfeit hundred-dollar bill. I'm told it was the first bill discovered in the Baton Rouge area that eventually linked Billy Cannon to his crime. In speeches, I sometimes embroider on the story, saying that I became suspicious when I looked at the bill. Where it should have said, "In God We Trust," it read, "Go to Hell, Ole Miss."

On this Halloween night, the rain did not let up. But I had the toughest election of my life coming up, and I wasn't about to pass up a crowd of potential voters. I stood outside the entrance at Gate 5, near the escalators on the west side of the stadium. I was drenched, but I shook every hand I could find, and asked thousands of Tiger fans (and probably a few Ole Miss fans) to vote for me. I certainly received my share of attention as I am easily recognized. For weeks, I have been the lead story on television stations throughout the state. I think I gained a little respect—and, I hope, a lot of votes—from the crowd. After all I had gone through, I was still there, standing in the pouring rain telling voters I needed their help. No other candidate for any office was there. I'm sure I looked pathetic, but the positive feedback I got told me I was doing the right thing.

**Tuesday, November 1, 1999**
**Baton Rouge, Louisiana**

Newspaper endorsements continue to come in. Forty-one different papers throughout the state have endorsed me so far. I expect additional endorsements in the coming week.

Of particular note was the editorial that appeared in three north Louisiana papers, the *Ouachita Citizen*, the *Franklin Sun,* and the *Concordia Sentinel*. Publisher Sam Hanna of Ferriday has traditionally made no endorsements on either the local or state level over the many years he has owned these papers. He is a highly respected publisher, whose weekly column appears in numerous parish papers, both north and south. It would have been easy for Sam to stick to his usual process and leave my race alone. His moving editorial helps tremendously, and means a lot to me.

### *BROWN'S INDICTMENT SHOULDN'T BE A FACTOR*

*Whether Jim Brown is guilty of the charges brought against him by the grand jury has not been determined and will not be determined until after the election. Until he is found guilty in court, Brown is an innocent man under the American system.*

*Thus, the indictment should not be a factor for the voters when they make their choice. Brown is accused of favoring an insurance company in a plan to liquidate a failed insurance company. He has pleaded his innocence in public remarks about the case.*

*Jim Brown should be judged by the voters on the merits of his performance as insurance commissioner, and in our view his performance has been creditable.*

*He joined hands with Gov. Mike Foster with a plan to lower insurance rates for the consumers of Louisiana, and although the decline of the rates has been gradual some progress has been made.*

*Brown also sponsored the impoundment law intended to remove the uninsured vehicles off the highways. It is a stringent approach, but, in our view, it is far better than one, which the challenger favors, a payroll deduction approach that would place more responsibility on the employers of the state.*

*Brown also has appealed to other states and Congress to support a system for insurers when damages from a natural disaster exceed $2 billion. Some insurance companies avoid hurricane-prone Louisiana.*

*And Brown is pushing another plan to spend some of the state's tobacco settlement windfall on health insurance for the working poor. Some of the windfall will be dedicated to healthcare.*

*On the whole, Brown has been a progressive commissioner. He should be re-elected for that reason and not rejected because of the indictment.*[100]

---

[100] *Concordia Sentinel,* October 27, 1999.

Also endorsing me was the *Colfax Chronicle*, a first-time endorsement for this central Louisiana newspaper.

> *The Chronicle would suggest that incumbent Jim Brown has been a fair and dedicated insurance commissioner, taking on the difficult tasks of overseeing a huge industry that touches the lives of almost every Louisiana resident, young and old.*
>
> *Louisiana's image as a safe haven for those who want to engage in insurance fraud has been improved under Brown's leadership. But his work is not done. More initiatives, and continued efforts to improve health insurance coverage for our state's young and old, keeping up efforts to protect our citizens against drunk drivers and keeping insurance rates affordable for all our drivers will keep Brown busy for another four years—and keep Louisiana on the right track in "cleaning up our image."*[101]

The good news is the *Chronicle* did not even mention the indictments. That will help me continue to build momentum in the last two weeks of the campaign.

Local columnist John Lockhart, writing in the *Riverside Reader,* said:

> *Brown has been in office going all the way back to 1972, and the people feel they know him. On the other hand the voters don't know Boudreaux, and Brown skillfully has painted the Metairie insurance man as untrustworthy.*
> *As it stands now, I'd say Brown has won himself another four years.*[102]

---

[101] *Colfax Chronicle,* November 10, 1999.
[102] (Baton Rouge) *Riverside Reader,* October 11, 1999.

**Friday, November 5, 1999**
**On the Road**

Down here, we don't get to see the leaves change color like they do in the northeast, but November brings a subtle variety of colors to Louisiana foliage, particularly in the northern part of the state. There is extraordinary beauty in the rolling hills of the parishes north of Alexandria. I think about the scenery I would miss if I were not re-elected. I could still travel throughout the state, but not as much as I have all these years in public life. Few states have the varied scenery that I have observed as I criss-crossed Louisiana during my 30 years in public life.

From the air, the beauty is even more breathtaking. Small lakes are scattered across north Louisiana like drops of dew. The lakes grow in size as you fly south. We are completely surrounded on three sides by water. Toledo Bend and the Sabine River to the west, the Mississippi River to the east, and the Gulf of Mexico surrounding our southern border. The waters grow as you fly over the Atchafalaya Basin and head through south Louisiana to the Gulf. The flat wetlands are a marked contrast to the lights that follow the Mississippi River at night and the breathtaking spectacle of New Orleans from several thousand feet up—then the great vastness of the Gulf of Mexico. This is a landscape I will never tire of.

My office faxed me an article by columnist James Gill in today's *Times-Picayune*. He raised the issue of how inconsistent it is for someone like me to be accused of the crime of false statements, while it is not a crime for the FBI to lie to any citizen. Gill pointed out that I was under no obligation to talk to the agents and that my statements were made long before the Cascade case was really developed. He went on:

> *Brown would have had to be pretty foolish to give the FBI statements that might be used to incriminate him. It seems a little harsh to put anyone in prison for electing not to be as foolish as all that. Some courts have adopted what is known as the "exculpatory no doctrine," which holds that a mere denial of guilt is not a violation of statute. Whether the exculpatory rule could work for Brown is a question that must be left to the lawyers, but it seems to the layman that*

*he was merely entering a perspective not-guilty plea. If that should turn out to be the only crime he could be convicted of, he will be one unlucky son-of-a-gun.*

*Such an outcome would be a great injustice, and no doubt Brown would kick himself for helping the government plot his own downfall.*[103]

James Gill makes a lot of sense. I'm already kicking myself.

## November 7, 1999
## New Orleans, Louisiana

Tonight, several television stations throughout the state carried a debate between Allen Boudreaux and me that was taped several days ago. Boudreaux immediately went on the attack, raising questions about the charges against me. I answered by raising the same questions Winston Riddick had asked in the first primary about Boudreaux's associates and his activities in the insurance industry.

Allen Boudreaux and I visit before one of our debates.

---

[103] *Times-Picayune,* November 5, 1999.

The debate went downhill from there.

I don't like the charges and countercharges, but this plays right into the strategy outlined by my campaign team. If Boudreaux is attacking me, he's not defining himself. In fact, Boudreaux is letting *me* define him. I am raising questions about him that are creating a negative public perception of him. As Rannah Gray puts it, why should the voters want to go from the frying pan into the fire?

There is some discussion of insurance issues, but they will be barely mentioned on the evening news tonight or in tomorrow's newspapers.

Jim Kitchens's polling indicates that I am staying in the 45-to-46-percent ranges, with Boudreaux polling in the mid-30s. That means there's still a large undecided vote that, so far, is not moving. The longer those voters stay undecided, the better it is for me. My media team feels we can "bring a large share of them home" with a strong positive message in the final days of the campaign.

## Sunday, November 14, 1999
## Baton Rouge, Louisiana

Jim Kitchens and I talked at length this morning about the daily tracking poll. With less than a week to go until the election, he has concerns about the undecided voters. The campaign has been so negative up until now that many voters will not vote at all in the insurance commissioner's race. We are still holding in the 46-47-percent range, but I'm stuck and not moving towards the magic 50-percent mark. The good news is that Allen Boudreaux is not moving either. Kitchens concluded that we have to cool our media down and come on with a strong positive in the final days. We agree that I should return to my original message, talking about the things I have done as insurance commissioner—touching the lives of senior citizens, working with Governor Foster to get uninsured drivers off the road, reducing the cost of car insurance, and being there for the average citizen who is often overwhelmed with insurance problems.

But how do you convey this in 30 seconds? Do I look directly at the camera, and make my final pitch? This approach worked effectively in the first primary, when I addressed the indictment head-on. Should I do it again? Rannah Gray argues that I may not be the most effective messenger. With the indictment and all the negative campaigning, how credible will I be making a plea for myself? But whom do we turn to? Rannah, Jim Kitchens, and Mike Mann will talk throughout the morning; then they will bring in George Kennedy, who will pull the television spot together.

We all hooked up by conference call in mid-afternoon. There was unanimous agreement as to who should deliver the final message. One person, and only one person, should be the voice on the spot and the face that looks into the camera. Gladys!

For the past 20 years, Gladys has campaigned with me throughout the state. She has even had to make speeches by herself when I had a schedule conflict. But being seen by millions of voters will be a new experience for her. She has been under the weather lately, but despite some reluctance, she agreed to do it. We all began working on the script. Rough drafts were faxed back and forth throughout the evening. We settled on a final script around 7:00, and the camera crew arrived at my house soon after. They set up their lights and equipment in our living room, and Gladys started working on her presentation. By 8:30 she had a slight fever and her voice was a little hoarse. We worried about whether she could tape the spot.

At 9:00, George turned on the cameras. Rannah hovered in the background. Gladys was so nervous she asked me to leave the room.

Gladys looked directly into the camera and spoke to the voters:

*I'm Gladys Brown. Jim Brown is my husband. Jim and Governor Foster have fought to make the insurance industry work for us. Forty-one newspapers have endorsed Jim. They know he's done a good job. And I know his heart. And he's a good man. On Saturday, give Jim a chance to keep working for us.*

Normally, a television commercial requires 20 or 30 takes. Gladys's voice held up for four, but George and Rannah agreed that was all they needed. Rannah's big smile expressed her satisfaction. "She was unbelievable," she declared. "This spot's going to be the most effective one you've ever done."

Gladys took a couple of aspirin and went to bed. Rannah and George headed for the production studio about a mile from my house. They would stay up all night to edit the spot and put the visuals together. Then they'll make copies for the TV stations. We have runners lined up to be at the studio at 4:00 A.M. to distribute the finished spots to television stations statewide. By 9:00 A.M. the new commercial will be on the air.

The spot opens with videotape of me talking to senior citizens, and then cuts to a shot of me talking to Governor Foster. The voiceover says, "Jim Brown and Governor Foster have worked together as a team to protect Medicare supplements. To give us the right to change our doctors and insure all of Louisiana's children." Then it cuts to Gladys, who looks into the camera and asks voters to give me a chance.

The spot was conceived, written, produced, delivered, and on the air in less than 20 hours. Very few political consultants, even in national campaigns, could accomplish that type of turnaround. Of course, we all think the spot is a home run. Tomorrow we'll find out what the viewers think.

**November 15, 1999**
**Baton Rouge, Louisiana**

Allen Boudreaux and I had our final debate today. The lead paragraph that went out on the Associated Press wire throughout the state summed up what happened pretty well:

### *BOUDREAUX LOSES HIS TEMPER*

*It got a little dicey as commissioner of insurance candidate Allen Boudreaux repeatedly interrupted the incumbent with cries of, "You're a liar" and "You're the crook."*

*The moderator at the Press Club of Baton Rouge luncheon tried to calm Boudreaux, who appeared as though he wanted to come out of his seat at Insurance Commissioner Jim Brown.*

It was our final debate, and Boudreaux apparently felt he should go on the attack. He looked out of control and on the verge of physically attacking me. My campaign staff could not have been more pleased. His screaming and out-of-control demeanor was the lead story on most of the state's television stations. This certainly will be picked up on by viewers and will do little to build any positive feeling for him.

Five days until Election Day. The undecided still are not moving. I have a major television buy beginning tonight. I just hope that Gladys can move them into my camp.

## Wednesday, November 17, 1999
## Baton Rouge, Louisiana

I spent the afternoon in New Iberia with an old friend, former state representative Ted Haik. He had lined up a noon speech for me to the Rotary Club and arranged a reception at the Iberia Parish Courthouse, with most of the elected officials of the parish in attendance. Ted and I met in law school in New Orleans, and we also served in the legislature together. He was chairman of the House of Representatives Insurance Committee during my first four years in office

Ted Haik hosts a series of receptions for me in New Iberia.

and has been there when I needed him on numerous occasions. As I left today, he handed me a bunch of checks from supporters who wanted to contribute. They will come in handy in the final television push.

Tonight, I was a guest on the "Weill, Weill World" radio show, hosted by LeAnn and Gus Weill. Gus is a prominent Louisiana author who has been a friend and adviser for many years. He predicted I would win going away. I wish I were as confident.

After being on the road all day, I was glad to get home. And the news could not have been better. Reaction to "the Gladys spot" has been overwhelming. My campaign headquarters has received numerous unsolicited calls from people who just want to tell us how moved they are by Gladys's message. Many of our friends have called to say her words brought tears to their eyes. Jim Kitchens will have solid polling numbers for us in the morning, but it looks like many of the undecided are finally moving in my direction. I will gladly take a one-vote victory, but I think it will be much bigger.

**Thursday, November 18, 1999**
**Baton Rouge, Louisiana**

*These are also sayings of the wise: To show partiality in*
*judging is not good.*
Proverbs 24:23

A neutral observer might well believe that Judge Frank Polozola is calculatedly interfering with the election and undermining my campaign. On several occasions since the indictment in late September, I've been ordered into court with the other defendants for a so-called "status conference." This is a meeting of the prosecutors and the attorneys for the defendants, along with the judge, to work out a schedule for the filing of motions and other pre-trial activities. Status conferences are routine in cases like mine. What is not routine is for the judge to order the defendants themselves to attend. That's why we have lawyers. In most courts in this country, the lawyers work out the details with the judge. But Polozola has felt it necessary that I be in court, even though I was right in the middle of the election. He knows full well that my entering the federal courthouse would be the lead story on any evening newscast. But the fact that he was creating negative publicity for me did not seem to bother him in the least.

Today it got worse. Polozola issued a new gag order that will take effect immediately after the election Saturday night. What he did today is to create a major news story that will be played on TV and in the newspapers throughout the state tomorrow, the day before the election. The judge is waving a red flag and telling everybody that I will be gagged and can say nothing more about the case.

If he genuinely wanted to issue a gag order in good faith, Polozola could easily have waited until next Monday, after the campaign. I

148

certainly could not have done any damage on Sunday, particularly since the gag order has not been in effect for the last month and a half. I guess it's payback time. I've been criticizing the gag order throughout the campaign, pointing out that this is something that you would assume would take place in a totalitarian South American dictatorship or in Nazi Germany. Not in America.

At a status conference several weeks ago, Polozola looked at my lawyer Bill Jeffress and expressed his concern over my comments about uncontrolled prosecutors and the government's acting in bad faith with selfish motives. (Lawyers throughout the country routinely refer to the prosecutors as "the government.") Polozola looked at Bill Jeffress and me and said, "He's criticizing the government. You know, that's directed at me. *I'm* the government." Several lawyers in the room rolled their eyes, and I was stunned. Judge Polozola is not part of the prosecution team. He's supposed to be a neutral arbitrator who ensures that all sides are treated fairly according to the law. But he said from the bench that this was not how he saw it. He *is* the government. His prejudicial attitude bothered all of us on the defense team.

Now, today, Polozola enters this new order, which I interpret as a direct effort to create negative publicity for me right before the election. His reputation among defense lawyers as a "prosecutors' judge" was certainly affirmed by his ruling today.

**Friday, November 19, 1999**
**Baton Rouge, Louisiana**

Jim Kitchens' was the first call I took today. His news was better than we had hoped for.

"You're moving the undecided significantly," he said. "The 'Gladys spot' was dynamite. Voters can identify with her and her message, knowing that she has been at your side all these months. You're going to win, and you're going to win big."

Jim predicted that I'd get 55 to 56 percent of the vote. We will know tomorrow.

Another note of interest – I've been reading the *Wall Street Journal* for years. It is the nation's premier daily business newspaper, and pictures on the front page are usually reserved for international business leaders and national public officials. I ran to the drugstore to pick up a prescription for Gladys this morning and glanced at the newsstand. There I was. My picture is on the front page of the *Wall Street Journal*, and the lead story is about tomorrow's election.[104] The story was merely a rehash of what has been written here in the state for months. And the picture was actually a drawing, done from a photograph. I didn't look bad. I guess this is my 15 minutes of national fame.

# THE WALL STREET JOURNAL

——

## Down in Louisiana, Insurance Regulation Carries a Strange Risk

——

Friday, November 19, 1999

Jim Brown

## Saturday, November 20, 1999
## Baton Rouge, Louisiana

Television cameras from around the state have been set up at Jumelle's Restaurant since early evening. There were only two statewide races on today's ballot, and my election was certainly the major story. My mother had come down for what we hoped would be an election-night victory. We also had my brother Jack and his wife Pam, my in-laws Ted and Doris Solomon, my brothers-in-law Gary and George, and a number of other family members. My sister Madalyne was looking after my business in Plaquemines Parish and also helping her husband, Sheriff Jiff Hingle, get reelected.

Jim Kitchens was wrong. It wasn't 56 percent. It was more than 57 percent! I won a resounding victory, but I couldn't fully enjoy the moment. I spent several hours after the polls closed and the results were in, talking to television stations, radio stations, and newspaper reporters throughout the state. I told them that Louisiana voters had sent out a strong message. Don't believe all the hogwash being put out by the U.S. Attorney's office in New Orleans. I have received an overwhelming vote of confidence, and I have passed the first

---

[104] *The Wall Street Journal*, November 19, 1999.

important test. This gives me excellent momentum as I start a third term, and begin preparing for the trial itself.

An election night victory celebration. My mother (far left), sister-in-law Pam, and Gladys join numerous supporters in celebrating my big victory.

Photo by Mark Salz
*The Advocate*

I have accomplished what no other official in Louisiana had done. I have been charged with these outrageous crimes yet still won a resounding victory. This sends out an important message. But I can't afford to slow down.

**November 24, 1999**
**Baton Rouge, Louisiana**

Political pundits have been analyzing my victory for days, and the stories have been generally positive. The *Shreveport Times* editorialized:

> *Many political supporters believe Brown's indictment is a politically motivated attempt to get at former Governor Edwards. Louisianans can hope that Brown's innocence is proved. Thousands of voters have put their confidence in*

*him. The last thing they need is to have that vote nullified later.*[105]

Columnist John Hill wrote in *New Orleans CitiBusiness*:

> *Brown is the first statewide elected official to be re-elected under the cloud of federal indictment charging him with 56 counts of wrongdoing in the liquidation of Shreveport-based Cascade Insurance Company.*
>
> *Political analyst Gus Weill of Baton Rouge said Brown successfully painted Boudreaux as the bad guy in the race, removing him as a viable alternative. "Brown turned the tables on him." Weill said.*
>
> *Brown agreed. "He never differentiated himself from me," Brown said of Boudreaux. "He let me define him instead of him defining himself."*
>
> *Pollster Vern Kennedy of Florida, who polled for Allen Boudreaux agreed: "That was the only way Brown could win," he said. "Brown fought back with an aggressive television media campaign."*[106]

Columnist James Gill in the *New Orleans Times-Picayune* pointed out what I've been saying all along: that I did not benefit in any way from the Cascade matter.

> *But voters were apparently inclined to give Brown the benefit of the doubt, perhaps because he is accused of offenses that are somewhat recondite. He is alleged to have helped fashion what prosecutors term "a sham settlement" with a liquidated insurance company, but not to have received any money in exchange.*

---

[105] *Shreveport Times,* November 23, 1999.
[106] *New Orleans CitiBusiness*, November 29, 1999.

*Voters might have concluded that any crooked politician worth his salt would at least have made off with an envelope or two stuffed with cash.*[107]

John Maginnis, in his *Louisiana Political Fax Weekly* column, summed up our strategy very well:

## POWER OF POLLING

*Despite the horrible publicity of his 56-count indictment and some pre-election anxieties over black turnout, the insurance commissioner's race was never close, says his consultant. He should know, for the campaign polled every night, with the most aggressive voter surveying of any candidate in this cycle.*

*Brown, running his sixth statewide race, waged a nearly flawless run-off campaign that managed to cast more doubt on opponent Allen Boudreaux's background and his associations than Brown's own legal entanglements with Edwin Edwards. The final score was 57-43 percent with a 27 percent turnout.*

*Early on, Brown committed to invest in nightly tracking polls from October 1 through election eve. That gave the incumbent a distinct strategic advantage, said consultant George Kennedy. "When you have numbers every morning broken down by key demographics and media markets, the moving average smoothes out the dips and you can make media decisions day by day based on rating points of what's playing where."*

*Brown assembled the same team he has used since he was first elected insurance commissioner in 1991. Jim Kitchens of Orlando did the polling. Press secretary Allan Pursnell took leave from the department to handle press, printing and mailing.*

---

[107] *Times-Picayune*, November 24, 1999.

*They communicated by conference call every few days to discuss strategy. When Kennedy shot a commercial, he sent it via Internet to the rest of the team, who could download and discuss revisions before approving a final print.*

*They braced for a plunge a few days after the candidate was indicted shortly after qualifying. The objective, said Kennedy, was "to stop anyone else from stepping into the breach. They (the Boudreaux campaign) didn't expect us to walk out our research like we did."*

*"We had more credible negatives," said Kennedy. "You have to have negatives the way a journalist does: who, what, when and where." The early and unrelenting TV attacks on Boudreaux prevented the challenger from establishing his own conservative Republican identity. Kitchens' polling showed Boudreaux was still unknown by 47 percent of the electorate in the final week.*

*But there can be too much of a bad thing. When polling in the final week showed a slight dip, Brown and Co., fearing backlash from their hard negative spots, decided to put Gladys Brown on the air talking about how her husband worked so closely with Gov. Foster. Not your ordinary stand-by-your-man spot. Kennedy said the ad was written at 7:30 a.m., shot at 8:30 p.m. and on the road the next morning to all TV stations. He added, "We may win or lose, but we ain't gonna get outfamilied."*[108]

Author Gus Payne, who has written extensively about the abuses of the Justice Department, also chimed in. His comments appeared in the *New Orleans Times-Picayune* on November 24:

*The public does not seek to elect federally indicted felons to office in Louisiana. Voters were asked to make a decision among the candidates and they decided on Brown. They*

---

[108] *Louisiana Political Fax Weekly*, November 24, 1999.

*knew about the indictments. Yet, the voters returned Brown.*
*Why?*

*The public is skeptical of the indictments and whether or*
*not they were politically motivated. This skepticism comes*
*naturally to a public fed up with past mistakes, lies and*
*obvious political actions from the U.S. Department of*
*Justice.*

*It is unfortunate. The U.S. Department of Justice should be*
*the one department of the government that we can trust.*
*That we must trust. Much needs to be done to restore the*
*integrity the department once had. Let it begin.*[109]

## Tuesday, November 24, 1999
## Baton Rouge, Louisiana

Thanksgiving week. It's time to take the next few days off.

I'm hoping for a speedy trial. The Constitution guarantees this, but Judge Polozola has indicated that he will try the Edwards riverboat-gambling case first. This, of course, is not fair to me. I want the trial as soon as possible. But Bill Jeffress says federal bureaucracy can grind this issue down. No matter how much I protest it may be a long time before I have my day in court.

My first order of business in the coming week: read the indictment! With the pressures of the campaign, I have not yet sat down and actually read, word for word, the charges against me. After that, I'll get some rest, some family time, some regular exercise, and then get back to work as insurance commissioner. And, of course, I must prepare for a bigger challenge than even the election—defending myself in federal court.

## Thursday, November 25, 1999
## Shreveport, Louisiana

The family has all gathered at my mother's house in Shreveport. This morning Mother and I drove out to Forest Park Cemetery to visit

---

[109] *Times-Picayune*, November 24, 1991.

my dad's grave. Dad picked out the site some years back, and being a perfectionist, he selected a wonderful location for a family plot. It's a corner plot with 10 individual gravesites. The big family tombstone is near a water line, and flowers and plants surround the entire area.

Dad and Mother with the President in the Oval Office back in 1974.

I wish Dad were here. In spite of the vicious campaign I've just been through, and the ordeal I face in the coming year, Dad would still have liked to be a part of it. He was, bar none, the best campaigner I have ever seen. With a Jim Brown button on his shirt and bumper sticker on his car, he never hesitated to approach complete strangers anywhere in the state to talk continually about his son, the candidate. To this day, people come up to tell me how Dad lobbied them to vote for me in an election.

Jack, Madalyne, and I took some time while we're all together to talk about the months to come. Jack has been an integral part of my

Brother Jack and wife Pam

Sister Madalyne and husband Jiff

156

defense team, reviewing every document and constantly second-guessing my lawyers. You need a devil's advocate in a fight like this.

Madalyne's husband, Sheriff Jiff Hingle from Plaquemines Parish, probably spent more time campaigning for me than he did on his own reelection. He has been effective in rallying elected officials and Republicans (he's the token in our family) to stand by me.

Gladys and I thought fleetingly about taking a week off to just get away. Hit the beach in Florida? Take a cruise? Head out west to ski? But there is simply too much to do. I need to sit down next week and start a detailed review of the specific charges against me. From my conversations with Bill Jeffress, I realize there are literally hundreds of thousands of documents to review. No trial date has been set, but we have to be ready. In a trial like this, information is power. We have to know more, and be better prepared, than the prosecutors. We will relax this weekend and get back to work on Monday.

## Monday, November 29, 1999
## Baton Rouge, Louisiana

> *Oh what a tangled web we weave*
> *When first we practice to deceive.*
> Sir Walter Scott[110]

I called my senior staff together this morning to talk about the coming year. I let them know that I wasn't going to be distracted from my job here at the insurance department, and they should not be affected by my trial. But I still need time for the massive preparation for what lies ahead.

All of my key staff members were recruited and hired by me. There are no holdovers from the previous commissioner's staff. They know my expectations; they know how I operate. I asked each of them to give me a weekly memorandum and to be prepared to update me in our weekly staff meetings. As I expected, they all are supportive. Now it's time for me to analyze just what I face ahead.

This afternoon, I sat down for the first time with a copy of the charges against me and the other defendants. I waded through a

---

[110]Sir Walter Scott, "Marmion: A Tale of Flodden Field," *The Poetical Works of Sir Walter Scott,* (Edinburgh J. Ballentyne and Co., 1808).

rambling 47-page document that continually repeated and contradicted itself. But, it's a tar baby I have to thoroughly analyze.

Even after reading the charges, it's hard to understand exactly what I am supposed to have done. As best I can determine, I am accused of having been involved in a plot to illegally help David Disiere and his insurance company, Cascade, reach a favorable settlement with the state. The settlement supposedly violated federal law and cost the taxpayers millions of dollars. That seems to be it in a nutshell. The conclusion is farfetched and, frankly, a bald-faced lie.

The charges against all the defendants include conspiracy, mail and wire fraud, insurance fraud, and witness tampering. I am also charged with 13 counts of making false statements to FBI agents.

I only had to read a few pages to determine that whoever wrote the document had a vivid imagination and is assuming or guessing about many things that supposedly took place.

Nearly every page of the indictment includes "facts" that just are not true. On Page 2 is the statement, "Brown had the power to award legal contracts to anyone Brown wished." False! All contracts to hire attorneys, by law, had to be approved not only by the attorney general but also by a judge of the 19th Judicial District Court.[111] In fact, the attorney general oversees and monitors the activities of the lawyers hired and approved their fees; he also has the authority to do the legal work with his own staff. Many outside lawyers working on contract for the insurance department were in place before I was even elected.

Furthermore, at the time of the Cascade settlement, there was very little contract work of any kind at the department. We were winding down all this work; there were no new contracts being recommended by my office or approved by the attorney general, the judges of the 19th Judicial District Court, or anyone else. Obviously, the prosecutors threw in this allegation to create an image of political patronage to benefit public officials. That's hogwash. There are specific checks and balances in place for the awarding of contracts, but in truth there was no work being given out.

On Page 5 of the indictment, the charge is made that "Brown planned to allow Bonneville to relocate to Louisiana even though Brown at all times knew that LRO and Sanders' Special Master were preparing a civil racketeering lawsuit against Disiere for personal

---

[111] La Revised Statute 22:743(B).

liability relating to transactions involving the Cascade Insurance Company."

The charge that my office or I personally, had any plans to allow Disiere to relocate an Oregon company to Louisiana is completely false. Disiere *wanted* to re-domesticate, or move his Oregon Company to Louisiana. He asked the department for permission to do so. His request was denied and never given serious consideration by the insurance department.

Any insurance company can make a request to move from one location to another. It's done all the time. There was nothing abnormal about Disiere's request. But my office had not been part of the final settlement reached by Disiere, Judge Sanders, Ed Gonzales, and the receiverships office. (Remember, at that time in 1996, the receiverships office was under the direct control of Judge Sanders.)

After the settlement was reached and all the controversy calmed down, if I had wanted to do Disiere a favor, it would have been very easy to allow his company to re-domesticate in Louisiana. But that was never done. Again these were false charges by the prosecutors.

On Page 10 of the indictment, charges are made that the defendants devised a scheme "To defraud the State of Louisiana and the citizens thereof, the Estate of Cascade Insurance Company, its creditors, claimants, and policyholders of money and property by means of false and fraudulent pretenses, representations, and promises."

In other words, the policyholders didn't get their money. The bills were not paid. There were significant losses. Again, hogwash. All were paid the money they were owed. They were not defrauded of "money and property" as alleged in the indictment.

On Page 12 of the indictment, allegations are made that "in or about May, 1996, Disiere sought Brown's help with the purpose of having the Disiere investigation terminated. Brown agreed to help Disiere and stated that he wanted Disiere to stay in the insurance business in Louisiana."

In fact, just the opposite happened. Disiere came to my staff to discuss the fact that he thought he was being improperly treated by Judge Sanders. He was told there was really nothing we could do. The judges of the 19th Judicial District Court had the final say-so, and they had delegated the approval process to Sanders. Disiere, in fact, left the meeting with my staff and complained to an FBI Agent in Shreveport,

159

and to his own lawyers, that my office would not help him fight Sanders. Again, false information from the prosecutors.

On Page 13, the charges state, "On or about June 19, 1996 Weems on behalf of Disiere requested and received from Brown's office a letter of good standing for Disiere and his companies when Brown knew, at the time, Disiere was under investigation for fraud and misapplication of funds regarding his operation of the Cascade Insurance Company."

Again, a fabrication by the prosecutors. At no time did David Disiere receive a letter of good standing from my office. We sent out a standard form letter regarding several companies, located in Shreveport and owned by Disiere, which said the companies complied with Louisiana law. These are routine letters often sent out by our office. In fact, Louisiana law *requires* that we send out such a letter when requested to by any insurance company.[112] But no good-standing letter was ever sent regarding Disiere personally. This conclusion shows either sloppy work by the prosecutors or an effort to outright lie about what happened.

The more the charges I read the more frustrated I became. False statement after false statement.

On Page 14, the indictment describes a telephone conversation between Edwards and me.[113] He had called while I was vacationing with my family in North Carolina. The indictment says the discussion was about "[how to] get a settlement which would be most favorable to Disiere;" "getting the investigation of Disiere terminated before Sanders retired as Judge;" and how to get rid of Ed Gonzales "in order to facilitate a settlement favorable to Disiere."

There is absolutely nothing in our taped conversation that remotely confirms these allegations. No such conversation took place. It just didn't happen. These are simply false statements by the prosecutors.

---

[112] La. Revised Statute 22:1461.

[113] *U.S. v. Brown, et al.* C.D. 99-151-B-M2, Wiretap Tr., No. 4, October 21, 1996.

Reviewing page after page of false charges.

There are a number of statements in the indictment that I am supposedly cooperating to bring the Disiere investigation to an end, or saying that "the Disiere investigation would be completed soon." Again, fabrication. There was no investigation of Disiere through the receiverships office. I initiated the only investigation of Disiere and his companies that ever took place in 1997 through our Fraud Division. At my request, my staff opened up a fraud file to look at this entire matter. After Judge Sanders agreed to a settlement with Disiere, my fraud investigation continued. The only major investigation ever undertaken of Disiere was by my office, not by the receiverships division.

On Page 19, the indictment talks about a lengthy conversation where Governor Edwards called me. But the prosecutors left out key parts of the conversation that clearly show I was trying to get the best settlement possible. Edwards had told me that one of the lawyers in the case was working on a report showing that from five to ten million dollars might be recovered from Disiere. The tapes clearly reveal that I said if the lawyer could do that, then let him go recover it. "I said, hey, if he can get ten million, go get the ten million."[114]

---

[114] Ibid. No. 32, November 18, 1996.

That sounds like a pretty strange comment from someone who was supposed to be trying to help Disiere settle the case for less than two million. My statement here completely undermines the prosecutors' assumption that there was an effort to do anything special for Disiere or to take any action that would keep policyholders from getting all the money they were owed. Why wasn't this put in the indictment? It's on the tapes. We know why it wasn't included. Because it shows I was innocent, and this was not what the prosecutors want to do. They continue to manipulate the facts to support the story they are trying to create.

On Page 20 of the indictment, references are made to a conversation where Edwards called me on November 19, 1996. The indictment reads: "Disiere was very pleased with what Brown was doing for him." If you listen to the tape, there is absolutely no reference to David Disiere being pleased with anything.[115] Disiere's name is never even mentioned in the entire conversation. Again, false information given by the prosecutors.

The indictment continues by alleging that, in the same November 19 conversation:

> *"Brown informed Edwards that the problem with the entire matter was getting Sanders' Special Master out of the investigation so that a favorable settlement for Disiere could be realized."*

No such statement was made, and there is nothing on the tape that is even remotely close.

A point to consider. Why is it a crime for anyone to give false information to the FBI, when it is apparently no crime at all for the prosecutors to file an indictment that, page after page, makes false allegations and gives false information? Shouldn't this be a crime? Of course it should. This is something on my list to share with our congressional delegation at some point in the future.

Shall I continue with this fairy tale? I'm trying to be objective, but it's difficult when I'm reading one false statement after another.

On Page 20 of the indictment, the allegation is made that "Brown assured Edwards that he would contact Bourgeois and tell Bourgeois

---

[115] Ibid. No. 35, November 19, 1996.

to settle the case." There is nothing on the tapes even remotely close to my agreeing to tell Bourgeois to settle the case. Not in this conversation or any other conversation.[116] Bob Bourgeois will so testify. In reality, Edwards told me he was having a difficult time arranging a meeting with Bourgeois and attorney Ron Weems. I told Edwards that I would be glad to call Bourgeois to see if a meeting could be set up. There was nothing in the conversation that referred to any settling of the case. Again, a false statement by the prosecutors.

Pages 36 and 37 of the indictment allege the crime of mail fraud. The indictment then goes on to list 37 different criminal counts involving the mailing of letters or checks. Disiere agreed to pay so much a month to settle his claims, and would send several checks a month to the receiverships office. The prosecutors are saying that every time a check was put in the mail, one more crime was committed. Now help me figure this out. The man is sending money to the receiverships office to pay the debt he owes. But he is committing a crime in doing so? This is really far-fetched. I'm charged with 56 criminal counts, and 35 of the counts involve mailing checks to pay the claims of policyholders. I had absolutely no knowledge the checks were being sent, and I was not involved in any of these negotiations. Yet I am charged with 35 criminal counts. Ridiculous? A waste of taxpayers' money? A blatant example of prosecutorial misconduct? All of the above. But it is happening!

Count 41 of the indictment is really bizarre. Witness tampering. Judge Sanders' friend Ed Gonzales was assigned by Sanders to work on the Disiere matter. Gonzales was being paid ninety dollars an hour for his work and was allowed by Sanders to receive a sweetheart fee of 20 percent of the final settlement. Supposedly, all the defendants conspired to give Gonzales this additional fee to prevent him from communicating any criminal concerns to law-enforcement officials. In other words, we are supposed to have bribed him. Well, then, why wasn't he charged with receiving a bribe? He took the money for whatever work he did. He did not stop the settlement. He did not write a formal complaint to any law-enforcement official. Yet all the defendants are supposed to be involved in some type of witness tampering. I never once talked to Ed Gonzales during the entire time he was working for Judge Sanders. I never communicated with him in

---

[116] Ibid. No. 40, December 2, 1996.

any way. Yet I'm supposed to be part of some type of witness tampering? Again, how absurd.

There are other convoluted charges that are unclear and make little or no sense. And when I finally was able to listen to the tape-recorded conversations, the charges became more unsubstantiated. Finally, there are the false-statement charges against me – 13 of them. And these charges are certainly the most disturbing.

FBI Agent Harry Burton came to my office in May 1997 to get what I assumed to be routine information about Cascade. I wasn't concerned about the interview, because I thought it had nothing to do with my office or me. I assumed it might have something to do with the puzzling contract that had been given to Ed Gonzales, and the fact that he made such large attorney's fees for so little work. Or perhaps it related to Judge Sanders and his involvement in the Arist property sale. In any event, I had talked to federal and state law-enforcement agents on numerous occasions about their investigations; I looked on the conversation as an effort by me to help an investigation. Little did I know that Burton had listened to all of the taped conversations of Edwards and myself and had done extensive research into what, if any, involvement I might have had. So when he came to my office he was "loaded for bear" and ready to jump on every word I said.

The reason these charges concern me so much is that they basically come down to his word against mine. In reading through these charges, it is clear that Burton is either incompetent at understanding insurance issues, or he is making a calculated effort to trip me up. Either way, his actions in crafting these charges are despicable.

The charges center around two basic questions. How much did I know about Cascade Insurance Company, and how involved was I in the final negotiations that actually settled the case?

The false-statement counts start with Count 44, which reads: "Brown falsely stated that he was only vaguely familiar with Cascade Insurance Company when in truth and in fact Brown well knew that he was very familiar with Cascade Insurance Company." In fact, when put on the stand at the trial, Agent Harry Burton said his question to me was how "familiar he was with David Disiere and his operations of Cascade Insurance Company."

I did tell Burton I was not overly familiar with Disiere's operations or the background of Cascade Insurance Company. Disiere had not been operating Cascade in any way from the time that I took office as insurance commissioner. So it was true that I had little knowledge or familiarity with how Disiere operated this company.

Frankly, I would have given the same answer to anyone who asked me about any other insurance company in the receiverships office, or for that matter, any other insurance company operating in the state of Louisiana. What does it means to be "very familiar?" As insurance commissioner, I have a large number of examiners who review the financial details and management structure of each insurance company. Only when there are major issues to be resolved do they bring me into the mix. Otherwise, the oversight of the operations of an insurance company is handled on a day-to-day basis by key staff assigned to the company. The same is true of the companies in receivership. There is an "estate manager" assigned to each company that is being shut down or rehabilitated by the receiverships division. The staff generally discusses major decisions with the director of receiverships for final determination. When my office ran the receiverships division, occasionally some issue *was* brought to my attention. But it would be unfair and wrong to say that I was "very familiar" with any company operating in the state. I would confidently say that any insurance commissioner in America could make the same statement. There is just no possible way that any insurance commissioner would be "very familiar" with the operation of any one company. I gave Burton an honest answer. And what does he do? He charges me with being "very familiar" with David Disiere and his operation of Cascade Insurance Company.

Remember, this conversation lasted no more than 30 or 40 minutes. It was not recorded by any tape recorder. The only true record made of what was said was the handwritten notes taken by Burton in my office. (Remember those notes. The notes taken by Burton will become the most important issue in the entire case.)

I am further charged with multiple counts of saying that I was not part of the settlement negotiations, when in fact I was supposedly an integral part of these negotiations. This is the basis of most of the false-statement counts against me.

Was I part of the negotiations? Absolutely not. There was discussion among the various parties for months about the problems of getting both sides together and trying to find a middle ground to discuss the negotiations. But the parties, for a variety of reasons, delayed getting together. I was involved in conversations with Edwards, Ron Weems, Sanders, and Bob Bourgeois about how to get all sides to the table to begin some type of orderly discussion.

When it came to the final negotiations in the Cascade case, however, neither my staff nor I was involved. Bob Bourgeois and Ron Weems set up two meetings with David Disiere and the various lawyers on December 18 and 19, 1996, at the receiverships office in downtown Baton Rouge. Neither my staff nor I was notified about the meeting, included in the meeting, or consulted about the meeting. We had no involvement in the meeting or the negotiations, and we did not even learn about the negotiations until several days after an agreement was reached. And this shouldn't be surprising to anyone. The receiverships office was under the direct authority of Judge Sanders and did not report to me. The final agreement would not have to be approved by the insurance department, so it was not our place to be involved. Yet I am charged with several counts of being intricately involved in these negotiations. I'm frankly dumbfounded at these false-statement charges. Obviously, it would have been much better for me not to have even met with Burton or told the FBI anything. But that would not have been the right thing to do. As insurance commissioner, I thought it was important that I cooperate. I just didn't know that my cooperation would lead to my being set up.

## Thursday, December 2, 1999
## Baton Rouge, Louisiana

> *The first principle of a free society is an untrammeled*
> *flow of words in an open forum.*
> Adlai Stevenson[117]

Bill Jeffress filed a motion today in federal court asking Judge Polozola to do away with the gag order he imposed on me election night. I had asked Jeffress to do this, arguing the effectiveness of my office will be compromised if the gag order keeps me from responding to the allegations in the indictment. Jeffress argued, "The public's interest in having an effective insurance department and Brown's own first amendment rights would require that he be free to

---

[117] Speech by U. S. Ambassador to the United Nations Adlai E. Stevenson, Jr., *New York Times,* January 19, 1962.

speak, and the public free to hear, his response to the allegations against him."[118] How can I run an effective office and build confidence if all I can say is, "trust me, I'm not guilty" or "no comment" when anyone asks about these charges. The insurance department deals with the insurance industry worldwide, and I need to clear up any concerns as I do my best to attract new companies to our state.

Besides, doing away with the gag order is basically a question of fairness. Day after day, news articles replay the fact that I have been indicted, and go into detail about the various charges. What am I supposed to say — "no comment?"

I'm not particularly confident that Polozola, being the prosecutor's judge that he is, will sympathize with my wanting to defend myself. But I hope we will have the chance to make a strong argument before a higher court in the months to come.

## Monday, December 13, 1999
## Baton Rouge, Louisiana

Today a lawyer in New Orleans faxed me a copy of an article that had appeared in the *Wall Street Journal* earlier this year titled, "What Justice Department Guidelines Say About Perjury." The article focuses on President Clinton's giving false testimony to the grand jury in the Lewinsky case. Remember, the president gave his false testimony under oath, on tape, before a federal grand jury. The article begins:

> *President Clinton's defense at the House impeachment hearings produced several former federal prosecutors who testified that they would have ignored Mr. Clinton's grand jury perjury as a trial matter. Several Democrats on the House Judiciary Committee asserted that, if prosecutor Kenneth Starr had only followed the Department of Justice procedures explicated in departmental policy, he too would have ignored presidential perjury.*

---

[118] *U.S. v. Brown, et al.* C.D. 99-151-B-M2, Motion by JHB to Vacate or Modify Gag Order, Docket Entry 57, 12/01/99.

*Furthermore, because federal prosecutors are busy trying matters that used to be the responsibility of state and local law enforcement (as Chief Justice Rehnquist recently complained in his annual Report of the Federal Judiciary), U.S. Attorneys are too busy to focus on lying.*

*Perjury is probably the most under-prosecuted of all crimes," James Stewart noted in 1987 in "The Prosecutors." "The offense is rampant but prosecutors rarely seek indictments." Line federal prosecutors repeat those thoughts today.*[119]

I have asked criminal defense lawyers in Louisiana and the rest of the country about how often federal prosecutors bring charges of perjury. Most cannot recall an instance in which federal charges were brought for perjury in Louisiana or anywhere else. This makes me even more certain that Burton came to my office with the specific intent to set me up and later accuse me of giving him false information.

The occasional perjury charges that are filed generally involve testimony given under oath and recorded before a federal grand jury. You just cannot point to another instance in Louisiana in which an FBI agent walks into the office of a public official, has a 30-minute conversation, and brings false-statement charges. What a tragedy if the testimony of one FBI agent would convict me of these charges. Prosecutors should look to the Old Testament, Deuteronomy 19:15:

*"One witness shall not rise up against a man for any iniquity or for any sin, in any sin that he sinneth: at the mouth of two witnesses, or at the mouth of three witnesses, shall the matter be established."*

Gag order or no, I want to say it as loudly and clearly as I can every chance I get. I did not give the FBI agent any false information. What I told him was the truth.

---

[119] *The Wall Street Journal*, January 18, 1999.

**December 20, 1999**
**Baton Rouge, Louisiana**

Several national insurance publications have commented on my indictment and my reelection. One noted example is *Business Insurance,* a bimonthly.

The cover story this week is a year-in-review article on the top ten newsmakers in the United States in 1999. Included is financier Warren Buffet, who is listed as one of the top two or three wealthiest Americans; notorious international stock swindler Martin Frankel; President Clinton; and Vermont Senator Jim Jeffords. But who topped the list as the newsmaker of the year? Yours truly! It's hard to imagine that, with all that is going on in the country, my re-election and the controversy surrounding me is the top story affecting the insurance industry.

The story is an example of the widespread interest in my case, and it shows that the entire country is observing the State of Louisiana. I am certainly not pleased by the intense review of my predicament. In the future, I hope I never again make the top ten list no matter what I do.

# 2000

**Department of Insurance doorway
looking toward the State Capitol.**

**Monday, January 10, 2000**
**Baton Rouge, Louisiana**

Inauguration day at the State Capitol. This is my eighth swearing-in ceremony as a public official. The only other elected official around the capitol who outranks me in years of service is Senate President John Hainkel. He was first elected to the Louisiana House of Representatives in 1968, and I came to Baton Rouge as a new senator in 1972. In years served, I outrank all the other state officials and our congressional delegation.

I viewed the day with mixed emotions. It's always enjoyable to be in the center of the day's activities, and I have fond memories of my past inaugurals. But I face trial in just a few months. I'm not just watching events take place, I'm right in the center of them. Today, I felt that I was more closely observed than anyone else except the governor.

Being sworn in for my third term as Commissioner of Insurance. Gladys and James stand by my side.

The day began with a prayer service at St. Joseph's Cathedral, where I've prayed on seven previous inauguration days.

At 10:00 both houses of the legislature were sworn in, and at noon statewide officials were inaugurated on the front steps of the capitol. Gladys and I were warmly received all day, and I tried to put aside my concern about the massive preparations for the trial ahead.

Immediately after the inaugural ceremony, my office was opened for a reception for the hundreds of friends, supporters, and well wishers who make the rounds of the state offices. I received overwhelming assurances of prayers, support, and encouragement and was repeatedly told, "Hang in there, Commissioner." But I also detect concern in the eyes of those who wish me well. They are looking for a sign, an assurance from me that this is all going to work out. Part of my daily burden is to reassure those around me. I know they are worried. They want this nightmare to go away. It will, but I have to keep reassuring them. This is something I will have to do for the rest of the year.

The day finally ends at the Governor's Soirée on the LSU campus. I still had enough energy to dance with Gladys and a few other ladies.

Tomorrow it's back to work—the familiar job as insurance commissioner and a brand new role, preparing for the trial of my life.

**Tuesday, January 11, 2000**
**Baton Rouge, Louisiana**

> *Delay in justice is injustice.*
> Walter Savage Landor[120]

Somewhat lost in the shuffle of yesterday's inaugural activities was the beginning of Edwin Edwards' riverboat-licensing trial. No one can even guess how long the trial will last. It may take several weeks just to pick a jury. With six defendants, and a multitude of witnesses on both sides, the jury might not get this case until late spring.

The Cascade case has been set for trial on May 15, with Polozola as presiding judge. Frankly, I think my case should have been tried before the riverboat case. Edwards is a defendant in both cases, and he will need a break after this trial to prepare for the Cascade case. At this stage, I'm worried that there will be additional delays, and we may not even try my case until the fall. So much for my right to a speedy trial.

---

[120] Upton Sinclair, *The Cry for Justice: An Anthology of the Literature* (New York: Barricade, 1915).

But at least there will be a reprieve from the daily stories about Cascade in the papers and on the evening news. The whole focus will be Edwards' involvement in riverboat licensing.

Bill Jeffress and I will meet next week to layout a time frame for preparing my defense. Just reviewing all the documents will be an enormous task. At least I will have some quiet time while the public focuses on Edwards and company at the federal courthouse.

## Thursday, January 13, 2000
## Baton Rouge, Louisiana

> *The orders in the Edwards case exemplify the trend towards secrecy in the courts. The jurors were anonymous, the media was ordered not to interfere with anonymity and the whole trial was cloaked in secrecy.*[121]
> Ashley Gauthier, Secret Justice

> *Everything secret degenerates, even the administration of justice.*
> Lord Acton[122]

Judge Polozola has ordered an anonymous jury in the Edwards trial. Like the gag order, an anonymous jury is extremely rare and normally only imposed when there is some perceived danger to the jury. One can understand the need for an anonymous jury in the Oklahoma City bombing trial of Timothy McVeigh, or when there are international drug lords or members of organized crime involved. But an anonymous jury for a Louisiana politician? How absurd!

The prosecutors apparently have made the accusation that, back in the 1980s when Edwards was tried twice in the hospital-permit case, his legal team did extensive research on potential jurors. So what? Background checks on jurors are done every day throughout the country. There is no justification for an anonymous jury in this case. And this development does not bode well for me in the Cascade case.

When jurors are told that they must remain anonymous, it sends a chilling signal that they or their families may be in danger. It certainly

---

[121] Ashley Gauthier, *Secret Justice: Anonymous Juries, The Reporters Committee for Freedom of the Press*, refp.org/secretjustice/anonymous juries. Fall 2000.
[122] Platt, Susie. *A Dictionary of Quotations:* Barnes & Noble, New York, 1993.

has to be troubling to an average citizen, with no experience in the courtroom, to remain unnamed.[123]

But the prosecutors have requested it, and Polozola is a prosecutor's judge. He's wrong, it's unfair, but that's the way it's going to be.

## January 18, 2000
## New Orleans, Louisiana

Bill Jeffress and his associate John Elwood flew down from Washington this morning to meet me at the FBI office in New Orleans. We had scheduled an appointment to review all the documents that have been seized in the Cascade case. The FBI had gathered financial and legal documents from all the defendants. File cabinets full of documents were taken from Judge Sanders' office. Virtually every financial document involving David Disiere, Cascade, and his financial dealings have been seized from Disiere's office in Shreveport. A number of documents were taken from my office at the insurance department, as well as my financial records and campaign files going back into the 1980s. It is obvious the FBI was throwing a net around anything and everything in the hope of finding something incriminating on each of us.

All told, more than 800,000 documents were subpoenaed. Imagine the effort it will take to go through it all so there will be no surprises at the trial. We have no choice but to wade through all those pages.

It is probably easier to get into the private quarters of the president than the file room at the FBI. We had to pass through guards at the gate, get parking permits, obtain IDs, go through metal detectors, and wait for some 30 minutes for an FBI monitor to accompany us. Finally, we were taken to the room where the documents are located. From that point on, it should have been easy. We should have been able to go through the index and pick out documents from boxes arranged in an orderly fashion. Good luck! There *was* no orderly fashion. There were four small rooms filled with boxes piled up in no particular order, often seven or eight boxes high. Some were

---

[123] A detailed discussion about why there was no justification for an anonymous jury in my case or the Edwards case appears in my appeal, *U.S.A. v. Brown, et al.,* USCA 5th Cir. No. 01-30173, Brief for Appellant, 46 et al.

unlabeled, and those that were labeled often were turned with the labeled side against the wall. In some instances, it took two of us to lift the boxes because they were so heavy and unstable. Numerous documents were missing, and many others were out of any type of listed order. Bill and I agreed it was going to be a gargantuan task to wade through this mess. Had the documents been purposely strewn about in disarray? Or was this a reflection of the general disorder of the FBI office in New Orleans? Who could say? We just knew we had a lot of work to do.

We worked all morning then headed to Whitey's Seafood on Downman Road for a lunch of crawfish and soft-shell crabs.[124] Then it was back to the FBI office, where we went through the entire routine again to get in the door. We stayed until we were told to leave at 4:30. As we left the building and went through another complicated procedure to check out, Bill, John, and I were disappointed and disgusted at the mess we will continue to face in the weeks to come. But the documents must be reviewed.

After finally clearing security, we drove toward the front gate with Bill at the wheel. There was one more security checkpoint, at a gatehouse with several guards inside. Bill had to stop the car, or we would have rolled over the large spikes at the exit gate. A guard lowered the spikes and raised the gate. Just as we started to drive off, there was a knock on my window. A guard was standing there. I looked at Bill and rolled my eyes, wondering what additional delay we faced now. As I rolled down my window, the guard gave me a big smile and said, "Commissioner Brown, all of us here who work security think you got a bum rap. You've done a great job as insurance commissioner. Hang in there. I just want to wish you good luck, and I'm sure it's going to work out okay."

I thanked the man, and we drove away. Bill shook his head and said, "In all my years of practicing law, I've never had someone working for the FBI say my client was innocent and was going to get off. This is a real first. Jim, it's got to be a good sign."

I hope he's right.

---

[124] I've been meeting friends at Whitey's for more than 40 years to eat boiled crawfish, crabs, and shrimp. Sadly, it closed in the fall of 2001.

## February 20, 2000
## Baton Rouge, Louisiana

*Without free speech no search for truth is possible.*
*Better a thousand-fold abuse of speech than a denial of free speech.*
Charles Bradlaugh[125]

---

The gag order remains, and I continue to be unable to talk about the outrageous charges against me. Judge Frank Polozola reaffirmed his ruling this week, upholding the gag order he imposed upon me as soon as the election was over.

Polozola has struck a stunning blow against freedom of speech and my right to a fair trial. As commissioner of insurance, I am expected to speak out and explain the charges against me. The prosecutors have made outrageous allegations, which are continually repeated in the press. But I can't respond.

What's even more disappointing is that high-profile trials take place all over America without the imposition of gag orders. The Unabomber in New York, notorious gangsters in Chicago, major drug lords throughout the country — all have been tried with no gag orders. But here in Baton Rouge, Louisiana, I am prohibited from protesting my innocence. Most of the news organizations in the state will join me in appealing Polozola's order to the Fifth Circuit Court of Appeals.

Predictably, Polozola's order has been criticized all over the country. Lucy Dalglish, the executive director of the Reporters Committee for Freedom of the Press, in Washington, said, "You gag the parties. You gag the lawyers. You effectively gag the press. It's the public that suffers. We are supposed to have public trials in this country. Judges are deciding they don't like media coverage. They are annoyed. "[126]

M.R. Franks, a Southern University law professor and former New Orleans prosecutor, also spoke up on my behalf. He strongly argued that gag orders harm defendants by keeping them from telling their side of the story to the public: "Prosecutors are able to get their side out through the indictment. Denying defendants the ability to tell

---

[125] Edmund Fuller , *A Thesaurus of Quotations* (New York Crown Publishers , 1941) p.398.
[126] *Sunday Advocate*, February 20, 2000.

their side of the story through the media taints the jury pool in favor of the prosecutors."[127]

New Orleans attorney Mary Ellen Roy, who represents several New Orleans television stations in this freedom-of-speech issue, also criticized Judge Polozola's order. She will fight the order at the appeal level, arguing, "The constitutional right to free speech and the public's right to know should prevail over all vague concepts of the administration of justice."[128]

The prosecutors say they can't get a fair trial without the gag order. But even former U.S. Attorney Ray Lamonica, who now teaches at LSU, disagrees: "While defendants have the constitutional right to a fair trial, there is no such constitutional protection for the prosecutors."[129]

My legal team will argue that I should be free to speak about the allegations against me to maintain public trust in my office. My attorney Bill Jeffress has written:

> If Jim Brown is free only to say "trust me, I'm not guilty," and to offer only "no comment" when asked about the merits of the prosecutors' allegations ... he cannot effectively combat the government's well publicized allegations against him in the eyes of constituents, insurance consumers, insurance companies, insurance regulators in other states, and the legislature.[130]

Stan Halpin, a constitutional-law professor at Southern University, argues that elected officials often have multiple audiences to deal with when charged: "In some cases, the bigger stake might be the reputation of the person or their political future. They have another forum outside the courtroom they must be concerned with."[131]

I know the public is strongly on my side. In America, you are supposed to have the freedom to speak out. Polozola's effort to gag me is wrong, unfair, prejudicial to my defense, and flies in the face of

---

[127] Ibid.
[128] Ibid.
[129] Ibid.
[130] *U.S.A. v. Brown, et al.,* C.D. 99-151-B-M2, Motion by JHB to Vacate or Modify Gag Order, Docket Entry No. 57, 12/01/99.
[131] *The Sunday Advocate,* February 20, 2000.

our democratic system of government. I can only hope a higher court will set me free to speak out.

## Tuesday, February 22, 2000
## New Orleans, Louisiana

A disappointing ruling from the Fifth Circuit today. In a divided vote, the three-judge panel turned down my request to immediately lift the gag order. But I am still optimistic since they granted my request to speed up my appeal so that another panel of judges can consider the matter in the next 45 days.

Without this early hearing, it could take six months to a year to have my appeal heard in the normal rotation. Numerous media outlets, both television and newspapers, were also granted the right to file written arguments in support of my request to throw out the gag order imposed by Judge Polozola.

One member of the panel, Fifth Circuit Judge Robert M. Parker, wrote a strongly worded dissent saying how unfair it is for me not to be able to speak out:

> *Brown, an elected public official, is unable to respond to the charges and public statements made against him.*
>
> *The prosecution has the luxury of well-publicized allegations against Brown, aided in large part by the government's release of sensitive wiretap material to the press and various public announcements regarding the "factual basis" for the indictment.*
>
> *By forbidding Brown to respond to the public statements, the order violates the Constitution's prohibition on prior restraints of speech.*

Judge Parker argued that my status as an elected official "provides further justification for his being able to publicly respond to the charges made against him."

> *Public officials have not only their personal reputation to defend, but also their public persona. This latter concern*

179

*dramatically affects a public official's ability to perform his duties to the public.*

*Brown's hands are tied by the district court's order that effectively limits his public comments, to "I'm not guilty."*[132]

Judge Parker, a Clinton appointee from Texas, strongly supported my appeal to abolish the gag order. I hope the new Fifth Circuit panel that will hear my request considers his solid reasoning.

## March 3, 2000
## Baton Rouge, Louisiana

The Edwards riverboat-licensing trial continued today with testimony from Baton Rouge attorney C.J. Blache. He had represented the Jazz Enterprises group back in 1993 in their effort to obtain a riverboat license on the Mississippi River in Baton Rouge. The FBI first interviewed Blache in September 1993. The agents interviewing him included Karen Gardner and, interestingly, Harry Burton. Blache gave a 16-page statement about what he knew about his efforts to obtain a license for his client. Some five years later, on June 17, 1998, different FBI agents met with Blache and asked him to review his earlier statement. They wanted to be sure the information was correct. Blache immediately told the agents that the original statement was riddled with errors, and they weren't minor errors. There was complete confusion about a number of people named, percentages were off by as much as 18 percent, and there were countless factual mistakes.

After Burton and Gardner interviewed Blache, the two agents took their handwritten notes back to their office and typed a transcript of the interview, which is referred to by the FBI as a 302. Burton and Gardner made 18 major mistakes in writing up the information they had received from C.J. Blache. When the new team of agents talked to Blache in 1998, they had to prepare an entirely new statement incorporating numerous corrections.

---

[132] *U.S.A. v. Brown, et al.,* C.D. 99-151-B-M2, Dissenting Opinion by Judge Robert M. Parker, Docket Entry No. 92, 2/22/00.

Blache's contention that Burton made numerous mistakes is critical to my case. Not only was Burton part of the team that interviewed Blache initially but also he signed a statement that the original information was true and correct. But other agents and prosecutors who interviewed C.J. Blache five years later found that much of the information that Burton had signed off on was, in fact, completely different from what Blache had told Burton and the other agent. Defense lawyers in the Edwards case today pointed out numerous mistakes made by Burton and the other FBI agent when they originally took the statement. The transcript from the Edwards trial shows attorney Ernest Johnson raising questions about Blache's statement:

> **Mr. Johnson:** W*ell, the purpose of the questions, your honor is to show that almost three – some years later, Mr. Blache is allowed to make adjustments and amendments to his 302[the typewritten statement]. Our client is charged with, under those false statements, for making false statements on the 302. And so, in terms of evidence for our clients, we would like the jury to know that there are other people who have been allowed to make those corrections or amendments or whatever they are.*

Almost unbelievably, prosecutor Todd Greenberg responded to Ernest Johnson by saying:

> **Mr. Greenberg:** *That's exactly what I asked the court to rule on. This was not his 302. This was the agent's 302. Until he read it and corrected it and adopted it, it was not his statement. So, he cannot be impeached and it cannot be implied that he provided any false information at all.*[133]

In other words, Greenberg is saying that the statement did not become factually correct until C.J. Blache actually reviewed and adopted it. I'd like to ask Greenberg why the FBI did not bring my statement to me so I could read it over and see the numerous mistakes that were made. If you follow Greenberg's logic, there was no

---

[133] *U.S.A. v. Edwards, et al.* C.D. 98-165-B-M3, March 3, 2000, Tr. 81-84.

justification for using Harry Burton's statement against me without letting me look at it first and correct his many mistakes.

Another lawyer for the defense, Pat Fanning, followed up Ernest Johnson's argument by telling the judge:

> **Mr. Fanning:** *Judge, the purpose for the use of this document, I understand from talking with Mr. Johnson is, that the agent interviewed Mr. Blache and upon receiving a copy of the interview to review it, he had to go back and tell them that they had made numerous mistakes. It's not to impeach Mr. Blache but simply to call—show that sometimes these agents do interviews, they make 302s, and they make mistakes. And so, it goes to the reliability of the document, the 302, which form the basis for the false statements.*[134]

The defense lawyers are saying that numerous mistakes were made, and they ought to be able to tell this to the jury. And they are absolutely right.

I've never seen the statements in my case. But the indictment charges me with 13 counts of giving false information. The same argument made by Ernest Johnson and Pat Fanning should apply to me when my trial comes up. If I am going to be accused of giving false information, I certainly should be able to review in detail the information taken down by Harry Burton, and I should also be able to point out to the jury that, in the past, Burton has made a lot of mistakes. That's a fact, and it is only fair that the jury hear this information. I hope Judge Polozola will be fair on this issue.

The prosecutors made another startling admission. The handwritten notes taken by FBI agents who interviewed defendant Bobby Johnson, were given to the defense. The defense received both the typed statement, or 302, *and* the handwritten notes.

I will watch this issue closely. So far, I have received nothing from the prosecutors. If they are going to give the handwritten notes to the defendants in the Edwards case, then I certainly should be given the notes taken by Harry Burton in my case. I assume the prosecutors will play by the same rules and give me the notes. The notes are the

---

[134] Ibid.

"best evidence" of what I said, because Burton took them as we were talking. It will be unbelievable if I am not allowed to have the notes. But it's obvious the prosecution team's priority is not to be fair or to see that justice is served. They want to win at any cost. A competent judge will insist that the prosecutors be consistent. If that happens, I will get the notes. If the prosecutors are not consistent, they will hide the notes from me. I remain apprehensive.

**March 17, 2000**
**Baton Rouge, Louisiana**

The prosecution continues to play tape recordings of Governor Edwards and the other defendants accused of criminal activity involving riverboat-gambling licenses. The highlight of the day was supposed to be videotape of a state senator receiving a stack of hundred-dollar bills from the former governor. I was not in the courtroom, but I read the account in the newspaper, the New Orleans *Times-Picayune*.

> *The videotape was shot by FBI equipment suspended in the ceiling of Edwards' law office…*
>
> *A key portion of the meeting does not appear on videotape. Lead FBI agent Geoffrey Santini testified that Harry Burton, the FBI agent who monitored the meeting, did not turn on the videotaping equipment until moments after Edwards gave the stack of cash…*
>
> *The lapse left a nearly two-minute gap at the beginning of the videotape displayed Wednesday. The words "video unavailable" flashed on the courtroom monitors while jurors listened to the beginning of the meeting…*
>
> *Burton is a 20-year FBI veteran. His long history with the agency took on greater significance because the revelation that he did not turn on the videotape came moments after Santini finished testifying that it is not uncommon for*

183

*young, inexperienced agents to make mistakes during surveillance operations.*[135]

I shook my head in dismay when I read that. Harry Burton, the same FBI agent who interviewed me. His own supervisor says he is "inexperienced, and can make mistakes." This "mistake" by Burton should certainly be presented to the jury at my trial. If only Judge Polozola will be fair and let us produce this evidence.

## Sunday, April 2, 2000
## New York City, New York

I've had four enjoyable days with Gladys and our son James in New York.

Friday, I spent the day at the New York Department of Insurance, where Neil Levin is the commissioner (called the superintendent in New York). We met with key members of his staff to update our joint efforts monitoring Lloyd's of London. The Surplus Lines committee that I chair has required Lloyd's to keep a trust fund in the United States in order to do business, so there is no question that policyholders will always be paid. The trust fund is kept in a New York bank and monitored by the New York Department of Insurance. Superintendent Levin and I have been talking or meeting about once a month for the past several years to be sure the trust fund is adequate and to monitor the progress of Lloyd's since its 1993 reorganization .

New York's insurance office is rather dingy; it's in a bland midtown office building. In Baton Rouge, I look out the windows of my office on the seventh floor across from the State Capitol and watch ships go up and down the Mississippi River. I can see several lakes, the site where Huey Long is buried, and the beautiful oak trees that surround the Capitol. In the coming months, Levin will move to the World Trade Center and have spectacular views of the whole city.

The highlight of our weekend was hearing James and other members of the University High School choir sing at Carnegie Hall along with several other choirs from around the country. Gladys and I were so proud to see our son on the stage of one of the premier concert halls in the world.

---

[135] New Orleans *Times-Picayune*, March 17, 2000.

This has been a pleasant respite from the Edwards trial and my all-consuming preparation for my own defense. But tomorrow it's back to the real world.

**Monday, April 3, 2000**
**Baton Rouge, Louisiana**

One of the jurors in the Edwards trial was dismissed this week after writing a scathing letter about the prosecutors to Judge Polozola. Because the jury is anonymous, he is known only as Juror 112. But his words certainly hit home.

> *Originally, I was asked if I could remain neutral throughout the course of this case. I originally answered "yes." My answer is now changed. Because I am upset with the government I no longer feel that I can remain neutral. It is just beyond my imagination that the government has the power to ruin the life of a citizen who has done "nothing wrong..."*
>
> *... I will forever hold a different view of my government.*[136]

I wonder what, exactly, Juror 112 meant when he talked about ruining the life of a citizen who has done "nothing wrong." That's exactly the way I see myself. I hope I have such an understanding jury, one that can sense the viciousness of the prosecutors who have brought these charges against me.

**Thursday, April 6, 2000**
**Gulfport, Mississippi**

Gladys and I drove to Gulfport today for a meeting of insurance commissioners from throughout the Southeast. The group generally gets together several times a year to discuss problems facing our region of the country. Hurricane protection is at the top of the list. The meeting begins tomorrow morning.

---

[136] *The Times*, April 2, 2000.

This evening, I spoke to the Louisiana Land Title Association, which is holding its annual meeting in Gulfport. After the meeting, Gladys and I joined some of the members, along with several insurance commissioners, for dinner at Morano's Italian restaurant. Altogether, there were about 40 of us seated around several tables. One of the female employees of the Land Title Association had brought a date. As we made small talk, someone asked the young lady's date what he did for a living. He was probably in his late 20s, but his crew cut made him look even younger. He said he was an agent with the FBI.

The conversation quieted down considerably. In the next few minutes, a number of people at the dinner, including Gladys and me, quietly made our excuses and left the table. We felt bad about abandoning our hosts, but the young man's presence had definitely put a chill on the room – the other commissioners and their staff members know what I have been going through. It was a strange, melancholy end to what should have been a pleasant evening.

## Saturday, April 8, 2000
## Alexandria, Louisiana

Reverend Anthony Mangun called me several days ago. He and his father, Reverend G.A. Mangun, have been friends of mine since the 1960s. Both have been major voices in the Pentecostal faith in Louisiana and the rest of the country for many years.

I heard Anthony give one of his first sermons when I was a newly elected state senator in 1972. He was a guest speaker at the Grayson Pentecostal Church in Caldwell Parish located in north central Louisiana. With him was his fiancée Mickie, whom he was to marry in a few months. She sang several solos that night, and I really believed I was listening to an angel. Hers was the most stunningly spiritual voice I had ever heard and it continues to be remarkable to this day. I believe Mickie has sung at every governor's inaugural for the last 25 years.

Anthony was calling to say that he and his dad were praying for me regularly and wanted to invite me to a special presentation of the *Messiah* at his home church in Alexandria. I had heard of the *Messiah* for years but had never actually seen it performed.

The Mangun family is close friends with President Clinton. Mickie's father was head of the Pentecostal association in Arkansas and knew Bill Clinton well when he was governor. Anthony told me there was a good chance the president would attend his church's performance of the *Messiah*. I knew such plans often change, and I really wasn't counting on seeing the president, but I feel honored to be invited. Gladys had a family commitment in New Orleans, so I went to Alexandria by myself. Many old friends from central Louisiana were there, including my lawyer Camille Gravel with his wife Evelyn. I was also happy to see Alexandria mayor Ned Randolph. We attended Tulane Law School at the same time and also served in the state senate together. Ned is a close friend, and we lamented the fact that we haven't seen much of each other recently.

The president did come, and without much fanfare. Apparently, the national press was told it was a private trip, and only a small entourage was with him at the Mangun Pentecostal Center. There was a small reception before the performance for the president and a few public officials. I chatted with President Clinton briefly, and he praised my daughter Campbell for the job she is doing covering the White House for NBC.

The performance of the *Messiah* was one of the most dramatic musical events I have ever seen. It rivaled the most elaborate Broadway production in its professionalism, and I joined the rest of the audience in being overwhelmed – a cast of several hundred performers, donkeys and goats on the stage, unbelievable lighting, and angels that soared 30 feet into the air. It was a spectacle I will never forget.

After the performance, the president joined Reverend Mangun on the stage. They prayed together and talked about their longtime friendship. Then the president spoke.

In all that I've read about the Lewinsky scandal, I've never heard him be so candid. He openly expressed pain and regret for the hurt he had brought to his family and the country. He talked about his religious convictions and how he had turned to Reverend Mangun and other close friends to help him through his crisis. Several people in the audience were openly crying as Bill Clinton talked for almost an hour. I wished that my family could have been there to share the moment. Whatever anyone there tonight thought of the president, you just couldn't help but hope and pray for restoration and healing, both for the president and for our country.

**Friday, April 14, 2000**
**Baton Rouge, Louisiana**

Governor Edwards and other defendants in the riverboat-casino trial ended their defense today. The only defendant to testify was Edwards himself.

From all I have read, and from what I have heard in discussions with my attorneys and other lawyers, there is a general feeling that Edwards' legal-defense team erred in not putting more witnesses on the stand. There was strong testimony against the group from others who had pled guilty, including riverboat-casino owner Robert Guidry; Ricky Shetler, a longtime friend of Edwards' son Stephen; and San Francisco 49ers owner Eddie DeBartolo. Where was the rebuke? All these witnesses have baggage that could have been brought out; the Edwards' team to refute what was said could have called other witnesses.

I think Edwards also made a mistake in not having character witnesses talk about his job as governor and the thousands of lives he has touched. Some of these jurors can't remember back to the 1970s, when Edwards did a lot of positive things for the state. Strong character-witness testimony would have presented a different side of him from what was portrayed by the prosecution. The problem he faces is that there are a number of witnesses saying one thing, while he alone is saying another. The scales don't balance. I'm sure there have been lengthy strategy sessions regarding these decisions, but if the group is convicted, there will be a lot of second-guessing.

**May 5, 2000**
**Baton Rouge, Louisiana**

One of the most bizarre things I've ever heard of took place today at the Edwards trial. The jury has been deliberating for two weeks. A juror was dismissed because he told the judge that his fellow jurors were intimidating him. The other jurors apparently told the judge that the dismissed juror is biased and will not join in their discussions and deliberations. Apparently, he has already made up his mind. In all my days as a lawyer and public official, and having followed trials throughout the country, I've never heard of a juror being thrown off a jury after sitting through the entire trial and deliberating for two weeks. Eleven jurors instead of twelve now will judge Edwards and the other defendants. This seems to be one more broken piece in the prosecutors' case; an anonymous jury, a juror kicked off while deliberations are going on — there are just too many holes. All this could come back to haunt the prosecution. If there are convictions, Judge Polozola could be responsible for a later reversal by the appeals court.

**May 9, 2000**
**Baton Rouge, Louisiana**

The jury came back with a verdict today in the Edwards case. Five defendants, including the former governor and his son Stephen, were found guilty of multiple charges.

Close observers of the trial seem to agree that Edwards and the other defendants did not adequately respond to the charges against them; they missed a number of opportunities to contradict the prosecutors' case.

My immediate concern is how this will affect my trial, which is coming up in mid-June. Will the taint of the Edwards conviction rub off on me? Will we all be lumped together as just another bunch of crooks? I hope not. The two cases differ like night and day. In my case, there were no suitcases of cash, no money vests, and no political wheeling and dealing. The Cascade case is not even close to the Edwards case. But can we be convincing as we make the distinction? I am still greatly troubled by the fact that the former governor has no lawyer. We don't have a lot of time, and there's a great deal of preparation yet to be done. But after the intensity of the convictions dies down, Bill Jeffress will talk to Edwards in hopes of convincing him to hire a lawyer.

I continue to wear multiple hats, doing my job as insurance commissioner, working with the legislature, trying to keep a high profile throughout the state, and spending hours each day preparing for my trial. There are thousands of documents to go through and additional witnesses to run down. As expected, the prosecutors continue to be uncooperative. They make no bones about the fact that they are in this matter to get people convicted, justice be damned. Winning is the only thing they care about. But I have known this from the beginning.

## May 12, 2000
## Baton Rouge, Louisiana

The jury in the Edwards' trial found Senator Greg Tarver of Shreveport innocent. Greg is chairman of the Senate Insurance Committee, and we have worked well together over the last eight years. The prosecutors made virtually no case against him, and it was obvious when the prosecution rested he that would be found not guilty. But it's a tragedy that he and his family had to go through this nightmare for the past year.

Predictably, the senator was extremely upset at U.S. Attorney Eddie Jordan. He didn't hold back: "A man in his position should never lie to the public. He just wanted to dirty and destroy my family name. He must have a personal vendetta against us."[137]

Senator Tarver also raised some troubling questions about Jordan's motives: "I think Eddie Jordan wanted to determine the Black leadership in Louisiana. What's frightening is, he might not be finished with other Blacks in this state."[138]

It seems that Eddie Jordan is trying to build his own political future by persecuting (not prosecuting) elected officials like Greg Tarver and me. I'm glad the senator had the courage to speak out against what he was put through.

The *Times-Picayune* has reported that before the trial Jordan and the U.S. Attorney's Office in New Orleans guaranteed that Tarver would spend no time in jail if he testified against Edwards. Tarver lashed back, "I told them I'm not doing anything because I didn't do anything wrong. They wanted me to lie on Edwin."[139] The senator further accused Jordan of using the prosecution of Edwards and the others to help Jordan's political friends gain prominence, which in turn would help Jordan's own political career.

---

[137] *The Times*, May 12, 2000.
[138] The *Times-Picayune*, May 12, 2000.
[139] Ibid.

Bad news on the scheduling of my trial. Judge Polozola has now pushed the date back to August 21. I suppose no one wants my trial to interfere with his or her summer vacations. I want a speedy trial, which I thought I was guaranteed by the Constitution. I strongly protested this two-month delay to Bill Jeffress, but he says there's really not much we can do.

## May 16, 2000
## Baton Rouge, Louisiana

Today I had my annual physical examination. Dr. Roy Kadair gave me the works, including a proctoscope. It was no fun, but the results were good. I'm fit, with no real problems, but I still complained to the doc about my knees and ankles hurting, and my other aches and pains. He was a bit exasperated. "You're sixty years old, for goodness sake. You cannot run marathons and climb mountains, unless you want to really hurt. Slow down a bit, exercise at a more moderate pace, and take care of yourself. You'll live to be a hundred, but not at the pace you would like."

I suppose he's right, but I don't want to admit it. I'm going to work out this afternoon.

## May 19, 2000
## Baton Rouge, Louisiana

There is speculation that Governor Edwards might plea bargain with the prosecutors rather than be tried again on insurance-fraud charges. U.S. Attorney Eddie Jordan told the press this week that he told Edwards "the door is always open" to making a deal in the Cascade case.[140] This, of course, gives rise to speculation that Edwards will testify against me.

I never have thought that Edwards would implicate me in any crime. He has repeatedly told me, and anyone else who asked, that I did nothing wrong. There is nothing secret about our discussions. Almost every conversation we had about Cascade is on tape. So I'm not sure what he could say that would bolster the charges against me.

---

[140] *Monroe News-Star*, May 11, 2000.

If Edwards can walk away from further controversy, if a plea bargain is in his best interest, then he certainly should consider it. I'm not concerned about what effect it will have on me. Our taped conversations speak for themselves. What Edwin Edwards does should not affect my future.

**Tuesday, May 23, 2000**
**Baton Rouge, Louisiana**

> *I'll be the Judge, I'll be the Jury, said cunning Old Fury,*
> *I'll try the whole cause, and condemn you to death.*
> Lewis Carroll, *Alice's Adventures in Wonderland*[141]

After following the Edwards trial, I have continuing concerns about Judge Frank Polozola. The same secrecy that surrounded the Edwards trial will no doubt surround mine. I'm not supposed to be living in a totalitarian atmosphere where everything is done behind closed doors. But most of the documents in Cascade are being filed under seal, which means they are being kept from the public. The gag order, the possibility of an anonymous jury (which makes potential jurors think they will be in danger)—all of this creates a cloud of secrecy and fear that is unfair; I am convinced it will prevent my getting a fair trial. The more I review high-profile trials around the country, the more puzzling it becomes. You just don't find the secrecy surrounding Cascade in other major criminal trials. Drug lords, mafia bosses, terrorists, even the Unabomber, do not face the secrecy I'm strapped with.

In commenting on Judge Polozola's approach in the first Edwards trial, New Orleans television reporter Scott Simmons summed it up pretty well:

> *Iron fist. Very pro-prosecution; aggressive. I lost count of how many defense motions he denied. The feds had an advantage because the judge definitely appeared to be learning toward the prosecution.*[142]

---

[141] Carroll, Lewis (author's real name Charles Lutwidge Dodgson): *Alice's Adventures in Wonderland and Through the Looking Glass*, Oxford University Press, London, England, 1971.

[142] *La. Bar Journal*, Vol. 48, No. 4, p. 285.

*Shreveport Times* reporter John Hill expressed concern over the secrecy Polozola imposes:

> *I have never been to a trial where there is a blanket order to file everything under seal and let the Judge decide later what will be made public.*[143]

My lawyers are defending me against both the prosecutors and the judge. Polozola's actions are costing my legal team enormous time and costing me a lot of money to oppose the gag orders, the anonymous jury, and other forms of secrecy. Defense lawyers regularly tell me that this type of prejudicial secrecy does not take place in courtrooms anywhere else in this state—or, for that matter, anywhere else in America.

It's wrong, it's unfair, but it's one more hurdle I have to overcome.

## Tuesday, June 6, 2000
## Baton Rouge, Louisiana

The Internet address **www.Deductbox.com** is where those who closely follow Louisiana political news begin their day.

The Deduct Box was the brainchild of former Shreveport newspaper reporter John Copes. He now lives in Covington, where he started this news service that provides links to websites containing articles about Louisiana politics. Besides the stories themselves, you get John's insights and opinions, which are filled with humor, sarcasm, and irreverence. Today's Deduct Box features a story that appeared in the *Baton Rouge Morning Advocate* covering a speech I had made to a local civic club. The story was positive, reflecting well on all of us here at the department, and went into some detail about our efforts to protect consumers and lower insurance rates. Copes summarized my speech like this:

---

[143] Ibid.

## YET ANOTHER EXAMPLE OF HOW A SHREWD
## MAN CAN RENDER A GAG ORDER USELESS!

*More good PR for Insurance Commish Brown! This story, in the newspaper that reaches the potential jury pool (assuming no change of venue), reinforces the notion that he's a man just going about his business, doing his job— Brown gets this message across without commenting on the impending trial or directly asserting his innocence. Congrats!*

Thanks, John. I plan to keep it up.

**Thursday, June 8, 2000**
**New Orleans, Louisiana**

Bill Jeffress called this morning to tell me the new round of indictments we had been expecting this week would probably come down later today. He anticipated no additional charges against me. But the mere fact that new charges are being levied against David Disiere and Ron Weems will certainly create a wave of publicity statewide. I will no doubt be mentioned prominently in the stories, and television footage of me will probably be aired, along with footage of Edwards.

Bill and I agree it is a real abuse of the process by the New Orleans U.S. Attorney's office to wait so long to release this information. Nothing new has been discovered. The prosecutors have known all the information in the new charges for months.

The only purpose in waiting so long to bring these charges is to influence potential jurors against all of us. The U.S. Attorney's office waited until the latest deadline set by Judge Polozola.

As expected, the evening television news was headlined "New Allegations Levied in Brown-Edwards Fraud Case." As the focus of the press turns from the riverboat-gambling case to the insurance case, I am taking the spotlight away from Governor Edwards; generally, my name is mentioned first in the various news stories.

I was not even mentioned in the new charges brought by the prosecutor's office today, but tonight most of the television stations throughout the state showed tape of Gladys and me walking into the courthouse a year ago.

I was in New Orleans to attend the grand opening of a new multi-screen movie theater built by my father-in-law Ted Solomon on the west bank in Jefferson Parish. Gladys and I were staying at her family home in New Orleans. When we got in around 11:00 P.M., I turned on the cable rerun of WWL's 10:00 P.M. newscast. WWL, the largest television station in the state, led the newscast with the blaring statement, "Brown and Edwards get additional charges in Cascade Insurance case." Of course, this was completely untrue; neither Edwards nor I has been charged with any additional counts.

I had the number for the WWL news desk in my briefcase, and I immediately called and complained. A young reporter working night duty heard my complaint and said someone would get back to me shortly. Ten minutes later, anchor Dennis Woltering called to acknowledge my complaint. He said he had reviewed the story, and he admitted that their conclusion was wrong. I told him I was concerned about the story running throughout the night and the next day on the morning news. To his credit, Woltering agreed to immediately stop the reruns of the story, so that no more damage would be done.

Earlier in the day, before I had any specific knowledge about the new indictments, my press secretary Amy Whittington had set up an interview with Julie Baxter, a news reporter with WAFB in Baton Rouge. According to Amy, Julie was assigned to cover my trial; Amy thought it would be in our interest for me to give an interview about how the impending trial was affecting my daily activities as insurance commissioner.

I have known Julie for several years, since she covered my office as a radio reporter for WJBO in Baton Rouge. Julie was generally fair in her coverage, although her questions would occasionally put me on the hot seat—which is to be expected when you are as controversial as I am. When she set up the

Baton Rouge TV reporter, Julie Baxter interviewing me about the coming trial.

interview, Amy made it clear that I could not violate the gag order and talk about anything specific regarding the Cascade matter. Julie sat down with me about midday and immediately started asking questions about Cascade. I repeatedly told her that I could not violate the gag order.

Julie led off with "How did you feel when you heard the news that Governor Edwards was convicted?" The gag order issued by Judge Polozola included the previous Edwards trial as well as my trial; I was prohibited from making comments relating to the merits of either case.

"I was glad to hear that the Edwards trial was over, and that I could finally get my day in court," I told her. "The U.S. Constitution says that anyone charged with a crime is entitled to a speedy trial. I was charged nine months ago, and I can't get my day in court. I'm ready to go to trial tomorrow, but apparently the prosecutors are not."

Julie followed up with, "Are you the insurance companies' fair-haired boy?" Without hesitation I replied, "I'm the fair-haired boy of anyone who will live with tough regulation. The vice president of the United States came to Baton Rouge last year and called me the toughest regulator in America. I have shut down more bogus insurance companies and made more criminal referrals than any insurance commissioner in America. Call me what you want, but I think people use any number of terms of appreciation and agree with the job I am doing in cleaning up the huge mess I inherited."

She followed up with several questions about how the Cascade controversy was affecting my ability to do my job. Several of my answers made the evening news

"Of course it is affecting me, and no doubt making me work a lot harder," I said. "You've got to remember the circumstances. I was charged four weeks before my election last year. My lawyers have researched this, and cannot find any instance in the history of our country where a statewide elected official was charged so close to an election. It obviously was done for the sole purpose of trying to get me defeated.

"Quite frankly, my family and I had some long discussions about getting out of my race for reelection. I had enough money in the bank to take care of a major part of my legal fees, and there was a certain question as to whether or not I could win with such a huge negative hanging over my head. No one could remember an indicted official, when the election was so close at hand, having survived. This seemed to be true in the case of Commissioner of Elections Jerry Fowler. He was charged about the time he qualified for re-election and didn't make the run-off. I had never considered myself a quitter. I knew I had done nothing wrong, and that I could possibly hang in there and win re-election. I felt an election victory would be a major rebuke to the prosecutors' case, and a reaffirmation that the public agreed I had done nothing wrong."

It was a fair interview, and it would help make my case to the public without directly violating the gag order.

**Friday, June 9, 2000**
**New Orleans, Louisiana**

I got up at dawn, and set off from the Solomon home on Bayou St. John by Lake Pontchartrain for a bike ride. I rode on a path laid out on the Mississippi River levee, beginning at the New Orleans–Jefferson parish line and traveling upriver about 20 miles. I usually take my bike along when Gladys and I plan to spend the night in New Orleans and take an early-morning ride. The rising sun glistens off the river and the dew is fresh on the grass along the levee. This is a bit of morning therapy before I begin my workday.

After my ride, I stopped at the GNO Cycle Shop owned by Billy Ruddy, from whom I bought my bike, a top-of-the-line triathlon bike by Cannondale. The shop doesn't open until 9:00, but Billy is generally at work by 6:30. When I'm in town, I often interrupt his solitude by beating on the door to get him to make some minor adjustment on the bike. I caught Billy's eye in the back of the shop around 7:00 and bent his ear about how to adjust my aerial bars to fit my elbows. You don't see many sixty-year-olds leaning forward on aerial bars with their elbows to cut down on wind resistance, but I wanted the option of using the bars. I am not at all mechanically inclined, but Billy patiently talked me through the procedure of adjusting the bars, which require maintenance once or twice a week.

With that task completed, I headed for Metairie to see Dr. Jerry Provance. Jerry is the chiropractor for the New Orleans Saints; he specializes in working with athletes. I go to him every three or four months for "general maintenance," particularly on my back. In 15 minutes, Jerry had "popped" my back, neck, hips, fingers, toes, and everything else that could be adjusted.

I complained about my knees. "You are not stretching enough, particularly your hips," Jerry admonished me. "That's why your knees are hurting."

"If my knees are hurting, what does that have to do with my hips?" I protested. He patiently put me through some contortions and convinced me that, although I stretch 30 minutes a day, I am missing some key stretches that could directly affect the pressure on my knees.

"Be realistic," he said. "You are sixty years old and are trying to perform like a thirty-five-year-old athlete. I'm not saying don't do it, but you have got to do a lot more to remain flexible." Jerry pointed out that professional athletes like Michael Jordan and Nolan Ryan, after a game, would stretch for 30 to 45 minutes to prevent tightening up of the muscles.

"Athletes in their mid-30s can't get away with what a twenty-five-year-old can when it comes to stretching and flexibility," Jerry told me. "It gets tougher each year. You can still do triathlons, and a lot of other activities, but stretching is the key. As you get older, you are going to have to stretch more—not just a few times a week but more than once a day. If you are as serious as you seem to be, you need to stretch several times a day."

As I left Jerry's office, I had to laugh at myself. Here I am, too old to be doing all the physical activity I want to do, with a high profile, high-pressure job under normal circumstances, about to face the biggest hurdle of my life—a trial coming up in two months. And what am I worried about? Trying to get more flexible so I can compete in some small-town triathlon!

Gladys and I left New Orleans this morning for Destin, Florida, where I will speak to the "Big I" (Independent Insurance Agents Association of Louisiana). During the drive, she read through some of the documents filed in my case by Bill Jeffress, as well as information about the plea bargain by Judge Foxy Sanders. She peppered me with questions about what the charges meant and how I was going to defend myself against so many allegations. It was good practice for me, and it made me think about all the work I still had left to do. Although I have gone over the indictment and listened to the tapes many times, it seems that every time I discuss them with another person, I gain a different perspective; I find new areas to research and new questions that need answers.

As soon as we checked in to the Hilton Hotel in Destin, I jotted down a few notes based on Gladys's questions. I called my office in Baton Rouge and dictated the notes over the telephone, then dropped Gladys at the local outlet mall near the hotel. With several hours to kill until my speech, I took a late-afternoon swim in the Gulf of Mexico. The salt water was cold and invigorating, and a brisk wind created high waves. Thirty minutes in the ocean gave me a solid workout.

When I got back to the hotel room, Gladys told me she was too tired to go to the dinner. The NBA finals were on television, so she opted to order room service and watch the game in bed. She's a big Indiana Pacers fan, and they are one game behind the Los Angeles Lakers. She curled up in bed to watch the game, and I joined the Big I board of directors for dinner.

This organization of insurance agents has been supportive of me since I first ran for insurance commissioner eight years ago. The group's executive director, Jeff Albright, gave me a warm introduction. Jeff took the job five years ago, replacing long-time director Tom Oglesby. When I first met Jeff, I thought he was a little brash, and I wondered if the Big I had made the right decision in hiring him. But he has become a close ally as we worked to solve problems in the insurance industry. Jeff is a quick learner, extremely personable, and he often knows more about the problem being discussed than anyone else at the table. He was one of the first persons to come to my defense when the indictment came down a year ago, and he persuaded insurance agents throughout the state to support me financially and in other ways. Although I have never made a decision that showed favoritism to the organization, I've enjoyed a strong working relationship with the Big I and have always appreciated Jeff's friendship.

After speaking to the Big I board for about 30 minutes, I thanked them for their many efforts on my behalf then left to attend several receptions sponsored by various insurance groups in the hotel. The receptions continued until past midnight. I made it back to the room just in time to see Gladys's team, the Pacers, get clobbered by the Lakers, 120 to 87.[144]

## Saturday, June 10, 2000
## Baton Rouge, Louisiana

> *My real quarrel, though, is with the arrogance and vaulting careerism of those in the Department of Justice—so skilled at spin, so brazen in their efforts to conceal their own mistakes, so intent on "winning"— who trashed the respect for the law, for fairness, and for the truth, which ought to be the hallmarks of their work.*[145]
>
> Attorney Stephen Jones

Front-page stories appeared all over the state today, supposedly making numerous new allegations against Governor Edwards in the Cascade case. Actually, there is nothing new. The allegations are merely an elaboration of what was initially charged last year. By bolstering the allegations and filing new charges in court, the prosecutors have accomplished exactly what they set out to do—get major headlines in the newspapers and have lead stories on the evening news throughout the state. It is nothing more than an attempt to get around the gag order. And they have succeeded. How unfair. I am gagged and can say nothing. Yet the prosecutors can fine-tune their charges, plaster these charges all over the state, and lead the public to believe there is some type of new crime.

This is the ploy they have used for months. They look for any reason to file some inflammatory motion that will be all over the papers the next day. No gag order is violated, they make no public statement, but they get the same result. There is no fairness here, no justice. It's just a tactic they use because they couldn't care less about the truth and want to win at any cost.

There are also lengthy news stories on how the Justice Department in Washington is supposedly investigating one of their own. L.J. Hymel is the U.S. Attorney for the Baton Rouge area. New

---

[144] The Los Angeles Lakers went on to win the NBA Championship, beating the Indiana Pacers four games to two.

[145] Stephen Jones, *Others Unknown: The Oklahoma City Bombing Conspiracy* (New York: Perseus Books Group, 1998.

Orleans television station WWL quoted sources who said that Hymel is being investigated at the request of the local office of the FBI.[146]

This is an obvious attempt by the U.S. Attorney's Office in New Orleans, and the FBI, to damage Hymel's credibility. His involvement in the Cascade case is nothing new. When the indictments were handed down last October, references were made to Edwards talking to Hymel at the request of Judge Foxy Sanders. I have listened to the two conversations Edwards had with Hymel. The U.S. Attorney could not have been more professional, and he treated the conversation with Edwards as another event in the normal course of his office activities. To infer that Hymel made a deal to help Sanders is ridiculous. Talk about eating one's own young. In this no-holds-barred effort, the U.S. Attorney's office in New Orleans is so desperate to get convictions in the Cascade case that anything goes. They will try to destroy a reputable U.S. Attorney in Baton Rouge if this can help them accomplish their goal. Truth be damned. Winning is not the most important thing, it's the only thing. Who cares who they destroy in the process. What a subversion of the judicial process.

## Sunday, June 11, 2000
## Orlando, Florida

My key staff at the insurance department was on their way to Orlando on Friday to attend the summer meeting of the National Association of Insurance Commissioners. All of the state regulators meet at least four times a year at various locations throughout the country. There is no federal regulation of insurance, so these meetings are important in our efforts to coordinate insurance regulation across state lines. Company representatives from all over the world attend these conventions to network with key regulators. We accomplish a great deal at these quarterly meetings.

I like to spend weekends with my family, so I usually wait until late Sunday to leave Baton Rouge. After a short workout in the pool, I attended church, stopped for Eggs Benedict at Louie's, and then drove to New Orleans for my flight to Orlando.

Some of the commissioners from the South had planned a surprise birthday party for former Alabama Commissioner Mike Weaver. He

---

[146] WWL-TV, New Orleans, LA., 6:00 P.M., June 20, 2000.

was the top insurance regulator in Alabama when I took office in 1992, and we became close friends right away. Although we worked hard at our quarterly meetings during the day, Mike and I would always find a sporting event to attend in the city where the meetings took place. Whatever the season—baseball, basketball, or football—we would slip out of the commissioners' dinner just before dessert and head to the local stadium.

When I was indicted, Mike was one of the first to call, saying he was ready to do whatever he could to help. "You may not know this, but I was one of the major witnesses against Doug Green [a former Louisiana commissioner who is still in jail] at the request of the prosecutors," Mike told me. "I was one of the strongest witnesses for their case, but I am ready to be an even stronger witness on your behalf. I'll testify to how ridiculous these charges are, and how you were only doing your job as commissioner." I hope to take Mike up on his offer.

Mike turned 50 today. About a hundred of his good friends gathered at, an Italian restaurant where the toasts and songs went on late into the evening. One of the persons at our table was insurance consultant Barbara Bain, a longtime friend of Gladys's and mine.

As we were leaving the restaurant, Barbara pulled me aside. "Jim, you may not believe this, but I get down on my knees every morning when I wake up and pray for you. I really do, and I know this is going to work out for you."

I do believe her—that she gets down on her knees and prays for me, and that this whole mess will be behind me soon.

## Monday, June 12, 2000
## Baton Rouge, Louisiana

My day started with breakfast at the Walt Disney Hotel with an old California friend, Ken Gibson. We worked together on the Lloyd's of London problem in the mid-1990s, when Ken was deputy insurance commissioner in California. His roommate in college was Ned Randolph, who is now mayor of Alexandria and one of my close friends and allies.

Ken updated me on the crisis facing California Insurance Commissioner Chuck Quackenbush. There were allegations that fines levied against California insurance companies were being diverted

202

into the pockets of Chuck's campaign consultants and supporters. Chuck is a Republican, but we built a close working relationship during the Lloyd's crisis, and I was sorry to see that he was in the middle of such a mess.

"I'll tell you how bad things are in California," Ken said. "If Chuck Quackenbush could change places with you, take on your burden and give you his, I think he would jump at the chance." I knew then that Chuck must really be in trouble.

After meeting with fellow commissioners all afternoon, I decided to catch a late flight back to Baton Rouge. Gladys has held up well throughout this nerve-wracking year, and she is always full of questions and suggestions when we are together. But I can tell that when I'm away the pressure gets to her. So I feel it's best to go home.

My plane was late getting to New Orleans, and we did not land until 1:00 A.M. After a quick cup of coffee at the airport, I picked up my car and headed for home. Just outside the entrance to the airport, I saw the flashing blue lights of a police car behind me. I didn't think I was speeding, but I pulled over. When the officer came up to my car, I handed him my license and he smiled.

"Commissioner, you weren't speeding, but I recognized you as you pulled out of the parking lot," he said. "I just wanted to tell you that we talk about you a lot here at the sheriff's office, and we really think you are getting a lousy rap. You're the one that's been shutting down all these crooked companies. They ought to be praising you instead of harassing you. I just wanted to wish you luck."

I assured him that his kind words had picked up my spirits and would make the drive back to Baton Rouge a lot easier. When I pulled into the driveway at 2:30, Gladys was waiting up for me.

**Thursday, July 6, 2000**
**Perdido Key, Florida**

For the past 40 years, my family and I have spent pleasant, if uneventful, vacations on the Gulf Coast at Gulf Shores and Perdido Key. In the old days, there were no condos, no Water Worlds, and no Putt-Putt golf. The few beach houses had no air-conditioning or telephones. Yet the two weeks we spent there each summer seemed to fly by. The children and I built sand castles, picked up shells during long walks on the beach, and caught crabs to boil for lunch and flounder to broil for supper. In spite of the dramatic growth here in the past 15 years, it's still an anticipated getaway for us.

Today, when I came back from an early swim, there was a message to call Bill Jeffress immediately.

"I have some news," Bill declared. "It may be good. Judge Polozola has just recused himself from our case."

"What? Did he give any reason?" I asked.

"None whatsoever. I'm getting a lot of calls, and I may know something later this afternoon. Apparently the other three judges—Tyson, Parker, and Brady—have also recused themselves. Right now, we don't have any idea who will try the case."

Earlier years spending summers with my children on the Gulf Coast.

Bill called back a few hours later. "The judge has filed a three-page statement saying he is stepping aside because he knows several potential witnesses in the case. He mentioned U.S. Attorney L.J. Hymel, and he apparently had a phone call from Foxy Sanders a few years back asking about the reputation of Ed Gonzales. They may be witnesses, so Polozola is stepping aside."

Bill added, "This probably means our August 21$^{st}$ court date will be delayed again, Jim. I know you're anxious to get this case moving, but without a judge there's not a lot we can do."

Bill said he had no idea who would be appointed to handle the case, but Carolyn King would make the decision, the chief judge of the U.S. Fifth Circuit Court of Appeals in New Orleans. "The judge could come from anywhere in the Fifth Circuit," Bill added. "Louisiana, Mississippi or Texas."

Throughout the day I talked to a number of attorneys and others interested in the trial. No one bought the reasons given by Polozola. The involvement of Sanders, Hymel, and Gonzales has been known for more than a year. In fact, when Foxy Sanders pled guilty to conspiracy back in October 1999, and his full involvement in the

Cascade case was laid out in some detail, it was in Polozola's courtroom.

Gannet columnist John Hill summed it up in his weekly column:

> *It is incredulous to believe Polozola suddenly realized these people would be involved.*[147]

Although the law says I am entitled to a speedy trial, Polozola has dragged this matter out for eight months. He should have recused himself from the very beginning and not put me through this draining process. The Cascade case should have been tried months ago.

On the other hand, it's hard to imagine that we can do any worse with a new judge. I've asked attorneys who practice before Polozola their views of his recusal. Their conclusion is almost unanimous: no matter what judge is selected it will be an improvement. Polozola has surrounded this trial with a shroud of secrecy and tied my hands with his gag order. His ruthless effort to directly inject himself into the final days of my election by publicly reinstating the gag order was a gross miscarriage of justice. He has certainly tainted his reputation by his actions in the Cascade case. Perhaps that's the reason he stepped aside.

In any event, I expect more delays in the weeks to come.

## Friday, July 7, 2000
## Baton Rouge, Louisiana

> *Free speech is the whole thing ...Free speech is life itself.*
> Salman Rushdie[148]

Bad news today from the Fifth Circuit Court of Appeals. A decision was handed down that maintains the gag order in the Cascade case. A three-judge panel concluded:

> *"While this case presents a somewhat close call, we conclude that the gag order is constitutionally permissible because it is based on a reasonably found substantial*

---

[147] *Monroe News-Star*, Sunday, July 9, 2000.

[148] *New York Times,* December 12, 1991. Rushdie's publication in 1988 of *The Satanic Verses*, about repression in Iran, resulted in continuing death threats.

*likelihood that comments from the lawyers and parties might well taint the jury pool.*"[149]

In other words, because a potential juror may hear something I say in the media, I will continue to be gagged.

We also continue to make new law as this case moves along. Bill Jeffress was quoted in a number of news stories saying, "It is the first time a federal appeals court has upheld a gag order against a defendant, as opposed to attorneys, when the defendant is the one to challenge it. It is a very important decision. We will consider whether to take it up to the Supreme Court."[150]

No consideration necessary. We are definitely going to appeal. It is just wrong for me not to be able to defend myself and speak out about my innocence in public.

Four major New Orleans television stations have joined my efforts to abolish the gag order. New Orleans attorney Mary Ellen Roy, representing the major stations, filed a supportive brief before the Fifth Circuit that said, "It is unfortunate because the public will get less information in important trials."[151]

A little movement forward, then you get knocked back a step or two. Major decisions are coming down everyday, and I'm becoming more and more consumed with preparing for my defense. The costs are mounting dramatically. But I really have little choice. I'm innocent, so I have to keep fighting one day at a time.

**Monday, July 10, 2000**
**Baton Rouge, Louisiana**

This morning I logged on to the Internet to check the website Deductbox.com. The morning headline flashed across my computer screen and jumped right out at me.

## *OUT OF THE FRYING PLAN, INTO THE FIRE FOR BROWN, ET AL?*

---

[149] No. 00-3-134, U.S.C.A. Fifth Circuit, July 6, 2000.
[150] *The Times-Picayune*, July 7, 2000.
[151] Ibid.

*The story announced that New Orleans judge Edith Clement has been appointed to handle the Cascade case. Clement was described by virtually every lawyer quoted as "conservative" and "pro-prosecution." The Times-Picayune quotes former U.S. Attorney Harry Rosenberg as saying, "I don't think the government is crying."*[152]

In the publication *Almanac for the Federal Judiciary,* which rates judges throughout the country, the conclusion was that Clement is "prosecution-oriented." The publication quoted a defense attorney who said, "She is not a good draw in criminal cases; she is much more inclined to believe the government and the police."[153]

Press reports continue to play up Judge Clement's right-wing leanings and pro-prosecution attitude. Today's Deduct Box ran a lengthy *Washington Post* story that said Clement had taken a free vacation to Montana, paid for by several conservative foundations that are funding lawsuits on important environmental issues in federal courts. In other words, companies give the money for the seminars to foundations with a significant interest in property rights and environmental-law issues. The *Post* story quotes a brochure given to judges: "Conference and travel expenses are paid and time is provided for cycling, fishing, golfing, hiking and horseback riding."[154]

It's hard to believe that a federal judge who might be ruling on key issues affecting the companies would accept the free vacations. Organizations throughout the country are criticizing judges who participate in these seminars. The *Post* article says: "Douglas Kendall of Community Rights Counsel, which helps local governments defend their activities against efforts by property rights advocates and provided information about the free seminars to *The Post*, called them 'junkets for judges, sponsored by the same foundations that are bankrolling taking cases before the same judges...At the very least, they create an appearance problem.'"[155]

The story quotes legal-ethics expert Stephen Gillers of New York University saying that he "felt uncomfortable" about the whole idea of such seminars.

---

[152] *The Times-Picayune*, July 10, 2000.
[153] Ibid.
[154] *Washington Post*, June 10, 2000.
[155] Ibid.

Everything I hear about Clement is troubling. We just want a decent judge to listen to our arguments and give us a level playing field on which to make a fair presentation to the jury. But the press reports overwhelmingly paint her as being solidly in the prosecutors' corner. One more mountain to climb.

## Thursday, July 13, 2000
## Baton Rouge, Louisiana

*An anonymous jury flouts the principle of open trials.*[156]
Douglas Lee

Judge Clement has quickly made it clear that the veil of secrecy in the Cascade case will remain in place. Today she ruled that there will be an anonymous jury, but she gave no reason why. Rather than reviewing the facts in the various pleadings that have been filed so far, Clement seems to be merely following in lock step with Judge Polozola's decisions. It is unbelievable to me that Clement would order an anonymous jury without allowing any evidence to be taken or any hearing to be held.

Clement has also moved our trial date back to September 18. Since she has just become involved in the case, I'm not surprised at the delay.

John Copes' *Deduct Box* column could not have summed it up better:

### NEW JUDGE IS SECRECY FREAK TOO!

*There is something un-American and sneaky about this whole process of secret trials, anonymous juries, sealed evidence, sealed motions, and iron-fisted information management in what is purported to be a system of public justice. The public still doesn't know why the government asked for and the judge granted an anonymous jury in the last trial.*

---

[156] Douglas Lee's article critical of anonymous juries was published by freedomforum.org on May 29, 2001. Lee is a legal correspondent for the First Amendment Center.

*Is there a fear of jury harassment by the media? Or jury harassment by the defendants? Is the government trying to claim the defendants might physically harm or intimidate the jury? Who knows?*[157]

The good news this week is that my fundraising activities have gone well. My events in Alexandria, Shreveport, Lake Charles, and Baton Rouge have been solidly attended, which is important as the trial nears and costs continue to rise. In spite of the daily deluge of front-page stories about Cascade, I still have strong public support.

## Friday, July 21, 2000
## Baton Rouge, Louisiana

David Disiere, the owner of Cascade Insurance Company, pled guilty today. But I'm not sure what he pled guilty to. Officially, it was "misprision of a felony," which means that he failed to report a crime. But Disiere told the court he was "unaware of much of the alleged illegal activity involving Edwards and the others."[158] As best I can understand, Disiere supposedly determined, more than a year after the Cascade settlement, that something had been done to settle the case of which he had no knowledge, and he did not immediately run to the FBI and report what he was thinking. Of course, it's all a sham. Disiere now walks away from the case with no jail time, and a fine of $100,000. It's obvious he did not want to go through the trial, and the prosecutors did not want him at the table.

I think he was afraid of taking his chances. If he were convicted, he would take heavy losses, like the rest of us. But he really knew of no crime, and would testify to that at the trial. The prosecutors just did not want his claim of innocence. They had their sights set on Edwards and me, with Ron Weems thrown in as lagniappe, and Disiere was in their way.

I have read over his "factual basis" several times and can find nothing that he or anyone else really did wrong. Of course, the media is having a field day with his plea, and the legal pundits are saying this is a big win for the prosecutors. The *Times-Picayune* quotes

---

[157] *Deductbox.com*, July 14, 2000.
[158] *The Times-Picayune,* July 22, 2000.

former U.S. Attorney Harry Rosenberg as saying, "It's a great coup for the government; that clearly is a way to sort of put a wrap around the case."[159]

Frankly, we don't see it that way. I immediately called a press conference and told the media, "It would seem that the key parties who have had any authority to settle the Cascade matter have now pled guilty. The indictment makes it clear that I had no authority to settle the case. I therefore hope the prosecutors will do the right thing and dismiss all charges against me."[160]

At least I got my point of view across; it ran in most of the news stories throughout the state.

Bill Jeffress and the rest of the defense team are pleased that Disiere is out of the case. The Cascade case is about benefits to Disiere, but his testimony is so useless to the prosecution that I doubt they will call him as a witness. My lawyers think it would be better to have him out of the case completely than to have him sitting at the defense table with us.

There are also rumors about other problems Disiere may be facing, problems that could come out before the trial. So it benefits us to have him out of the way.

## Wednesday, July 26, 2000
## Baton Rouge, Louisiana

The blows from Judge Clement continue. She has ruled against my request to dismiss nine criminal counts involving the false-statement charges against me.

Bill Jeffress had accused the prosecutors of trying to "bludgeon" me with a number of different charges that were all or part of the same subject. FBI agent Harry Burton asked me whether I had talked to anyone about the settlement involving Cascade. I truthfully told him that I had not been at the settlement, was not notified of the settlement, and did not have a chance to talk to anyone about it. He then mentioned specific names, including Ron Weems, Edwin Edwards, Bob Bourgeois, and Judge Sanders, and asked if I had talked to them about the settlement. I gave him the same answer: I

---

[159] Ibid.
[160] Ibid.

hadn't talked to anyone about the final settlement. Instead of making one charge, the prosecutors made nine different charges against me for saying I had not talked to anyone about the settlement. This was overkill, and Bill Jeffress made a proper request to dismiss a number of these charges. Clement, taking a pro-prosecution stance, disagreed. In the scheme of things, it's not a huge defeat, but its one more indication that we are going to be fighting not only the prosecutors but also the judge in the months to come. Her ruling today was wrong.

In separate conversations with Jeffress and Camille Gravel, I again raised the question of Edwards representing himself. He's a good lawyer and quick on his feet, but this case is extremely complicated. He has not practiced criminal law in many years, and I think he would be making a mistake to argue his own defense.

Edwards believes his defense will come down to a swearing contest between himself and Foxy Sanders. This may be true, but he's also going to have to wade through mountains of paperwork involving contracts, investigations, and other material important to his defense. Jeffress, Gravel, and Ron Weems' lawyer Eddie Castaing say that if any one defendant is convicted on insurance fraud, we will all be convicted. So Edwards must be concerned with more than just "who said what." He needs to immerse himself in the minutiae of this case.

Bill and Camille will talk to Edwards soon. There is a lot of preparation to do, so if he's going to hire another lawyer he'd better do it soon.

## Thursday, July 27, 2000
## Baton Rouge, Louisiana

The news media are on my side in opposing an anonymous jury in the Cascade trial. Lloyd Lunceford, an attorney for the *Baton Rouge Morning Advocate,* filed a strongly worded motion this week, asking Judge Clement to reconsider her decision to make the jury anonymous: "The press and public can't emphasize enough how fundamental it is to our American system of justice that trials be held openly. An anonymous jury is simply contrary to that. The courts have made clear that anonymous juries are only allowed in the most extraordinary of circumstances, none of which are present here. Anonymous juries go against First Amendment values and open judicial proceedings. Open court proceedings foster public confidence in the judicial system and provide citizens with information about their government."[161]

A pattern seems to be developing in Louisiana federal courts of using anonymous juries, and this should concern the Fifth Circuit and the U.S. Supreme Court. Hopefully, this will not be an issue I will ever have to address, because I am sure I will be found not guilty. But I have to assume the worst and keep a list of these errors as a basis for appeal.

The press is also raising concerns about the unfairness of all the secrecy. John Copes in *Deduct Box* said today:

> *"There's a perverse and unfair and Un-American quality about the secret fetish surrounding the coming trial; feds allege and judges agree that Edwards, and [Brown] and possibly the media all pose such threats to justice that the jury may be anonymous. In fact, they are so dire they can't even tell you what they are and they can't explain their reasoning? Trust us!"*[162]

Copes, with his witty sarcasm is reflecting what a number of other reporters throughout the state are saying: that there is no reason for an anonymous jury, and that no explanation is forthcoming from Judge Clement.

## Thursday, August 10, 2000
## Baton Rouge, Louisiana

Camille Gravel came to my office this morning to discuss recent events related to the trial.

The first thing we reviewed was a copy of the reasons Judge Clement made public today for having an anonymous jury. She says she has seen some evidence that "the defendants may be willing and able to interfere with the judicial process,"[163] but she gives few specific examples.

---

[161] *U.S.A. v. Brown et al.* C.D. 99-151-B-M2, Notice of Appeal by *The Times-Picayune*, Docket Entry No. 300, July 27, 2000.

[162] Deductbox.com, July 27, 2000.

[163] *U.S.A. v. Brown et al.* C.D. 99-151-B-M2, Order and Reasons as to JHB, et al. Granting Anonymous Jury by USA, Docket Entry No. 312 (August 10, 2000).

One example she does give is that during the earlier riverboat-licensing trial "certain members of the media" apparently contacted several jurors in violation of an order earlier signed by Judge Polozola. Now let me get this straight. Members of the press talked to jurors during a completely different trial, so I have to be tried by an anonymous jury in the Cascade case? The judge also says that the severity of the punishment we face is another reason to have an anonymous jury. I've talked to a number of defense attorneys who are puzzled by this reasoning, including Camille Gravel. Her decision is poorly reasoned, cites few specific examples of any possible threat, and she does not cite legal cases from other districts to support her decision. Most of the lawyers with whom I have discussed this issue agree that she has committed an error that could cause reversal if any convictions take place. As *Deduct Box* editorialized: "The problem with Clement's anonymous EWE-Brown jury ruling is secrecy only works where there is a sufficient level of trust in and respect for authority."[164]

The overwhelming majority of observers looking at the issue, including defense lawyers, the press, and the public aren't buying Clement's reasoning that we should "trust her." So far, I've seen very little to trust.

An interesting story is also developing about a dispute between Ed Gonzales and U.S. Attorney L.J. Hymel. Gonzales billed large attorney's fees in the Cascade settlement and signed off on the final agreement. But then, in a strange twist, he apparently went to the FBI to raise questions about possible criminal activity. Again, this is hard to swallow. He gets paid the big fees, negotiates the settlement, signs off on it, and then has the audacity to say that something was wrong? Several news stories quote Gonzales as saying that he gave sensitive information about Cascade to the U.S. Attorney's office. But Hymel flatly denies that his office received anything from Gonzales. The *Baton Rouge Morning Advocate* reported: "Ed Gonzales, who investigated Cascade's finances at the behest of a state judge, claims in a sworn affidavit that twice in 1996 he reported to federal prosecutors in Baton Rouge wrongdoing on the part of David Judd Disiere, the one-time owner of Cascade Insurance Company. U.S. Attorney L.J. Hymel of Baton Rouge said he finds no record that

---

[164] *Deductbox.com*, August 11, 2000.

Gonzales ever spoke to anyone in his office about Cascade. 'We're not able to find any documentation that he ever did that,' Hymel said."[165]

Camille told me that Edwards has been talking to Alexandria attorney Mike Small about possibly representing him in the coming trial. I have known Mike for a long time and think he would be an excellent choice. He's an aggressive, articulate defense lawyer with a strong enough backbone to stand up to both the prosecutors and the judge. That's just what Edwards' needs, and I hope Mike joins the defense team.

Camille Gravel has served as my advisor, counselor, mentor and friend for many years.

Photo by John H. Williams
*The Advocate*

Camille and I also talked at length about the recent loss of his daughter Eunice, who died of cancer at 51. He said it was much more of a shock when his son Camille, Jr. died suddenly of a heart attack. He said at least he had had some time to prepare for Eunice's death and come to terms with the loss as she struggled through her final weeks.

I spend part of every day relating in some way to my four children, hoping they are living full and successful lives and trying to figure out what I can do to help them along. Camille has 10 children.

---

[165] *Baton Rouge Advocate,* August 9, 2000.

How much more difficult, yet how much more rewarding, that must be. I feel lucky to have him as a part of my team.

## Tuesday, August 15, 2000
## Baton Rouge, Louisiana

> *Secrecy rulings do not serve as future guidelines, even in the same court. Secrecy enables guides to ignore the law knowing that justice is hidden. Feedback to the public, necessary to correct abuses, is prevented.*[166]
>
> Michael Schmier

The secrecy from Judge Clement continues. She ruled today that the audiotapes of Governor Edwards and all of us discussing the Cascade matter would not be made public. The defense team wants the tapes made public, as does the press. Clement gave no reasons for her ruling and kept everything involving the tapes under "seal." As the *Deduct Box* headline said, the "secrecy fetish" continues. The sarcastic analysis concludes that:

### SECRECY FREAKS STILL RULE
### IN COMING TRIAL

*Clement rules surveillance tapes still bear seal of double-super-secret-stuff because the sheer power of the images they contain might taint the tiny minds of potential jurors in coming Edwards (Brown) trial.*[167]

Several of the defense lawyers are jokingly wondering: Where's the Ayatollah Polozola when you need him?

## Wednesday, August 23, 2000
## Baton Rouge, Louisiana

I had a full day today, beginning with a 6:00 A.M. interview on a local television station. I'm still trying to give attention to the issues that face me daily as insurance commissioner. That means less sleep

---

[166] Candidate for Attorney General in California in 1998. Fas.org/sgp/news/secrecy/2001.

[167] *Deductbox.com*, August 15, 2000

and many more phone calls, but I'm able to balance both schedules. I do worry about family commitments, particularly spending time with my son James. The girls and I talk several times a week, and I can hook up with them by phone in the car or wherever I happen to be. But teenagers need time. Not necessarily quality time—just time.

While serving as a state senator in the mid-1970s, I attended a conference at the upstate New York mansion of former governor Averill Harriman. Over dinner one evening, I had a discussion about raising children with a Nixon cabinet member and her husband. They traveled extensively, but they said they always found time each month for "quality time" with their kids— a special lunch or an evening out. Making the most of their time was their child-rearing creed. At the moment, it seemed to make sense.

But in the years since, I've learned that quality time is important, but "a lot of time" is much more necessary. Sure, there should be family discussions about current issues, and there should be special nights out. But just "hanging out" together as a family is every bit as important. Watching old movies and ordering pizza, riding bikes in the neighborhood, shooting baskets in the back yard, and just "chilling out, doing nothing."

Simply put, I've learned way too late that children spell love T-I-M-E.

I'm "compromising" now, spending too little time with my family. I know it, and I hope they understand. There is so much to do in preparation for the coming trial.

Our first pre-trial hearing before Judge Clement took place this morning in New Orleans. In addition to some routine matters that were handled, the prosecutors are trying to keep Baton Rouge lawyer John DiGiulio[168] from testifying for the defense. John had represented Bob Bourgeois before he pled guilty; if allowed to testify, he will state that Bourgeois felt the settlement "was and still is an excellent one."

It will not surprise me if the judge rules that DiGiulio cannot testify. So far, she has been in lock step with the prosecutors, agreeing to their every request, and they certainly don't want this type of testimony. I even wonder if they will call Bourgeois himself. I really

---

[168] John also owns a well-known Baton Rouge restaurant, DiGiulios, where Gladys and I eat lunch every Monday, when the daily special is baked oysters.

think he will tell the truth and say the settlement made sense. I still can't see what Bob did wrong. It looks to me like Sanders scared him and made him think he may go to jail for a long time. I'm sure Bob Bourgeois regrets that he pled guilty, and he will tell the truth on the stand. If he does, it will dramatically undermine the prosecutors' case.

Governor Edwards acted as his own lawyer at the pre-trial hearing and did some cross-examination. He's entertaining but a little rusty. The talks with Mike Small are going well, and I hope Mike will be representing him at our next court appearance.

**Friday, August 25, 2000**
**Baton Rouge, Louisiana**

There was good news and bad news today.

Edwards has hired Alexandria attorney Mike Small to represent him in the coming trial. Trial date is September 18, so Mike has his work cut out for him. He's going to have to work seven days a week around the clock to prepare a proper defense. But he is capable and should do an effective job. I asked Bill Jeffress to call Mike and bring him up to date.

On the downside, Judge Clement has fined Edwards seventeen hundred dollars, holding him in contempt of court for violating her gag order in the Cascade case.

When the pre-trial hearing was held in New Orleans last week, apparently Edwards stood on the courthouse steps and referred publicly to a letter Bob Bourgeois had written saying the settlement was excellent. According to press reports, Edwards said the letter "totally undercuts the government's position that this was a scam." He also referred to several people who had recently pled guilty saying, "now we have the dirty dozen."[169] The judge fined him a hundred dollars for each word she says violated the gag order. She said the next fine would be a thousand dollars a word. I suppose if he violates the gag order again, Clement will get out the cattle prods. The defense team agrees that her actions are unconstitutional and have put a cloud over our entire case.

My legal team also filed a motion with the U.S. Supreme Court requesting a decision that the gag order violates my First Amendment

---

[169] *The Times-Picayune,* August 26, 2000.

right to free speech. I was quoted in press reports throughout the state: "I truly believe the Constitution requires free speech. To gag me is not only an abridgment of my First Amendment rights, but of the right of the people of this state to hear the truth. I must have the freedom to talk about these false allegations in order to properly do my job as Insurance Commissioner. And the people should be free to hear the facts."[170]

However, it is highly unlikely the Supreme Court will hear my case before the Cascade trial begins.

## Thursday, August 31, 2000
## Baton Rouge, Louisiana

No word yet on any additional delays in the starting date of the Cascade trial. I won't be surprised if the case is put off another month or so. Clement's appointment has dragged this matter out longer with a number of pre-trial meetings that should have been held months ago.

The *Baton Rouge Morning Advocate* editorialized today about the delays in the trial: "which brings to mind another old saying about our legal system. That one holds that justice delayed is justice denied."[171]

I agree. I've certainly been denied justice as I've waited for this trial to begin. Judges have come and gone, as have witnesses and defendants. The financial cost has been tremendous, yet the matter drags on. In spite of constitutional guarantees, I have been denied my right to a speedy trial. Any citizen deserves better.

Dove season opens Saturday. As we do every year, James and I will drive up to Jonesville, spend the night at Elmly Plantation, and go hunting with Jimmy Lossin, an old friend from Catahoula Parish. I bought a .410 pump shotgun last year from Guy Coates, an Associated Press reporter assigned to cover the State Capitol. James and I will give the gun a good test. He is a far better shot, but I generally bring down my share of doves. Whatever our luck, it will be good to get away for the weekend.

---

[170] Ibid.

[171] *Baton Rouge Advocate,* August 31, 2000.

## Wednesday, September 6, 2000
## Opelousas, Louisiana

Another day of contrasts, filled with good news and extremely bad news.

Bill Jeffress called this afternoon to report on his lengthy meeting with U.S. Attorney L.J. Hymel. Far from being a problem for us, Hymel knows of no crime and has no knowledge of any problems with Edwards in their conversations—or for that matter, anything else relating to Cascade. Several news articles have indicated that Hymel will be called as a prosecution witness, but I doubt it. He may be the U.S. Attorney in Baton Rouge, but Bill and I don't think the New Orleans prosecutors will touch him. He won't help them one bit, and he could actually hurt their case. I was surprised Hymel even met with Bill, and we both feel Hymel is not at all happy about the way he has been treated by the U.S. Attorney's office in New Orleans. The prosecutors have obviously leaked information in the past to embarrass him, and he seems quite bitter about it.

The bad news is that I've lost Camille Gravel as one of my attorneys. He called me this morning and asked to meet with me today. I suggested that we split the difference and meet in Opelousas, about halfway between Baton Rouge and his home in Alexandria. Gladys drove to Opelousas with me, and Camille brought his wife Evelyn.

Evelyn is having some health problems and has had no significant improvement for several months. Camille is understandably concerned, and he has reservations about embarking on a trial that could last five or six weeks. He knows the lawyers will be working nights and weekends as the trial progresses. Of course I understand, and I agree that Camille has no choice but to step down. Still, it's a huge blow to my defense.

Camille and Bill Jeffress have worked on several trials together, and they balance each other's strengths and weaknesses. Camille has a knack for stepping back a bit and giving a solid overview of cadence, direction, and priorities as the case unfolds. He has given me excellent legal advice over many years, always right on target. We agree that he will come to Baton Rouge when he can and stay in touch with Bill by phone. But his loss will be significant; Bill and I will look for additional help on the case.

Gladys has become extremely close to Evelyn over the past 10 years. She shares my concern for her and my disappointment at losing Camille. It's just one more obstacle we must overcome.

**Wednesday, September 13, 2000**
**Baton Rouge, Louisiana**

Final press conference before the trial begins.

Photo by Bill Feig
*The Advocate*

The news media turned out in numbers for a press conference I held this morning. There has been a lot of speculation as to how the insurance department will be run during my trial. I wanted to assure citizens throughout the state that the office will continue to run smoothly and function well, and that I will still be there on a daily basis. The federal courthouse in downtown Baton Rouge is just a few blocks from my office. I told the press that I would be in the office each morning before trial and each evening afterwards. I will also be working there on weekends.

*"There's a lot of average, decent people out there whom have some concerns about who will protect them and take care of them," I said. "This trial will not have any effect on this office. We're not going to slow down the functions of this office one iota."*[172]

Frankly, it wouldn't matter if I were not there at all for the next few weeks. I have a well-trained staff, and over the past 10 years I have built a system of checks and balances. My job has evolved into making long-range policy decisions rather than tending to the daily functions of the office. But I still felt it necessary to reassure everyone that I will be there on a regular basis.

---

[172] The Associated Press, September 13, 2000.

The press asked lots of questions about the trial, but all I could do was refer to the gag order. Remembering Judge Clement's threat to fine anyone who violated the gag order a thousand dollars per word, I told the media, "I've got better ways to spend a thousand dollars especially as expensive as this has been." I added, "I stand by my previous statements."[173] Although I didn't say it, later news reports would refer to my earlier comments that the indictment was "a political drive-by shooting, the work of out-of-control prosecutors, and secrecy that would make the Gestapo proud." That would have been an expensive few words, so I'm glad the press filled in the gaps.

I was also fortunate to find office space across the street from the courthouse to use during the trial. Each lawyer has paralegals and assistants, and we need a place to start off the day, meet for lunch, and work in the evening. Gladys has a lot of old office furniture stored in a local warehouse, so we can give the whole legal team adequate backup facilities. Gladys and Gloria have agreed to have their restaurant, Jumelle's, cater lunch. We anticipate feeding about 50 people a day, including the lawyers, their backup staff, family members, and a few close friends. We will also provide a light breakfast each morning. I don't want the legal team bogged down trying to grab a sandwich, or traveling any distance during the trial. This office will be a great resource for all of us.

## Monday, September 18, 2000
## Baton Rouge, Louisiana

"It's show time, Dad." My son James was trying to loosen me up as we walked toward the federal courthouse on the first day of the trial. He had taken the day off from school to be there to support me. My daughters had checked by phone in over the weekend. Other family members wanted to come to Baton Rouge for the first week of the trial. I suggested they wait a while and come later. With the pressure of jury selection and all the decisions to be made, I won't have much time to visit with family, but I really appreciate their offers to be here.

Gladys was with James and me as we headed to the courthouse, along with her twin sister Gloria (who would be there with Gladys

---

[173] *Baton Rouge Advocate,* September 14, 2000.

every day of the trial). My brother Jack was also with us, along with my brother-in-law, Sheriff Jiff Hingle. (Both would also be regulars throughout the trial.). As we approached the open door of the courthouse, about 40 members of the press were waiting for us with still cameras flashing and television cameras rolling.

"There's not a whole lot I can tell you because of the gag order," I told the press. "But I'm glad the day has finally come when I can have my day in court and get this matter moving along. I am completely confident I will be found not guilty." As reporters shouted questions, we entered the courthouse and took the elevator to the third-floor courtroom that would be my "home" for the next few weeks.

Gladys and James share a lighter moment outside the Federal Courthouse in Baton Rouge as Candy Edwards, the Govenor's wife waits for the jury to be picked.

Photo by Arthur D. Lauck
*The Advocate*

The first thing Judge Clement did was to banish my family, the press, and almost everyone else from the courtroom. All jurors were to be interviewed in secret. Bill Jeffress raised concerns on my behalf, but the judge dismissed his protest by saying there could be "potential bias" if the public hears the questioning of the jurors.

The state's major daily newspapers and television stations, arguing that the questioning of jurors should be open to the public, immediately filed legal motions. Clement promptly denied their motions; the media lawyers are appealing to the Fifth Circuit Court of Appeals in New Orleans.

Several lawyers questioned Clement's decision. Ray Lamonica, a former U.S. Attorney who is now an LSU law professor, said Clement's action is "unusual." And an attorney for the *Baton Rouge Advocate*, Ed Fleshman, criticized Clement's ruling by saying that there is a "presumption of openness" during the jury-selection process, and that a "judge should not close the courtroom unless the rights of the defendants or the interests of jurors are at stake."[174]

In any event, all questioning of potential jurors will be done in private, whether we like it or not. We spent the rest of the day watching the judge ask potential jurors about any bias or prejudice they might have and whether they know any of the parties involved in the case.

This continued until seven o'clock when the judge shut down proceedings for the day. Bill Jeffress filed a motion at the end of the day asking for the handwritten notes taken by FBI agent Harry Burton during my interview in May 1997. Bill said in his motion, "Minor variations in the language between the handwritten notes and the final memorandum of interview could make the difference between a statement that is demonstrably true and one that is false. Thus, the notes are very much material to Mr. Brown's defense."[175]

In commenting on Bill's motion, the New Orleans *Times-Picayune* said, "The FBI agent who took the notes, Harry Burton, is probably best known for forgetting to turn on a video camera clandestinely hidden in Edwards' law office in time to catch the former governor handing State Senator Cleo Fields, D-Baton Rouge, then out of office, a wad of cash. This incident was recounted in testimony during Edwards' previous trial in which Edwards was convicted."[176]

After an hour-long meeting with the defense team to analyze the responses from potential jurors, I had a late dinner at Jumelle's with Gladys, Gloria, Jack, Jiff, and a few friends. It's been a long day, no doubt the first of many.

## Thursday, September 19, 2000
## Baton Rouge, Louisiana

> *Secrecy and a free, democratic government don't mix.*
> President Harry S. Truman[177]

---

[174] *Baton Rouge Advocate,* September 19, 2000.

[175] *U.S.A. v. Brown et al.* C.D. 99-151-B-M2, Notice of Memorandum Regarding the Production of Interview Notes by James Harvey Brown, Docket Entry No. 393 (September 1, 2000). Also see *Times-Picayune,* September 19, 2000.

[176] *Baton Rouge Advocate*, September 19, 2000.

[177] Merle Miller, *Plain Speaking: An Oral Biography of Harry S. Truman* (New York: Berkley Books, 1960).

A picture of Gladys, James, and me walking up to the courthouse was splashed across the front pages of most of the state's newspapers this morning. But the headlines were troubling. "Brown Case Off to a Secret Start" was the banner in the largest paper, the *Times-Picayune*. Most of the other papers took the same approach.

Potential jurors are not supposed to read newspapers or watch television news, but invariably they do. And family members often discuss their views with potential jurors. This "aura of secrecy" that Clement has put around the trial deeply concerns me. It sends a chilling message to jurors that the defendants could be dangerous and the jurors have something to fear. There is no reason for any of this secrecy, and it's so unfair. Far from creating a level playing field, Clement has consistently tilted the balance of favoritism toward the prosecutors. We have a lot to overcome.

## Tuesday, September 19, 2000
## Baton Rouge, Louisiana

The 12-person jury was picked today. I am uncomfortable with the process used in picking the jury and with the group that was finally selected.

The prosecutors have hired two jury consultants from California, Steve Patterson and Norma Silverstein. They sat right next to the prosecutors at the table before the jury, and they were allowed to give advice and make recommendations as the jury process continued through the day. There is something inherently wrong in the federal government's being able to bring in high-priced jury consultants, paid for with my tax dollars, to help them pick a jury slanted toward their point of view. My feelings are well expressed in criminal expert William Pizzi's book *Trials Without Truth*, which strongly criticizes the use of jury consultants:

> *"Sometimes a jury consultant with a background in psychology may sit in the courtroom in order to study the body language and manner of speech of a potential juror and thereby help the trial lawyer determine which jurors should be struck from the panel. This focus on who gets on the jury is demeaning to the entire system. It reinforces the view that trials are just a "crapshoot" or "a roll of the*

*dice" and that the right or wrong juror can determine the outcome despite the evidence. A rethinking of our jury system is long overdue."[178]*

Judge Clement gave the jury a long rambling explanation of why they would be anonymous. The very words and phrases she selected sent a message that the jurors should be worried. Of course, their apprehension will be directed toward the defendants, which is why having an anonymous jury is so unfair. The judge kept telling the jury that they should "not be concerned," then she repeated a number of specifics that obviously made them more concerned:

> *"It's not being done because of any apprehension on the part of this court that you would have been endangered or subject to improper pressures if your names had been disclosed. You should not be concerned about your safety or the safety of anyone connected with this trial...You must not allow these obvious security measures to influence you in your deliberations and your verdict...You must not allow these security procedures to suggest that you have any fear of the defendants."[179]*

On and on, obviously <u>raising</u> concerns among the prospective jurors.

She then announced, "I'm going to seal the courtroom during this follow-up questioning so everyone except the potential jurors, the parties, and their lawyers please leave the courtroom."[180]

As the courtroom was cleared, the potential jurors were obviously wondering why all this was being done in secrecy. Clement was implying that there was potential danger and indicating that "these three defendants" have done something that requires extraordinary protection which is normally not found in any courtroom in America.

When the courtroom was cleared, Judge Clement started questioning jurors one at a time. Before the trial began, every potential juror filled out a detailed questionnaire about what

---

[178] William T. Pizzi, *Trials Without Truth* (New York: New York University Press, 1999).
[179] U.S.A. v. Brown et al. 99-151-B-M2, Tr. P. 10.
[180] Ibid. 179.

knowledge he or she had about the Cascade case and the individuals involved. The judge's questions were generally directed at the written comments of the potential jurors.

In reviewing the questionnaires, and listening to the questioning of potential jurors by the judge, I see two problem areas that could affect my defense: the jurors' feelings about Edwin Edwards and their opinion of the FBI.

Questions about Edwards elicited a variety of responses, as I expected. Jurors expressed wide-ranging opinions: he was "a great governor;" he "finally got caught with his hand in the cookie jar;" he was "a flamboyant person who used his position for personal gain;" and his race against Klansman David Duke was like "choosing your wife in a whorehouse."

I'm not that concerned about Edwards' riverboat-gambling conviction. Cascade is an entirely different matter, and I did not benefit in any way. I am worried that several potential jurors admitted that their strong negative feelings about Edwards could prejudice them against me. Several examples emerged today:

**Judge Clement:** *Do you think once a criminal, always a criminal, or do you think people sometimes commit crimes, sometimes don't?*

**Juror 201:** *I think it's difficult to change, for a dog to change his spots.*

**Judge Clement:** *Then in response to one of the questions, you said you weren't sure that you could be fair and impartial to Edwin Edwards and you weren't sure that you could be fair and impartial to the co-defendants, Jim Brown and Ronald Weems. Is that your position today?*

**Juror 201:** *Yes. Ma'am.*[181]

**Judge Clement:** *Then you answered a question about the co-defendants, Jim Brown and Ron Weems, because of your opinion of Edwin Edwards and the recent conviction,*

---

*whether it would be difficult for you to be fair and impartial to these other two defendants who are on trial with him today, and you said, "Jim Brown appears to be an intelligent man. He must be aware of Edwin Edwards' reputation. It's hard not to question his association with Edwin Edwards."*[182]

**The Court:** *Then there was a question about the co-defendants, Mr. Brown and Mr. Weems, being involved in this indictment with Mr. Edwards and knowing Mr. Edwards is a convicted felon. The question was whether it would be difficult for you to be fair and impartial to the other two defendants, and you said that you weren't sure, "It's hard to separate a man from the company he keeps." Have you been thinking about that?*

**Juror 484**: *Yes, I have.*

**Mr. Castaing [Ron Weems' attorney]:** *Is it fair to say you would treat someone differently who was on trial because they had been co-counsels or had some association with Edwin Edwards than someone who has not?*

**Juror 484:** *I might look at them a little different. I think I would pay more attention to—I would probably tend to scrutinize the evidence maybe a little bit closer, hold it up to a magnifying glass a little closer.*[183]

**Mr. Castaing:** *You said it is hard to separate a man from the company he keeps.*

**Juror 484:** *True.*

**Mr. Small [Edwin Edwards's attorney]:** *Apparently, based upon your answer to question 107, your opinion of him is so strongly held—and I'm not saying this critically*

---

[182] Ibid. 226.
[183] Ibid. 74.

*because you are entitled to your opinion, but it is so strongly held, that it might even rub off on the two that are charged with him because of your opinion about Mr. Edwards, is that true?*

**Juror 67:** *That's true.*[184]

Other jurors did not come right out and strongly express their opinions about my being associated with the former governor, but we sensed that these feelings are not isolated among this jury pool. My concern is that the evidence won't make a lot of difference. If the jury finds Edwards guilty of any crime, Ron Weems and I could also be convicted based on guilt by association.

Then there is the potential jurors' attitude toward the FBI. On the questionnaire, they were asked about their feelings toward the FBI. Jurors had to note whether they strongly agreed, agreed, disagreed, or strongly disagreed with various statements. Nearly every juror on the panel "strongly agreed" that the FBI is "very thorough and accurate" in its work. Potential jurors have made it clear that they will give strong preference to any testimony by the FBI.

**Judge Clement:** *Would you require a witness who is testifying on behalf of the FBI to be evaluated in the same manner you would any other witness? In other words, would you test their veracity, evaluate the evidence in light of the other testimony in the trial? Would you treat that person the same as any other witness…?*

**Juror 234:** *No. I would think the FBI would be thorough on a witness, you know.*[185]

**Mr. Jeffress:** *With respect to {Juror 83}, could you ask her about the "agree strongly" on the FBI question; what is that based on? Is it on personal experiences or what she has read or opinions of others or what?*

---

[184] Ibid. 233.
[185] Ibid. 41.

**Juror 186:** *I guess it's just on the reputation of the FBI. It's not really any personal experience. I don't know any FBI agents. I don't really keep up with the cases. It's probably just based on their reputation.*[186]

**Judge Clement:** *Do you believe the FBI is very thorough and accurate in its usual investigations? You said you strongly agreed with that. What do you base that answer on, any personal experience or just a general belief or what?*

**Juror 90:** *I have no personal experience at all, just a general belief that the organization would be as thorough as any organization could be.*[187]

**Judge Clement:** *Had you had any professional or personal dealings with an FBI agent at work?*

**Juror 118:** *Not really, it's just from what I have seen in the past they have done a good job.*[188]

**Judge Clement:** *Would you be more likely to believe a law enforcement officer or another government agent than another witness," and you said, "Yes." What is the basis of that?*

**Juror 114:** *...because how else would you get the evidence.*[189]

**Mr. Jeffress:** *In answer to another question on the questionnaire, whether you believe that the FBI is very thorough and accurate in its usual investigations, you said you agree strongly with that proposition.*

**Juror 321:** *It's their job. I would hope so.*[190]

---

[186] Ibid. 110.
[187] Ibid. 110.
[188] Ibid. 187.
[189] Ibid. 243-44.

(At another point in the questioning, Juror 321 responded: "It's their job to make sure they are thorough in their investigation. You would want to believe somebody in that type of position.")

> **Judge Clement:** *You indicated that you agreed strongly that the FBI is very thorough and accurate in its usual investigations. What do you base this belief on?*
>
> **Juror 333:** *On the evidence that they find.*
>
> **Judge Clement:** *Could you give me some particular examples? Have you had any dealings with the FBI?*
>
> **Juror 333:** *No ma'am.*
>
> **Judge Clement:** *What particular facts are you referring to or cases or what is the basis for your belief?*
>
> **Juror 333:** *Just stuff that I hear and stuff, really, not too much. I really don't know too much about stuff like that.*[191]

There were many similar comments from potential jurors. What this tells me is that I go into this trial "presumed guilty" on the false-statement charges. This seems likely in light of the 12 jurors and four alternates who were selected today. The 11 women and one man who will decide my fate seem to be decent, hardworking citizens who believe in their government, accept the system, and like structure in their lives.

What I mean is, they all receive paychecks from a company or organization. None of them is a business owner who has to make a payroll or deal with government bureaucracy. None of them questions higher authority in their work. They accept the "system" and seem to have no personal experience with federal agencies or the federal bureaucracy. So they would probably believe someone who represents the government. Because of these attitudes, I do not start off on an

---

[190] Ibid. 303-04.
[191] Ibid. 386.

equal level with the FBI agents who will testify against me. They have a "presumption of truthfulness" that I will have to overcome.

I need to give strong testimony in my behalf. I have worked with law-enforcement agencies to develop insurance-fraud cases, and I have put evidence together that led to the conviction of numerous crooks in the insurance business. If I'm allowed to enter this information into evidence, it should give a significant boost to my credibility compared to the FBI.

At least, we have a jury. Tomorrow Bill Jeffress and I will meet for breakfast to evaluate today's activities and decide how to deal with the new stumbling blocks that seem to lurk in our path each day.

## Wednesday, September 20, 2000
## Baton Rouge, Louisiana

My longtime friend Bill deLaunay, who will be a character witness for me in the trial, faxed me the lead editorial from the *Alexandria Daily Town Talk* this morning. Judge Clement was strongly criticized for the secrecy surrounding this trial:

> *"While this latest federal trial of statewide interest may provide cause for extra caution, we fail to see how it differs from any other trial which is supposed to be public. Public means public. What's worse in this case is that the judge has imposed a gag order on all involved in the trial. That means that we the public have no means of finding out what is going on."*[192]

Clement so far seems oblivious to, or at least unconcerned about, the barrage of criticism she is receiving over the secrecy issue. And we continue to hear from both lawyers and the general public how disturbing it is that such secrecy is allowed.

---

[192] *Alexandria Daily Town Talk,* September 20, 2000.

**Friday, September 22, 2000**
**Baton Rouge, Louisiana**

The last three days have proceeded about as expected with no bombshells or unpredictable events.

Both sides gave opening statements on Wednesday. Assistant Prosecutor Jim Mann attempted to explain this complicated case to the jury. He told them he would not "present you [with] a lot of arcane insurance law" because "that's not what this case is all about." He then proceeded to demonstrate on the TV screens set up in the courtroom all types of insurance documents. It was so confusing and boring that the judge finally told the prosecutors that the proceedings were "getting painful." Several jurors seemed to be dozing, and the judge admonished them to keep their heads up and "pay close attention."[193]

My lawyer Bill Jeffress, Edwards' lawyer Mike Small, and Weems' lawyer Eddie Castaing seem to be working well together. All three gave solid opening statements blaming Foxy Sanders for the bulk of the controversy and claiming that the prosecutors, either through ignorance or calculation, were wrong in their interpretation of what took place. All three defense lawyers came down hard on Sanders, labeling him "the fox in the henhouse."

Bill Jeffress strongly defended the Cascade settlement, belittling the prosecution claim that it was a sham. "It was a settlement like any other settlement," Bill said.

Eddie Castaing told the jurors, "The only sham in this courtroom is the indictment against the defendants."[194]

Following opening statements, the prosecutors called their first witness, Foxy Sanders.

When discussing specifics of the settlement, Sanders said he wasn't even part of the final negotiations. So he did very little to help the prosecutors in outlining any "fix." Several times during his testimony, he rubbed his fingers together, implying that Edwards had tried to bribe him. Sanders said he told several people about the purported bribe, including Bob Bourgeois. Then he said, "I told my

---

[193] *Times-Picayune,* September 21, 2000.
[194] *U.S.A. v. Brown et al.* C.D. 99-151-B-M2, Tr. p. 551.

father and I told a friend, Joseph Cannella ... I told all three of them within a couple of days of him asking me, 'Do you want money?'"[195]

Surprisingly, Sanders' father and Cannella are not listed as witnesses. The prosecutors have said they will not call Bob Bourgeois. Three people could support Sanders' testimony that he was bribed; yet none will be called. This certainly should hurt Sanders' credibility.

The consensus is that Sanders does not come across as believable. He was confrontational with the defense lawyers and often shot questions back at them.

By his third day of testimony, Sanders had grown significantly more combative, apparently uncomfortable being at the mercy of lawyers when he is used to controlling them as a judge. At one point, when Sanders told Jeffress he wanted to present a court transcript to the jury, Jeffress said, "Well you're not a lawyer."

Sanders also lobbed questions back at the lawyers on occasion; prompting Judge Clement to tell him that defense attorneys can't "testify" during the trial. The former judge was also uncomfortable admitting that he had failed at least twice to tell federal agents about an alleged bribe attempt by Governor Edwards, when Sanders was trying to plea bargain with the feds. Mike Small, Edwards' attorney, confronted Sanders head on. "Is this something that just slipped your mind?"

Sanders responded: "No, I did not want to let them know that I had not reported a crime. I know I should have reported that but I didn't."[196]

John Copes, in *Deductbox.com*, summed up Foxy's performance this way:

## FOXY! IS HE REALLY AS NUTTY AS HE LOOKED ON THE STAND? OR WAS THAT ALL JUST AN ACT?

*In a strangely Biblical twist, feds had to ask him three times before he told them about EWE bribery attempt, rubbing thumb and fingers together, finger laid along*

---

[195] Ibid. 681.
[196] *Times-Picayune,* September 23, 2000.

*nose, etc. Also, Sanders' testimony doesn't match court transcripts used by Brown's lawyer."*[197]

Bill Jeffress did an effective job of cross-examining Sanders about his dictatorial control over the receiverships office. We all believe that because Sanders continued to be defensive and confrontational, he lost credibility with the jury. It is certainly going to take a lot more than his testimony to convict any of us.

One surprising admission by Sanders is that he met with FBI agents in Mobile, Alabama in September 1997, and Harry Burton played several of the tapes for him. At this point, Sanders had not been told he was a target of the investigation but merely that the investigation was ongoing. So in his first discussion with the FBI, Sanders listened to the tapes. Burton showed me no such courtesy. Even though he knew all the information on the tapes, he quizzed me in detail without allowing me to refresh my memory about a lot of what was said.

Sanders testified, "They, the FBI, asked me to come over, and they wanted to present something to me. They played two tapes to me. After they played the two tapes, they told me I didn't have to say anything."

Sanders further testified that Harry Burton had put wrong information in his typed report following an interview with Sanders. Sanders testified, "But what it was, to the best of my recollection was that I was saying one thing; they were saying

My lawyer, Bill Jeffers, looks on as Governor Edwards shouts to the press.

*Photo by Patrick Dennis*
*The Advocate*

---

[197] *Deductbox.com,* September 25, 2000.

another thing. We didn't have a meeting of the minds. I said, 'I didn't say that.'"

FBI agent Harry Burton continues to make mistakes.

We will work through the weekend at the trial office, anticipating what may be asked of prosecution witnesses and outlining our questioning of the defense witnesses. The case is moving faster than anticipated. The original consensus was that the trial would go six weeks, but the prosecutors could well finish up their case next week. So we have a lot of preparation to do.

Sitting in a chair all day long, with no time to exercise, is starting to have its effect. My knees hurt, and my legs often go to sleep. Despite the workload, I've got to find some time for exercise over the weekend.

## Tuesday, September 26, 2000
## Baton Rouge, Louisiana

Yesterday was fairly uneventful. The tapes were played from beginning to end, which took most of the morning. The jury showed little interest.

Press reports on last night's evening news and in today's morning papers played up my conversations with Edwards about my interest in being appointed U.S. Senator. It was interesting to those of us in political life, but our conversation should really have no effect on the outcome of the trial.

The only witness to testify today was Baton Rouge attorney Wade Shows. He was another lawyer hired by Sanders to work with Ed Gonzales in negotiating a Cascade settlement. He initially testified that he had some misgivings about the final settlement. But on cross-examination, he admitted that he signed off on the settlement. *Deductbox.com* concluded, "Lawyers will overlook a lot to generate those billable hours, huh?"[198]

Shows did testify that he knew I had objections to a contingency-fee contract for him and Gonzales, both in this case and in the case of another defunct insurance company. He's right about that. I consistently opposed lawyers making a windfall without doing a great deal of work.

---

[198] Ibid.

Today the prosecutors announced they would not call David Disiere or Bob Bourgeois as witnesses. I'm not surprised. Neither will say the settlement was either fixed or bad. It's obvious they both pled guilty out of fear of long jail terms and heavy fines. If they were sitting here at the table today, having heard the case put on by the prosecutors, I am absolutely sure they would withdraw their guilty pleas, and fight to prove their innocence. Mark my words they both will say in the future that they made a big mistake by pleading guilty.

The pace of the trial is picking up, and we may have to start our defense on Thursday or Friday. We have lots of witnesses to call, to notify them when they may testify. I predict late nights ahead.

## Wednesday, September 27, 2000
## Baton Rouge, Louisiana

> *The justice and the truth o' th' question carries; The due o' th' verdict*
> *with it: at what ease; Might corrupt minds procure knaves as corrupt;*
> *To swear against you! Such things have been done.*
> William Shakespeare, Henry VIII[199]

FBI agent Harry Burton took the stand today. He started out by rehashing the charges in the indictment and actually read word for word from the indictment itself. Bill Jeffress called his hand on this and told him to not read the prosecutors' words, but testify about what he remembered. Burton said he could not remember everything, and was "refreshing" his memory.

Judge Clement has refused to give us the handwritten notes that Burton took at our interview. I don't know the exact number, but there had to be about 11 pages of notes from Burton's interview with me. What better possible evidence could there be of what was actually said than what he wrote down in the notes? The prosecutors have given Ron Weems the notes Burton took when he interviewed Weems. Why are they afraid to give me the notes Burton took when he interviewed me? Do they think the handwritten notes contradict Burton's statement, which was prepared a few days later?

Burton has obviously been well coached and has spent a lot of time rehearsing his testimony. He almost seems like an actor who has memorized his lines. He speaks in a rote, methodical way, spitting out

---

[199] *Henry VIII,* Act 5, Scene I.

his answers. It's obvious to the defense lawyers that he is repeating what he's been told to say. But I'm concerned about how his testimony is being viewed by the jury. They don't deal with rehearsed testimony on a regular basis, and they believe the FBI normally does the right thing. There are 13 charges of false statements against me, and Bill Jeffress did his best to pick each charge apart. In one particular charge, the prosecutors allege I stated to Burton "the only thing I knew" about a particular subject. Burton admitted that the word "only" was not in his report.[200] Burton also confirmed that, although every other conversation in this case was tape-recorded, he did not record his interview with me. He did not write up his report until several days later, relying on his notes. But I don't have the notes. In answer to several specific questions, Burton merely read his answers from the charges in the indictment.

"You weren't testifying from your memory?"[201] Bill Jeffress asked him. Burton said he was trying his best to testify from memory but was relying on the indictment as a record of what was said. In other words, he was reading the lines written by the prosecutors.

I honestly do not know how to evaluate Burton's testimony. There are a number of holes in what he said. Bill was hampered in a major way by not having the notes, and also by not being able to go into Burton's background.

It's a plain fact that Burton makes a lot of mistakes in his work. But Judge Clement would not let us review these mistakes. There is a question about his truthfulness when it comes to his testimony about Ed Gonzales and FBI agent Karen Gardner. But, again, the judge is stonewalling us. Burton can make outrageous allegations against me, and all I can say is "No, no, no, they are not true."

Not only would Judge Clement not give us Burton's notes, we were prohibited from even asking him whether he wrote down certain things that I said. At one point, Bill Jeffress asked Burton, "Now did you write down in your notes . . ." and before he could even finish the question the prosecutors objected. Clement upheld their objection and would not let my lawyer ask Burton about what he wrote down. The Sixth Amendment makes it clear that someone charged with a crime has the right to "confront his accuser." But I was not able to

---

[200] *U.S.A. v. Brown et al.*, C.D. 99-151-B-M2, Tr. p. 1616.
[201] Ibid. 1591.

"confront" my accuser. My lawyer could not even ask what Burton wrote down. This is an outrageous violation of my constitutional rights, and will certainly be grounds for an appeal if one is necessary.

During the trial, one of the prosecutors told the judge: "All credibility calls go to the witness, Harry Burton, who took the statements."[202] In other words, Burton's testimony gives him credibility, yet we cannot cross-examine him about his credibility! The prosecutors can call any number of witnesses to make vague allegations about me, yet my lawyers can say nothing about Burton's questionable background, relationships, and competence. Burton makes numerous mistakes in his work and may well have perjured himself on the stand. Yet we are unable to cross-examine him about any of these activities. All the jury will see is his methodical, rote responses to questions from the prosecutors.

I certainly have a big job ahead of me when I take the stand next week.

## Thursday, September 28, 2000
## Baton Rouge, Louisiana

The headlines in the morning papers quoted Judge Clement saying, "The tapes are so strong."[203] Her comments were also widely reported on radio and television. Although she did not make the statement in front of the jury that did not give the defense team much comfort. In spite of the judge's order, it is common for jurors to continue to read the papers and watch television. Their families talk to them about the case. To say that jurors can stay insulated from news reports just isn't realistic.

This is not the first time that the judge has let her personal prejudices influence the case. She rolls her eyes in disbelief when certain witnesses make statements. She has been extremely harsh on the defense attorneys, often making wisecracks when rebuking them. She has earned her reputation as a "prosecutors' judge," and her comments in the paper were certainly out of line.

Ron Weems took the stand today and did a first-rate job of calmly and methodically rebutting the prosecutors' case. He reviewed in

---

[202] Ibid. 1816.
[203] Ibid. 1820.

detail the personal animosity that existed between Sanders and him and how vindictive Sanders had been, even trying to put Ron in jail. He commented at length on why Edwards was hired by the Disiere team. Ron was also able to use the actual notes that Harry Burton took when he interviewed Ron. The prosecutors have continually argued that they were following a rule in this judicial district, which allowed them not to have to produce the actual notes. But they didn't follow the rule in Ron Weems' case. Of course, there is no such rule, but the "double standard" is inexplicable. Ron Weems can see the actual notes taken by Harry Burton when Ron was interviewed, but I cannot see the notes taken in my interview. What are the prosecutors trying to hide?

"I was getting hammered in Judge Sanders' court," Weems testified. "We were trying to find some way to hand-to-hand combat in this war that was going on with Judge Sanders."

Ron testified that Edwards made it clear his job was to act as an intermediary and that he was not going to be involved in filing court documents or doing research.

Ron's professionalism, his knowledge of the events that took place, and his believable testimony gives him enormous credibility. He did a good job in refuting most of the insurance-fraud charges against us.

Several of Ron's law partners, including Shreveport District Attorney Paul Carmouche, testified that Sanders was out of control whereas Ron was following the law in all he did.

The handwritten notes of Harry Burton were of significant help to Ron's defense. Ron not only received the typewritten statement made by Burton (which is called a 302), but the prosecutors also gave him the actual handwritten notes. And there were significant differences between the notes and the typed statement.

Ron testified that Edwards was hired to "mediate" the controversy between Sanders and the Disiere group. This was certainly one of the most important statements made by Ron in all of his interviews. In Burton's notes, he wrote that Edwards was hired to "mediate." But in his typewritten statement, Burton omitted the word "mediate."

On two other occasions, Burton's notes included statements from Ron regarding the Cascade settlement and Edwards' specific role in it. On neither of these occasions was my name mentioned. But when Burton typed his statement, he injected my name, although it appears nowhere in his notes. In other instances, Burton typed lengthy comments, purportedly from Weems, saying that discussions were held that included me. But there are no such references in his handwritten notes.

In his handwritten notes, Burton wrote "Bob Bourgeois," who was heading up the receiverships office. In his typewritten version, the name became "Jim Bourgeois."

The typewritten statement includes numerous phrases and comments that do not appear in Burton's handwritten notes.

It is obvious that there are dramatic differences between Burton's handwritten notes and the final, typed version. The handwritten notes are certainly critical to Ron's defense. Unfortunately, I will not have the same advantage, because I can't have my notes.

## Friday, September 29, 2000
## Baton Rouge, Louisiana

> *If the government becomes a lawbreaker it breeds contempt, it breeds contempt for law; it invites every man to become a law unto himself; it invites anarchy. To declare that in the administration of the criminal law the end justifies the means—to declare that the Government may commit crimes in order to secure the conviction of a private criminal—would bring terrible retribution.*
> Justice Louis D. Brandeis[204]

Prosecutor Sal Perricone physically assaulted my lawyer Bill Jeffress today. It was simply unbelievable.

Late in the afternoon, Judge Clement called Bill, Perricone, and several federal marshals into her office. The prosecution team was trying to keep an important witness for the defense from testifying. After a general discussion, Clement ruled that the witness would be allowed to testify. As Bill rose from his chair to return to the courtroom, Perricone was obviously angry. He became belligerent, yelling that Bill was misleading the jury. Without any warning, Perricone roughly shoved Bill backward. Bill stumbled then regained his balance. The federal marshals quickly intervened and kept Perricone from continuing his attack.

---

[204] Olmstead et al. v. United States, 277 U.S. 485 (1928).

When everyone returned to the courtroom, the story of Perricone's attack quickly spread. We waited for the judge to admonish Perricone and sanction him. We wondered if he would even be allowed to continue handling this case. But Judge Clement resumed the trial proceedings and said absolutely nothing. At the next break, Bill rose to his feet and said he wanted to make a record of the incident. "It's the first time in my 28 years [of practicing law] that I have been physically assaulted by a prosecutor or any opposing counsel," he said. "I don't appreciate it. It's totally unprofessional. Other defense lawyers get sanctioned very heavily for exactly the same thing. When prosecutors do it, I think the court needs to know it and a record needs to be made."

Clement responded: "I was there, Mr. Jeffress, as you recall. It was appalling. You don't call people names." She turned to Perricone and said, "Stop calling people names, Mr. Perricone." She went on, "I will not tolerate any sort of physical abuse; any slight indication that it's about to happen again and the lawyer's off the case." [205]

If it happens *again*, the lawyer is off the case? My lawyer was physically assaulted and the judge sat there and did nothing. Under federal law, any assault on a prosecutor is a felony. [206] If Bill Jeffress had shoved Perricone, he would have been arrested on the spot.

In the same courthouse, other lawyers have been sanctioned merely for verbally castigating a prosecutor. Michael Fawer is one of Louisiana's top criminal-defense attorneys. In this same courthouse, he was fined ten thousand dollars and suspended from practicing law for a year because he had verbally challenged one of the prosecutors. The federal judge took immediate action against Fawer. Yet Perricone is allowed to physically attack Bill Jeffress and nothing is done. This double standard undermines any sense of fairness in the federal court system. The same federal laws that prohibit a prosecutor from being attacked should also protect a defense lawyer in the courtroom. Judge Clement's failure to take swift action against Perricone is certainly one of the low points of this trial.

---

[205] *U.S.A. v. Brown et al.* C.D. 99-151-B-M2, Tr.,. (September 29, 2000), Status Conference, pp. 42–43.
[206] 18 U.S.C. Sec. 111.

**Monday, October 2, 2000**
**Baton Rouge, Louisiana**

As my son James would say, today really was "show time." I was on the stand all day, outlining why I believe I had done nothing wrong and answering questions about my involvement in Cascade.

I made it clear from the beginning that any settlement involving Cascade was out of the hands of the insurance department or me personally. I was doing my best to keep all sides communicating, knowing that if a fair settlement was reached, the problem would be put to rest, and the State would ultimately save money. I reviewed the bizarre behavior of Judge Sanders, outlined the initial calls from the former governor, and made it clear that when the settlement negotiations were under way in mid-December 1996, I was not included.

Tomorrow, I will no doubt face a barrage of accusatory questions from the prosecutors. I'm concerned about the repeated playing of the taped conversations between Edwards and me. If you add up all the time we talked about Cascade, it comes to less than 45 minutes. I doubt I spent more than a total of three or four hours in personal and telephone conversations with Foxy Sanders, Ron Weems, Edwin Edwards, and anyone else involved in Cascade. But the tapes don't give this impression. Listening to the prosecutors, and hearing the tapes played over and over again, you would think that I was consumed with the Cascade matter. The prosecutors have unfairly thrown a barrage of information at us. With 56 charges against me, each requiring a detailed response, there is so much to cover. I am concerned that the jury will become confused and perhaps not realize how little I was actually involved.

I did my best to answer the charge that I did not have a lot of knowledge about Cascade Insurance Company. The settlement issues were focused on one small part of the company's overall operations going back to the 1980s. But the prosecutors keep hammering the fact that I was intricately involved in day-in, day-out details for over a decade. This is just not true. But I'm not sure what impression the jury received.

There is so much for the jury to absorb, and so many questions to answer.

242

Bill Jeffress took me through each of the false-statement charges. In Count 45, I was charged with telling Burton that I had no specific knowledge of Cascade Insurance Company's having any problems with the Oregon Insurance Commissioner's Office. That's absolutely true. Cascade was a Louisiana insurance company, and it was not involved in any way in Oregon. So how could Cascade have problems in the state of Oregon? There were sister companies involved in Oregon, but Burton did not ask me about them. It's obvious now that Burton himself was confused when he asked many of these questions. But he made it even more confusing by the rambling, disjointed way he wrote up his statement of what I said. In short, his incompetence is making it all the more difficult for me to defend myself and explain what happened to the jury.

A number of family members and friends had packed the courtroom to lend their support. I have encouraged those close to me not to come, because I don't want to be distracted. But I must admit it was reassuring to have smiling faces to look up to as I went through my testimony. My in-laws Doris and Ted Solomon were there, as were my brother-in-law Jiff, my brother Jack, many friends from throughout the state—and as always, on the front row, never missing a minute, was Gladys.

Between the brutal campaign and this trial, Gladys has certainly shouldered more burdens than any husband could expect. She regularly asks for back rubs, which is difficult because I have arthritis in my hands. After the ordeal she has been through, she will be entitled to all the back rubs she wants.

## Tuesday, October 3, 2000
## Baton Rouge, Louisiana

Today I underwent strong cross-examination by the prosecutors. Under heavy questioning, I told the jury that Cascade was a minor issue compared to the many other major problems I faced as insurance commissioner. We had a number of companies whose losses were much greater than Cascade's. When all was said and done, all the policyholders had been paid in the Cascade case, and the taxpayers had not lost a penny. This success story was a marked contrast to stories of failed companies like Champion, and Southshore, in which policyholders received virtually nothing and the state treasury lost millions of dollars.

Prosecutor Jim Mann sounded accusatory as he asked me why I would return calls to Edwin Edwards, Ron Weems, and others, when I was outside the state, particularly when I was in London. He implied that the Cascade matter was so important that I would put other matters aside and take phone calls involving Cascade at all hours of the night. I calmly told him that London time was seven hours ahead of Louisiana time. When I was in London on insurance business, I would generally get back to my hotel room around 11:00 P.M., which is 4:00 P.M. in Baton Rouge. I would check in with my office and have my secretary hook me up by phone with the people who had called me that day. I felt I was making the best use of my time by taking care of insurance business even when I was halfway around the world. But Mann implied that I was involved in some type of evil plot.

At another point in the cross-examination, Mann raised questions about political contributions I had received and implied that I had granted favors to contributors. I told him firmly, "No campaign contribution ever influenced me, and that includes the contribution from the U.S. Attorney, Mr. Jordan, when he was at a private law firm."[207] Mann quickly changed the subject.

Few questions are being asked about the false-statements counts. But I'm not sure that's a good sign. I would rather defend each count in detail. Bill Jeffress quizzed me about each charge, but I was expecting more questions in cross-examination by the prosecutors. I believe I handled the insurance-fraud issues well and bolstered the testimony given earlier by Ron Weems. But I continue to have an uneasy feeling about the fact that I was not given Harry Burton's notes and that Bill was not allowed to cross-examine him about his questionable past.

It is a relief to be off the hot seat and out of the witness stand. I am cautiously optimistic but still apprehensive.

The former governor began his testimony this afternoon, outlining his role as a peacemaker in the Cascade matter. He strongly denied that he tried to bribe Judge Sanders. His testimony will continue tomorrow.

---

[207] *U.S.A. v. Brown et al.* C.D. 99-151-B-M2, Tr. p. 2562.

After court adjourned for the day, I went to the trial office to review the day's activities with my legal team. Gladys had left earlier to check on James and prepare dinner. After about an hour of talking over the day's events with my lawyers, I got in my car and headed home on the interstate.

I popped in a Tom Waits CD I had picked up a few weeks earlier, called *Heart Attack and Vine*.[208] I have always liked Waits' combination of blues, folk, and rock sung in a deep, raspy voice. One of the songs on the CD was a lullaby about little boys growing up. As I drove home, I listened to the phrases — "ring around the rosy," "sleepin' in the rain," "little boys who never comb their hair." Then came a verse I had never really listened to before:

> *So you better bring a bucket,*
> *there's a hole in the pail,*
> *and if you don't get my letter,*
> *then you'll know that I'm in jail.*

For the first time, that song really hit home. He was singing about his son, and the fact that he may be going to jail. James is 16. We've always done so much together—going one-on-one on the basketball court, hunting, fishing, and wrestling matches that make it clear he's now stronger than I am, helping him with his homework, having him teach me about the computer. Suddenly, as I headed for home with Tom Waits on the CD player, I faced the fact that I could lose all that.

I rarely express my emotions. I don't cry often. The last time I cried was when my father passed away over three years ago.

When my brother called to tell me that my dad had died, we were immediately immersed in the details of comforting my mother and making funeral arrangements. I made numerous calls back and forth between Baton Rouge and Shreveport as all the plans were made. Later that evening, when I went to bed, the reality finally hit me. My dad had died. I said it out loud three or four times as Gladys tried to comfort me. All the emotion of losing someone who had been such an important part of my life came out. My dad had died. I lay there with Gladys holding me, and I cried, and I cried, and I cried.

---

[208] Tom Waits, "On the Nickel," *Heart Attack and Vine,* Electra Entertainment, 1980.

Those feelings returned as I drove home, realizing that I face the possibility of losing years of my life. I could go to jail. I could be forcibly taken from my son, my daughters, and my wife - my entire family.

I was so overcome with emotion that I took the College Drive exit, pulled into a supermarket parking lot, and turned off the ignition. It was starting to rain. I put my head down on the steering wheel and closed my eyes. I cried, and I cried, and I cried.

**Thursday, October 5, 2000**
**Baton Rouge, Louisiana**

Closing arguments were completed today, and the case is almost ready to go to the jury. The lawyers for the defense did an effective job of referring to the tapes, pointing out that the recordings did not support much of Fox Sanders' testimony. Mike Small, representing Edwards, hit hard on the fact that Bob Bourgeois and David Disiere were not called as witnesses, obviously because their testimony would have helped the defense more than the prosecutors. Earlier in the trial, the prosecutors had said, "We hid nothing from you." If that is true, then where were Disiere and Bourgeois? Their absence should certainly have an effect on the jury. In this morning's *Times-Picayune*, columnist James Gill outlined what many courtroom observers felt: *"You won't catch me predicting how any jury will vote, but what we have here is reasonable doubt out the wazoo."*[209]

Gill also reached an interesting conclusion that I hope the jurors will consider in rendering their decision: *"The feds also did the defense a great favor by allowing Sanders to plead guilty to greatly reduced charges in making him their star witness against Edwards and Brown. An admitted corrupt judge is always an inviting target on the witness stand, and there were plenty of tapes to support the defense's contention that Sanders was the real villain of the piece. He would have been a real liability at the defense table, but he was easy to beat up on when he switched sides."*[210]

The jury really has two questions to answer. First, whom do you believe, Sanders or the three of us? Second, whom do you believe,

---

[209] *Times-Picayune*, October 5, 2000.
[210] Ibid.

Burton or Brown? After all the charges and all the testimony, this is what it's coming down to.

## Tuesday, October 10, 2000
## Baton Rouge, Louisiana

We waited all day with no word from the judge or the jury. A group of some 50, including the three of us on trial, plus the lawyers and family members waited at our defense team office across from the federal courthouse. Around 7:30 this evening we received a disturbing call.

The jury was still out, and Judge Clement's assistant was calling to say that the jurors had sent a note to the judge saying they would like to have a copy of my testimony. Clement will tell them that my testimony on the stand is not available.

Why can't my testimony be transcribed? It's not that long. The jurors could be excused for the evening, and the court reporter could transcribe what I said overnight and have it ready to give to the jury tomorrow.

Even more disturbing is the fact that the actual transcript of my testimony is available on the court reporter's computer, which is referred to as "Realtime Production." All the court reporter has to do is print out her transcription, and my testimony would be available to the jury.

I sense that the jury is reaching out. They want to give me the benefit of the doubt, but they have some specific concerns. I can only assume that those concerns relate to the false-statements charges.

I asked Bill Jeffress to go over and talk to the judge. But it did no good. She has sent the jury a message that my testimony is not available and there's nothing she can do about it. It's another sideswipe from Clement. In fairness, she should make my testimony available to the jury. I only wish I knew why the jury wants the testimony.

We've been told that the prosecutors, supposedly by accident, allowed Harry Burton's typewritten statement to be given to the jurors, although it was not admitted into evidence. The jurors gave it back, but this "mistake" compounds the problem. The jurors read Burton's statement about what he claims I said, but they have nothing from me in response, even though they have asked for it. This is nothing less than a double standard. Judge Clement should stop the proceedings, transcribe my testimony, and give it to the jury.

I tried not to show my disappointment, but the defense team realizes I am bothered by the call.

## Wednesday, October 11, 2000
## Baton Rouge, Louisiana

At 4:00 P.M. we got the call. The phone rang in our legal office across from the courthouse. It was for Bill Jeffress. I happened to pick up an extension just as Bill heard the words from the judge's assistant, "I think we have a verdict."

It took about 10 minutes for all of us—Edwards, Ron Weems, our families, our lawyers, and me—to get across the street to the federal courthouse.

After a seemingly endless 10-minute wait, the judge entered the courtroom, called in the jury, and asked, "Have you reached a verdict?" They sent up a long legal-size form for her to review.

I turned to smile at Gladys and the crew of family and friends who had been with me from the beginning of this ordeal. One of James' teachers had heard on the radio that the verdict was in and he had immediately driven down to the courthouse. He was sitting on the front row next to his mother, holding her hand.

When the judge read over the verdict form, she frowned. I hoped that this was a good sign. She has been so unfair in handling our case I thought her disappointment might mean a favorable verdict for all of us.

"The defendants will rise as the verdict is being read," she said matter-of-factly.

On Count One, conspiracy involving all three defendants, the verdict was Not Guilty.

On Counts Two through Forty, mail fraud and wire fraud involving all three defendants, the verdict was Not Guilty.

On Court Forty-one, witness tampering, the verdict was Not Guilty.

Count Forty-two, insurance fraud, Not Guilty.

Count Forty-three, insurance fraud, Not Guilty.

On the counts relating to Commissioner Brown:
Count Forty-four, Guilty.

My stomach tightened and I reached down to steady myself by grabbing the edge of the table. Guilty? How could I be? Why on earth?

Count Forty-five, Not Guilty.
Count Forty-six, Guilty.
My head was spinning, and I fought to keep my composure.
Count Forty-seven, Not Guilty.
Count Forty-eight, Guilty.
County Forty-nine, Not Guilty.

I felt like I was in the middle of a whirlwind, being hit from one side and then the other. It was almost as if someone on one side of me was slapping me and hollering YES, and on the other side someone was shouting NO.

Count Fifty, Guilty.
Count Fifty-one, Guilty.
Count Fifty-two, Not Guilty.
Count Fifty-three, Not Guilty.
Count Fifty-four, Guilty.
Count Fifty-five, Guilty.
Count Fifty-six, Not Guilty.

I felt like every eye in the courtroom was looking at me, and I could only stare straight ahead in disbelief. This couldn't be happening! What could the jury have been thinking? Why didn't they believe me? What could have been going through their minds?

The judge quickly dismissed the jury. "The defendant will be allowed to stay free on his own recognizance, and lawyers will be notified of a sentencing date. If there is no other business, this court is adjourned."

Ron Weems hugged his lawyer Eddie Castaing, and Edwards grabbed the hands of his attorneys, Mike Small and Phyllis Mann. Both were obviously elated over their not-guilty verdicts. But they quickly made their way toward me, knowing the weight on my shoulders.

Out of the corner of my eye, I could see that Gladys and several members of my family were in tears. The courtroom slowly emptied as I talked with each member of the legal team who came up to offer sympathy.

Gladys came over and hugged me. "It's so unfair, but it will work out," she said bravely. I asked her to have our group of friends and family wait for me in the hallway while I sat and composed myself. I knew I had to go downstairs and face the barrage of media on the front steps of the courthouse.

Almost everyone had left the courtroom. I sat there in disbelief, trying to think through what to say. I turned and noticed James, standing right behind my chair. He bent and kissed me on the cheek.

"Dad, you know I'm here for you. I'm right by your side. Just tell me what you need me to do."

I had to fight back tears, but I was so proud of him.

After a few minutes, James and I walked out in the hallway. There were hugs and reassurance from numerous members of my family and friends who had been there for the verdict. We took the elevator to the main lobby and found a throng of reporters waiting.

Governor Edwards was just finishing up his comments. At the time, I didn't hear what he said, but I later learned that he had blasted the secrecy of the entire proceeding and said how wrong it was that I had been convicted of the false-statement charges. I also appreciated the governor's words of support:

> *"Whatever joy I and my family experience from this verdict, we are heavily depressed by what happened to Jim Brown. I feel it was an unfair allegation."*[211]

Ron Weems and the prosecutors had already had their time at the mike. Now it was my turn. With Gladys and James at my side, I talked of my reaction to what happened to me.

> *Okay, folks, well, obviously I am disappointed at what happened here today. I was surprised and did not*

---

[211] WWL-TV Online, October 12, 2000.

*anticipate it. I think that the jury did a good job, and tried their very best in probably as complicated a case as has been held in this courthouse in Louisiana in some time.*

*It's interesting that the tapes were to play this big role. Every charge that related to the tapes we were found innocent of. The only thing where I was found guilty involved a conversation that was not taped. And I think that was ironic, that the taped conversations, everybody is found not guilty, including me, but the non-taped conversations, and then only half of the charges. So I can't explain it and I don't know what was going through the jury's mind, but that will come out.*

*I am very sorry that my 30-year career in public life has this damper on it, and having said that I respect the system and we are obviously going to appeal. And let me say this about my attorneys. My lead attorney Bill Jeffress, over here on the side, John Elwood, Mary Jane Marcantel, the whole team has done a marvelous job. They are very confident about the issue on appeal. There are some issues that I will not get into with you now. You will have plenty of time to write about, that we think cries out for a change to be reconsidered and thrown out. In the meantime, I can't tell you how supportive my family has been—my wife Gladys, my son James, all of my relatives and friends that are here have been so supportive and I am glad that they are here. And so we are going to deal with that.*

Someone tried to interrupt by asking a question.

*Let me finish now folks, this is my few minutes to show you how I feel. I'll give you a statement tomorrow as to what happens with the office. It is not what a lot of you have written about. I don't resign, the governor doesn't appoint. There's a procedure by law, where I step aside. I am still the insurance commissioner, although technically I step aside from the office. I've got a marvelous staff that does a first-rate job. As you know we are the envy of America in terms of how we run our office. The office is going to continue to run very well as I step aside, on a temporary basis, as I get on with my appeal.*

*So, temporarily I am not going to be acting insurance commissioner, although I still hold the position, and that statement will be out tomorrow in terms of how the whole thing works. We will give you the law. We will release that in the morning. So, in the next few days, I will meet with my staff in the morning, go over the good things they've done in the past and keep them focused and directed. And we'll still be doing the first-rate job. As you know, we've done [that] in the past, so that's the best overview I can tell you. I'm sure I'll have a press conference here in the next few days and get into some of the specifics with you about thoughts concerning the trial.*

*Obviously, I don't want to get into a lot of that right now, but that's the best overview to tell you right now. Sure, I am disappointed, but the end of the world has not come. I have served 30 good years in public life. I am very confident that this appeal's going to work out. I'm glad it's over; because I am anxious to get back to exercising and spending time with my family and doing some things that I've missed out doing the last few months. So I'll keep a buoyant attitude. As I've done in the past, I will take all of your phone calls when you give me a holler. And we'll continue to move forward. Get this major bump in the road behind me and we move toward the appeal. I am confident that the appeal will be successful. I am confident that I will be restored as insurance commissioner. There are three years and three months left in my current term so, it's going to take some months to get all of this behind me, but that's the decision. You know, I am sixty years old and there are a lot of things I want to do with my life, so that is not really a concern or an issue right now.*[212]

---

[212] My comments were carried live by a number of television stations throughout the state. WAFB-TV, Channel 9, graciously supplied film of my comments for my use.

I stood there for 45 minutes, answering questions as frankly as I could. There was no political spin. This was not a political crisis in which I was trying to put the best face on what had happened to me. The jury's verdict had certainly changed my life. I spoke as candidly as I could while trying to keep my emotions at bay. The anger, hurt, and grief could come out later.

Members of my family stand with me as I talk to the press after the jury verdict.

Photo by Bill Feig
The Advocate

One final question was asked. "Do you expect to go to jail?"

I answered: *"I don't. I didn't. I've never considered the possibility that I would let this happen, this whole trial, not when I was called. And you know what? I still don't. I still don't."*

That was about all I had left in me to say. I told the press I would talk with them at length tomorrow.

With family and friends accompanying me, I headed back to the trial office across from the courthouse. The TV crews walked with us, and the interviews continued the whole way. Some of the questions were hard, but I felt that the press had been fair to me throughout the trial. Most of the reporters covering the trial had also spent time with me during the campaign. A number of TV and news reporters have expressed their support during this ordeal, and several of them expressed regrets during our walk back to the office.

Gladys, James, and I were headed for home when, on the spur of the moment, we decided to stop for dinner at Jumelle's, which is near our house. It was early on a Wednesday evening, and I doubted many people would be there. When we walked into the restaurant, only a few tables were filled.

Within 30 minutes, the restaurant was jammed with our family and friends. The entire defense legal team was there, as well as Edwin Edwards and his wife Candy, Ron Weems and his wife Rose, and several members of the press who had filed their stories and wanted to come by and offer support.

Although my first reaction had been to go home and be alone, I really wasn't disappointed that so many people joined us. Throughout this ordeal, one of the keys to my reelection and to my defense was to be available, to never shy away from those who had questions. So perhaps it is fitting that supporters should surround me as the case comes to an end.

It was a bittersweet evening. The Edwards and Weems families were celebrating, while my family was trying to deal with what had happened to me. Bill Jeffress made the point that I was found innocent of all the serious charges, and that things could have been much worse. But that's not much consolation.

The large group of family and friends continued to socialize, but Gladys, James and I slipped out the door and headed home. Each of my three daughters had called and left messages on the answering machine. Campbell had seen the news come over the Associated Press wire in her office at NBC News in Washington. My brother Jack had called Gentry and Meredith.

The first person I called was my mother in Shreveport. I had been worried about her, but she sounded buoyant and upbeat. I had thought I was going to have to pick up her spirits, but she actually picked up mine. For the rest of the evening, I made phone calls to my three daughters. By the time I fell into bed at midnight [or whenever], I was numb with exhaustion. Normally, I fall asleep within a minute or two. Not tonight. I lay there for more than an hour, my mind spinning. Over and over, I asked myself, "Why?"

**Thursday, October 12, 2000**
**Baton Rouge, Louisiana**

I spent a full day in the office to plan a transition. Under the law, even though I have been convicted I continue to hold the title of

254

insurance commissioner. But I must step aside, receive no compensation, and take no part in the daily activities of the office.

I hired nearly every key employee in the office, and I've set out their training schedules. So there should not be any problem with continuity in the months ahead. I met with senior staff members and told them to carry on as usual. I will receive periodic reports, and I will be available to give advice.

Final calls and goodbyes as I prepare to leave my office.

Around mid-afternoon, I gathered all 300-office employees in the Insurance Building auditorium and gave a farewell pep talk. There were lots of tears and condolences from the dedicated employees I have worked with for the past 10 years. I urged them to keep doing the fine job they have been doing and suggested that, if asked, they should say that I am taking a temporary break to pursue my appeal. Many reporters had asked for individual meetings, and I met with TV and newspaper reporters all day. The phone desk was flooded with calls, not just from within the state but from throughout the country—and throughout the world. I was gratified that there was so much interest and support. It would take me days to return the phone calls from people I had worked with over the past 10 years.

I wanted to roll up my sleeves and start catching up on all the requests, memos, and issues on my desk. But for the time being that part of my life is over. It's time to start winding down.

**Monday, October 16, 2000**
**Baton Rouge, Louisiana**

You don't ever really "get away" from a conviction. But over the weekend we tried. Gladys, James, and I, along with our good friend

255

Denise Cassano,[213] drove two hours to Fouchon, a small fishing village at the southern tip of the state. We were the guests of another longtime friend, Baton Rouge attorney Mary Olive Pierson, better known as MOP. She has an exquisite, well-stocked fishing camp that most folks would love to have as their permanent home. Two days of catching redfish and speckled trout gave me some diversion from the drama of the week before. And at least I will eat fresh fish every night this week.

Columnists and political pundits have begun weighing in with their newspaper commentary. There has been some negative press, but the general consensus is that I got a bum rap. There seems to be general astonishment that the jury concluded there was no crime, yet convicted me of making false statements about a crime that never happened. Most of the commentators also conclude that I was entrapped.

*Times-Picayune* columnist James Gill wrote:

> *Brown was the victim of an FBI trick, which may not meet the legal definition of entrapment but would strike any fair-minded layman as dirty pool. When the FBI interviewed Brown it was not as he would naturally have assumed to gather information.*
>
> *Thanks to bugs in Edwards 'office and on his home telephone, the feds already knew all the answers, and the only point in questioning Brown was apparently to catch him stretching the truth. With the dual advantage of the secret tapes and the law that says they can lie to us but we can't lie to them, the feds managed to reel their man in.*
>
> *He had, after all, done nothing wrong.*[214]

Jim Leggett wrote in a Sunday column in the *Alexandria Daily Town Talk*:

---

[213] Denise Cassano is executive director of the Louisiana Health Care Commission, which is part of the insurance department.
[214] *Times-Picayune*, October 12, 2000.

*Insurance Commissioner Jim Brown was convicted by a federal jury of lying to an FBI agent—seven times.*

*That is a fact. Period.*

*But it's an alarming fact.*

*Why, you might ask?*

*It's alarming because Brown was convicted because the jury took the word of the FBI agent over his.*

*So?*

*Well, FBI agents, for the most part, take handwritten notes of interviews, and in the Brown case, the notes were transcribed three days later. Neither Brown nor his attorney was allowed to see the handwritten notes.*

*That is frightening!*

*And in this case, it was the same FBI agent who forgot to turn on a hidden camera when former Gov. Edwin Edwards handed over a fist full of bucks to Cleo Fields, then between terms as a U.S. Congressman and a state senator.*

*The lesson here, perhaps, is Brown should never have talked to the FBI agent.*
*There is no way to know from this distance exactly what happened between Brown and the FBI agent. But it is a given that an agent is free to draw his own conclusions from his own notes.*

*Even the most senior of reporters often relies on tape recordings, especially on lengthy interviews.*

*It is too bad Brown went down like this—although he may
well win on appeal. He has done a good job as insurance
commissioner.*[215]

Former New Orleans U.S. Attorney Harry Rosenberg told the
*Times-Picayune,* "It was perplexing that the jury found him [Brown]
guilty on virtually half of the false statement charges but found him
innocent on the others. It was almost as if they reached a compromise
so that they would not have to call an FBI agent a liar."[216]

And John Volz, who unsuccessfully prosecuted Edwards in the
mid-1980s said, "I don't think it was clear Jim Brown got anything
tangible out of this, and it surprises me that they convicted him."[217]

With his usual wit, John Copes in Deductbox.com summed it up
pretty well in his headline:

## MEMO TO ALL LOUISIANA POLITICIANS:
## THIS IS WHAT HAPPENS WHEN YOU'RE DUMB
## ENOUGH TO SIT DOWN WITH THE FBI

Copes went on to say:

*And we further understand that Brown's hubris got the best
of him when he decided to sit down and talk with an FBI
agent, with no counsel, no recorder, no nothing. Having
said that, isn't there something sort of disturbing about a
public official maybe going to jail for lying to an FBI agent
about matters that may not be material? The word "lame"
keeps coming to mind here. Does this not sort of parallel
the situation with our prez, when he was found to have lied
under oath, but since his lies were immaterial to the
proceeding they handed him a get-out-of-jail-free card.*

*What's worse, the only record of the conversation in
question is the feeb's based on handwritten notes, typed up*

---

[215] *Town Talk*, October 15, 2000.
[216] *Times-Picayune*, October 12, 2000.
[217] Ibid.

*days after the actual conversation. Then the handwritten notes were destroyed, per FBI policy.*

*Every day here at Deductbox, we compare multiple stories about the same event, and marvel at the different versions of the same quote, or the different ways reporters see the same event. The point is, it's a long journey from ear to pen to paper—even for reporters who do this for a living. FBI agents are supposed to be somehow better or more accurate at taking dictation than reporters.*[218]

Judge Clement had made it clear that the parties involved in the case could not talk to the jurors after the trial. As I understand her order, I cannot talk to a juror for the rest of my life. But I would like to sit down with several of them and have a candid discussion of what more they wanted to know from me.

One juror did talk to a reporter for the *Times-Picayune* several days after the trial:

*The juror said she also was distressed the jury was not allowed to see the typed report that FBI agent Harry Burton prepared after interviewing Brown in May 1997. That interview formed the basis of 13 counts of making false statements that were leveled against Brown. Defense attorneys sought to get Burton's handwritten notes entered into the record, but Clement ruled against them.*

*In an interview Thursday, Brown said the jury sent out a note at one point asking to see a transcript of his testimony about the FBI interview. But because the transcripts were not yet prepared, Brown said jurors had to rely on their memories or notes they took during the trial.*[219]

The juror interview confirmed the fears that I had when the jury had asked to see my testimony. They wanted to see Burton's handwritten notes and they wanted to hear what I had to say. I felt

---

[218] *Deductbox.com*, October 12, 2000.
[219] *Times-Picayune*, October 13, 2000.

then, and I feel now, that they were reaching out for some way to give me the benefit of the doubt. But Judge Clement blocked the jurors from getting the vital information they needed. This should be an important issue on appeal as we again ask for the notes taken by Harry Burton. Just about everyone who talks about the case finds it incredible that a man who testified against me had taken detailed notes of the conversation, yet to this day I've never seen the notes.

Judge Clement also came under heavy criticism in Sunday's *Times-Picayune*. The paper concluded, "The level of secrecy surrounding this particular jury has been extraordinary."

> *Not only did U.S. District Judge Edith Brown Clement take the unusual step of keeping jurors' names secret, she prevented the public from knowing even general information about them such as what jobs they do or whether they are married. Worse, their views on all sorts of important questions relating to the case at hand—any preconceived notions about former governor Edwin Edwards and the other defendants, the prosecutors or the use of wiretaps, for example—were shielded as well.*
>
> *It doesn't end there. The Judge forbade the media to identify jurors, even if their names were obtained outside the courthouse and through legal means. She also took the unprecedented step of suggesting that the media call her to get permission before publishing anything of the sort.*
>
> *But the idea of the media or any citizen having to ask the government for permission to exercise free speech is patently un-American.*[220]

Deductbox went a step further, asking, "Is Judge Clement a closet fascist?"[221]

---

[220] *Times-Picayune*, October 15, 2000.
[221] *Deductbox.com*, October 16, 2000.

**Friday, October 20, 2000**
**Baton Rouge, Louisiana**

Today marks the end of a long week of cleaning out my desk and bringing my daily office schedule to an end. I will continue to talk daily by phone with key staff members. Various insurance publications, correspondence, and memos will be delivered to me each day. I really don't believe I will have to give much advice on daily office activities.

The staff knows what to do, and I have confidence in their abilities. There are some national issues where I may be of assistance. Also, there will be questions about proposed legislation to introduce in the spring.

Bill Jeffress will be preparing motions for a new trial, as well as a separate motion to throw out several of the counts that led to convictions. My sentencing date is set for January 31. So at least I will be able to spend the Christmas holidays with my family. I will also do a detailed analysis as to exactly what happened, what we could have done differently, and how we can prepare for the future appeal. The Deductbox concluded, "Brown's defense failed to see the danger in the 13 lying counts and perhaps did not focus as much time and effort into defending them as they spent on the substantive charges."[222]

I think he's right, but we are all great Monday-morning quarterbacks. The good news is that columns in newspapers throughout the state continue to raise questions about what happened to me. A column by New Orleans newspaperman Clancy Dubos is being taped to the walls of elected officials throughout the state.[223]

> *Years from now, they're going to call it the Jim Brown Rule: if you're a public official in Louisiana, do not talk to the FBI.*
>
> *Not under any circumstances.*

---

[222] *Deductbox.com*, October 16, 2000.
[223] *Deductbox.com*, October 13, 2000.

261

*Not even if you're innocent and have nothing to hide. Especially if you're innocent and have nothing to hide. Brown's conviction last week of seven counts of making false statements to an FBI agent sets a low watermark for the federal government's otherwise valiant attempts to clean up Louisiana politics. For Brown, the guilty verdict is especially hard to bear because he was cleared of all 43 substantive charges in the Cascade Insurance Case. There's little justice to be found in his conviction.*

*Brown was not under oath at the time of the interview, and he was being asked to recount things that had transpired months earlier. The agent also had the benefit of having listened to taped conversations between Brown and Edwards—but he didn't tell that to Brown.*

*Most of all, the agent did not tape-record his conversation with Brown, so at trial it came down to the agent's word against Brown's. The only "record" of Brown's alleged lies was the agent's notes, which were dictated and then typed days after the interview.*

*FBI agents, however, are just as human as the rest of us. If the government could record every other important conversation in the case, why not Brown's interview as well?*

*Worst of all for Brown, Judge Edith Clement denied his attorney's request for the agent's hand-written notes from the interview. That effectively killed Brown's best chance of fighting the charges.*

*Brown now stands convicted of collateral charges, based on what one FBI agent says he remembers hearing Brown say, using notes typed days after the interview, which could have been tape-recorded but wasn't, and which covered events that occurred months earlier.*

*The feds shouldn't be doing any victory laps on this one, because from now on, the Jim Brown Rule is in effect across Louisiana.*[224]

I even had a call from a Louisiana district attorney on the Dubos article. It is being copied, framed, and placed prominently in his office where all can see it.

Columnist John Maginnis, who writes for several Louisiana newspapers, continued the skepticism by writing:

*"When FBI agent Harry Burton, Jr., showed up at the Department of Insurance on May 2, 1997, he already knew the answers to the questions he would pose to Brown. He knew them better than Brown did, having listened to the wiretapped conversations that had taken place six months earlier. It's as though Burton were grading Brown on a pop memory quiz, with each wrong answer scoring an indictment. It was a sad, sorry case all around, in which the law and justice were used more than they were served."*[225]

Sam Hanna, the publisher of several north Louisiana newspapers, said in his column, which appears in papers throughout the state:

*"... Brown worked diligently to set the Department [of Insurance] straight. He worked at it with a great amount of energy, and according to people in the insurance business, he was a good commissioner. Brown apparently has a good chance for appeal, because the statements he made to the FBI agent were not taped."*[226]

I'm not sure how important these various commentaries are to my future appeal efforts, but they certainly give comfort to friends and supporters who have believed in me all these years and are confused about what happened.

---

[224] *Gambit Weekly*, October 17, 2000.
[225] *Gambit Weekly,* Baton Rouge, October 19, 2000.
[226] *Concordia Sentinel,* October 18, 2000.

Both Ron Weems and Edwin Edwards called today to express their concern. Both have told me that, if I have to be tried again, they are willing to testify and to help in any other way they can. They both testified at the trial that they did not talk over any negotiations of the Cascade settlement with me. Two of my convictions were based on my having had settlement-negotiation discussions with them. No doubt we should have spent much more time questioning both of them about this important issue. I will definitely need their help if I win a new trial.

## Wednesday, November 1, 2000
## Baton Rouge, Louisiana

Bill Jeffress filed a motion for a new trial today. He alleges that Judge Clement allowed a number of mistakes to take place that prevented my receiving a fair trial. First, Bill pointed out that an FBI typewritten report that was supposed to be withheld from jurors was sent to the jury room while deliberations were taking place. One of the jurors noticed it and admitted that she read a good bit of the report before it was called to the judge's attention. She was not able to say whether any other jurors read the report, but it is blatantly prejudicial to me for the FBI's version to be in writing and given to the jury, without the jury's hearing my testimony, seeing anything in writing from me, or having the actual notes from the FBI agent.

In addition, Bill says that I am entitled to a new trial because I did not see Harry Burton's notes. And finally, there are a number of allegations against Harry Burton that we were not allowed to raise at the trial. Bill argues that Clement should have let us cross-examine Burton on a number of inconsistencies in his testimony about his past, but we were not allowed to do so.

I'm not that optimistic about Clement giving us a new trial based on our saying that she made a lot of mistakes. She will have to have the courage to admit that she was in error if she is to order a new trial.

I also have to deal with her political considerations. There are rumors that if Governor Bush wins the presidential election tomorrow, Clement may be appointed to the Fifth Circuit Court of Appeals. I don't believe her ego will allow her to admit that she made substantial mistakes in my trial, because she doesn't want to tarnish her image. But it's important that Bill file the motion anyway as we prepare for an appeal later down the road.

There was a nice column this week in the *Shreveport Times* by editorial writer Wiley Hilburn. My brother and my mother live in Shreveport, and they really appreciated Hilburn's words as they face their friends and acquaintances.

> *Though profoundly shocked and saddened by Jim Brown's conviction, I come to praise—not to pile on—the fallen insurance commissioner. The FBI and the American justice system remain responsible, if inevitably flawed, to me. Brown has made a positive contribution to Louisiana that ought to be acknowledged. The Louisiana insurance industry and many people affected knew Brown was doing a superb job. The 60-year-old Brown is appealing his case, in my opinion, with reason.*[227]

Hilburn also addressed the obvious pain that my family and I are going through.

> *But unlike Edwards, I know Brown. And whatever the outcome, I know there has been a death in the Brown family with all the agony implied. That's how such a verdict feels.*
>
> *For Brown, in the words of his favorite author [Charles Dickens], these are the "worst of times."*[228]

Wiley summed it up pretty well.[229]

---

[227] *Shreveport Times*, October 21, 2000.

[228] Hilburn quotes from one of my favorite Dickens novels, *A Tale of Two Cities*.

[229] Besides editorials and columns for the *Shreveport Times*, Hilburn has written a book called *Fragments* that vividly and humorously describes the personalities and the landscape of north Louisiana. I reread it once or twice a year.

**Thursday, December 14, 2000**
**Baton Rouge, Louisiana**

After numerous requests from the press, Judge Clement finally released transcripts that revealed information about the 16 jurors and alternates in my case. At the time of the trial, all the questioning of potential jurors took place in secret with the media and general public removed from the courtroom.

Unfortunately, I was so overwhelmed in preparing my testimony for the trial that I didn't spend as much time as I should have reviewing potential jurors. At the time of the questioning, with jurors behind closed doors, the judge and the lawyers asked numerous questions. Some of the potential jurors' comments should have caught my attention, but they didn't. A few examples:

Juror 265, the foreman and the only man on the jury, said he blamed the insurance commissioner when rates were high.

Juror 186 said her father's company had once been involved in a lawsuit with my wife Gladys.

Juror 191, when asked her feelings about politics, said, "I just feel like if a person contributes to a candidate's campaign, at some time down the road it may be a payback or favor." A number of people involved in the trial had given me campaign contributions, so her comments should have concerned me more.

Juror 449 said she disapproved of towing the cars of uninsured drivers. I was the leading proponent of this plan.

Juror 47 had done some work for the FBI.

This is not to say that these jurors didn't try their best to be fair. But we are all affected by relationships and experiences in forming our opinions. Most of these jurors should have been removed for cause, which Judge Clement would not do.

The general profile of this jury also leads any neutral observer to conclude that they don't question the actions of their government. None is a business owner who has to deal with the bureaucracy and red tape of government. None has ever had to make a payroll. They are hardworking people who do what their bosses tell them to do, never question company decisions, and feel their government always does the right thing.

But that alone is not the reason I was convicted. After spending hours reviewing the trial, I have my own opinion about what happened to me.

The jury had to make two major decisions. First, whom should they believe—Foxy Sanders, or the combined testimony of Ron Weems, Edwin Edwards, and me? Not only did the three of us refute Sanders' testimony, but other witnesses also cast him in a negative light. Ron Weems' law partners, former receivership employees Gene Broussard and Randal Beach, and of course, our legal defense team continually made the point that Sanders had his own agenda and could not be believed. It was Sanders against all the rest of us.

The jurors didn't believe Sanders. But the combination of his testimony, the outrageous attacks on me by the prosecutors, and several other prosecution witnesses whose motives were questionable, resulted in a lot of criticism of Edwards, Weems, and me. We were "muddied up," if you will. One observer told me that when it came to deciding whether the former governor had been bribed by Sanders, the jurors "held their noses" and found Edwards and the rest of us not guilty.

But the fact remains that I was muddied and bloodied by the Edwards-Sanders controversy. So the jury already had some reservations about me by the time they had to decide the second question: whether to believe FBI agent Harry Burton or me.

Bill Jeffress was prepared to give evidence raising serious questions about Burton's competence as an FBI agent, his propensity to make mistakes in his job, and his truthfulness on the witness stand. But Judge Clement stopped Bill in his tracks. We were not allowed to put on any evidence questioning Burton's competence or veracity. We couldn't tell the jury that he had made numerous mistakes in interviewing witnesses. We couldn't say that Burton could not even remember to turn on his camera to tape the Edwards meeting with Cleo Fields. We couldn't put on witnesses who would testify that Burton had been untruthful in his statements on the stand. With Judge Clement's help, he came across as "Mr. Clean."

In spite of all this, the jury tried to give me the benefit of the doubt. They wanted to hear my testimony. Out of all the information that had been thrown at them, they specifically asked to review what I had said. But Judge Clement would not let them see any of it. They were left with a choice between what they remembered about my testimony and the words of Harry Burton, which had been pounded home by the prosecutors.

These 12 decent jurors, who generally believe and accept whatever the FBI says, determined that no crime had been committed—no insurance fraud, no witness tampering, no wire and mail fraud. None of the charges against us held water. We were completely innocent.

Yet, even though there had been no crime, I was convicted of giving false statements to an FBI agent—an agent with a questionable background—over a misunderstanding about the interpretation of a few words. Actually, the jury found me innocent of half of the false-statement charges. It was as if they "split the baby down the middle," saying the agent was wrong on half the charges and I was wrong on the other half.

Do I accept and agree with what happened? Of course not! My fight will go on. I will ask for a new trial and will continue to appeal—if necessary, to the highest court in the land. My job is far from done.

## Monday, December 18, 2000
## Baton Rouge, Louisiana

Bill Jeffress called today to tell me that his law firm is merging with one of the country's largest firms, Baker Botts, LLP. The senior partner is James Baker III, who was the lead attorney and strategist in President-elect George Bush's legal fights in Florida and the rest of the country. Bill assured me the change would have no effect on my legal representation. His hourly rate will increase dramatically, but that won't affect our agreement.

We talked for quite a while about the possibility of asking President Clinton for a pardon. Last week, several friends with close ties to the White House called me to suggest applying for a pardon. Although his time in office is running short, they felt the facts of my case did not justify a conviction, and they think I have a good chance of being pardoned by the president.

A number of prominent public officials have received pardons when they were charged with giving false statements. Former Defense Secretary Casper Weinberger and former Assistant Secretary of State

Elliott Abrams were pardoned by former President George Bush in 1992.[230]

Bill told me that a pardon would only clears up the penalty phase of my conviction. In other words, I would not face any jail time or fine. But a pardon would not remove the fact that I had been convicted.

> *A recent study by the <u>National Law Journal</u> concluded, "Contrary to general perception, a pardon does not wipe a defendant's slate completely clean. Not only does the defendant have to live with the social consequences of a prior conviction, there may be lasting legal consequences as well. A pardon may protect a defendant from criminal punishment for his actions, but it does not rewrite history."[231]*

In fact, the U.S. Supreme Court reached this same conclusion in the 1915 case of *Burdick v. U.S.* The court's ruling stated that a pardon "carries an imputation of guilt, acceptance and confession of it."[232]

So a pardon alone is unacceptable. I did nothing wrong, and I want my name cleared. I want my job back. I want all my benefits restored. And I want my legal bills paid. None of that would happen if I were given a pardon. So, in spite of the fact that my chances for a presidential pardon look good, we agreed not to pursue it.

---

[230] *Washington Post*, February 26, 2001.
[231] Laurie Lebensen, *National Law Journal* "Criminal Law Pardon Me," March 5, 2001.
[232] *Burdick v. U.S.*, 236 U.S. 79 (1915).

# 2001

**The ruins of the old Department of Insurance building at the foot of the State Capitol, torn down to become a parking lot. Good riddance! It was the scene of a terrible miscarriage of justice.**

**Wednesday, January 10, 2001**
**Baton Rouge, Louisiana**

Today Bill Jeffress sent down a stack of more than three hundred letters written to Judge Clement by friends and associates on my behalf. It is fairly normal for letters to be written to the judge, sharing personal relationships, giving testimonials, and urging leniency.

I have been reluctant to ask friends to write letters for me. Such letters often become public, and many people just don't want to be put on the spot. So I am gratified that so many people have volunteered to write for me. Former New Orleans mayor and court of appeals judge Moon Landrieu; New Orleans District Attorney Harry Connick; Jim Donelon, the chairman of the House Insurance Committee; a number of legislators and retired judges; prominent lawyers from throughout the state and the country; and a number of people in the insurance industry have all written on my behalf.

It's hard to know what effect the letters will have. Given the cold, crusty attitude Judge Clement has shown toward me throughout this ordeal, I suspect I may be wasting my time gathering the letters. But how can it hurt?

**Wednesday, January 17, 2001**
**Baton Rouge, Louisiana**

*A gag order is more redolent of a non-democratic state.*
Stanley L. Tromp[233]

Bad news from the U.S. Supreme Court today. The nation's highest court refused to hear my appeal of the gag order issued before my trial began. We were all surprised by their decision.

John Elwood, a co-counsel working with Bill Jeffress, wrote a well-reasoned 30-page brief outlining why the nation's highest court should hear my appeal and why the court should rule that the gag order was a violation of my First Amendment right to freedom of speech.

John effectively used the words of Fifth Circuit Court of Appeals Judge Robert M. Parker who had previously stated that "the [gag]

---

[233] Stanley L. Trump (journalist) mpsonaccess.ca/Submissions/StanleyTromp.htm.

272

order violates the Constitution's prohibition on prior restraints of speech."[234] Judge Parker concluded:

> *The government has already tilted the scales in its favor...with well-publicized allegations against Brown, aided in large part by the government's release of sensitive wiretap material and various public announcements regarding the "factual basis" for guilty pleas. Brown's interest in replying to the charges and the associated adverse publicity...is at its peak because the full spotlight of media attention with the full weight of the government is upon him...Brown's status as an elected official provides further justification for permitting public response, because the inability to defend the integrity of the office dramatically affects a public official's ability to perform his duties to the public.[235]*

Judge Parker went on to call the gag order imposed by Judges Polozola and Clement, "the most draconian remedy possible—a direct prior restraint. Brown's hands are tied by an over broad gag order that effectively limits his public comments to bare denials of guilt."[236]

John Elwood effectively argued that various courts of appeal throughout the country are sharply divided on the issue of gag orders. Several circuits allow the gag order, but four circuits—the Third on the East Coast; the Sixth, (Kentucky, Michigan, Ohio, and Tennessee); the Seventh in the Midwest; and the Ninth in the West—allow no gag orders unless there is a specific "clear and present danger" or "imminent threat" of prejudicing a fair trial. There was certainly no threat or prejudice in my case by the defendants. If I had been charged in one of those four districts, I would be able to speak out.

When courts of appeal throughout the country are divided, the Supreme Court will traditionally hear oral arguments and decide whether the gag order is constitutional. But not in my case. The U.S.

---

[234] Elwood John, William H. Jeffress Jr., and Scott Nelson, *James H. Brown Jr. v. United States of America: Petition for a Writ of Certiorari.* Washington, D.C.: Wilson-Epes Printing Co., 2001.

[235] Ibid. 10.

[236] Ibid.

Supreme Court refused to consider any evidence on the gag order but gave no reasons for its decision. John Elwood speculates that the high court may have decided the issue was moot, since my trial is already over. But if, for any reason, I face trial again, we will have to move quickly and try to get the court to consider the unfairness of my being gagged, with no way to effectively defend myself.

**Friday, January 19, 2001**
**New Orleans, Louisiana**

I spent today in Judge Clement's New Orleans courtroom as we argued our case to throw out several of the conviction counts and give me a new trial.

My lawyers and the prosecutors spent most of the morning quibbling about what words were used in my interview with the FBI, and just what the prosecutor's interpretations were supposed to mean. This shows how ridiculous the convictions are. The jury concluded that no crime had taken place, yet I was convicted based on a misunderstanding by the FBI agent over what type of adverb I used.

James Gill, writing in the *New Orleans Times-Picayune*, summed up what happened pretty well:

> *"The hearing quickly degenerated into semantic quibbling as Clement and counsel pored over the words in trial transcripts, the indictment and Burton's report of his interview with Brown. One of Brown's convictions was for using the wrong adverb in his interview with Burton."*[237]

Gill's column, laced with sarcasm, summed up the morning's activities:

> *The longer Assistant U.S. Attorney Jim Mann argued in court Wednesday, the more likely suspended Insurance Commissioner Jim Brown seemed to get his convictions overturned.*

---

[237] *Times-Picayune*, January 19, 2001.

*"That makes no sense. Sorry," Judge Edith Brown Clement told Mann at the end of one particularly opaque sequence of fractured sentences. Don't blame Mann, though. This case has been an embarrassment for the government from day one.*

*The prosecution team at last year's trial never came close to proving that Brown and former Gov. Edwin Edwards had been part of a conspiracy to let David Disiere stiff creditors of his liquidated Cascade Insurance Company.*

*Brown says he told Burton the truth, and it is indeed hard to see what motive he had for doing otherwise. Had he thought he had committed a crime, Brown presumably would have had more sense than to talk to the FBI in the first place. Come to think of it, he should have had more sense regardless.*

*Jeffress wants the convictions overturned because Clement refused to lose time by allowing Burton's handwritten interview notes into evidence.*

*Jeffress figures his client has a right to check all the evidence against him and let a jury decide whether any disparities exist. If the law does not give Brown the right to Burton's notes, the law's a bigger ass than we thought.*[238]

*Brown's convictions are a meager return for all the money taxpayers spent on the Cascade case. If Clement, or the appeals court, does overturn those convictions, the government would merely look petty and vindictive if he were put on trial again. Don't bet against it.*[239]

---

[238] Gill, who is British, is paraphrasing from Charles Dickens's *The Adventures of Oliver Twist*: "If the law supposes that," said Mr. Bumble..."the law is an ass—an idiot."
[239] *Times-Picayune,* January 19, 2001.

275

Clement made no decision today and will take the matter "under advisement." There is no deadline for her to rule. My sentencing date is only 12 days away. Whatever the news, I just hope we hear it soon.

**Wednesday, January 24, 2001**
**Baton Rouge, Louisiana**

> *With what judgment you judge, yet shall be judged; and with measure ye met, it shall be measured again.*
>
> Matthew 7:3

More concern is being expressed about the secrecy in the first Edwards trial. I am getting calls from lawyers all over the country. Some are asking for information to help in defending a client. Others, who don't even know me, are calling, just to express sympathy about the secrecy. One New York lawyer told me, "Now I see why Louisiana is considered a Banana Republic. It's not all your people's fault down there. This kind of secrecy reminds one of Gestapo tactics."

This week's *New Orleans CitiBusiness* published a lengthy commentary by columnist John Hill. He is extremely knowledgeable about the first Edwards trial as well as my trial, and he has continually expressed concern about all the secrecy. He was there daily during the Edwards trial, but he was (successfully) battling cancer during my trial and missed most of it. But he has reviewed the results of my trial at length and written a series of articles about improprieties by both the prosecutors and the courts. His most recent commentary concerns the secrecy provisions installed by Judge Polozola, whose rulings on the gag order and the anonymous jury made it extremely difficult for me to defend myself. John continues to raise questions about the improprieties of the prosecutors and the courts. He perceptively commented this week on all the secrecy. Although he is writing about the first Edwards trial, remember that it was Judge Polozola who instituted all the secrecy provisions that rolled over into my trial, gagging me, tying my hands, and making it difficult to defend myself.

> *Forget about Edwin Edwards. Your feelings about him color all your reasoning about everything concerning his trial. Just put yourself as a defendant whose trial was*

276

*handled—mostly secretly and often arbitrarily—by the trial judge. Harvard Law Professor Alan Dershowitz, who is handling the appeal of Edwards and his son Stephen, and his New York law firm were incredulous about the things that went on in U.S. Judge Frank Polozola's courtroom. The appellate specialists had never heard of such things as a blanket order for everything to remain under seal, and reviewing and "redacting" (read editing out items) from the official trial transcript. The complaints Dershowitz made about the prosecutors and Polozola in the Edwards trial are in fact alarming in a country founded on public and fair trials.*

*Again, forget the defendant is Edwin Edwards. Think of the defendant as yourself or a relative you love. How would you like for such things to happen to you?*
*Dershowitz...listed the following "areas of concern that may raise appellate issues."*

*The wiretap authorizations were "based on information obtained from a cooperating witness the government believed was a liar. The prosecutors made an affirmative decision not to question this witness about his continued illegal activity" to avoid having to disclose this to the judge in a wiretap application.*

*The Judge's gag order prevented the defense from speaking about the case publicly.*

*Polozola required all pleadings to be filed under seal, and he alone would decide what would be made public. "This essentially made the proceedings secret to the press and to the public."*

*The judge denied a motion to recuse himself and, "In a fit of anger...he stated that he knew the defense hated him but that was too bad because they were stuck with him."*

*Polozola recommended an anonymous jury to the prosecution; then when the prosecution filed a motion for one, granted it. "Everything was sealed, so the press and the public speculated that an anonymous jury was ordered because the evidence at trial would reveal threats, or violence or ties to organized crime." Because of the gag order, no one could comment on the reasons for the anonymous jury.*

*After the trial was over, but before filing his written reasons for an anonymous jury, Polozola recused himself from the Jim Brown insurance fraud charge. He said his previous professional relationship with two prosecution witnesses might cause some people to question his impartiality when making rulings concerning those witnesses. In writing about his reasons for the anonymous jury, Polozola relied on charges in the insurance case, including the testimony by the same witnesses.*

*Polozola repeatedly barred both defendants and their lawyers from proceedings he held in his chambers, then barred three lawyers and one defendant from a closed court proceeding over defense objections. Polozola continues to hold many trial documents under seal, away from public inspection, even though the verdict came down last May 9, the insurance trial ended in October and sentencing occurred Jan. 8. What possible reason could there be for maintaining secrecy of proceedings and pleadings when the U.S. Constitution calls for public trials? That is the state of the U.S. court system. How would you like to be tried under similar circumstances?*[240]

Judge Polozola's decisions in the Edwards case, as well as his rulings on preliminary motions in my case, are quite simply, unconscionable.

---

[240] John Hill, *New Orleans Citibusiness,* January 22, 2001.

Other newspaper columnists have commented on Polozola's antics. In the *Crowley Post-Signal,* Robert Walters gave his views on the controversial Baton Rouge judge:

> *"I've got about as much respect for Judge Polozola and his band of thugs as I have for a carrion eating coyote! The judge thinks the federal judgeship put him just to the right of the Messiah."*[241]

Sometimes I feel like I am shouting in the dark about the secrecy and the "Gestapo tactics." But John Hill, Robert Walters, and others agree that what is happening in these trials is an outrageous abuse of the basic constitutional rights of any American. I just hope that someone with higher judicial authority is listening.

## Friday, January 27, 2001
## Greensburg, Louisiana

My son James was warming up on the basketball court of the Greensburg High School gym with his University High teammates. The bleachers were packed with locals from St. Helena Parish, who were there to cheer for the Greensburg Hornets. Gladys and I had just arrived for the game when my portable phone rang. It was Amy Whittington, my press liaison, saying we had been getting a number of calls from the press.

Judge Clement has thrown out two of the charges against me but refused to grant a new trial on the other five counts. That means I will have to immediately start preparing to appeal her decision. Amy's evaluation is that the press considers this to be good news for me. I started out with 56 counts against me, and now I'm down to five. Of the 13 charges of making false statements, I now stand convicted of only five. That means that the jury and the court have rejected the prosecutors' and FBI agent Harry Burton's testimony on eight of the 13 counts. We still have to quibble over interpretations of verbs and adverbs in the other five counts.

The evening news played the story of the judge's decision as a big victory for me. But I know better. It doesn't make a lot of difference

---

[241] Robert Walters, *Crowley Post-Signal,* September 24, 2000.

whether you are convicted of 13 counts or five counts. Even if you're convicted of only one count, you are still a convicted felon, and you still face the same basic sentence.

I suppose I should find some solace over how far I've come. I have been cleared of more than 90 percent of the charges. But it's so unfair to have a system in which the prosecutors can throw every conceivable charge at you, hoping that something, anything, might stick. I had no choice but to go down every alley, read every document, and aggressively defend myself against every charge. The task has been monumental. I suppose I'm making some progress, but it's a great disappointment that I did not get a new trial.

But really, it was unrealistic to expect the judge to give me a new trial. To do that, she would have had to admit that she made a number of wrong decisions. Once she refused to give me Harry Burton's notes, her later rulings compounded the problem. Clement's ego just will not let her admit she made a mistake. It's going to take a higher court to do that. She would have grown in stature by admitting the mistake and correcting it to see that I was treated fairly. She belittles herself by digging the hole deeper. Interestingly, her written opinion reaffirms the fact that the jury did not believe Burton on a number of counts.

In Count 44, the judge concluded that I did not give false information when I said I was only "vaguely familiar" with David Disiere and his operation of Cascade Insurance Company. In her opinion, Judge Clement says: "The Court believes that the jury might have <u>misunderstood a portion of Agent Burton's direct testimony</u>." Judge, you are right. The jury did misunderstand, on this count and on a number of others.

The Judge goes on to write in her opinion:

Thus, the jury

- Believed Mr. Brown's—<u>and disbelieved Agent Burton's</u>—explanation of what Brown meant when he stated he was "out of the loop" concerning any settlement issue between LRO and Cascade (Count 47);
- Believed Mr. Brown's—<u>and disbelieved Agent Burton's</u> explanation of what Brown meant when he told Edwin

Edwards that he would "tell Bourgeois he's gotta do it." (Count 53);

- Believed Mr. Brown's—and disbelieved Agent Burton's statement that Brown did not know who "drove the Cascade settlement." (Count 49);

- Flatly rejected Agent Burton's assertion, as memorialized in his 302, that Mr. Brown had told him that he had not had "any specific conversations with **Bourgeois** concerning **Cascade Insurance Company** and/or **David Disiere**." (Count 52); and

- Flatly rejected Agent Burton's assertion made during direct examination and suggested by his 302, that Mr. Brown had told him that the only thing he knew about a contingency fee contract for Edward Gonzales was information he had learned from a Louisiana Assistant Attorney General (Count 56).[242]

The judge in this case said it well. The jury "disbelieved" agent Burton, "flatly rejected" agent Burton's assertion, "misunderstood" agent Burton. Isn't that all the more reason to give me a new trial? Since such a tremendous amount of material involving so many people presented so much confusion, doesn't fairness demand that I have a chance to zero in on just these charges? The judge has concluded that time and time again, the jury did not believe the FBI agent. She has also concluded that they misunderstood what he said. In the atmosphere of all this rejection and misunderstanding, mixed in with all the secrecy, it seems logical and fair for justice to cry out (for me to cry out) that I was wronged.

The ordeal continues; my sentencing takes place in five days.

## Wednesday, January 31, 2001
## Baton Rouge, Louisiana

> *"This is a court of law, young man; Not a court of justice."* [243]
> Oliver Wendell Holmes

---

[242] *U.S.A. v. Brown et al.* C.D. 99-151-B-M2, Order & Reasons, January 26, 2001.

[243] Lawrence J. Peters, *Peters' Quotations: Ideas For Our Time* (New York: Morrow, 1977), 277.

Today I received my sentence!

My youngest daughter Meredith flew in from Portland, Oregon, where she is an emergency room nurse, to be here with me. She sat next to Gladys and James in the front row of the spectators' area, surrounded by the same loyal family members and friends who have been there throughout the trial.

The sentencing hearing was short, with no speeches or arguments from either the prosecution or the defense. Judge Clement asked me repeatedly if I wanted to say anything. Before the hearing, Bill Jeffress, Camille Gravel, and I had talked about my making a statement, but we agreed that I should say nothing. If I spoke the truth, I would lash out at the unfairness of what had happened to me, and I would question the judge's decision in not giving me the notes. I am innocent, I've done nothing wrong, I did not violate the public trust, and I should have been given the notes. I also should have been allowed a detailed cross-examination of Harry Burton, who was not forthright in his testimony.

We all agreed that Judge Clement had already made up her mind what sentence to give me. My comments would certainly not endear me to her. By speaking, I would possibly spark her temper and I would appear to question her judgment. So it was best that I say nothing. Unfortunately, a judge is given vast discretion in sentencing any defendant. There are specific judicial guidelines, but there are numerous exceptions that allow a judge to alter those guidelines. The federal sentencing guidelines, which give so much discretion to the judge, are so draconian that even though I was found innocent of 41 insurance-fraud counts, the judge can still look at those counts in deciding what my sentence will be. She could let me go free on probation, or she could give me up to five years in jail.[244]

The judge announced her decision matter-of-factly: "You are sentenced to six months confinement, and a fifty-thousand-dollar fine."[245] Bill Jeffress immediately requested that I be free on bail while I pursue my appeal. Clement refused. Bill then asked that I be assigned to a federal prison camp in Pensacola. Often a judge will make a recommendation based on a request from the defendant and his family. Gladys's parents have a house near Pensacola, and it

---

[244] William T. Pizzi, *Trials Without Truth.* New York: New York University Press, 1999.
[245] *U.S.A. v Brown et al.* C.D. 99-151-B-M2, Sentencing Hearing, January 31, 2001.

would have been convenient for my family to stay there on weekend visits. Otherwise, they would face a lengthy drive to another state and have to stay in a motel. Clement refused, saying it was her policy not to recommend where anyone serves his time. (Six months later, when sentencing Cecil Brown in the Edwards riverboat case, Clement granted Brown's request that he be sent to the Federal Bureau of Prisons in Oakdale. So much for her not making recommendations.)

Bill then raised questions about the fine. I had not benefited from the Cascade settlement in any way and had certainly not received any money. The fine was significantly above the guidelines normally used by courts in this country. My legal fees have mounted dramatically, and the fine would be a strain. Bill Jeffress told Clement: "He's had to borrow substantial money against assets from his family because he no longer has a job, a paying job." Clement responded: "There's always the option of the attorney cutting his fees."

That was a cheap shot at Jeffress that disgusted a number of attorneys in the courtroom.

Following the hearing, joined by my family and numerous well wishers, I headed out the front door to again talk with the media, who have been at the courthouse for the past four months. I reiterated what I have said all along: "I did not violate the public trust. What's happened to me certainly cries out for a new trial."

Numerous questions were thrown at me. "Will you appeal?"

"Of course I will. What's happened to me is wrong, and I'm convinced I will be exonerated by a higher court."

"Are you concerned about going to jail?"

"I've never thought about it. Even though Judge Clement did not grant my request for bail, I'm convinced a higher court will. Too many wrongs took place in this case that she should have corrected. I'm convinced the Fifth Circuit Court of Appeals will let me stay out on bond."

I then went on to field questions about how my office is running, and how I will spend my time.

"I'm going to write a book about everything that's happened. Tell it like it was and how it is. I'm sure I will offend a few people, but I am offended about what happened to me. I will have a lot to say. What's happened to me today is a stumble on the road to clearing my name. This is one more step in the process I have to go through to be found innocent. I'm convinced when all is said and done, that I will be cleared. This is a bump in the road, and I can deal with it."

Press conference after sentencing.

## Wednesday, February 21, 2001
## St. Francisville, Louisiana

I am one week away from beginning my six-month prison sentence at the federal facility in Beaumont, Texas, unless the Fifth Circuit Court of Appeals lets me remain free on bond.

The Fifth Circuit is noted for never granting bond appeals. There have only been two exceptions that anyone can remember in this century. But I do have strong hopes.

First of all, it takes about a year just to get your appeal heard by the Fifth Circuit. By that time, my sentence would have been completed many months over. How unfair it would be for anyone to serve their entire sentence, and then have their conviction reversed. That's exactly what happened to Governor Buddy Roemer's father, Charles Roemer. He was convicted of conspiracy to violate the Racketeering Influenced and Corrupt Organizations (RICO) Act and served 18 months at the federal prison in Fort Worth, Texas. After he had completed his sentence and returned home, the U.S. Supreme Court threw out his conviction. He was innocent, yet he was forced to spend a year and a half in a federal penitentiary.[246]

The second reason I hope I won't be going to Beaumont next week is that my appeal is so strong. I continue to talk to lawyers throughout the country who are stunned by my not receiving Burton's notes, and not being able to cross-examine him about the inconsistencies of his statements.

One thing that may hurt me is lack of time. Bill Jeffress has filed my request to stay out on bond, but the prosecutors have the opportunity under the law to answer. They have not filed their answer yet. They will no doubt exaggerate their claims about me dramatically, so we will then have to file a response to their answer. At the very best, the judges assigned to my case in the Fifth Circuit will only have a few days to review our argument. I lose time because February is a short month, and next Tuesday is Mardi Gras. I hope the three-judge panel assigned to my case will get all the briefs by this Friday. If I'm lucky, they will read my argument over the weekend and give me a decision early next week. If the Fifth Circuit does not act by March 1, I could even be forced to go to the Beaumont penitentiary, stay for a few days, and then be turned loose.

The bottom line is, I have no choice but to assume the worst and start planning for a six-month departure. I've located several persons who have served time in Beaumont. Initially, I had hoped to go to the Pensacola Federal Penitentiary at Saufley Field Air Force Base. My Tulane Law School classmate Carl Cleveland spent 28 months there after he was convicted in a video-poker investigation back in 1995. His conviction was eventually overturned. Carl gave me a detailed assessment of how he coped with prison life, which was very helpful. He wrote a monthly newsletter to his friends about his prison experiences. That is a good idea that I want to adopt.

Former Senator Larry Bankston, who spent 18 months at Beaumont, has been extremely helpful in outlining the routine at the facility. Prisoners are allowed no hardbound books, only paperbacks, apparently because drugs can be hidden in the binding of a hardback. More notes from Larry: search out a good job and keep yourself busy; don't participate in any organized athletic events—that is where

---

[246] *U.S. v. Roemer and Marcello,* 703 F.2d 805 (1983).

grudges are played out and revenge exacted; your family can visit you every weekend; you can take absolutely nothing with you, with the exception of a religious ornament (a cross, rosary beads) and a pair of reading glasses. That's it, nothing else. Larry went on and on about all the rules and regulations.

It's troubling to think about going there, but as several people have told me, you can stand anything for six months. As one Baton Rouge television reporter commented, "Six months. That's only a basketball season!"

I have been getting this information together just in case. But I really have a solid feeling that three fair-minded judges are going to give me a decent hearing and let me stay home to carry on with my appeal. If not, I have one week of freedom left. If you eliminate Saturday, Sunday, and Tuesday (Mardi Gras), I have four working days. But I have a good hunch, a good feeling. One way or the other, I'll know in a week.

## Monday, February 26, 2001
## Baton Rouge, Louisiana

*I only ask to be free.*[247]
Charles Dickens

The phone rang in my car as I was heading home from a morning workout at the Louisiana State Police training facility. It's just a few blocks from my house, and my caller ID told me that Gladys had called twice in the last few minutes. I returned the call, and Gladys picked up on the first ring. Her voice was jubilant.

"You're out! You're free! Bill Jeffress just called. The Fifth Circuit judges unanimously said that you have a good appeal, and you don't have to go to Beaumont!"

By the time I got home, numerous calls were coming in from the press. I contacted my office and asked my staff to set up a press conference in the late afternoon. Then I called Bill Jeffress for the details.

"The three judges on your panel unanimously voted to let you stay out on bond," he said. "They didn't give any reasons, so I'm not sure

---

[247] Charles Dickens, *Bleak House* (London: Dent Press, 1907).

which of our appeal issues sparked their interest." Bill explained that he thought the judges must have been convinced that I had substantial grounds for appeal that could result in a reversal of my convictions.

Bill said the three judges are all conservative Republicans, two appointed by Reagan and one by George Bush. To his knowledge, during the time they have served on the Fifth Circuit Court of Appeals, none of them has ever voted to let any defendant stay out on bond. At 4:00 P.M. I held a press conference outside the insurance department. I chose that setting because, symbolically, I wanted to send the message that I intend to fight to get back the full authority of my office.

Some people said I was checking for rain; others said I was giving thanks for relief as I received news that the Fifth Circuit Court of Appeals had let me stay out of jail on bond until my appeal had been heard.

Photo by Arthur D. Lauck
*The Advocate*

The press corps was out in force. I stood and gave them my thoughts: "Three fair judges…made a determination I had not been treated fairly in having to go to jail over this matter, and that there were substantial issues the court should look at in terms of what happened at my trial."

I was asked if I thought the anonymous jury had been a major issue in the judges' decision. "Any time there is an anonymous jury, there is a chilling effect," I said. "It sends a signal to the jury that they may be in danger that the defendants could be threatening in some way. In my case, such a signal is ridiculous. I don't know what concerned these three judges. I do know they have never voted to let someone stay out on bond before. They must feel strongly [that] I was not treated fairly."[248]

Gladys and Gloria joined me at the press conference. Afterwards, we celebrated over dinner as numerous family and friends called or came by the house to discuss the news and wish me well.

Tomorrow is Mardi Gras. I've been celebrating Fat Tuesday for 45 years, but this year will undoubtedly be the best.

## Tuesday, March 20, 2001
## Baton Rouge, Louisiana

The press reports and letters to the editor in newspapers throughout the state have been overwhelmingly positive about the decision to let me stay out of jail while I appeal. The articles and columns have ranged from encouraging to humorous.

John Hill, the Baton Rouge bureau chief for Gannett, interviewed former U.S. Attorneys Harry Rosenberg and John Volz, both of whom have experience with bail issues, about what it means for me to stay out of jail.

Rosenberg thought it was encouraging that I have been granted freedom by three appellate judges: "The fact that both motions were granted by what most people consider very conservative judges who are historically known as pro-government judges is very significant."[249]

Volz, who was U.S. Attorney in New Orleans for more than 10 years said, "If Edwin's [Edwards] got a shot on appeal, Brown has an even better shot." Volz added that, because I was not under oath when my interview was held with the FBI agent, he never would have taken the case to trial. "I don't think they would retry him. I thought their case was very weak."[250]

In the Ruston paper, columnist Paul Pennington analyzed:
*I also don't understand Jim Brown's problem. He was convicted of failing to tell an FBI agent the truth. One has to wonder how many people know that a lie to an agent can land you in the pokey.*

---

[248] *Times-Picayune,* February 27, 2001.
[249] *Shreveport Times*, March 5, 2001.
[250] Ibid.

*It has to be tough on FBI agents' families. If an agent asks his son if he has done his homework and the kid lies about it, does the kid face serious jail time? If his wife tells him about her tough day, could he send her to prison if he finds out it wasn't so tough? Those suckers have power.*[251]

*Concordia Sentinel* publisher Sam Hanna went the furthest out on the limb:

*"Thus those of us who thought Brown was finished in politics were wrong. With two years left in his term, Brown could very well seek re-election if he is successful with a new trial. And, who knows? At the age of 60 and apparently in excellent health, Brown could run for governor again."*[252]

There's little chance of that, but boy, what a turnaround. A few weeks ago, I was headed to prison. Now I'm being discussed as a possible candidate in the next governor's race.

## Friday, June 8, 2001
## Baton Rouge, Louisiana

Fox McKeithen called today to discuss the proposed Louisiana Hayride Museum in Bossier City. Fox, the son of former governor John McKeithen, succeeded me as secretary of state when I did not run for reelection in 1987. The museum will be part of the State Archives and museum activities that are managed by the secretary of state's office.

When I served as secretary of state, I arranged the funding to build what many consider to be the finest state archives building in the country. It is state of the art, and archivists from throughout the world regularly come to Baton Rouge to study our approach to protecting Louisiana's historical documents. I spent a great deal of time with the architects designing the building in the mid-1980s. I learned that

---

[251] *Ruston Morning Paper*, February 9, 2001.
[252] *Concordia Sentinel*, March 21, 2001.

289

intense light can hasten the deterioration of paper documents, so we installed special lighting in the archives. I also learned that protection from sound is important. Exposure to excessive noise over a number of years can affect the integrity of paper, so we built special soundproofing into the walls of the State Archives.

The Louisiana State Archives under construction during my tenure as Secretary of State.

The "Louisiana Hayride" was a traditional country music show broadcast throughout the country from Shreveport back in the 1950s. Many famous country singers performed there, including Hank Williams, Ernest Tubbs, and Elvis Presley. All received significant boosts in their careers by appearing on the "Hayride." Shortly before leaving office as secretary of state, I learned of the existence of hundreds of hours of audiotape from the radio show, which were owned by the Kent family of Shreveport. I asked them to donate this important collection to the State Archives, and eventually they did. For years, the tapes were stored at the archives building. Recently Fox McKeithen learned that new technology was available to digitalize the tapes and to transfer them onto CDs. He's in the process of doing that and wants to have a major release of the tapes next spring. I agreed to work with him on the project and join him on a statewide tour. He also wants to emphasize songs from my old hometown of Ferriday, namely the music of Jimmy Swaggart, Jerry Lee Lewis, and Mickey Gilley. The state has acquired an old post office in Ferriday to house the music museum.[253]

Louisiana's country-music heritage is an important asset for the state, and it makes sense to highlight our well-known performers, both locally and throughout the country.

Stories also appear in newspapers throughout the country today that a former federal prosecutor was sentenced to two years' probation for withholding information involving the deadly siege at

---

[253] Al Ater is first assistant secretary of state.

Waco.[254] Former U.S. Attorney Bill Johnston admitted to withholding a key page of pre-trial notes from the defense back in 1993. U.S. District Judge Charles Shaw also sentenced Johnston to two hundred hours of community service to talk to high school students. The judge told him, "Maybe you can help somebody not to make a similar mistake."

A prosecutor withholding notes? This is a crime? A prosecutor is now a convicted felon? Isn't this exactly what happened to me when both the FBI agent and the prosecutor refused to make available the notes from my interview? Justice moves slowly, but perhaps soon I will prevail. What was done to me was wrong. There was no justification for not giving me the notes.

An interesting event took place in the Louisiana legislature yesterday that has a bearing on my case. A new law was passed that allows jurors in criminal cases to take notes during trials and use them while deliberating.[255] It would have been extremely helpful to me if the jurors in my case could have taken notes. The decision to allow note taking by the jury was up to Judge Clement. But she never gave the jurors permission to take notes.

There was "information overload," a massive amount of material given to the jury. It was not reasonable to expect any juror to follow and understand all the documents being presented to them. With 800,000 documents, hours of tape recordings, numerous witnesses, and 56 criminal charges, the jury needed every tool at its disposal to keep focused on the events that transpired. Taking notes would have been extremely helpful and would have helped the jury remember my testimony. Since the court reporter failed to transcribe the testimony and make it available as the jury requested during the trial, their notes would have given them some of the details of what I said. The fact that they could not take notes certainly hurt my defense. I hope that, in the future, the jury will be allowed to take notes. It's only fair.

National publications this week reported mounting criticism of the Justice Department and the FBI. In Saturday's *Washington Post*, Representative Dan Burton (R-Ind.), Chairman of the House Government Reform Committee was quoted:

---

[254] *The Advocate*, June 8, 2001, *The New York Times*, February 7, 2001, *The New York Times*, September 2, 2000.
[255] *Times-Picayune*, June 8, 2001.

*"[There is a] pattern of prosecutorial misconduct that threatens to undermine the integrity of the FBI. People should have confidence in their law enforcement agencies including the FBI, Burton said. And if these atrocities or these mistakes are being made intentionally, that are taking people's liberty away, we need to clean it up."*[256]

The *Washington Post* story also quotes Burton as saying he wants to look at several cases where the FBI did not give evidence to defense attorneys that would have helped the accused.

Such stories concern me. All along, I thought I was unique as a defendant—having an FBI agent give false testimony against me, and having prosecutors who would not provide information that could prove my innocence. In all these news reports, there is a pattern of FBI and Justice Department wrongdoing that apparently takes place throughout the country. This is scary, and it should deeply concern every law-abiding citizen. It is a sad state of affairs when you have to be afraid of your own government.

## Sunday, June 10, 2001
## New Orleans, Louisiana

Gladys and I had dinner this evening at one of New Orleans's newer celebrated restaurants. (To those of us in Louisiana, and I imagine throughout the South, you go home at night for *supper*, but you go out at night to *dinner*.)

Insurance commissioners and insurance executives from throughout the country are in New Orleans for the summer meeting of the National Association of Insurance Commissioners. Friends who regularly attend these quarterly meetings, whom we enjoy seeing socially, joined Gladys and me.

Delmonico's is the recent creation of Emeril Lagasse. He has emerged as one of the nation's premier chefs; it was recently announced that he would have his own television sit-com this fall on NBC. I have been hosting a cable-television show in Louisiana for 14 years. It's an hour-long program that focuses on insurance issues, but

---

[256] *Washington Post*, June 2, 2001.

I have always had well-known Louisianans as featured guests. Back in the 1990s, Emeril appeared on my show often. We would talk about Louisiana cooking, and he would prepare something tasty. Gladys's brother Gary Solomon and his son Gary Jr. were guests on Emeril's national cooking show last fall. Having such a close family friendship with Emeril, we were excited about our first visit to his new restaurant.

Attorney Kevin Salter, an old friend from New York, joined us for dinner. He told me that a day does not go by in which my name does not come up among his clients. He said that the general view in the insurance industry on the East Coast is that I got a "bum rap." He echoed the thought I hear regularly from lawyers when he told me that he always advises his clients not to talk to the FBI. Kevin summed it up bluntly: "Jim, ol' buddy, the consensus is, quite simply, that you got royally screwed." Apparently, my case is a classic example of how you can get set up, how innocent business people can be ensnared in legal, criminal "quicksand" by a simple conversation with an unscrupulous FBI agent.

Last night, we ate at the House of Jaeger Restaurant in the French Quarter as guests of our longtime friend Barbara Bain of Miami. Mississippi Insurance Commissioner George Dale and his wife Yvette joined us, and George had plenty of stories to tell about his unfair harassment by the FBI and the Justice Department. Bill Bailey, who hosts a weekly nationwide radio show on insurance issues, was also with us. He is the brother of one of the nation's top criminal attorneys, F. Lee Bailey. Bill shared similar stories of the Justice Department's unscrupulous behavior in its all-out effort to get his brother.

It seems that everyone has a story to tell of mistreatment by federal officials. Gladys told me later that she wishes we could just enjoy dinner and stay away from the subject, but she also knows that it's not to be.

**Thursday, June 14, 2001**
**Baton Rouge, Louisiana**

Today is my oldest daughter Campbell's birthday, but I won't be able to call her. She is on Air Force One, somewhere between Brussels and Poland, traveling with President George Bush. It is incredibly satisfying to see her grow in poise and confidence and to see her on national television almost daily. But today all I can do is to e-mail her my love and birthday greetings.

I've been staying up late to catch up on reading the newspapers I had let pile up the past few days. Monday the *Washington Post* did an updated story on former Housing and Urban Development Secretary Henry Cisneros. He was indicted in 1997 on 18 felony charges of making false statements to the FBI. Cisneros admitted he lied repeatedly yet was only given probation.[257] This confirms what we all know—that justice is not fair, and that sentences are given at the whim of a federal judge. What better example can one point to than President Bill Clinton's grand-jury testimony in the Monica Lewinsky case? His admitted false statements, made under oath before a federal grand jury, netted him nothing more than losing his law license in Arkansas for five years. Since he had no plans to practice law anyway, this amounted to a slap on the wrist.

I have an unrecorded casual conversation with an FBI agent that lasted approximately 30 minutes, and I'm sentenced to six months in jail, and a fifty-thousand-dollar fine. Where is the due process? Where is the equal justice?

Also, I read today that New York Governor George Pataki is proposing that the legislature pass tougher penalties for perjury in criminal cases when an innocent person is convicted.[258] In other words, under New York law, an FBI agent who gives false information leading to the conviction of an innocent person can be criminally prosecuted and face punishment of up to 15 years in prison. Louisiana needs such a law, and after I get all this behind me, I certainly want to propose that our legislature support such legislation in the coming session.

**Thursday, July 5, 2001**
**Baton Rouge, Louisiana**

*Justice delayed is justice denied.*
Attorney General John Ashcroft[259]

---

[257] *Washington Post,* June 11, 2001.
[258] *New York Times,* June 13, 2001.
[259] Speech to the American Bar Association, Chicago, August 7, 2001.

Almost seven months have gone by since my conviction, and, unbelievably, I am still unable to obtain a copy of the transcript from my trial. The appeal cannot be filed until a transcript is prepared by the district court in Baton Rouge. I was sentenced on January 31, and my attorneys immediately asked that a full transcript be prepared as required by the Fifth Circuit. Unfortunately, there's not a lot my lawyers can do until we have the transcript. My appeal is based on erroneous rulings by Judge Clement that often were determined by the interpretation of a few words. Therefore, the exact words used by FBI agent Harry Burton, and even by the judge herself during bench conferences with only the lawyers present, need to be reviewed in some detail by my lawyers. But first, we have to have the transcript.

It does no good to complain; in fact, you can dig a deeper hole for yourself. I was told I would be wasting my time to protest and that the complaints would only drag my request out even longer.

I'm hopeful the Fifth Circuit will throw out my conviction, and I'm anxious to get back to my job as insurance commissioner. But the waiting continues. Think how unfair it would be if I were in jail waiting for my appeal to be heard. That happens to many defendants who are convicted in federal court. They wait, and they wait.

## Saturday, July 7, 2001
## Baton Rouge, Louisiana

I took an early morning swim today—a mile and a half, which is a good distance for me. Several weeks ago I strained a muscle on the right side of the kneecap of my left leg. Despite my following a daily stretching routine given to me by an orthopedic surgeon, the knee has been slow to respond. Swimming is one exercise I can do that doesn't bother the knee, but I'm eager for it to heal. At my age, it's not good to do just one exercise. Cross-training is all the more important as you get older, and I've found my body responds best to a combination of biking, swimming, and running.

Before hitting the pool, I had a light breakfast of juice, wheat toast, and honey and did a quick review of the newspaper headlines. All the daily papers had front-page headlines that blared: "Ex-FBI

Agent Pleads Guilty." The stories were about agent Robert Hansen, who pled guilty to spying for the Russians.[260]

For the past month, there have been daily stories of incompetence within the FBI. The piling on continued yesterday in front-page stories announcing the new director of the FBI, a San Francisco prosecutor named Robert Mueller. A typical analysis in the New York Times: "Senate Judiciary Committee Chairman Patrick Leahy, D-Vt., said:

> *'Unfortunately the image of the FBI in the minds of many Americans is that this agency has become unmanageable, unaccountable and unreliable.'*"[261]

Leahy was also quoted in the *Washington Post*: "There's a management culture with an air about it that the FBI can do no wrong. That attitude is at the root of the problems we've seen in high-level cases."[262]

I'm not using the FBI as a scapegoat for my problem. But our nation's top law-enforcement agency is riddled with incompetence and outright fraud. I can't help but feel that I am one of its victims.

I hope the new director will build in some checks and balances so that other public officials won't be targeted as I was. Regardless of my problem, our country is being short-changed by a federal agency that has proven to be inept, incompetent, and outright vicious in profiling innocent victims.

## Friday, July 13, 2001
## Las Vegas, Nevada

Gladys and I thought it would be fun to spend five days in Las Vegas with James and several friends from Baton Rouge—just get away from home for the week and take in the sights. We quickly found out that Las Vegas is not the place to "get away." Louisiana tourists wanting to wish me well have stopped me repeatedly in the hotel and in restaurants.

---

[260] *Times-Picayune,* July 4, 2001.
[261] *New York Times,* June 21, 2001.
[262] *Washington Post,* July 6, 2001.

The *Las Vegas Sun* had a front-page story today about a local FBI agent who was arrested for selling confidential investigative information.[263] There continue to be daily stories in papers throughout the country that are heavily critical of the FBI. My personal criticism is, of course, directed at one FBI agent. But I was certainly hurt at my trial by the positive feelings most people had then about the FBI. Today, the agency's reputation has been tarnished dramatically. The *Baton Rouge Advocate* ran a recent editorial headlined, "FBI in Shambles."[264] And a *New York Times* editorial-page headline called the agency the Federal Bureau of Incompetence.[265] I suppose I am a little bitter that all these blunders by the FBI were not made public before my trial.

The Bellagio Hotel, where we are staying, has two Olympic-size swimming pools. I took out my frustrations with a mile-and-a-half swim this morning. Then my daughter Gentry tracked me down with big news. I'm going to be a grandfather—my first grandchild. Gentry and my son-in-law Michael are expecting in early April next year. Of course, we are all thrilled. Gentry has been on a career path as a successful advertising executive. Campbell and Meredith are unmarried and focused on their jobs. I was wondering for a while if I was ever going to have any grandchildren.

Campbell called shortly after did Gentry to be sure we had heard the news of the new baby. She leaves later today to cover the President's European summit. We will be seeing her on the NBC Nightly News all next week.

Tonight Gladys had planned dinner with several of her girlfriends, and James was off with friends to see

My Dad and I share an enjoyable moment at one of my many golf tournaments. He was always my number one fan.

[263] *Las Vegas Sun,* July 13, 2001.
[264] *Baton Rouge Sunday Advocate,* July 22, 2001.
[265] *New York Times,* May 16, 2001. *Newsweek Magazine* used the same description of the FBI in its publication of June 17, 2002.

magicians Siegfried and Roy at the Mirage Hotel. I opted for several hours at the Bellagio Art Museum, where comedian Steve Martin is exhibiting paintings from his private collection. Martin has been an art collector for years, and the exhibit includes the work of a variety of artists, from Picasso to David Hockney. I rented a cassette on which Martin leads you throughout the gallery and with simplicity and humor, outlines the history of each artist and what motivated him to buy the painting. It was several hours well spent.

From the gallery, I took a cab to the Mandalay Bay Hotel a few blocks away, where singer Dan Fogelberg was performing a concert at the House of Blues. I was able to get a good seat close to the stage for his intimate concert. Like so many others, his songs have been a part of my life from the early 1970s. He sang and played the guitar and the piano for several hours. He ran through "Hard to Say," "Longer," "Run for the Roses," and ended with his best-known song, "Leader of the Band."[266] *I thank you for your kindness and the times when you got tough, And Papa I don't think I said I love you near enough.*

I lingered for a while after Fogelberg left the stage. Dad would have been 88. Although I am glad he was spared the hardship of all I've gone through during the past three years, I wish he had been here with me—through the good times and bad. The older I get, the better I understand my father, because I find more and more of him in me. I still miss him a lot.

## Tuesday, July 17, 2001
## Baton Rouge, Louisiana

> *Decency, security and liberty alike demand that government officials shall be subjected to the same rules of conduct that are commands to the citizen. In a government of laws, existence of the government will be imperiled if it fails to observe the law scrupulously.*
> Justice Louis D. Brandeis[267]

I read the news accounts today of an attorney friend in Covington, Mike Fawer. He had been suspended from practicing law in federal court in Baton Rouge for a year because he used "foul

---

[266] Dan Fogelberg, "Leader of the Band," *Very Best of Dan Fogelberg.* Sony/Legacy, 2001.
[267] Olmstead et al. v. United States, 277 U.S. 485 (1928).

language" in talking to one of the prosecutors. A lawyer for the Justice Department argued that his behavior was "inappropriate and unacceptable." Not only was he suspended from practicing law in the Baton Rouge courts, Mike was fined five thousand dollars.[268] "Sticks and stones can break my bones, but words will never hurt me." In a Baton Rouge federal courthouse, that saying is only half right. Mike Fawer's words *have* hurt him.

Do I see a double standard here? Do the rules apply differently depending on whether the "unacceptable behavior" is by a prosecutor or a defense attorney? The answer of course is yes.

In the same Baton Rouge courthouse, a prosecutor in the U.S. Attorney's office physically attacked my attorney Bill Jeffress. Pushed! Shoved back! Physically assaulted! Judge Clement turned her head and did nothing. Bill certainly could have been hurt in the attack, but there was not one word of admonishment from Judge Clement. Bill had to bring up the attack in open court, and all Clement would say then was that it had better not happen again. Such double standards are certainly contemptible, as is the judge's failure to control her courtroom and prevent such irresponsible, unprofessional actions.

## Thursday, August 3, 2001
## Perdido Key, Florida

Every year around this time, the Brown family converges at Orange Beach on the Florida-Alabama border. We started this tradition about 20 years ago, before my father passed away. My sister Susie (Madalyne to her friends) brings her family, including her husband Sheriff Jiff Hingle and their daughters Carrie and Katie (my goddaughter). Mother comes from Shreveport with my brother Jack, his wife Pam, and their daughter Amanda. Parker, their thirteen-year-old son, is still at camp in North Carolina and won't join us this year.

We all pitch in. Jiff and Susie bring Creole tomatoes, shrimp, and oysters from Plaquemines Parish. Gladys and I stop at Joe Patti's[269]

---

[268] *The Advocate*, May 29, 2001.
[269] Joe Patti's has been owned for years by Frank Patti, who pleaded guilty to tax fraud in April 2002, and is serving a six-year and seven-month sentence at a federal prison in Fort Worth, Texas. He walks the prison yard each day with former governor Edwin Edwards who is also serving his own sentence there.

seafood market in Pensacola and load up on seafood, olive oil, and fresh bread. I have spent part of my last 40 summers along this strip of the Gulf Coast. There is lots of time to read, catch flounder and sea trout off the beach early in the morning, and take long bike rides with Gladys along the backwater canals in the afternoon. In spite of several recent shark attacks, I still work up the courage to take an ocean swim every afternoon.

Family beach picture.

At the beach, I usually attend mass each day, even though I'm not Catholic. The 9:00 o'clock service at St. Thomas by the Sea Catholic Church is a special way to begin the day. The church is just a few miles from our condo, and the mass is no more than thirty minutes long, but I generally linger for a while to meditate. Sometimes I read from the Bible or inspirational literature that I take along.

Catholics throughout our country, and often throughout the world use the same daily missal.[270] Anyone attending mass today in any location will share the same scripture readings. I was particularly attentive to the reading of Psalm 84:2, "My soul yearns and pines for the courts of the Lord," and Psalm 84:10, "I had rather one day in your courts than a thousand elsewhere."

I would have no problem making a case for my innocence before the Lord, although I might find it a challenge, as Job did.

> *I swear by God, who has denied me justice,*
> *So long as there is any life left in me*
> *And God's breath is in my nostrils,*

---

[270] *Today's Missal.* Volume 68, Number 5. Portland, Oregon: Oregon Catholic Press, 2001. 151-152.

*No untrue word shall pass my lips*
*And my tongue shall utter no falsehood.*
*I will not abandon my claim to innocence.*
*I will maintain the rightness of my case,*
*I will never give up.*

Job 27: 2 (5–6)


Today I stayed awhile after the service to read more of Job's trials. When I left the church and headed for my car, I heard a voice call out, "Excuse me, would you mind if I visited with you for a moment?"

I looked back to see a middle-aged lady dressed in yellow wearing a wide-brimmed hat, with a big smile on her face. "I have a message for you," she said. "I've been asked to tell you something."

I paused and turned to listen.

"I sat right behind you during the service, and the Lord spoke to me about you," she said. "I don't want to bother you but I felt you should know this. I know you've gone through a difficult trial, and it has been very hard on you. But the Lord told me to tell you that this is all going to work out, and you will be stronger because of what happened. Things are going to be okay for you."

I assumed that she had recognized me and knew about all that had happened to me during the past year. But as we talked for a while, a few things she said made me a little unsure.

I finally asked her, "You do know who I am, don't you?"

She shook her head and said, "No, I have no idea. I'm merely relating to you what I was told to tell you. The Lord told me to pray for you every day, and to take you under my wing. But I don't know who you are."

She told me her name is Mary Bond, and she is an interior decorator from Thibodaux, Louisiana. I told her I was Jim Brown, the insurance commissioner who was tried and convicted last year.

"Oh, yes, now I remember," she said. "But I didn't recognize you. I really didn't follow the trial that closely. But now I remember who you are."

We talked for a while longer and agreed to stay in touch. I don't know what to make of what she told me. I really believe she did not know who I was when she approached me. A lot of us have gone through trials in life. Perhaps I looked a little down and she wanted to pick up my spirits. Was it divine intervention? Whatever it was, I take it as a good sign. She seems to be a decent woman who obviously was concerned enough to talk to me about a crisis in my life. Not being Catholic, I don't have a godmother. But Mary Bond will hold that place in my heart for years to come. It's comforting to know that I have someone praying for me and looking out for me in a special, spiritual way.

## Tuesday, August 14, 2001
## Baton Rouge, Louisiana

Bill Jeffress called today to give me an update on our appeal. After waiting seven months to have the transcripts typed by the court reporter, we are close to having the documents filed with the Fifth Circuit Court of Appeals. This is the first required step before I can actually file my written appeal. It certainly should not have taken this long to prepare a transcript from a three-week trial.

The transcript was available on Realtime immediately after the trial was over. The computer could have printed out what was said throughout the entire trial. We could at least have had an unoffical record, which would have helped immensely in preparing our brief. It's a travesty of justice to wait so long for a transcript of the trial.

In the New Orleans courtroom of Federal Judge Morey Sear, the entire trial is videotaped. At the end of each day, each lawyer is handed videotape that contains all the discussions that took place. That is a much better way to do it. The system should not force defendants to wait months for a simple transcript that should take a few days to produce.

Bill and I discussed filing a memorandum requesting a copy of Harry Burton's notes before our actual appeal is heard. What possible motive could there be for keeping the notes secret now? The trial is over, and there is certainly nothing that needs to be protected. Why are the prosecutors fighting so hard to keep us from seeing the notes? What is in the notes that concern them so much? Why are they using every trick in the book, filing every conceivable motion, to keep the notes from being made public?

It seems as if every week I hear about another controversial case in which the actual notes are an important component of what happened.

302

Bob Bourgeois, who pleaded guilty in the Cascade case just this week, filed a motion to throw out his guilty plea. He claims that his lawyer had discussions with the prosecutors in which they offered him full immunity, but he was never told of such an offer. In support of his motion, Bourgeois has asked the court for the right to take the statements of the prosecutors in the Cascade case and to also make them produce <u>all notes</u> that were taken.[271] Bourgeois believes—and any fair-minded person would agree—that the actual notes are the best evidence of what agreement took place. Bourgeois wants the notes of the prosecutors. I should get Harry Burton's notes.

In a related story, newspapers throughout the country have been running stories about Houston English teacher and freelance writer, Vanessa Leggett, who is writing a book about a murder case in Texas. The prosecutors tried to get the tapes she had made in interviewing the accused as well as her actual notes. She refused and a federal judge held her in contempt and sent her to jail. She went to jail for not turning over <u>her notes</u>. You have to turn over the notes.[272]

Remember Ruby Ridge, where FBI agents stormed the Idaho home of Randy Weaver, killing his unarmed wife and their baby, as well as shooting his fourteen-year-old son in the back? In his explosive book *Ambush at Ruby Ridge,* author Alan Bock paints a picture of FBI agents who lose or purposely hide notes of interviews with key witnesses.

> *New evidence and witnesses emerged in a way that enraged the defense team and caused Judge Lodge to suspend the trial.*
>
> *Ron Howen [one of the prosecutors] also told the judge that a set of notes of an FBI agent...had been missing, but had been found weeks before in an FBI agent's desk drawer.*
>
> *The defense lawyers "accused the prosecution of purposely hiding evidence that would bolster the defense portion of the case." Judge Lodge flushed red as the evidence was*

---

[271] *Baton Rouge Advocate,* July 13, 2001.
[272] Molly Ivins, "From Journals to Jail," *Washington Post,* August 11, 2001.

*described, and then delivered a stern lecture from the bench. "I'm really disturbed by what appears to have happened here," he said.*[273]

Because the notes were not given to the defense, nationally renowned defense attorney Gerry Spence told the court: *"We are being ambushed. We may have further motions to dismiss based on prosecutorial misconduct."*[274]

The notes in the Ruby Ridge case were finally produced after the judge threatened sanctions against the Justice Department for prosecutorial misconduct.

You have to produce the notes.

## Friday, August 17, 2001
## Port Eades, Louisiana

Yesterday I joined a group of friends on a boat owned by my father-in-law Ted Solomon and New Orleans attorney Phil Wittman for three days of fishing offshore at the Empire Southpass Tarpon Rodeo. We caught a few black-fin tuna this morning and a barracuda this afternoon. We searched for tarpon and dolphin but with little luck so far.

The marina is only accessible by boat, and the closest road is in Venice, 35 miles north of the mouth of the Mississippi River.

I'm not a diehard big-game fisherman, so I took along several books to keep me company during the slow fishing days. But it can be hard to read when you are fighting three-foot seas with choppy water. Thank goodness for the transderm scope patch behind my right ear, which continually releases a chemical (scopolamine) that prevents seasickness.

Late this afternoon, Campbell called from New York and reached me on my portable phone out in the Gulf. She will host the weekend edition of the "Today Show" tomorrow and Sunday; then she'll take a plane to Waco, where she will join the national press corps covering President Bush's vacation in Crawford, Texas. I checked on the TV

---

[273] Alan W. Bock, Ambush at Ruby Ridge: How Government Agents Set Randy Weaver Up and Took His Family Down. (New York: Berkley Books 1995) p. 173, 196.
[274] Ibid.

reception at the New Orleans Big Game and Fishing Club near the marina, where we have dinner each night. The NBC affiliate is not picked up here on satellite, so I will cut my fishing trip short and head home later this evening. I'll stop in Buras and spend the night with my sister Susie and her husband Jiff. I'll be home tomorrow morning in time to watch Campbell on "Today" and play golf with my son James.

Since the fishing was slow this afternoon, I read a recent book by Bob Woodward of the *Washington Post*. In *Shadow: Five Presidents and the Legacy of Watergate,* Woodward recounts several examples in which presidents and other high government officials have been investigated for giving false information. In every instance, handwritten notes became critical and had to be produced.

Woodward writes that in 1987, Special Prosecutor Lawrence Walsh was investigating the Iran-contra affair. Woodward concludes:

> *"Walsh's team discovered that [Secretary of State] George Shultz had not produced all of Charlie Hill's notes and Walsh thought of indicting him. Shultz had in fact tried to keep the Special Prosecutor from receiving over 10,000 pages of notes, but he was unsuccessful."*[275]

Secretary of Defense Casper Weinberger also tried to hide notes he had taken. According to Woodward:

> *"Weinberger repeated his earlier denials in an interview with Walsh's prosecutors, claiming he hadn't really taken any notes since 1981." Walsh's investigators finally found the notes. "In all there were 7,000 pages, nearly 1,700 of them from the Iran-contra period." Robert Bennett, Weinberger's lawyer, argued that since the note taking was habitual, "like brushing his teeth," Weinberger's repeated denial of having notes was innocent. He simply forgot about them. Bennett produced a report by a so-called memory expert who argued the note taking was routine and*

---

[275] Bob Woodward, *Shadow: Five Presidents and the Legacy of Watergate* (New York: Simon & Schuster, 1999), 154.

*virtually unconscious so it was not stored in the memory bank for easy retrieval.*

*Walsh was amused and astounded. When he threatened indictment, Bennett looked at him and said smiling, "Of course, you know this means nuclear war."*
*On June 16, 1992, Walsh had his grand jury indict Casper Weinberger on five felonies, including obstruction of justice, making false statements and perjury."*

*The Weinberger indictment was designed to bring to justice someone who had, in Walsh's eyes, consciously and deliberately <u>concealed his notes</u>.*[276]

You have to make the notes available. You can't hide them. You can't hold them back. You have to give up the notes.

As part of his investigation, Walsh also wanted to look at the personal diaries of Ronald Reagan. Not the typed version, but the actual handwritten version. The notes that were written by hand at the exact time the thought took place.

*"As a preliminary step Walsh and Barrett demanded access to the actual pages of Reagan's personal diaries—not the typed excerpts that White House Counsel Culvahouse had prepared back in 1987. Having been burned by Shultz and Weinberger, they threatened to subpoena the diaries. Finally, Barrett flew to Los Angeles and was allowed to review the full photocopied pages from Reagan's handwritten diaries."*[277]

Not a summary, not a typed copy, but the actual handwritten diaries.

Once Weinberger's notes were finally discovered, their effect was bannered in headlines all over the country. The *New York Times* headline read, *"86 Weinberger Notes Contradict Bush Account on Iran Arms Deal."* The *Washington Post* said, *"Bush Stance, Iran-*

---

[276] Ibid. 156.
[277] Ibid. 157.

*contra Notes at Odds, Weinberger Memo Says President 'Favored' Arms-Hostage Plan.*"[278]

All these headlines refer to the <u>notes</u>. The notes are critical and must be reviewed.

What did President Bush say about the notes? Woodward states:

> *"In one entry in the [President Bush's] diary, Bush voiced astonishment that Shultz had turned over 200 pages of notes. Bush said he would never do that."*[279]

Of course he wouldn't. He didn't want the notes read. There were contradictions in them.

Some may say I'm beating this horse to death, but presidents, secretaries of state, secretaries of defense, and a cross-section of other officials <u>have all had to turn over the notes</u>. The only person who doesn't have to turn over his notes is one Baton Rouge FBI agent. Why not?

Woodward also writes that Bush was extremely angry when the special prosecutor indicted Weinberger, Bush's secretary of defense, <u>shortly before</u> Bush was up for reelection. How well I can identify with this. Woodward's book gives the details of President George Bush's reactions after Bill Clinton defeated him in 1992. Bush had just returned from Houston to the White House, and he gave a pep talk to his cabinet members and White House employees.

> *As [Bush] walked into the White House, he spotted Attorney General William Barr in the crowd. With an index finger motion of "follow me," the president summoned Barr. The affable 42-year-old intellectual, conservative legal strategist stepped in behind Bush and walked with him up to the Oval Office.*
>
> *When they were alone in the Oval Office, Bush exploded about the Weinberger indictment.*

---

[278] Ibid. 203.
[279] Ibid. 209.

*"It appears this was very political!" he bellowed, following up with a string of very pungent remarks. "Cost me the election," he said furiously. He felt he had been tricked. A pivotal event, he said, citing the polls and the loss of momentum. "What is your reaction?"*

*Barr said he thought it was a crude political act with a political motive. Career Justice Department prosecutors would never bring out such information in an indictment just before an election. Barr said he wanted to dismiss [Special Prosecutor Lawrence] Walsh. He knew the law well. He could remove Walsh for "misconduct."*

*"Walsh has abused his power!" Bush said, inviting the attorney general to fire Walsh.*

*Bush remained convinced that Walsh issued the indictment to influence the election.*[280]

The president of the United States, George Bush, was deeply upset that an indictment was brought just before the election. In his opinion, it was a calculated effort to influence the election, and it played a part in his defeat. He concluded that this action was outrageous.

Mr. President, I could not agree with you more. You and I are a part of a group of elected officials who were targeted by unscrupulous prosecutors who wanted to see us defeated at the polls in an effort to further their questionable agenda. You were wronged, and so was I. What U.S. Attorney Eddie Jordan did to me by bringing indictments right before my election was an outrageous abuse of his authority. So, welcome to the club, Mr. President.

President Bush, by the way, had very little respect for the FBI. Woodward recounts how upset Bush became when he found out the FBI was trying to set up his Texas campaign manager in his re-election campaign.

---

[280] Ibid. 205-07.

*[Bush] was especially incensed at the FBI. During the campaign, the FBI had tried to pull one of their famous undercover sting operations on Bush's Texas campaign chairman James Oberwetter, who was a friend of his son, George W. Bush. When he learned what the FBI had done, Bush was as angry as his advisors had seen him in 12 years.*

*The former president said he would never forgive the FBI. "I always defended the FBI, but not any more," he said.*[281]

My slim catch from the Gulf of Mexico

Presidents forced to give over actual notes, the Justice Department directly interfering in a major election, the president's personal experience with the FBI's dirty tricks—there certainly are similarities in the issues that affected the Bush White House and those that affected me.

Reading about this affords me some consolation as I sit 50 miles offshore in the Gulf of Mexico. If the tuna and tarpon were biting, I wouldn't be reading about others who have been abused by our federal criminal-justice system.

## Tuesday, August 28, 2001
## Baton Rouge, Louisiana

This morning I did my usual exercise routine: a 20-minute stretch, a one-mile swim, and 30 minutes on an elliptical trainer (which is similar to a Stairmaster but easier on my sixty-one-year-old knees. For breakfast, I mixed a fruit drink in the blender—papaya, strawberries, an apple, nonfat yogurt, soy protein powder, apple-cider vinegar, orange juice, and ice.

More than seven months have passed since my sentencing, and we still haven't received the official transcript of the trial. Mary Jane

[281] Ibid. 220.

Marcantel called to say it should be filed by next week. So we are close to a date for filing my appeal.

Bill Jeffress and I talked at length this morning about appeal issues. We are limited to 50 pages in our brief to the Fifth Circuit Court of Appeals. That sounds like a lot, but we have a number of issues to cover and will have to work hard to get all of our support data into the 50-page limit.

Whether a defendant has one issue or 40 to appeal, he is still limited to 50 pages. This makes no sense, but neither do many of the rules I must live with. Every time I read the 3,000-page transcript of the trial, I discover some new issue that could be helpful.

In reading over FBI agent Harry Burton's testimony, I note that he states that he never goes back to a witness after an interview to see if the information he has written down is correct. Bill Jeffress quizzed Burton about this procedure on the witness stand during my trial:

**Question:** *Agent Burton, when you made your 302 [typewritten statement], did you show it to Jim Brown and ask him, "Is this accurate?"*

**Answer:** *No, sir.*

**Question:** *Did you go to Mr. Myers, Mr. Brown's attorney, and show him the 302 and ask, "Brad, is this accurate?"*

**Answer:** *No, sir, I have never done something like that.*[282]

Burton is saying that once the interview is completed, the policy of the FBI is that agents do not go back to someone being interviewed to be sure what they put down was correct. Of course, Burton is wrong! That's why we wanted to call attorney C.J. Blache as my witness. When Burton interviewed Blache in the Edwards riverboat-gaming trial, he made numerous mistakes. By Blache's count, 18 major mistakes were made in the notes that Burton wrote down. The FBI later sent another agent to re-interview Blache and make corrections.

In the Edwards riverboat trial, defense attorney Pat Fanning questioned FBI agent Hillary Rossman about her interview with C.J.

---

[282] *S.A. v. Brown et al.* No. 99-CR-151-B, MDLA, September 27, 2000, Tr. p. 1603.

Blache, in which she corrected the mistakes made by Burton and another FBI agent.

> **Question:** *Agent Rossman, does it happen from time to time that FBI agents such as yourself find it necessary to write supplemental 302s in order to correct mistakes made in prior interviews?*
>
> **Answer:** *I'm sure that happens from time to time.*
>
> **Question:** *It's not always the 302s are accurate. Would you agree with that?*
>
> **Answer:** *We're all human, and we write a lot of 302s and I'm sure there are some that have errors in them.*[283]

Rossman, of course, found numerous errors in the C.J. Blache statement taken by Burton and another FBI agent. Yet Judge Clement would not allow Bill Jeffress to put C.J. Blache on the stand to talk about the errors made by Burton. This should be a strong issue for us on appeal.

I also pointed out to Bill Jeffress several errors made by Judge Clement that I had discovered in reading the transcript. Clement told the jury I was not to get Burton's handwritten notes because that's the law in the Fifth Circuit Court of Appeals, which includes the courts in Louisiana. Clement looked right at the jury and told them that.

> **The Court:** *Ladies and gentlemen, before trial we had a pre-trial motion in limine as to whether handwritten notes that are recorded contemporaneously with the FBI interview are something that needs to go to the defense lawyers, and the law in the circuit is that they do not because what they get is the finished product, the typed product.*[284]

---

[283] *U.S.A. v. Edwards et al.l. No.* 98-165-B-M3, MDLA, March 3, 2001, Transcript p. 142.

[284] *U.S.A. v. Brown et al. No.* 99-165-B-M3, MDLA, September 27, 2000. Tr. p. 1609

Unfortunately, Clement was dead wrong. The Fifth Circuit has never ruled on a defendant getting handwritten notes involving false statements. When Clement told the jury that my not getting the notes was "the law in this circuit," she was giving false information to the jury. This also should be an important issue in my appeal.

When it came to the handwritten notes that Burton took in his interview with Ron Weems, Judge Clement had no problem with letting the notes go to Weems. As Clement said in open court: "If the notes are consistent with the 302, what's the harm?" Well, Judge, let me ask you a question. If it were okay for Ron Weems to get the handwritten notes of Burton, then why wouldn't you allow me to have the handwritten notes from my interview? I would agree with the judge that if the notes are consistent with the typewritten statement (the 302), then "What's the harm?"[285] But what if the notes are not consistent? What if the notes taken by Burton were different from what he typed out? Wouldn't that be all the more reason to make them available? It would show that Burton was writing one thing at the actual interview and something different when he typed his statement. And that's exactly what happened in the case of Ron Weems.

In the handwritten notes that Burton took during his interview with Ron, words "mediator" and "to mediate" were used in describing the role that Edwards played in the Cascade case. Yet the words "mediator" and "mediate" do not appear in the typed 302.

But there are even more astounding inconsistencies. In the handwritten notes, Burton quotes Ron Weems as saying that Edwards was "hired by Disiere" for $100,000. But the typewritten statement makes no mention of Disiere hiring Edwards. In fact, Burton's typed statement says, "Weems acknowledged that he hired Edwin Edwards to assist him." There is no mention in Burton's typed statement that Disiere hired Edwards. When Ron Weems took the stand to testify, he stated that Shreveport attorney Joe Cage had actually hired Disiere.[286]

The indictment itself also contradicts what Burton wrote in his typewritten statement. The prosecutors charged in the indictment that Disiere hired Edwards.[287] Burton's handwritten notes were contradicted three times – by Ron Weems on the stand, by the

---

[285] Ibid. 1610.
[286] Ibid. 2038-39.
[287] Ibid. Indictment, September 24, 1999, p. 13.

indictment prepared by the prosecutors, and by Burton's own typewritten statement.

The conclusion is obvious – whether on purpose or through sloppiness – Harry Burton makes a lot of mistakes.

## Saturday, September 1, 2001
## Baton Rouge, Louisiana

If I had been forced by Judge Clement to actually go to prison on February 1$^{st}$, I would just be finishing my six-month term and returning to Baton Rouge today. What a blessing that fairness and justice prevailed and I was allowed to stay free on bond and work on my appeal. How sad it would have been to miss out on so many things during the past six months.

I have spent literally hundreds of hours working on my appeal with needed resources. I could have done limited research in prison but would not have had access to a computer, a fax machine, a full library, immediate telephone access to my attorneys and other advisers, and other important tools that are part of the research effort.

And I would have missed time with family and friends. I wouldn't have seen my son James take the basketball the length of the court and score an important basket against archrival Episcopal High School. I wouldn't have enjoyed weekend visits with my daughters, flying in from around the country, hearing their successes, sharing in their experiences, and trying to be an important component in their lives.

I would have missed out on spending a week at the beach with my mother and our family at the annual Brown vacation. I would have missed dinners with Gladys, family, and friends as we tried out every new restaurant in Baton Rouge. I would have missed our exercise sessions at the LSU stadium twice a week, walking up and down the steps with Gladys and a host of friends, followed by Saturday morning breakfast at Louie's and Wednesday night dinner at Serrano's.

I would have missed Friday night movies; Sunday morning visits to Coffee Call with the regulars, and reading hardbound books. That's right! In prison, you cannot receive hardbound books in the mail unless they come directly from the publisher. I always have a backlog of books to read and a personal library of several thousand books. But prison regulations would not allow me to receive any of these books by mail or through delivery by a family member.

It's good to have been free these past six months. I guess everyone remembers Janis Joplin's "Me and Bobby McGee," where she sings about being "busted flat in Baton Rouge." She sings, "freedom's just another word for nothing left to lose."[288] But she's wrong. I had a great deal to lose. I'm glad I had the time to do whatever I wanted to do, time to be free.

## Thursday, September 6, 2001
## Baton Rouge, Louisiana

After waiting for more than seven months, I got word today from the Fifth Circuit Court of Appeals in New Orleans that the transcript is finally complete. So much for speedy justice! My legal team of Bill Jeffress, Camille Gravel, and Mary Jane Marcantel must have my legal brief, outlining all the reasons why I should have my conviction thrown out, prepared and filed by November. The prosecutors will have 30 days to respond, and we will then have 15 days to reply. So, the Fifth Circuit should file all documents for review by early next year. A three-judge panel will be selected, and a date will be set when both sides will present oral arguments. I've said all along that I hope to be back in my job as insurance commissioner by the summer. I'm still hopeful that will happen.

Bill, Mary Jane, and I had a lengthy phone conference this morning about Harry Burton's interview with Ron Weems. Mary Jane has made a detailed, side-by-side comparison between Burton's handwritten notes and his typed 302. There are numerous differences. In fact, it's obvious that Burton has embellished his 302 and added many things that Ron Weems never told him.

The most glaring contradiction is who hired Edwards. In his handwritten notes, Burton writes that Disiere hired Edwards. In the typed version, done three weeks later, Burton says that Weems hired Edwards.

There are a number of such inconsistencies, but the major differences that jump out to any observer is how Burton injects my

---

[288] Joplin, Janis. Me and Bobby McGee. Pearl, words and music by Kris Kristofferson, Columbia Records, 1971.

name into the typewritten statement when no references to me appear in the handwritten notes. In one dramatic instance, the handwritten notes state, "He [Edwards] was asked to try to communicate with Judge Sanders to see if we could settle the matters." When Burton typed up these notes, he changed the context to read, "Edwards was asked by Weems and Disiere to communicate with Judge Sanders and Insurance Commissioner Jim Brown to see if they could help settle the matter of Cascade." I'm not mentioned at all in the handwritten version written when Burton was talking directly to Weems. But when Burton typed up his own version three weeks later, he conveniently injected my name.

Later in the typewritten statement, Burton says, "Edwards on a number of occasions told Weems of his efforts on their behalf, indicating to Weems that he had discussions and meetings with Sanders and Brown concerning the civil issues and the desire of Weems and Disiere to settle the matter out of court." There is no reference in the handwritten notes to Edwards making any such statement about my having discussions about settling the matter. Again, this information was injected by Burton.

Burton was either confused about what he had written down, or he purposely distorted what Ron Weems said. I have recommended to Bill Jeffress that he use this information in the appeal.

Friends in Memphis forwarded an Associated Press article to me in today's e-mail:

> *"A federal judge has agreed to take a six-month leave and receive counseling to avoid a hearing for alleged mistreatment of lawyers, including a claim he grabbed an attorney by the lapels during a courtroom altercation."*[289]

Now let me get this straight. The judge takes a six-month leave of absence, no doubt to avoid sanctions by a higher court and possible impeachment, because he "grabbed an attorney by the lapels." Talk about uneven justice. In my case, a prosecutor physically assaults my lawyer and is not even admonished by Judge Clement. I've made a note to buy a pair of boxing gloves and send them to Bill Jeffress for

---

[289] Associated Press, August 31, 2001.

Christmas, just in case he ever appears in Judge Clement's court again.

## Tuesday, September 11, 2001
## Baton Rouge, Louisiana

*I have watched through a window a world that has fallen.*[290]
W. H. Auden

Today's date, 9/11, turned into the frantic dialing of 911. A surreal feeling of shock and helplessness enveloped me as I watched the day's events unfold. Denise Cassano called at home a little after 8:00 A.M. central time to tell me about the first plane's crashing into the World Trade Center. Like millions of Americans, I turned on my television just in time to see the second plane hit the second tower.

I was home alone, so I immediately felt the need to call the people closest to me. I was able to reach my mother, my brother Jack, and my daughters Gentry and Meredith; I told them all to turn on their TV sets. I reached James on his portable phone as he was entering the LSU Lab School. But, what about Campbell? I knew she had flown back to Washington late last night from California, where she was doing a story on the retirement of the president's plane, a former Air Force One. Perhaps she was still home. I called her apartment but got no answer. Then the third plane hit the Pentagon in Washington. Thoughts raced through my head. Was there a fourth plane—or more? Wasn't the White House a likely target? Was my oldest daughter sitting in her NBC office in the White House?

Her portable phone didn't answer. I called the White House switchboard, which is noted for being efficient. There was a brief recording saying to hold on for an operator; then the line went dead. For a moment I feared the worst: a plane crashing into the White House, my daughter inside. Then I heard Matt Lauer on the "Today Show" say, "Now let's go to Campbell Brown for an update across the street from the White House." Campbell told a national audience that the White House had been evacuated and she was broadcasting from a nearby hotel. She gave hourly reports throughout the day and late into the evening.

---

[290] W. H Auden, *The Age of Anxiety* (New York, Random House, 1946).

After staying glued to the TV all day, Gladys and I kept a long-standing dinner date with friends at Chris's steakhouse. Halfway through dinner, around 9:00 o'clock, my portable phone rang. It was James. "Dad, I'm still watching everything on television," he said. "I just need to do something. Do we have an American flag here at home?" I told him we had one stored in our "flag box," where we keep banners for the various seasons, as well as holiday flags for Christmas, Halloween, and Easter. When Gladys and I drove into our driveway that night, a large American flag was hanging from the front porch, waving in the wind.

## Wednesday, September 12, 2001
## Baton Rouge, Louisiana

It's still not possible to reach offices and homes in New York City by phone, but I was able to reach several friends on their portable phones. Many of them work in the Wall Street district, and we have often gathered at the top of the World Trade Center for lunch during insurance meetings.

The news is not good concerning my friend Neil Levin, who until recently was New York's insurance commissioner. Several months ago, he took a new job as executive director of the Port Authority of New York and New Jersey, which is the landlord for the World Trade Center complex. His new office was on the 53 floor of the North Tower, the first tower to be hit. Neil is missing, and there is little hope that he will be found.[291]

When I talked to friends in New York, we speculated about the insurance costs that were incurred. Hurricane Andrew, who hit the Gulf Coast in 1992, cost insurance companies more than fifteen billion dollars. We all agree that the catastrophe at the World Trade Center will cost significantly more than this, perhaps approaching twenty-five billion.

I called key staff members in my office and suggested they contact the National Association of Insurance Commissioners. A task force should be formed immediately of key insurance regulators throughout the country to anticipate the wide range of problems that

---

[291] Neil's body was never found in the wreckage. A lengthy obituary, which paid tribute to his many accomplishments, appeared in the *New York Times* on September 22, 2001.

must be dealt with. Who has the responsibility to pay? Are there exclusions that will be asserted by insurance companies because the president has called this disaster "an act of war?" Are such clauses legal? Issues like these have never been faced in our country.

Is there liability on the part of the airlines? Should they have done more to protect against this type of terrorist activity? Does the United States government have that responsibility? What about the businesses in nearby buildings whose operations have been shut down? Do they have "business loss" claims? Numerous issues need to be addressed, and key commissioners should start gathering vital information as soon as possible. I also suggested that Louisiana should be made part of any such task force.

Since I was first elected commissioner in 1991, Louisiana has always participated in task forces and committees dealing with the national and international insurance problems. We are one of seven states that are part of the International Holocaust Commission, and we are one of several key states that worked out solvency problems affecting Lloyd's of London and other giant insurance companies. In fact, it was on such task forces that Neil Levin and I first started working together, and we became good friends. My department has always been part of finding solutions to these major problems, and I want Louisiana to be part of the solution to this overwhelming crisis.

Heavy criticism has been directed at the FBI for its failure to anticipate the acts of these terrorists. National newscasters have interviewed experts on international terrorism who question how these terrorists could so easily make their way in to the United States, use American schools to learn how to fly, and create such destruction and terror.

The *New Orleans Times-Picayune* was particularly critical of the FBI. Their "slash and burn" columnist, James Gill, didn't hold back:

> *But the FBI is supposed to keep tabs on terrorists. If they can be caught entirely unawares by a foreign plot that obviously required meticulous planning and constant radio and telephone contact, then we are entitled to ask what they are good for.*
>
> *The FBI has been more or less a laughing stock in recent years.*

*Not long after planes hit both towers of the World Trade Center, viewers might have been startled by news that the FBI's counter-terrorist hotshots were "stranded" in California, where they were apparently studying what to do in the event that a bunch of zealots should decide, say, to blow up buildings in New York and Washington.*

*We may never know whether it was just coincidence that these attacks came when the terrorism specialists were on the other side of the country. All we know for sure is that the terrorists could not have known less about American intelligence than American intelligence knew about the terrorists. Nobody was talking about the "efficiency" or the "sophistication" of the FBI yesterday.*[292]

Several friends have asked if I relish the criticism being directed at the FBI, but I find no solace or satisfaction in it. No, they were not at all fair with me. Yes, significant internal housecleaning is being called for, and rightly so. But we need an organization like the FBI to effectively protect all of us from similar future catastrophes. I hope Congress will scrutinize these numerous past mistakes and see that the proper safeguards are put into place.

In the meantime, we have a lot of questions to ask, and a lot of consoling to do. How can it be possible that there is such intense hatred for our country? Who is our enemy, and how do we do battle with them? Just a few days ago, life was so normal and ordinary. Now, for many of us, life will never be the same.

## Monday, October 15, 2001
## Baton Rouge, Louisiana

There have been a number of news stories over the past few weeks analyzing the physical and emotional health of Judge Frank Polozola. It is alleged that, at the same time Polozola was making key decisions in both the Edwards case and my case, he was claiming "impairment of function" in a lawsuit over a 1997 auto accident. The judge claims in his lawsuit (against his own insurance company) he

---

[292] *Times-Picayune,* September 12, 2001.

319

had severe injuries including, "impairment of function," "mental anguish," and "pain and suffering" as a result of the multi-vehicle accident.[293] Columnist John Hill of the Gannett News Service wrote, "Prescription records show that Polozola filled prescriptions for Oxycontin, a prescription painkiller, in late spring and the summer of 1999."[294]

Deductbox.com reported, "During the EWE case, Polozola was seeing a psychiatrist, two psychologists, an internist, a urologist, others. Two of his doctors have said in deposition they advised Polozola to reduce his workload."[295]

Oxycontin is being investigated all over the country. Just recently, Attorney General Mike Fisher of Pennsylvania stated, "Oxycontin is a highly addictive drug which, when abused, can produce the same effect on a person as heroin." Fisher said that it is increasingly being sold on the black market and is known as "hillbilly heroin."[296]

Judge Polozola's physical and mental state certainly concerns me, because they could have had an effect on decisions he rendered in my case. It was Judge Polozola who issued a gag order minutes after I was indicted. It was Judge Polozola who would not even have a hearing on the legality of the wiretaps. If he was under the influence of drugs that affected his physical and mental condition, then a serious question can be raised about whether his decisions were fair to me.

John Hill raised these issues in a Sunday column that appeared in Gannett newspapers throughout the state.

> *The long-running serio-comedic story took a surprising twist this past week when Gannett newspapers reported U.S. Judge Frank Polozola was pressing a personal injury lawsuit saying he was impaired and mentally anguished at the same time he was making decisions in the case.*
>
> *Subpoenaed records from a drug store showed Polozola filled prescriptions for the powerful painkiller Oxycontin in 1999. Those records indicate he may have been taking the*

---

[293] *New Orleans Citibusiness,* October 1, 2001.
[294] *Monroe News-Star,* September 26, 2001.
[295] Deductbox.com, Wednesday, September 27, 2001.
[296] Political1.com/Pennsylvania, July 25, 2001.

*prescribed medication at the time he suggested the use of an anonymous jury.*

*Now, it seems the case also includes a deposition, which is sworn testimony, of Polozola in October 1999 about his claims of impairment. That's a very important time because of its relationship to his decision-making timeline.*

*A public servant's own words about the state of his health should be open to public scrutiny. A federal judge may have an appointment for life, but he still is a government employee accepting a rather substantial part of our federal tax dollars.*

*But Polozola wanted the deposition sealed because it contained "personal" information. Information about a politically appointed public official is of intense interest to those who go before him.*

*Under the U.S. Constitution, everyone is entitled to a fair trial.*

*The issue of Polozola's physical and mental acumen deserves public scrutiny. Polozola obviously doesn't want the scrutiny or he would not have asked it be sealed.*

*That's why Gannett's Capital Bureau requested...to allow the deposition to be made public.*[297]

I've asked my lawyers to monitor the Polozola investigation. We've known all along that he is considered a "prosecutor's judge." But if, by his own admission, he was "impaired and mentally anguished" because of his pain, if he was using a highly addictive drug and under psychiatric care, then serious questions can be raised about whether or not he issued fair rulings on issues I am now appealing.

---

[297] John Hill, *Louisiana Gannett News,* September 30, 2001.

A major ruling was issued today by the United States Court of Appeals for the Ninth Circuit (western states). The court reversed a conviction because of the "trial judge's alleged use of and addiction to marijuana during pre-trial, trial and sentencing proceedings, as evidenced by the judge's admission . . . deprived [the defendant] of due process of law."[298]

If the Ninth Circuit Court of Appeals was worried about marijuana, I wonder how they would feel about "hillbilly heroin" – just one more puzzling aspect of the soap opera that has become my life.

## Thursday, October 18, 2001
## Baton Rouge, Louisiana

Today, a brief, two-paragraph order came down from the Fifth Circuit Court of Appeals.

> *IT IS ORDERED that the motion of appellant [Brown] for leave to inspect and copy handwritten notes of FBI agent Harry Burton contained in the record under seal and to address their content in briefs and argument in this court is GRANTED.*[299]

After three years of continual efforts to obtain the handwritten notes of Harry Burton, the Fifth Circuit finally granted me relief. Judge E. Grady Jolly, a Mississippi Republican who was appointed by President Ronald Reagan, signed the order.[300] Two other members of the court joined Judge Jolly but his was the only signature on the order. It would be an understatement to say that I am delighted with the decision.

---

[298] *Summerlin v. Stewart*, No. 98-99002, U.S. Court of Appeals for the Ninth Circuit, 2001 U.S. App. LEXIS 21773, October 12, 2001.

[299] *Brown v. United States of America*, 01-30173, U.S. Court of Appeals for the Fifth Circuit, October 18, 2001.

[300] Judge Jolly also signed the February 26 order allowing me to stay out of prison. For a colorful account of how Jolly was appointed to the Fifth Circuit Court of Appeals, over the initial opposition of Mississippi Senator Trent Lott, see New Orleans author Curtis Wilkie's recent book *Dixie*. This political and social history of the Deep South also reviews the Edwards-Duke gubernatorial race of 1991. Curtis Wilkie, *Dixie* (New York: Scribner's, 2001).

This is the second time that Judge Clement has been reversed by the Fifth Circuit. There obviously is a feeling that I was unfairly denied these notes, and I hope this is a sign that there will be a favorable decision by the court once my appeal is filed. Bill Jeffress called to discuss the logistics. The notes will have to be sent from the District Court in Baton Rouge down to the Fifth Circuit, and it may take a day or two before we actually see what Burton wrote. There is no doubt in my mind that much of what Burton put in his typewritten report will either vary from his handwritten notes or not be written down at all.

This was a big victory. I believe I'm starting to see some light at the end of this long, long tunnel.

**Friday, October 19, 2001**
**Baton Rouge, Louisiana**

Each of my three daughters called this morning to talk about my good news from the Fifth Circuit.

Gentry is over her morning sickness and regaining her appetite. Her position as an advertising executive requires a lot of travel, and she is obviously pleased that her diet will now include more than mashed potatoes and oatmeal. The due date for my first grandchild is March 15, 2002.

Meredith called from Portland, where she is an emergency room nurse. She is dating a doctor who has season tickets to the Portland Trailblazers professional basketball team, and she has become a fan. I told her to insist that he take her to the Washington Wizards game when Michael Jordan comes to town.

Campbell just returned from China, where she was covering the president's visit. She hasn't received any mail in several weeks; all mail has been shut down at NBC News because of the anthrax scare. The terrorists are starting to hit close to home, and I can tell she's apprehensive.

I should get my copy of Burton's notes late today. I'm setting the weekend aside for a detailed review. I've also gone into the files and acquired a copy of attorney Brad Myers's notes. In retrospect, I realize that we made a strategic mistake in not calling Brad as a witness at my trial. My legal team mistakenly believed the prosecutors had done a poor job of arguing the false-statement counts, and they thought Brad's testimony would not be necessary. The prosecution did not call the second FBI agent who was at my interview, and my lawyers decided not to call Brad so as not to draw attention to the false-statement counts. My lawyers thought that if Brad were called as a witness, the other agent would be called in an attempt to contradict Brad.

In reviewing Brad's notes, I see that they could have been of great help. His testimony and his notes certainly would have made a significant difference. That's water over the dam, but I do want to compare the Brad Myers notes to the Burton notes. My gut feeling is that both sets of notes will dramatically differ from Burton's testimony at the trial.

## Friday, October 26, 2001
## Baton Rouge, Louisiana

> *I had found the truth, I had dug the truth up out of the ash pile, the*
> *garbage heap, the kitchen midden, the boneyard...I couldn't cut the*
> *truth to match his ideas well he'd have to make his ideas match the*
> *truth. The truth shall make you free.*
>
> Robert Penn Warren[301]

After trying repeatedly for more than two years to obtain the handwritten notes of Harry Burton, I was finally able to read them today. I was stunned! In statement after statement made by Burton, the notes do not back up the testimony he gave at the trial. In many instances, his own notes contradict Burton. And in other instances, his testimony at the trial about statements I supposedly made to him is found nowhere in the notes. Simply put, the notes dramatically undermine what Burton said at the trial, and they would have been devastating to the prosecution's case.

It is now quite obvious why the prosecutors fought so long and hard to keep me from seeing the notes. They knew full well that the notes differed dramatically from Burton's testimony and would contradict his typed statement prepared several days after our interview. His own notes contradict every charge against me, directly contradict his typewritten statement, and undermine his testimony at the trial.

---

[301] Robert Penn Warren, *All the King's Men* (New York: Harcourt Brace Jovanovich, 1946).

A typical example is his saying that I had not discussed "settlement issues or what it would take to settle the matter." At the trial, Burton swore that I made precisely this statement, and he further testified it was "contradictory to his [Brown's] own words on the tape and represents another false statement."[302]

He gave similar testimony about my denying discussing "settlement issues or what it would take to settle the matter" with Ron Weems, Judge Sanders, Edwin Edwards, and anyone else. I, of course, never told Burton that I had not discussed settlement issues or what it would take to settle the matter. I denied <u>negotiating</u> with these people or being part of the final settlement negotiations.

Burton insisted during the trial that I used the words "settlement issues" during my interview with him. His typewritten report on four

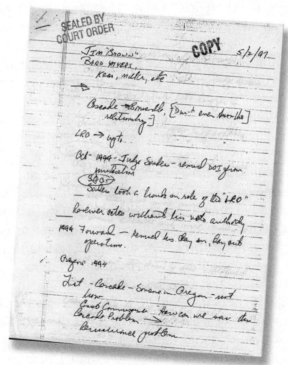

I finally receive a copy of the actual, handwritten notes.

---

[302] *U.S.A. v. Brown et al.*, No. 99-CR-151-B-M2 Tr. pp. 1578-7.

different occasions says that I denied discussing "settlement issues" with any of these individuals. <u>Four times.</u> But his contemporaneous notes make no reference to "settlement issues." That phrase appears nowhere in his notes. This is one of many glaring discrepancies between Burton's notes and his testimony that would have been devastating to the government's case and to the agent's credibility.

Burton also testified at the trial that I told him I was "only vaguely familiar with the Cascade Insurance Company,"[303] and he added, "He [Brown] was not telling me the truth." Yet his notes do not reflect any such statement by me, or anything remotely like it.

Additionally, Burton testified that I told him I "was not aware of any federal civil action that had been contemplated against David Disiere in December of 1996." Then Burton added, "He [Brown] lied."[304] Burton's own notes, however, reflect that I told him I had never <u>seen</u> the draft RICO suit. The tapes, and every other witness, back me up on this. Burton's own notes contradict his testimony at the trial.

In another charge, Burton testified, "Brown stated that he had not directed Robert Bourgeois to settle the Cascade matter."[305] Burton's notes, however, record a very different statement by me. "Never directed Bourgeois to settle the matter for a <u>specific amount</u>." This was another dramatic contradiction between Burton's testimony and what he wrote in his notes. There was no evidence whatever that I had directed Bourgeois to settle the Cascade case at all, let alone "for a specific amount." Burton's notes, if they had been made available to me, would have shown that his testimony at the trial was false.

On Count 51, I was convicted of denying to Burton that I had gone by Edwards's office to discuss the Cascade Insurance Company. Burton's exact testimony at the trial was, "I think I specifically asked him [Brown] if his conversations at Edwards's office related to Cascade, and he said, 'No.'"[306] Burton's own notes give a quite different version of what I said. The notes do not reflect any denial by me of discussing Cascade at Edwards' office.

Burton's notes reveal that I told him I had visited at Edwards' office while going out to my wife's restaurant, and that Edwards had

[303] Ibid. 1574.
[304] Ibid. 1575.
[305] Ibid. T. 1571.
[306] Ibid. Tr. 1572.

asked for some type of "form," and that the form had nothing to do with Cascade Insurance Company. I told Burton, as reflected in his notes, that I could not recall the nature of the form but it was "somewhat innocuous."

Burton's testimony, and his later typewritten statement change and distort what is in the notes by saying that I visited Edwards' office on "one occasion" and that the "conversation had nothing to do with Cascade Insurance Company or David Disiere." If we had had Burton's notes at the trial, my lawyers could have pointed out the direct contradiction between what Burton testified to and what his notes said. Bill and I talked at length this afternoon about the impact of the handwritten notes. We agreed that their importance in this appeal couldn't be overstated. We also agreed that our not having the notes undermined a central theory of my defense, which was that Burton, knowing exactly what was contained on the tapes and having a bias against me, deliberately crafted his typewritten statement to make up these false-statement charges.

As Bill Jeffress said in his opening statement, "After the interview, Mr. Burton twisted and misrepresented practically everything Jim Brown said in that interview in an effort to prosecute this offense called false statements."[307] But because we never were able to get Burton's notes, and were not even allowed to question him about their content, my defense was unfairly undermined. Virtually every damaging statement that appears in Burton's typewritten statements is not contained in the handwritten notes. Fortunately, we can argue all these issues at my appeal.

I have won an important victory by gaining access to the notes. But how unfair to have to wage such an effort over such a long period of time, and at such great personal and financial cost. Any American citizen deserves better.

**Tuesday, October 30, 2001**
**Baton Rouge, Louisiana**

*What we are obliged to do is make sure the truth comes out, not some exaggeration that would distort the truth.*[308]
William Safire

---

[307] Ibid. Tr. 477.
[308] William Safire, *Full Disclosure* (Garden City, N.Y.: Doubleday, 1977).

327

After reviewing thousands of documents, reading and re-reading the complete transcript of the trial, and doing months of research, my appeal brief is finished. Our appeal argues that the nondisclosure of Burton's notes was unlawful and denied me a fair trial. We argue at some length that the prosecutors had no choice but to give me Burton's notes and that numerous court decisions, federal laws, and judicial rules require these notes should have been made available to me.

In addition, we argue that Judge Clement's ruling forbidding my lawyers to cross-examine Burton on the content of his notes was a direct violation of the Sixth Amendment of the Constitution.

There is a detailed analysis of the notes. I felt our case for appeal was extremely strong without the notes. But the notes themselves should be devastating to the prosecution's case and to the credibility of Burton. It's hard to imagine the Fifth Circuit will not agree.

Our inability to call other witnesses who would challenge Burton's credibility was also raised. C.J. Blache would have testified in detail that Burton did not take accurate notes. Mistake after mistake was made by Burton in signing off on an interview he did with Blache. Yet Judge Clement would not let us cross-examine Burton on his past sloppiness in note taking.

We also raised the issue of why it was necessary for Judge Clement to order an anonymous jury. The Fifth Circuit Court of Appeals has never allowed an anonymous jury when the defendant was not in jail before the trial took place. In other words, it was allowed only when the person charged was so dangerous that he was not allowed to make bond and had to stay in jail until his trial. Usually, an anonymous jury is ordered in cases involving drug lords or mass murderers. As we stated in the brief: "Charging that a potential civil lawsuit was settled for less than it was worth is hardly the kind of case likely to stir the 'deep passions' that might call for an anonymous jury." Our brief went on to argue: "Many public officials in Louisiana and elsewhere have been tried on criminal charges generating extensive publicity without the 'drastic measure' of an anonymous jury."[309]

---

[309] *USA v. Brown*, USCA, 5th Cir., No. 01-30173.Brief for Appellant James H. Brown, 49.

Finally, my brief raises questions about the legality of the wiretaps themselves, particularly as they relate to Cascade Insurance Company. We argue that it is unlawful for the FBI to go on a fishing expedition and start listening in on private conversations of people they think may possibly have some criminal intent. And we argue that even though a federal judge authorized the wiretaps (months after the agents began listening in on Cascade conversations), the information given to the judge by the FBI was, in many cases, false.

The brief is 60 pages long, and I have been receiving requests throughout the day for copies. Lawyers and other interested citizens, both in Louisiana and throughout the country, are eager to hear my side of the story.

I am sure there will be commentaries by the news media. Their take will give some indication of public sentiment toward my appeal and the degree of support I can count on.

## Saturday, November 3, 2001
## Baton Rouge, Louisiana

I worked 16 hours a day this week helping Bill Jeffress and my legal team put the final touches on my appeal. It will be filed early next week.

I needed a way to let out pressures that have built up and my frustration (and sometimes outright rage) over all I had to go through to get Burton's notes. This morning, I found a diversion that temporarily took my mind off my legal challenges. I completed my first triathlon of the year.

At 8:00 A.M., I joined a pack of mostly Louisiana State University students in a sprint-distance triathlon that began on the LSU campus. It combined a 500-yard swim, a 15-mile bike ride, and a three-mile run. I completed the distance in a little less than two hours—not bad for an old guy. Halfway through the run, with my back aching, my knees throbbing, and my ankles in agony from pounding the pavement, the pressures of Cascade were far from my mind, at least temporarily.

Tomorrow morning, it's back to working on the appeal.

**Monday, November 12, 2001**
**Baton Rouge, Louisiana**

My appeal has officially been filed, and reaction has been swift. The press commentary has been quite favorable. *Times-Picayune* columnist James Gill made no bones about his take on my case:

> *Whether he wins or loses his appeal, Jim Brown got a raw deal in his federal trial last year.*
>
> *It was a cockamamie trial in any case, prosecutors adducing no credible evidence for their theory that Brown, former Gov. Edwin Edwards, and Shreveport attorney Ron Weems had concocted a sweetheart deal for the owner of a bankrupt company.*
>
> *Brown was the only defendant not to walk away scot-free, because before his indictment, he had agreed to an interview with FBI agent Harry Burton.*
>
> *Evidently Brown, not having committed any criminal offenses, did not suspect a trap. Poor sap. He should have learned at his mother's knee that innocent or guilty, you never, ever take chances with the FBI.*
>
> *Brown had no obvious reason to lie to Burton since, as the jury verdict established, he had nothing to hide. What Brown did not know, however, was that the feds had a bug on Edwards' phone and Burton was therefore asking questions to which he already knew the answers. The interview seems to have been little more than a trick to catch him in a lie.*
>
> *According to the defense, Burton, "having a bias against Jim Brown, deliberately crafted [his summary] to assist a false-statement prosecution." The appeal claims that Brown was convicted for statements that either do not appear at all in the handwritten notes or were doctored in the typewritten summary to make what was true appear to*

330

*be a lie. The appeal also argues that Brown was legally entitled to the handwritten notes at trial. Either way, it sure would have saved a lot of time and money if [Judge] Clement had let him take a gander.*[310]

Numerous headlines have summed up what happened to me. The *Monroe News Star* captioned its story, **"Brown Clearly Tried Unfairly."**

In Opelousas, the headline read, **"Tape Your FBI Chats,"** and the *Shreveport Times* also cautioned, **"If You Must Talk to the FBI, Tape the Conversation."**

John Hill's column in Gannett newspapers throughout the state concluded:

*Those who sat through the [Cascade] trial or followed it closely in the media quickly realized there was nothing to the charges. Some even felt the wrong persons were on trial.*

*Brown, Edwards, and Weems were acquitted of all substantive charges that they committed a crime. Brown, however, was convicted of lying to an FBI agent. (The government, fond of saying they "send a message" to the public with convictions succeeded only in sending the message no one should talk to an FBI agent.)*

*Now, here's the gig: Brown was convicted of lying to an agent – his word against the agent's.*

*And the convictions were based on the FBI agent's formal notes of an interview in Brown's office shortly after the case became public knowledge with the April 1997 raid of Edwards' home and offices.*

*There existed the agent's handwritten notes that were taken contemporaneously with the interview.*

---

[310] *Times-Picayune,* November 9, 2001.

331

*Now, here's a clear-cut violation of fair play and equal treatment under the law; the judge granted Weems' motion to get the handwritten notes of the agent who interviewed him—and he was acquitted of a charge of lying to an FBI agent. But Brown was consistently denied access to the original handwritten notes of his FBI agent.*

*So, what we had was one defendant gets the notes and was able to cross-examine the agent about the differences between the handwritten notes and the notes typewritten later. That defendant was acquitted. But Brown, the other defendant, doesn't get the notes—in the same trial, in the same courtroom. That immediately should violate everyone's sense of fair play.*

*The Fifth Circuit Court of Appeals ruled Brown should not serve six months in jail pending his appeal. That means the court reached the legal conclusion Brown had raised issues that are "likely" to result in a new trial or a judgment of acquittal. Strong stuff.*

*The message out of all of this is don't ever talk to an FBI agent. Or if you must talk to the FBI, have your attorney and a tape recorder right there.*[311]

Other media outlets throughout the state expressed similar views. I just hope that the strong public opinion in my favor will be acknowledged by the Fifth Circuit Court of Appeals and reflected in their opinion.

Good news also came today from my pollster Jim Kitchens in Orlando, Florida. My favorability rating is the same as it was just after my last election. The trial and my conviction have not eroded the public support I have maintained over the past two years. It's a good sign that Louisiana citizens understand; they know I did not get a fair trial and are hanging in there with me.

---

[311] *Shreveport Times*, November 12, 2001.

# 2002

The new Department of Insurance Building. I conceived the idea to build it, helped design it, and found the money from non-state sources to pay for it. Yet I will never serve the public here.

**Sunday, February 16, 2002**
**St. Francisville, Louisiana**

May 8th has been set as the date for oral arguments in my case—two days after my birthday. I hope that's a good omen.

My lawyers will travel to New Orleans to argue my case before the Fifth Circuit Court of Appeals. I have sent my appeal brief to interested lawyers throughout the state and the country. There is a strong consensus that my appeal has merit and that my conviction will be overturned. I suppose this reaction is to be expected from friends who are pulling for me. But it is good to know that respected lawyers share their view. I have three months to wait—time to read, to exercise, to "optimistically" prepare for my return to the insurance department, and to hope.

My daughters all called today.

Campbell leaves tomorrow with the president for a week's tour of Asia. She will be traveling 24 of the next 28 days, criss-crossing the country and the world. Even at her age, I ask, how does she like the hectic pace? Her response is immediate. "Dad, I'm having the best time of my life!"

Gentry is still working, with only three weeks to go until my first grandchild is due. She is putting up a good front, but I can tell from her voice that she is uncomfortable. We talked over names for the new baby, particularly if it's a girl. I'm lobbying hard for "Sweetie Pearl," which was the name of my dad's mother. It's a tough sell. But whatever Gentry and Michael name her (assuming it's a girl), I'm sure I will call her Sweetie Pearl.

Meredith announced that she is quitting her job in Portland and hopes to leave soon to travel throughout South America. She plans to study Spanish and work as a nurse in rural areas. Her mother is apprehensive about this plan, and so am I. But I still give her encouragement. This is the time of her life when she has the freedom to seek out special experiences. Besides, she's bullheaded like me, and she seems to have her mind made up.

Three months seems like a long time until I realize that it has been 15 months since my conviction. The time will pass rapidly.

**Wednesday, March 20, 2002**
**Memphis, Tennessee**

My first grandchild arrived at 3:24 this afternoon—a baby girl weighing eight pounds, fourteen ounces. Her name is Baylor Hayes Brann, but I've already started calling her Sweetie Pearl.

Gladys and I drove up this morning from Baton Rouge, arriving an hour before our newest family member was born. Gentry's induced labor lasted all day, but she handled the procedure well and was greeting all of us with smiles and hugs shortly after Sweetie Pearl's arrival. She has lots of dark hair, long fingernails, and she started nursing right away.

Holding my first grandchild. What a blessing and a great joy for our family.

This experience was very special. It's like I moved up another notch when I became a grandfather. I wonder what she will call me? Probably "Papa Jim," which is what my children called my dad.

I'm really looking forward to being a grandfather. This experience will be more meaningful than anyone really knows. I loved the early years of my four children and have many fond memories of their childhoods. But I also realize how quickly they grew up while I was spending lots of time—too much time—slaying dragons and jousting with windmills. I am excited about the possibilities of her life

335

stretching far out in the years to come. And I hope I can play a significant role in helping to mold a bright future for her.

But I also had another reaction—I'm not old enough to be a grandfather. Doesn't being a grandfather mean that the clock is past high noon and I am in the afternoon of my life? I swim two miles a day and run triathlons—but I am sixty-two years old. That's not really old, and I actually have a better perspective on the things that are really important – the chance to reach for whatever I have missed along the way. So maybe it really is the best time to be a grandfather.

Second, there is nothing like having grandchildren to restore your faith in heredity. She really does look like me. (I wonder if her eyes will stay blue?). So do all of my four children. It looks like the genes have come through well.

And third, I've already decided which new responsibilities I will take on. When Sweetie Pearl comes to visit, Gladys can be in charge of toilet training and tantrums. I will be in charge of treats and tall tales. Now *that* seems like a pretty good arrangement.

As grandparents, siblings, nieces, and nephews gather around her bed, Gentry holds and nurses our new family member. My daughter glows, she seems to radiate with feelings of continuity and belonging. As I watch her, the message is clear: this is my family. These are the ones who love me and will stand by me. This is how we do things. This is where we matter so much and where we get the strength and pride we need to carry on.

I don't think a father could be more proud.

## Saturday, April 13, 2002
## Oxford, Mississippi

This is my second day at the University of Mississippi, where I'm attending the Oxford Conference for the Book, a series of lectures and panel discussions on contemporary southern literature. There have also been seminars by prominent southern reporters on regional and national issues.

After yesterday's program, I made the 45-mile trip to Memphis to spend the night with Gentry, Michael, and "Sweetie Pearl." My three-week-old granddaughter spent most of the evening in my arms, giving Gentry a needed break and allowing me the pleasure of holding one of my own, something I had not done for many years.

I drove back to Oxford this morning. During a mid-morning lecture on Tennessee Williams, my portable phone buzzed. Campbell had been the sole host on the "Today Show" earlier this morning, and she was calling for a critique. I had watched her as I sipped coffee at a local restaurant, and I reported that she seemed relaxed and solidly in control. I slipped out of the auditorium and we talked for a while, particularly about our mutual concern of Meredith's going to Guatemala. Campbell will spend a week with her there in July.

Louisiana author Curtis Wilkie moderated an afternoon panel on "Covering Times of Trouble." His introductory remarks included comments about the "deceit of the Justice Department," particularly in times of war. "In war, truth is the first casualty," Wilkie said. (He later told me of his friendship with Judge Grady Jolly, who had allowed me to stay out of jail, and said Jolly would not have signed such an order unless he believed my trial had not been conducted fairly.)

*Los Angeles Times* columnist Jack Nelson was on the panel and talked about his experience with "the lies of the FBI." Nelson published a book in 1970, *The Orangeburg Massacre,* about student discontent relating to the civil rights crisis in the late 1960s. He talks at length about "FBI agents who misled Justice Department officials during a federal investigation," and "obvious lying by FBI agents to cover up a deadly assault" at South Carolina State College. Nelson, who won a Pulitzer Prize for local reporting in 1960, made no bones about what happened. "The FBI set up a death trap," he said. "They stood by while South Carolina State Troopers shot innocent people in the back."

I'm making no special effort to gather information about abuses or atrocities by the FBI. My problem has been with one local agent. But it amazes me that I can't even slip away to a college book conference without hearing about illegal activity by the FBI.

## Monday, April 29, 2002
## New Orleans, Louisiana

The three-judge panel that will hear my appeal was announced today. The consensus among the lawyers who argue cases before the Fifth Circuit is that my panel has moderate to conservative leanings. Every state in the country is part of a specific circuit to hear all appeals. There are 12 circuits throughout the United States; the Fifth Circuit is made up of 20 judges from Louisiana, Texas, and Mississippi. There is a balance in the number of judges from each of these states, although the Fifth Circuit is based in New Orleans. Under the rules of each circuit, a three-judge panel is normally randomly selected to hear cases on appeal from any district court.

Two of the three judges on my panel are from Louisiana, and I consider this is a slight advantage. The facts of my case are complicated. Normally, the judges in question know nothing more than what they read in the transcripts, and this can sometimes be confusing. But there is some chance that two of the three judges have followed my case in the Louisiana press. Since there have been so many supportive columns on my behalf, I hope the panel gets the full picture of my unfair conviction.

Judge Eugene Davis is based in Lafayette, although he lives in New Iberia. He was appointed by President Ronald Reagan in 1973 and is a Republican. Judge Carl Stewart is from Shreveport and was appointed by President Clinton in 1994. The third judge is from Texas, Emilio Garza of San Antonio. He was appointed by President Bush in 1991 and is viewed as perhaps a little more pro-government. A Texas magazine recently reported that President Bush as a possible future appointment to the U.S. Supreme Court would consider Garza. The magazine refers to him as "a hard-shell conservative."[312]

A number of press reports refer to the Fifth Circuit as "a conservative body that tends to favor prosecutors." The news stories generally go on to point out that several major rulings in my favor have been made by conservative Republicans.

*In fact, three Republican judges on the Fifth Circuit signed the February 2001 order allowing Brown to remain free while he challenges his appeal. And in October, another Republican, Judge Grady Jolly, forced federal prosecutors to let Brown see the FBI agent's handwritten notes that were used to convict him of lying.*

*During the trial, Brown was limited to a typed report, adapted from the notes of the agent who interviewed him.*

---

[312] *Shreveport Times,* November 12, 2001.

> *"Judge Jolly is viewed as a conservative member of the court and a judge who frequently votes to support the government's position," Rosenberg said. Since he voted against the government on a key issue such as the notes, Rosenberg added, "This seems to be a race you can't really handicap."*[313]

We have also been concerned about the fact that Judge Edith Clement is now a member of the Fifth Circuit Court of Appeals. This means that colleagues with whom she serves on a regular basis will review her work and, I hope, conclude that she made major errors in her rulings on the district court. We are concerned that she may try, in some way, to influence my panel merely by her presence. It will be a major blow to her reputation if my panel rules against her.

Former New Orleans United States Attorney Harry Rosenberg was quoted in the local press as saying that he doesn't think this is a problem.

> *"Rosenberg said he does not think Brown needs to be concerned that Edith Brown Clement, who presided over the trial while a U.S. district judge and originally denied him access to the handwritten notes, has since been appointed to the Fifth Circuit. 'When you get to any court of appeals, I don't think they're going to let personalities or deferences to their colleagues affect how they interpret the law.'"*[314]

I remain skeptical of Rosenberg's conclusions. These judges are going to have to work with Clement not just on one case and not just for a few years. They all have lifetime appointments; they are going to have to work with her for the rest of their lives. Anyone who thinks her influence won't be felt on the decision in my case is not being realistic.

Our oral argument before this panel of judges has been set for next Wednesday, May 8. My lawyers tell me that each of the three

---

[313] *Times-Picayune*, April 30, 2002.
[314] Ibid.

judges will read all the briefs and support documents and be well prepared to ask questions.

## Thursday, May 2, 2002
## Baton Rouge, Louisiana

Today Bill Jeffress sent down a lengthy internal analysis of my appeal prepared by one of his partners in the Washington office. The lawyers are trying to anticipate questions that may be raised by the three-judge panel next week.

One of the points made by the prosecutors in their written argument was that it would be extremely burdensome for FBI agents to have to keep all the rough notes they made in an investigation. In support of their position, their brief cites a commentary to Rule 16 of the Federal Rules of Criminal Procedure. When these rules were written in the early 1990s, an advisory committee of attorneys and judges added a written commentary explaining the intent of the rule. The explanation by the advisory committee states:

> *"The written record need not be a transcription or summary of the defendant's statement but must only be some written reference which would provide some means to identify the statement. Otherwise, the prosecution would have the difficult task of locating and disclosing the myriad oral statements made by a defendant, even if <u>it had no intention of using the statements at trial</u> ... that task could become unduly burdensome."*[315]

Of course the prosecutors are stretching beyond the limit what the advisory committee is saying. No one expects the prosecutors to turn over every single scrap of paper, or a record of every oral statement, particularly if they have no intention of using the statement at trial. But what I am asking for is a far cry from the limitations suggested in Rule 16. My lawyers have pointed out in my brief that there are certainly legitimate reasons to give the defendant the handwritten notes of an FBI agent. In my case, the handwritten notes were the

---

[315] Federal Rules of Criminal Procedure, Rule 16(a)(1)(A), Advisory Committee, (1991 Amendment).

foundation for a typed statement that was used as evidence against me, evidence that I had made false statements. In my case, the handwritten notes are the <u>only</u> contemporary evidence available.

If the notes had been destroyed, so be it. But they were not. They were preserved. And, lo and behold, they dramatically differed from the typewritten statement prepared three days later by the FBI agent.

The actual notes were not just important to my case; they were much more than that. They were the very foundation on which my defense rested and on which the prosecution's case should have been made. Rule 16 is a "good faith" test that is clear to any neutral reader. If the notes are available and critical to the prosecution's case and the defense's case, they should be produced.

Bill Jeffress will have to make the strong distinction when he presents his oral argument next Wednesday.

**Monday, May 6, 2002**
**New Orleans, Louisiana**

Today, an extraordinary letter was sent out that raises my hopes and gives me some encouragement. The deputy clerk of the Fifth Circuit Court of Appeals sent the letter to Stephen Higginson with the U.S. Attorney's Office in New Orleans. Higginson handles appeals for the prosecutors, and he will be arguing their case before the Fifth Circuit on Wednesday. The letter reads:

*Dear Mr. Higginson:*
> *The court has directed that you respond to appellant's reply brief and present your specific arguments as to why the discrepancies between Agent Burton's notes and his 302 listed in Appendix A of that brief would not have been helpful to appellant's counsel in impeaching Agent Burton's testimony. Your letter of response should be filed by 4:00 P.M., Tuesday, May 7, 2002.*
>> *Charles A. Fulbruge, III, Clerk*
>> *United States Court of Appeals*
>> *Fifth Circuit [316]*

---

[316] *USA v. Brown et al.*, No. 013-173, U.S. Fifth Circuit Court of Appeals, May 6, 2002.

The letter from the three-judge panel is saying they have concluded there are discrepancies between Burton's notes and his 302. Until now, the prosecutors and Burton have said repeatedly that there were no discrepancies, that the notes and the typewritten 302 statement were the same. But it is obvious from reading the two documents that they are vastly different. It seems that, for the first time in this terrible process, judges who are at last raising questions that should have been addressed at my trial are reviewing my case.

**Tuesday, May 7, 2002**
**New Orleans, Louisiana**

Gladys and I met my legal team this evening for dinner at Antoine's in the French Quarter. Upon arriving, Bill Jeffress handed me the prosecutors' response to our argument that Burton's handwritten notes would have been extremely helpful to my defense.[317] As expected, it was 10 pages of rambling references, often to testimony or law that was irrelevant to the judges' request. The judicial request was very clear: tell the court why the obvious differences between Burton's handwritten notes and his later typewritten statement would not have been significantly helpful to Brown's defense. You really couldn't get an answer by reading the prosecutors' response. The document was full of errors, often contradicted itself, and certainly gave a false impression of what happened at the trial.

But the brief was cleverly misleading, and it could confuse the judges about what actually happened. The brief is strong on the point that the judges do not have that much discretion. The prosecutors argue that federal rules allow only the typewritten notes, not the handwritten notes. What they want the court to conclude is that the handwritten notes are irrelevant. Whatever the notes say, even though they contradict the typewritten final statement of the FBI agent, they can't be used to help me. What a terrible injustice it will be if the court accepts this view.

Camille Gravel and his wife Evelyn Gravel joined us at dinner, as did Mary Jane Marcantel and my brother Jack. Bill Jeffress pointed out that we are not going to have enough time tomorrow to do much

---

[317] Ibid, Prosecutors Response to the Court, May 7, 2002.

342

more than answer specific questions from the judges. Each side is only given 20 minutes, and any judge can jump in at any time and ask questions, related or unrelated to what is being argued. I hope Bill's strong brief will have already answered a number of questions that could be asked. We should get some indication of the judges' leaning by the tone and tenor of their questions. What issues concern them? Are there any danger signs? Are there differences of opinion among the judges that might split their vote? By tomorrow, these questions should be answered.

## Wednesday, May 8, 2002
## New Orleans, Louisiana

Gladys and I arrive at the Fifth Circuit Court of Appeals in New Orleans.

*Photo by Travis Spradling*
*The Advocate*

There was standing room only in the Fifth Circuit courtroom on the second floor of the courthouse. Gladys and I arrive 15 minutes before the 9:00 A.M. hearing, along with our son James, Gladys' sister Gloria and my brother Jack. I was gratified that many friends from both New Orleans and Baton Rouge were there; so many, in fact, that half of them could not get into the courtroom and had to stand in the hallway. Attorneys Mike Small from Alexandria and Eddie Castaing from New Orleans were both there. Mike had represented Governor Edwards in the initial trial and Eddie had represented Ron Weems. Just before the trial began, my legal team counted the prosecutors and FBI agents in the courtroom. They recognized 26 different employees of the Department of Justice. It's ironic—we can't find Osama bin Laden, we have no idea who is sending mail laced with anthrax all over the country, drug dealers are overrunning our state, yet 26 prosecutors and agents have nothing better to do than to hang out at my appeal hearing. I didn't realize I was such a major threat to the safety of our country.

343

The judicial panel entered the courtroom, and Judge Eugene Davis of Lafayette gave a few opening instructions. He sat in the center and is apparently the chief judge of the panel. He immediately called on Bill Jeffress to begin his argument.

Bill explained that I was denied access to the handwritten notes until well after the trial. He argued that the handwritten notes varied significantly from Burton's later typewritten notes. "It was simply not a fair fight," Bill said. "This would have been a far different case with a different outcome if we could have seen the notes, and how they differed from the typewritten statement."

Twenty minutes went by quickly, and Bill got no further than a discussion of the notes. In our written brief, we had raised a number of other issues, including the legality of the wiretaps, how improper an anonymous jury was in my case, and the unfairness of our not being able to fully cross-examine Burton. I hope the panel will reread our written brief in some detail.

Assistant U.S. Attorney Steve Higginson began his argument for the other side. He continued his "bob and weave" approach and did not actually address the issue of how the notes would have helped me. It's hard to read what the judges are thinking, but each member of the court asked positive questions. Judge Garza, for instance, asked Higginson, "Would it not have been fairer for prosecutors to give Brown's attorney Burton's handwritten notes?"[318] When Higginson answered that I was not entitled to the notes, and that they wouldn't have helped that much, Judge Stewart spoke up, asking, "Shouldn't the ultimate determination be in the hands of defense counsel?"[319] Judge Davis added, "Some specific statements included in the report aren't written in the notebook. Why wouldn't this have helped a lawyer cross-examine him?"[320]

Again, I don't want to read too much into the judges' questions. But it seemed the hard questions were directed more at Higginson and the prosecutors' actions, rather than at what I did or didn't do.

When the hearing was over, the judges quickly left the courtroom, and that was it. My whole future seemed to be hanging on less than an

---

[318] *Shreveport Times*, May 9, 2002.
[319] *The Times-Picayune*, May 9, 2002.
[320] *Baton Rouge Advocate*, May 9, 2002.

hour of arguments, plus the written briefs that we had put together over the last six months.

Supportive attorneys and friends lingered a good while outside the courtroom. There was a general feeling that the arguments had gone well and that it was a matter of time before my conviction would be set aside. I did some perfunctory interviews with newspaper and television reporters on the steps of the courthouse. All I could say was that I was "optimistic, confident, and sure that I will be back at my job as insurance commissioner in the near future." The 26 Department of Justice employees quickly slipped away with no comment to the press. I hope that was a good sign. I think they know that their arguments did not go well.

Now the waiting begins. Two months? Four months? It's hard to say how long it will take the judges to render a decision. My friends who practice before the Fifth Circuit tell me the judges probably have their minds made up by now. But they know this is an important case. Precedent will be set that will affect future cases not just in this part of the country but all over America. I can expect a lengthy written opinion that will cite old law and perhaps make new law. Judges have "pride of authorship," as do many of us who put words on paper. These judges will probably meet on numerous occasions to discuss not just individual issues but paragraphs and even lines in the opinion. They are going to be "stuck" with the opinion the rest of their lives, so they want to be confident in what they are writing down.

I should probably use the summer to finish up some personal projects, spend extra time with my family, and not worrying about "when and if." I'm confident my conviction will be overturned. The time frame will take care of itself.

## Thursday, May 9, 2002
## Baton Rouge, Louisiana

Bill Jeffress and I talked by phone today about additional case strategy. Since the prosecutors were allowed to file their 10-page motion a day before my hearing on the difference between Burton's notes and his typewritten statement, Bill feels we should be able to give our response. Higginson's brief on behalf of the prosecutors was confusing, and he didn't address the question the court raised. Bill and I agree that we should file a short, simple answer to the prosecutors' brief, pointing out that it was not responsive to what the court requested, that it was confusing, and that we should have a chance to present specifics about the discrepancies between Burton's handwritten notes and typewritten statements.

## Monday, May 13, 2002
## Baton Rouge, Louisiana

Bill filed his response today, and pointed out that the prosecutors had not submitted what the court asked for.[321] In addition, he alleged that the government's brief "contained additional arguments not specifically addressing discrepancies between the notes and the typewritten statement." Bill went on to point out how, count-by-count, the prosecutors failed to answer the court's questions, and he spelled out specifically how the notes would have dramatically helped my defense.

The U.S. Attorney's office immediately objected to our filing additional information. But Judge Davis, representing the three-judge panel, dismissed the objection and agreed to let us file our statement. Every time Bill Jeffress has made a request to the Fifth Circuit on my behalf, it has been granted. The prosecutors have objected to every request we have made—letting me stay out of jail on bond, giving me Burton's notes, and now letting us present additional information to the court. We have won every step of the appeals process, and I certainly look at this as a good sign.

It was a good move on our part to get the last word in before the judges go through the decision-making process. Now there is nothing to do but wait.

## Monday, June 3, 2002
## New Orleans, Louisiana

Governor Edwards appeared at the same federal courthouse where I was a month ago, and his lawyers argued his appeal on his

---

[321] *USA v. Brown, et al.,* No. 013-173, U.S. Fifth Circuit Court of Appeals, Appellant's Motion to File Response to Government's Letter of May 7, 2002, and Response, May 13, 2002.

conviction in the riverboat-gaming case. I wasn't there, but I got a full report this afternoon by phone from Mary Jane Marcantel.[322]

The Edwards team is pleased with the three randomly selected judges who will hear their case. All three are considered moderates who should hold the prosecutors to a high standard and make them prove that the trial was fair. It is no secret that a number of judges on the Fifth Circuit are considered "pro-prosecution," but none of three judges picked for the Edwards appeal fits that mold.

Former federal prosecutor Shawn Clark was quoted as saying:

*"There is a perception among some defense lawyers that certain judges in the Fifth Circuit are biased toward the government. I don't think any of those lawyers would have such concerns of this panel."*[323]

And former U.S. Attorney Harry Rosenberg stated:

*"For a circuit that is known for being historically pro-government, these three judges should certainly keep the flames of hope alive for these defendants."*[324]

Of course I share the former governor's concern about having a fair group of judges who will not be biased in their ruling. Although my case has nothing to do with the first Edwards trial, we are appealing several similar issues that will affect us both in the same way. Judge Polozola ordered anonymous juries in both the first Edwards trial and in my trial. He used the same criteria and the same set of facts to make the jury anonymous. In addition, he allowed the prosecutors' illegally obtained wiretaps to be used without so much as giving either one of us a hearing.

The consensus of both legal teams is that the two panels of judges will rule the same way on these issues. I doubt that my panel of judges will rule one way on the anonymous jury and the Edwards panel will rule another. The feeling seems to be that both panels of judges will get together and reach a consensus.

---

[322] Mary Jane worked for both my and Edwards's defense teams. She's a paralegal, not a lawyer, but she is as knowledgeable and competent as any lawyer in the state.
[323] *Times-Picayune*, May 29, 2002.
[324] Ibid.

Flamboyant Harvard Law School professor Alan Dershowitz leads Edwards' defense team. He made no bones about his feeling that "Judge Frank Polozola was 'hell-bent' on getting a verdict and avoiding a hung jury in the riverboat corruption trial of the former governor."[325] Edwards has what most people agree is a strong issue— that Polozola removed one of the jurors after almost two weeks of deliberations. The juror was supposedly dismissed because he took a dictionary into the jury room and walked out with notes. What was particularly strange was the fact that the juror did these things weeks before he was kicked off the jury.

"This judge was hell-bent on removing this juror," Dershowitz said. "Both the government and the judge were determined to get rid of the holdout juror."[326]

Several lawyers on Edwards' team strongly attacked the prosecutors' use of secret recordings supplied by confidential informants during the1996 investigations. The judge who gave the authority for the wiretaps was never told of the "extensive criminal backgrounds of the informants." As Dershowitz said, "You can't trust anything they say."[327]

Many of the judges' questions focused on the use of the anonymous jury. In both the first Edwards trial and in my trial only numbers identified the jurors, and we had no knowledge of who they actually were. This flies in the face of the constitutional guarantee to be "tried in public" by "a jury of your peers." As one columnist put it:

> *"Polozola had already put the defense at a disadvantage by impaneling an anonymous jury, as though this were a mob trial and desperate characters threatened to pervert the course of justice."*[328]

The Edwards defense team seemed pleased, and most neutral observers feel that a strong case was made for reversal of his conviction. Normally the court hands down a decision in seven to eight weeks. But with so many important issues at stake, and the fact that both my appeal and the Edwards appeal raise similar issues, there

---

[325] *The Advocate*, June 4, 2002.
[326] Ibid.
[327] Ibid.
[328] *Times-Picayune,* June 5, 2002.

is little doubt that these judges will take their time. They know very well that lawyers and non-lawyers alike throughout the country will review their opinion. They will be making law and setting precedent that will be followed in hundreds of cases in the months and years ahead. So far I've waited a month for a decision in my case. I'll no doubt wait a lot longer.

## Friday, August 23, 2002
## Baton Rouge, Louisiana

How quickly things change. The "worst of times" happened today.

The phone rang at 5:00 P.M., just as I was on my way out the door for a 45-minute bike ride followed by dinner with friends in the neighborhood. The call was from Lauren Teague, an administrative assistant at the insurance department.

"I thought you would want to hear the news. I've been watching the Fifth Circuit Court of Appeals website on my computer. It just came up. The Edwards conviction was affirmed."

I was surprised at the result and puzzled by the timing of the decision. The consensus of most lawyers who had followed the Edwards case was that the defendants had some strong issues, and there was an excellent chance of a reversal in this case. And the timing was strange.

My appeal was argued four weeks before the Edwards appeal. Yet there had been no decision in my case. What did this mean? Was it good news for me, in the sense that the Edwards case was now out of the way? Was it possible I might be receiving a reversal of my conviction next week? It was after 5:00 P.M. and the courts were closed until Monday. I thanked Lauren for the information and decided I would enjoy my weekend and be prepared for a possible decision sometime next week.

I walked outside and was just getting on my bike when my nephew, Solomon Carter, came to the door. "Uncle Jim, there's someone on the phone, and he says it's really important."

I went back inside and took the call in my office, assuming that someone was calling about the Edwards verdict. It was Jim Donelon, the chief deputy at the insurance department.

"Bad news, Jim. The Fifth Circuit just affirmed your conviction. I'm really sorry."

I was stunned! Really stunned!

There had been any number of reasons to believe over the past few months that my conviction would be reversed; the strong defense that had been made by my attorneys, both in the written brief and at the oral argument; the overwhelmingly positive response from lawyers and judges throughout the state who had read the briefs; the questions asked by the three-judge panel at the hearing in May; and the press speculation over the past few months, which was virtually unanimous in stating that my conviction would be thrown out.

I was prepared for a reversal of my conviction. I had even fleetingly thought about what I would say to the press and how quickly I wanted to return to my job as commissioner of insurance. I had never even considered a decision upholding my conviction. It just couldn't happen. But it had!

My first call was to Gladys. She was in her car about 30 miles away, heading back to Baton Rouge with several of her girlfriends. When I gave her the news, she was silent. I'm sure she was just as shocked and surprised as I was. Finally, she said, "I'm on my way home and will be there as soon as I can. We'll get through this."

Bill Jeffress called from Washington, having just read the entire 44-page decision. "Jim, they just got it wrong. It's puzzling how these judges disregarded the confrontation clause of the Sixth Amendment to the Constitution, as well as their misinterpretation of some of the basic rules that should allow you to have the notes."

Bill and I agreed that we should move for a quick rehearing on the decision. He will reread the decision tonight and work this weekend on an evaluation of how the decision contradicts decisions by other courts throughout the country.

Gladys arrived just minutes before a barrage of neighbors and friends drove up to the house. Cars lined both sides of the street and parked on the neutral ground in front of our house. Without being called, several Baton Rouge police officers showed up to help with the traffic. I wasn't particularly comfortable receiving condolences, but it was reassuring and moving to Gladys and me that so many people came by and stayed throughout the evening. Longtime friend and neighbor Janet Crawford showed up with large quantities of cheeses, chips, dips, and desserts. By the end of the evening, little was left.

James arrived from his dorm at LSU shortly after we received the news. He continues to be at my side offering strong support. It's almost as if his adolescence has passed and he has become a man as he has stood by me during crisis after crisis.

Campbell and Gentry both called before I got a chance to call them. Campbell was in New York preparing for the "Weekend Today" show and had seen the news on the Associated Press wire. She had alerted Gentry, and they both called to offer family support. I didn't have a number for Meredith, who is now in Santiago, Chile, but I sent a quick e-mail, telling her what had happened and asking her to call me when she could. When I reached my mother, she had already heard the news from my brother Jack, and she was obviously having a difficult time. Like the rest of us, she had been confident of a reversal. Now she was trying to make sense of what had happened. All of us in the family need to rally around Mother, more than around me, as she deals with this difficult blow.

After talking to my daughters and my mother, I went back to greet a continual flow of friends until around 10:30. I was wearing down, and I needed to be alone.

I need to think through this tragic turn of events, try to make sense of what had happened to me, and ponder what options I now had. I also need to write down my reaction to the day's news. I wonder if I will ever receive justice?

When I was studying at Cambridge in the early 1960s, I remember hearing the words of the Lord Chief Justice of England. "A judge is not supposed to know anything about the facts of a case until they have been presented in evidence and explained to him at least three times."[329]

Next week, we start the process of asking for a rehearing and a hearing before the entire Fifth Circuit Court of Appeals. It's late in the game, I'm a little behind, but I haven't struck out yet.

---

[329] Hubert Lister Parker, Lord Chief Justice of England. "Single Quote Sayings of the Week," *The London Observer,* March 12, 1961.

**Sunday, August 25, 2002**
**Baton Rouge, Louisiana**

It would be an understatement to say that my heart was not in the 1:00 P.M. press conference at the insurance department today, but there really wasn't a choice. The working press has been supportive of me in my predicament, and most of the daily newspapers in the state have written columns about the injustice of my conviction. In almost every interview, reporters have taken the time to tell me they think I was unfairly convicted and to wish me success in the appeal process. Since Friday night, reporters have wanted to know my reaction. I had considered waiting until Monday to speak to the press, Governor Edwards was addressing the Press Club on Monday, and I knew his comments would dominate the evening news and the next day's newspapers. I wanted a chance to give my reaction to the public, so it made sense to hold the press conference on Sunday. I was surprised at the large turnout on what is normally a day off. Most of the South Louisiana television stations were there, as well as the working press that covers the State Capitol for papers throughout the state.

What could I say that I hadn't already said 50 times over during the past two years? I called the decision by the three-judge panel "puzzling," "novel," "unprecedented," and "ripe for a challenge." I pointed out that there had never been a decision in this country in which someone accused of giving false statements could not confront his accuser and see the notes in question.

"The court, we think, got the facts wrong," I said. "My lawyers as we speak are at work on my appeal and we will first ask the three-judge panel that unanimously decided the case to reconsider their ruling. Failing that, we will ask for an en banc hearing, which includes all the judges of the court. Beyond that, if necessary, I will take the case all the way up to the United States Supreme Court. Whether I am here, in jail, or wherever, I'm going to keep fighting this to the end. There's a strong general feeling from anyone who looks at my case that I received a bum rap."

Numerous questions were asked about my thoughts on going to prison, and I tried to answer them honestly: I still don't think it's going to happen. But if it does, well look, six months in a minimum-security prison—I'm not making light of it. It would be terrible for anyone to be away from their family and have to experience something like that. But a lot of you folks have known me over the years, and I like to curl up with a good book and keep to myself. I'll do whatever I'm called on to do. I'm a pretty good cook. I might be a good hand in the kitchen. But I'm not dismissing it or not taking it seriously."

Asked if I would resign from office, I said, "If I thought I had done something wrong, I would have resigned several years ago."

I talked on for about 30 minutes, quoting William Faulkner, Garth Brooks, and anyone else who came to mind.

I was stunnd.

I was asked my feelings about potentially being one of several Louisiana public officials who were serving jail time. "I hope that I will be looked on individually, not lumped with other officials," I said. "No one has ever accused me of taking one red cent or benefiting in any way. In most of the other instances, the officials involved were accused of taking some type of kickback, or enriching themselves. There has never been such an accusation toward me in all my time in public life. Basically, my 30-year career in public life will be judged on a 30-minute, non-taped conversation with an FBI agent who, for whatever reason, did not accurately report what was said. I think I deserve better than that."

Several department employees had taken time out of their Sunday afternoon to be there as a show of support for me. Gladys, James, and I visited with them for a while before leaving for lunch. I spent a quiet afternoon with my family, knowing I'll be back at work on the appeal tomorrow.

## Monday, August 26, 2002
## Baton Rouge, Louisiana

There were front-page stories about yesterday's press conference throughout the state this morning. The headline in the *Baton Rouge Advocate* simply stated, **"I was stunned."**

The various stories and television reports outlined my surprise at the court's decision and my commitment to take the appeal all the way to the United States Supreme Court.

A number of papers ran large color photos of me with Gladys and James at my side. This disturbs me, because I have tried to protect my son and keep him out of my controversial public life. He's off to a good start as a freshman at LSU, and I don't want to cloud what should be some of the most enjoyable years of his life. He's made it clear that he wants to be with me during court appearances, press conferences, and any other time when family unity is important. In so many ways, each of my children has made me so proud. Since James is the only one living with me, in a special way he has gone the extra mile.

## Tuesday, September 3, 2002
## Baton Rouge, Louisiana

I got some good news today that offers a degree of encouragement about my future appeal. Right after the decision came down upholding my conviction last week, the U.S. Attorney's office in New Orleans asked the Appeals Court to revoke my bond and start the process that would send me to jail. In a one-sentence entry into the court record, the Fifth Circuit simply denied the motion filed by the prosecutors.

Bill Jeffress and I responded to numerous press calls with "cautious optimism." I'm not sure you can really read anything in to the court's decision, but they are not going to rush my sentence and will apparently give me time to ask for a rehearing and appeal to the full panel of judges on the Fifth Circuit.

Bill e-mailed me a rough draft of the petition he will file to the whole Fifth Circuit Court. (When you ask every judge on the court of appeals to hear your case, it is called an "en banc" request.) It's a

354

well-written petition that simply states that the three-judge panel misinterpreted the clear rules of criminal procedure. In addition, the brief points out that no person in this country has ever been convicted under circumstances like mine, and that in any other part of the United States the notes would have been given to me.

He also points out that one of the defendants in my case, Ron Weems received his notes from the same FBI agent who interviewed me and was found not guilty. This is unequal protection under the law. The brief is thorough, well written, and reaches a logical conclusion that my conviction was unjust. I've shown the brief to about 20 lawyers and friends, and they all have a strong feeling that we are right, and the conviction should be reversed. But we all felt the same way when my initial appeal was filed to the three-judge panel.

Bill tells me our argument is probably stronger if we have to make it to the U.S. Supreme Court. When a circuit in the United States rules one way, and there are conflicting decisions in other circuits, the Supreme Court normally hears such a case to set rules of uniformity. My case certainly fits this criterion. Unfortunately, it takes a long time to get a case heard by the Supreme Court, if the Court agrees to hear it at all. Therefore, I face the egregious possibility of serving my six-month prison sentence and then having the Supreme Court throw out my conviction. I remember writing about the "light at the end of the tunnel" in my diary several years ago. The light is still there, but the tunnel is so long.

## Monday, September 9, 2002
## Baton Rouge, Louisiana

Today a period of uncertainty begins for me. My brief to all the judges on the Fifth Circuit Court of Appeals was filed last Thursday. There is no deadline by which they must act. At least five of the judges must agree to give me a hearing before the entire court. Their decision could come in a few days, a few weeks, or even longer. If the court agrees to hear my case, then the process will no doubt take several additional months. If I am turned down, I might have to report to prison in a few days.

Even though I remain optimistic, I also have to be realistic. Several lawyers have told me that having Edith Clement on the Fifth Circuit hurts my case. It is almost unheard of for a judge to try a case

355

in which a defendant is convicted; the defendant challenges many of the rulings of that judge; the trial judge moves up to the court of appeals; and then the defendant has to go to that court of appeals to ask for relief. The odds against me rose significantly when Clement moved up to the Fifth Circuit. The judges hearing my case all have lifetime appointments, and the other members of the Fifth Circuit will be dealing with Clement for many years to come. Cases like mine come and go. I hope the members of the court will be fair, but they are aware that if they reverse my conviction, Clement will no doubt take it personally, and they will have to deal with her in the future.

Frankly, I think an entirely different circuit in some other part of the country should have heard my appeal so there would not be any appearance of impropriety. But I am struck with Clement, including the strong feelings she displayed against me at the trial and the fact that her presence casts a shadow over the other members of the Fifth Circuit.

Of course I will take my case to the U.S. Supreme Court if the Fifth Circuit does not reverse my conviction. But I have to be realistic about my chances there as well.

Our Constitution gives any individual the right to appeal a case in a lower court to the nine justices who sit on the Supreme Court. But it is up to the judges to decide whether to hear a specific case. Last year more than 8.000 appeals were presented to the court, but the court only picked about one percent of these cases to review. In fact, the Supreme Court gives consideration to even fewer cases now than in the past. In 1970, the Supreme Court considered 151 cases. Last year, only 79 cases were reviewed.

In spite of these long odds, my legal team still feels we have a fair shot for consideration by the country's highest court. What happened to me in not receiving the notes of the FBI agent, and not being able to cross-examine him on the stand would not have taken place in virtually any other part of the country. Since the Supreme Court often insists on uniformity in how the lower courts operate, my legal team will, if necessary, make an argument that there was no equal justice in my case. If a federal court in California or New York would have allowed me to confront my accuser and given me his notes, why shouldn't a federal court in Louisiana do the same? This would probably be the issue that would pique the interest of the justices.

But the fact remains that I face a tough battle before both the Fifth Circuit and the U.S. Supreme Court. I need to start making preparations in case I'm given short notice to report to prison.

When my daughter Gentry visited last weekend, she gave me a book, written by a former federal inmate, about what to expect in prison. I've had several such books sent to me. Their advice is generally common sense—don't rat on anybody, don't cut in line, don't reach for anything, don't whine, and mind your own business.

Bill Jeffress has received letters from former prisoners who have started counseling services. They can be hired to sit down with someone who is going to prison, as well as the prisoner's family, to outline what that life will be like. But I will only be gone for six months—a basketball season. I can handle just about anything for that long. So I will pass on the various offers and opt to spend what time I have left with family and friends.

### Tuesday, September 10, 2002
### New Orleans, Louisiana

Today was a long and bittersweet day. *Best Week*, a major national insurance publication, summed up my feelings well.

> *If weren't for the federal conviction hanging over his head, suspended Louisiana Insurance Commissioner Jim Brown would be hosting the fall national gathering of his peers in his home state.*
>
> *Instead of basking in the glow of having a major industry event in a showcase city such as New Orleans, Brown expects to learn soon whether the Fifth U.S. Circuit Court of Appeals will hear his case.*
>
> *"It's painful," Brown said. "This should be a great moment for me, to have the insurance industry in my home state talking about the success of my state and solutions to problems. I should be hosting this convention and hosting every reception."*[330]

---

[330] *Best Week,* September 10, 2002.

But since my case is still in limbo, I have stayed away from all the official meetings. Instead, over the past two days Gladys and I have attended several dinners and receptions given on my behalf by people we have known and worked with over the years. It has been good to see so many old friends who want to show their support for me. But it's been hard, particularly for Gladys, to show much enthusiasm. We had expected this ordeal to be over by now, but it just keeps grinding on.

Still, there continues to be favorable press coverage throughout the state as my efforts to appeal move forward. *Gambit Weekly* in New Orleans newspaper wrote:

> *When state Insurance Commissioner Jim Brown was convicted of lying to FBI agents, I wrote that henceforth Louisiana politicos would do well to think of Brown before agreeing to talk to the feds—and then invoke "the Jim Brown Rule."*
>
> *The Jim Brown Rule is very simple: if you're a public figure in Louisiana, do not talk to the FBI.*
>
> *I certainly don't advocate obstructing federal investigations, but the plain truth is that FBI agents have no legal duty to tell people the truth. On the other hand, if the FBI is interviewing you, you have a legal duty to tell them the truth. As Brown found out the hard way, you can go to jail if you don't.*
>
> *That hardly seems fair, but fairness won't get you very far in a criminal trial. Brown found that out the hard way.*
>
> *I thought Brown raised some interesting points in his appeal, particularly his request to view FBI Agent Harry Burton's handwritten notes from the Brown interview. Typically, such interviews are not tape-recorded. FBI agents take notes by hand, then transcribe them neatly onto a form known as a "302" back at the office.*

*The trial court gave Brown and his attorneys copies of Burton's 302, but not his handwritten notes. On the witness stand, Burton used his 302—not his original notes—to refresh his memory of the interview and the specific instances in which Brown allegedly lied. Neither the 302 nor the handwritten notes were introduced as evidence. It was Burton's word against Brown's and the jurors believed Burton.*

*But my point is one of fairness, which sometimes has little to do with the law. It isn't fair that government agents can lie to us to see if we're telling them the truth. And it isn't fair that the government can use its own handwritten notes to create a formal document that later could help send us to jail—but not let us see the handwritten notes.*

*I just hope the FBI will understand where I'm coming from if agents ever try to interview me. After all, in upholding Brown's convictions, the Fifth Circuit has affirmed the Jim Brown Rule as well.*[331]

In a story headlined, **"Jim Brown Politician, But No Edwards"** Roy Pitchford wrote in the *Alexandria Daily Town Talk*:

*While it's easy to simply lump Brown in with the other insurance commissioners, agriculture commissioners, and other public officials who have been convicted of criminal offenses, Brown's case is different.*

*He was acquitted of the criminal accusations that started his entanglement with the criminal justice system, but was found guilty of lying to an FBI agent.*

*Many observers have suggested that had Brown, who first approached the FBI, simply said that he wouldn't talk to them without his lawyer present, he would likely still be in office.*

---

[331] Clancy Dubos, "Affirming the Jim Brown Rule," *Gambit Weekly,* September 10, 2002.

*That may be an oversimplification, but there is a ring of truth.*

*It's one thing to vote out of office an elected official who violates public trust. It's another thing to see him arrested, tried, and convicted.*

*In the case of Brown it will truly be sad.*

*Make no mistake; Brown was a Louisiana politician in every sense of the word. But on his worst day he was no Edwin Edwards.*[332]

## Monday, September 16, 2002
## Baton Rouge, Louisiana

We have filed a new petition to the Fifth Circuit Court of Appeals asking for an en banc hearing. I'm requesting that the entire court hear my argument.

We have raised the same basic question that I was denied my right under the "confrontation clause" of the Sixth Amendment, since I was not allowed to see the FBI agent's notes or to cross-examine him about what he wrote down in my interview. As Bill Jeffress states in my petition:

> *There has never been a reported case when a defendant accused of false statements was denied access to the FBI's contemporaneous record of the alleged false statements, much less a case where the defendant was denied the opportunity to confront the testifying agent with his own notes, or to ask him any questions about the content of those notes.*[333]

The earlier three-judge panel's decision concluded that the Federal Rules of Criminal Procedure did not automatically give me

---

[332] *Alexandria Daily Town Talk,* September 7, 2002.
[333] *USA v. Brown,* No. 99-151-B-M2, Appellant's Petition for Rehearing En Banc, 9/5/2002.

360

the right to see the notes. My lawyers think this decision is wrong and blatantly unfair. We have not found a legal brief, a legal article, or a legal decision in which any lawyer or any knowledgeable person concludes that I should not have gotten the FBI agent's notes. This is particularly germane because we have found that the notes differ dramatically from the agent's testimony at the trial.

In response to our argument, the prosecutors have filed 30 rambling pages rehashing what happened at the trial and quoting the opinion by Edith Clement when she was the trial judge on my case. But they won't address head-on the issue of how I could be the only person in this country ever convicted of giving false statements to an FBI agent without receiving the handwritten notes of that agent. It just hasn't happened anywhere else. The prosecutors won't address this; they just keep saying that the notes wouldn't have made a difference. If they wouldn't have made any difference, then why not, in fairness, give them to me? The answer is obvious. The notes would have made a dramatic difference; they would have caused any reasonable jury to set me free. The prosecutors knew this, and that's why they tried so hard to keep the notes away from me.

Bill Jeffress offers some encouragement based on the fact that the prosecutors had to file an answer to my petition. He says that in 90 percent of the cases in which an en banc hearing is requested, the prosecutors are never asked to file an answer. Bill argues that at least the judges are looking at my case.

I'm not that optimistic. I've been a realist through this entire process, and the numbers don't bode well for me. It would take a majority of the judges to grant me a new trial. There are 19 members on the Fifth Circuit. But four of the judges serve in a "senior status," only taking a few cases because of their advanced years. Those four will not vote on whether to give me a new trial. This reduces the number to 15, but currently there is one vacancy on the court. Judge Clement, who served as my trial judge, will be required to recuse herself. That means I must convince a majority of the 13 judges left.

Unfortunately, three of the 13 judges have already voted not to give me a new trial. I need seven judges out of 13, but I've lost those three votes, which means I actually need seven judges out of 10. Put another way, 70 percent of the judges who have not made a decision on my case must rule in my favor. Those are steep odds, but they get even steeper when you consider the role that Clement plays in this entire affair. I am basically asking 10 judges to rule that Clement made a wrong decision and failed to properly interpret the law. I'm asking them to "pass judgment" on her.

These judges will only have to deal with me on one occasion. They will never hear from me again, and I will soon be a distant memory. But Clement is their colleague. She will work with them on a daily basis. Month after month for the rest of their lives, the 10 judges who hold my fate in their hands (who have a lifetime appointment to this court), will have to look Clement in the eye, work with her, and get along with her. Their lives are certainly going to be much more difficult if they rule against her in my case.

I don't want to make a blanket charge that all the judges in the Fifth Circuit are influenced by personal relationships and the politics of getting along. But it's an accepted fact that Clement's presence puts an additional roadblock in my path. When I add all this up, it seems unlikely the Fifth Circuit will overturn my conviction. So what's the next step? The Supreme Court of the United States.

Of course, I plan to appeal to the country's highest court. There is good reason to do so. I hope the issue of basic fairness and equal justice will pique the interest of the Supreme Court and persuade them to hear my case.

Unfortunately, no one has the "right" to appeal to the Supreme Court. I have the right to ask, but there is no guarantee that the high court will consider my case. And the judges themselves don't even decide whether to hear my case. According to a recent story in *USA Today*:

> *Law clerks from eight of the nine justices work together to assess which appeals to the court should be heard and then write memos that are shared among the eight chambers. Only Justice John Paul Stevens, appointee of President Ford at 82, the eldest justice declines to use the clerk pool. He relies only on his own clerks for guidance as he weighs the filings.*

> *"I think the less judicial work that is delegated, the better for the court and the country," he says.*

*The justices are highly selective; less than 1% of the appeals filed annually are granted reviews.*

*"They take the earth-shattering cases, but they also take some cases that we would think of as 'little,' when lower courts have ruled differently on similar issues," says Thomas Goldstein, a Washington lawyer who has argued several cases before the court.*

*"The justices are trying to make our legal system uniform," Goldstein said.[334]*

My only real hope is to spark an interest in a few of the judges that the Fifth Circuit decision does not "make our legal system uniform." I would have received the notes in any other court of appeals in the country. But not the Fifth Circuit.

It has to be considered a "Hail Mary pass," but there really is no choice. What happened to me was wrong, and I will push my appeal to the end.

While my appeal moves forward, the debate over what has happened to me continues in the press.

From the Houma, Louisiana, *Business News,* August 28, 2002, in an editorial by publisher Darrin W. Guidry Sr.:

*A friend asked if I would ever get into politics? My answer was "no, I don't want to go to jail."*

*What concerns many potential candidates today is what is happening to people like Jim Brown. It seems that there is a rush to convict politicians on just about anything.*

*They tried to send Bill Clinton to jail a few years back for lying, but Jim Brown wasn't so lucky. He faces jail time for "lying to an FBI agent."*

*I told my son the other day that he had better be good because Santa Claus was watching. I hope he doesn't press*

---

[334] *USA Today,* September 17, 2002.

*charges. Good luck to those running for political office this Fall ... I hope you have good lawyers.*[335]

From the *Baton Rouge Advocate,* letters to the editor section, September 13, 2002:

*Recently, a three-judge panel ruled it was appropriate for our government to withhold from Jim Brown an FBI agent's notes of their conversation, seriously hampering his ability to defend himself. Obviously, that decision has been appealed to the full court in hopes that it will see the blatant unfairness, and the basic right one has to confront one's accusers. After all, embarrassing errors made by the agent in question have been widely reported and are known to even the most casual political observers. And the defendant who was given the notes was acquitted on all charges.*

*If you doubt that this is a sad time for our government, go to lunch with Jim Brown and watch the steady stream of people stop by to say how wrong they believe his conviction was. Listen to them thank him for cleaning up the insurance industry and bringing sound business practices to a beleaguered state department.*

*If forced to serve six months in prison, Jim Brown will do it with grace. But he will never ever give up fighting to correct this grievous mistake, a quality that made him an effective public servant for 30 years. We should expect nothing less now.*

*There is a scar on the face of our justice system so ugly that common citizens feel a burning shame.*[336]

Tomorrow we will spend the day in New Orleans, remembering the events of September 11 a year ago at a

---

[335] *Houma Business News,* August 28, 2002.
[336] *Baton Rouge Advocate,* September 13, 2002.

memorial service. Then back home to Baton Rouge, and back to work on the appeal process.

**Wednesday, September 18, 2002**
**Baton Rouge, Louisiana**

Bob Hayes, my former teammate and roommate on the U.S. track team, died today. "Bullet" Bob was fifty-nine years old. He had been battling liver and kidney ailments, along with prostate cancer, for some time. I got a call this afternoon from a mutual friend in Florida, where Bob was living, that his kidneys just gave out.

We had traveled throughout Europe as teammates in 1963 and had roomed together in Germany and Scandinavia. I handed off the baton to Bob on the four-hundred-meter relay team in numerous races that summer. I always worried he would leave me before I could get the baton in his hand.

Besides winning the Olympic gold medal for the hundred meters in the 1964 Olympics, Bob also had a successful career as a wide receiver for the Dallas Cowboys. But he never made it into the Pro Football Hall of Fame. A drug and alcohol problem got the best of him, and he served 10 months in federal prison on narcotics charges. We stayed in touch over the years, and I called him from time to time to offer encouragement as Bob tried to rebuild his life by working in a drug clinic in Jacksonville, Florida. But the tragedy of his drug conviction always hovered over him.

Whatever happens to me in the future, I'm not going to face the emotional and physical tragedy that Bob Hayes went through. One thing that makes it much easier for me to deal with my unjust conviction is the continuing public support I receive. Many people have faced tragedy in their life and suffered much more than I have or probably ever will. Whatever happens to me through the judicial system will take its toll. But with the support of so many family members, friends, and members of the general public, I still have a long, productive life ahead and much to be thankful for.

**Monday, September 23, 2002**
**New Orleans, Louisiana**

Today, as I had feared, the full Fifth Circuit denied my request for an en banc hearing. No vote was listed in the order, so I don't know which judges voted for me and which voted against me. But whatever the vote, my only recourse now is the Supreme Court.

Whatever happens now will take time. There is a strong possibility that the Supreme Court will hear my case but not let me stay out on bond. I could have my conviction reversed but still have to serve my sentence. It's time to start preparing for six months in a federal minimum-security prison.

Once the hearing was denied, it didn't take long for articles to appear about my looming prison term. But even with the stigma of prison hanging over my head, most of the news coverage has been fair and even a little upbeat.

From an editorial in the *Ruston Daily Leader*, August 28, 2002, headlined, **"Now Brown Reads Faulkner":**

> *During Jim Brown's promising political years, he would indulge himself in the writings of Charles Dickens.*
>
> *Now in what could be the dark years of his political career—and his life—he turns to the writings of William Faulkner. The erudite Brown, Louisiana's suspended insurance commissioner could be only weeks from spending time in a federal prison after he was convicted for lying to the FBI about his role in a state settlement with a failed insurance company.*
>
> *And in the last couple of weeks, as serving prison time may be inevitable, Brown has been spending a great deal of time reflecting on his 30 years in public service and taking time to read, too.*
>
> *His novel of choice in these dark times—Faulkner's "The Sound and the Fury."*

*His office said he received about 150 calls each day;*
*mostly those calls come from district judges, district*
*attorneys and others who know him and want to express*
*remorse or wish encouragement.*

*But just as if it were another campaign year, Brown*
*seemed to be accessible to all media and returned my*
*phone call two hours later.*

*"I'm hanging in there," Brown told me via phone in his*
*polished Southern accent. "But I've had better months."*
*Those better months include terms as a Ferriday state*
*senator, a career as, in my opinion, the best secretary of*
*state in Louisiana's history and gubernatorial hopes in*
*1987.*

*Brown, the consummate politician, has Constitutional*
*hope. It is based on the fact Brown never got to review the*
*notes—handwritten notes FBI agent Harry Burton took in*
*a May 2, 1997, interview; instead he was able to review a*
*report supposedly based on "what is in the notes."*

*Brown is depending on the Sixth Amendment, which says*
*you have the right to confront your accuser, and in his*
*opinion view those notes.*
*"If the notes say the same thing that he (Burton) said on*
*the stand, then why not let me see those notes?"*

*"How outrageous, how un-American, how un-democratic*
*is that?"*

*Hopefully, for Brown's sake, the Supreme Court will*
*review his case and determine that.*

*One thing admirable about Brown is his positive*
*demeanor despite his career and life slowly crumbling. He*
*attributes his "prevailing" spirit to Faulkner.*

*"What Faulkner said is that if you are going to live a full life, you've got to do more than just survive—you've got to prevail," Brown said.*

*"And that is exactly my philosophy. I'm not just going to survive this, but I'm going to prevail."*

*In a short time, Brown will find out if the Supreme Court will hear his case. In a short time, Brown will know if he faces prison time, and he will know if his political career in Louisiana is salvageable.*

*But only history will be the judge as to whether or not Jim Brown prevails.*[337]

## Saturday, September 28, 2002
## Baton Rouge, Louisiana

Today was jam-packed from dawn to dusk. It's only 7:00 P.M., but Gladys has already fallen asleep.

I got bad, but predictable, news yesterday as the three-judge panel of the Fifth Circuit, which had turned down my appeal two weeks ago has now ruled that I cannot stay out on bond while I pursue my appeal to the United States Supreme Court. I wasn't surprised. These three judges have voted against me on two other occasions so far. Why should I have any hope that they would let my bond continue and allow me to stay free as I attempt to argue my case to the nation's highest court? Monday Bill Jeffress will start preparing my final request to the Supreme Court. He will ask the presiding judge, Justice Antonin Scalia, to allow me to stay free while we are waiting on the high court's decision.

In the meantime, I'm trying to make the best use of my time in case prison is inevitable. I am hoping for the best but assuming the worst. I should have about 30 days to put my affairs in order.

This morning I had a 7:30 golf lesson with University Club pro Shane Warren. I was candid with him about my situation and asked for his help. As I get older, I'm enjoying golf more, particularly

---

[337] *Ruston Daily Leader,* August 28, 2002.

368

playing with my family. I think it's a game I can play for years to come. But how do I carry on with my golf drills and related stretches if I have to go to prison? Shane agreed to give me some suggestions. (I should add here that I'm about as good a golfer as I am a fly fisherman. Even Gladys, who rarely plays, gives me a good match. I'm sure Shane looks on me as quite a challenge.)

After a quick shower, I headed to Tiger Stadium with Gladys for the LSU–Mississippi State football game. Over the last few days, news coverage about the possibility of my going to prison has been extensive. We spent most of the first half of the game in the hallway on the way to our seats. One after the other, people stopped us to express their sympathy and concern.

A local contractor made no bones about his opinion. "You're a POW, Jim. You've become a prisoner in the government's efforts to get Edwin Edwards at any cost. It's totally unfair, and the prosecutors should be ashamed."

A local chiropractor came up to shake hands with me and give Gladys a hug. "Commissioner, this is the worst of times and the best of times for you. It's the worst for the outrageous thing that has happened to you. But it's the best because anyone who has followed your case knows how unfairly you were treated and supports your efforts to clear yourself. You are in every conversation I have, and there's a strong feeling that you were wronged in the worst way. Hang in there! We're for you."

A couple from my former home of Ferriday wished me well and gave me an editorial that appeared in a number of north Louisiana newspapers this week:

> *Unless the U.S. Supreme Court rules against the Fifth Circuit Court of Appeals, James H. (Jim) Brown, Louisiana's suspended Commissioner of Insurance, will serve time in a federal prison for lying to an FBI agent.*
>
> *Brown's attorney failed to convince the federal courts that Brown was entitled to see the notes which the agent took during the interview and which Brown was denied.*
>
> *Thus, the matter became Brown's word against the agent's word.*

*Was that fair?*

*It doesn't seem to us to be fair.*

*Brown could have refused the interview with the FBI but he didn't. That later proved to be a mistake.*

*Brown was acquitted of the criminal accusations brought against him by the government, which failed to prove him guilty in the settlement of the insurance company.*

*But he now faces six months in prison because the courts accepted the word of the FBI agent while denying Brown access to the agent's written notes. The agent, incidentally, testified in court with a typed version of the interview, not with his hand-written notes.*

*More than any other reason, it appears Brown was found guilty of association.*[338]

In spite of all the favorable articles and solid expressions of support from the public, it looks like I'm only a few weeks from going to jail.

## Wednesday, October 8, 2002
## Baton Rouge, Louisiana

A probation officer who has been assigned to me called to tell me to report to a federal prison camp at Oakdale, Louisiana, next Tuesday by noon. I have little chance of a reprieve from the U.S. Supreme Court. It seems that, by Washington standards, my case is not seen as all that important.

If I have to go to prison, there are some advantages in going to Oakdale. It is only a two-hour drive from Baton Rouge, which will be a reasonable trip for family and friends. Shreveport, where my mother

---

[338] "Brown's Conviction Doesn't Seem Fair," *The Concordia Sentinel*, September 25, 2002.

and brother live, is a little more than two hours north. So I suppose I should give thanks for small favors.

I will take the next few days to clear off my desk at home, paying bills, and organizing the personal effects I will leave behind. We will spend the weekend visiting with family and friends at home.

One thing I will surely do in prison is read and write. As I understand the rules of federal prisons, an inmate can receive only paperback books through the mail. By a stroke of luck, the annual LSU Book Bazaar was held a few weeks ago. I bought 125 paperbacks. I took pleasure in picking out older books I read many years ago, which I plan to reread, as well as some I have always wanted to read but never got around to.

I have only a few more days of freedom. Then I go on to a new experience that will forever change my life.

## Tuesday, October 14, 2002
## Oakdale, Louisiana

My first day in prison.

What an unbelievable day!

In my lifetime, I have experienced major challenges, controversies, and conflicts. I went into the military knowing I might go to war, although fortunately I never did. I knew every time I ran for office that I might face defeat. And like everyone, I have had my share of personal tragedy to deal with. But never in my worst nightmares did I ever think I would end up in federal prison.

Gladys and I got up at 4:00 A.M., and I packed the few items I was allowed to take with me:

- A pair of reading glasses;
- A religious ornament (I chose a small silver cross given to me by my wonderful friend, Mary Bond of Thibodaux, the lady who sought me out to pray for me.);
- My wedding ring (Gladys had one specially engraved for me to wear while I'm away from home);
- A religious book (I chose *The Book of Job: His Struggle against Injustice*); and

- A tube of Chapstick (I've been hugging and kissing a lot of family and friends in the past week, and my lips are chapped.).

That's it. Nothing more. Everything else I might need will presumably be given to me at the prison.

Our first stop was at Coffee Call to say goodbye to our close friends and my key staff members from the insurance department. The press was aware of our plans, so they were all there for my sendoff. I gave a short press conference and then spent 30 minutes saying goodbye to the people who have stood by me during this terrible, unfair ordeal.

I'm told that most of the evening TV news stories showed my son James and me sharing a private moment and a hug. He has been at my side unwaveringly during this crisis in my life.

By 8:30, I was on the road with Gladys, my sister-in-law Gloria, and family friend Janice Shaab. My first stop was the federal courthouse in Baton Rouge to pay my fifty-thousand-dollar fine.

As I started to write a check, the clerk said, "No personal checks. Only money orders, cashier's checks, or credit cards."

Credit cards! "Do you take American Express?" I asked. The answer was yes. I paid my fine with the card and chuckled at the thought that I will get 73,000 frequent-flyer miles courtesy of the government. I guess I can file that information under the heading "Every Cloud Has a Silver Lining!"

We set out for Oakdale with a caravan of reporters following. The press even joined us when we stopped at the Popeye's in Oakdale for a quick lunch of barbequed chicken and coleslaw. After that, there was nothing left to do but drive up to the gates of the Oakdale Federal Detention Center.

A swarm of reporters and television crews from throughout the state were waiting to record my arrival. Before I went in, I stopped the car and got out to share a few final thoughts.

"My feelings are bittersweet. What happened to me is an outrageous injustice that I hope never happens again to any American citizen. Going in these prison gates, I feel like a prisoner of war."

"I'm the only person in the country who has ever been convicted in a federal court where I could not confront my accuser, nor see the handwritten notes that were the basis of the charges against me."

"But I'm blessed by the support I have received from the people of Louisiana. I've seen recent polls showing an overwhelming opinion that I was not treated fairly, and that I should not be in prison. And if an election were held today, I'd be reelected."

"I will go through those gates with dignity and will get along fine. But I'll be back soon. I've written one book about my ordeal. And I will continue to speak out for years to come to oppose the abuses allowed by the prosecution in my case."

With those final words, I drove through the prison gates, and toward a whole new way of life for the next six months.

Several prison cars and trucks escorted us through the prison-camp entrance. Gladys was allowed to walk with me through the front door, where we said our goodbyes.

What could I say to the woman who has stood by me through this terrible ordeal, who has never wavered in her love and support? I am truly blessed to have her. We shared a few quiet moments, and then she left.

I underwent a friendly but professional orientation and a strip search, changed into the green prison uniform, and was escorted to my camp building—my new home.

So now I begin my personal experience of Purgatory.

# EPILOGUE

I served six months in federal prison. I could write hundreds of pages describing my experiences there, experiences most people would find hard to believe. But that's another story for another book.

A day does not pass that I am not asked about the injustice that took place. I would like to put the whole experience behind me, but it's not that easy. I will always have to live with the fact that I was violated by the legal system.

Halfway through my prison term, one of the jurors who passed judgment on me spoke out publicly. She had finally seen the handwritten notes that were kept from the jury at my trial. She had e-mailed me a few weeks before going public, telling me that she thought the jury had been misled and that they had made a mistake in convicting me. A number of news reports covered her public statements.

From the WAFB Television news broadcast, January 31, 2003:

*It started with this email . . . "As one of those 12, I so thought you would win your appeal. I believe in the system far less after being on that jury. I know this doesn't mean much to you now but I wish you and your family all the best under the circumstances. There has not been much peace of mind from this juror since the day we left the courthouse. Keep up the good fight. God be with you."*

*It has been almost three years since Jim Brown was convicted and to this today "Beth"—as we will call her— says she regrets her decision to vote guilty. Even on verdict day Beth says she walked into the courtroom thinking, "You know if you fight it hard enough you can get it on appeal."*

*Beth says when called to be a juror in 2000 she was both scared and nervous. For days and weeks she and the other jurors heard from witness after witness. Including key prosecution witness FBI agent Harry Burton, who testified that Brown lied to him about being involved with the Cascade Insurance scheme.*

*"Harry's a pretty good witness. Harry's convincing," said Beth. However, she still says jurors wanted to see Burton's notes of his conversation with Brown. "We requested to see these notes and we weren't allowed. We were told that basically the notes reflected what the FBI agent had told us."*

*So even though the jury found Brown not guilty of the bigger charges including conspiracy, on the counts of lying to an FBI agent, they voted guilty. Still she thought he could win on appeal. Beth's reasoning, "We weren't allowed to see the FBI notes so if there are notes and if anyone is allowed to see them he can beat it on appeal. Surely, he can."*

*But of course that hasn't happened. And as she thinks of Brown now serving a six-month sentence in federal prison she says, "Under the same circumstances I wouldn't have done it the same way. I wish I could go back and change it. I never thought he would go to prison."*

But as grateful as I am that the juror vindicated me and acknowledged that I was wrongfully convicted, it really makes no difference. There is no legal procedure to reopen the case and reverse my conviction. What's done is done. The truth doesn't matter. Justice be damned.

I have found a degree of peace. But looking back, I often wonder if we worry too much about the dangers abroad and not enough about the injustices that take place at home.

Is my heart still full of bitterness? Not often. I have accepted the fact that what happened to me was an aberration. I happened to be in the way when the Justice Department unloaded on Edwin Edwards. I was caught in the crossfire.

Tolstoy wrote that chance played an important role in every historical event. Bad things can happen without rhyme or reason, just because someone is in the wrong place at the wrong time. In the words of Ecclesiastes, "I returned, and saw under the sun, that the race is not to the swift, nor the battle to the strong, neither yet bread to the wise, nor yet riches to men of understanding, nor yet favor to men of skill: but time and chance happeneth to them all."

Was the time I spent in public life worth all the tragic events that happened at the end? That's not a hard question to answer. I can't look back and change what happened. And I can't deny the fact that I thoroughly enjoyed my 28 years as an elected public official. I have had the opportunity to touch the lives of millions of people in positive ways, throughout Louisiana and throughout this country. In doing so, I had to accept the bad times with the good. There is no one-way street in public life. Garth Brooks said it pretty well: "Our lives are better left to chance. I could've missed the pain, but I'da had to miss the dance."

It's time to move on, and I hope to do so in a positive, productive way. So many people have believed in me, and no doubt they expect me to continue making a meaningful contribution. I just hope I can live up to their expectations.

I am convinced that, despite my being a little older, the possibilities for renewal and wonder are not gone. Public life takes quite a toll. You can never get away from it. I look forward to experiencing life in a broader way. I want to see more, feel more, question more, and experience more.

I have lived through my darkest hour. I can only hope that the recent difficult years are part of a larger story that will overflow with faith, family love, good health, curiosity, and a full engagement with whatever comes next in my life.

I will always be sustained by the belief that I was right and by knowing that, even when justice failed me, I didn't back down.

## Final Thoughts

There were lessons to be learned in the Cascade trial about how justice could be much better served. Here are my conclusions and recommendations.

## I. <u>Prosecutorial Misconduct</u>

*A prosecutor may prosecute with earnestness and vigor—indeed, he should do so. But, while he may strike hard blows, he is not at liberty to strike foul ones. It is as much his duty to refrain from improper methods calculated to produce a wrongful conviction, as it is to use every legitimate means to bring about a just one.*

—Justice George Sutherland
Berger v. United States, 1935[339]

There is little doubt that the prosecutors obstructed the search for truth, both in the initial investigation of Cascade and at the trial itself.

If fairness was a consideration, there was no legitimate reason for the prosecutors to fight as hard as they did to keep important and relevant information away from the jury.

Why wouldn't they turn over to me the handwritten notes of Harry Burton? Why were they so afraid to have Burton explain what his notes said? The Sixth Amendment to the United States Constitution guarantees that, "In all criminal prosecutions, the accused shall enjoy the right ... to be confronted with the witnesses against him." The handwritten notes of the chief witness against me, was an important tool with which I could "confront" the witness and cross-examine him.

The Sixth Amendment also guarantees to any accused a "compulsory process for obtaining witnesses in his favor." In questioning the credibility of Burton, basic fairness calls for me to have the right to present key witnesses who would contradict both his competence and his truthfulness. FBI agent Karen Gardner, attorney C.J. Blache, Bob Bourgeois, and others would have been able to undermine Burton's

---

[339] *Berger v. U.S.*, 295 U.S. 78, 55 S. Ct. 629.

credibility. But the prosecutors fought long and hard to keep key witnesses from testifying about Burton's mistakes.

A prosecutor using false testimony by a witness to gain convictions is certainly not unique in this country. A recent national survey indicates that of all the prosecutorial misconduct that takes place, 22 percent involves the knowing use of false testimony by prosecutors.[340] Isn't this all the more reason why the prosecutors' key witness, Burton, should have been open to rigorous cross-examination about statements he has made in the past and mistakes he has made in both this case and previous related cases?

The use in my trial of information gathered through wiretaps also raises serious questions of prosecutorial abuse if not outright lying on the part of the prosecutors.

The prosecutors based their entire case for obtaining a judicial order to wiretap Edwards's office and home on information provided by two con men, Patrick and Michael Graham. The Graham brothers were facing serious criminal charges in Texas. They had their lawyer approach federal prosecutors in Louisiana to offer information about Governor Edwards in exchange for their receiving immunity for their crimes. They then confected an unsubstantiated story about paying Edwards a bribe to receive a contract to build and operate a juvenile prison in Jena, Louisiana. Based on these allegations, the prosecutors were able to get a federal judge in Shreveport to approve a wiretap of Edwards. To this day, no charges of any kind have been brought involving a prison facility in Jena. Apparently, it was all hogwash.

To get authority for the wiretap, the prosecutors had to convince the judge that the Grahams were a credible source. Even though the prosecutors knew that the Graham brothers were involved in numerous schemes of fraud and deception, none of this was information was told to Shreveport federal judge Don Walter. The prosecutors had no evidence of any wrongdoing by Governor Edwards except the Grahams' story.

---

[340] Jim Dwyer, Peter Neufeld, and Barry Scheck, Actual Innocence: *Five Days to Execution and Other Dispatches from the Wrongly Convicted* (New York: Doubleday, 2000), 265.

So the whole justification for obtaining the wiretaps depended on the credibility of the Grahams.

An FBI agent told Judge Walter that the Grahams were completely trustworthy and that Patrick Graham "has never been known to provide false or misleading information."[341] But at nearly the identical time in a hearing before a bankruptcy judge in Texas, another Louisiana federal prosecutor told this Texas judge that the Graham brothers had done "some horrible things;" that they were "as bad as they come;" that they were "the most manipulative con men probably on the face of the world;" and that "the things that we were not able to independently corroborate we believe are lies, and that is the way it has to be when you deal with the Grahams."[342]

Supreme Court Justice Antonin Scalia in the case of *Morrison v. Olson* summarized the dangers of prosecutorial abuse recently. Scalia quoted the words of the late Supreme Court Justice Robert Jackson:

> *Therein is the most dangerous power of the prosecutor; that he will pick people that he thinks he should get, rather than cases that need to be prosecuted. With the law books filled with a great assortment of crimes, a prosecutor stands a fair chance of finding at least a technical violation of some act on the part of almost anyone. In such a case, it is not a question of discovering the commission of a crime and then looking for the man who has committed it, it is a question of picking the man and then searching the law books, or putting investigators to work, to pin some offense on him.*[343]

---

[341] *U.S. v. Martin et al.* U.S.D.C. Eastern District of La., Criminal Docket No. 99-069, Sect. G (M5-Motion to Suppress Wire Interceptions. P. 18, Exh. 5-B (p. 9).

[342] *Rosalind L. Graham v. Fred Hofheinz as Trustee et al.*, U.S. Bankruptcy Court, Southern District of Texas, Houston Division, 96-4528

[343] *Morrison v. Olson*, 108 S.C. 2597 (1988). Also see a similar discussion of Justice Jackson's quote in Joe Conason and Gene Lyons, *The Hunting of the President: The Ten-Year Campaign to Destroy Bill and Hillary Clinton.* New York: St. Martin's Press 2000 p.185.

This stinging rebuke to prosecutorial misconduct is a strong warning that when prosecutors cross the line, as they certainly did in the Cascade case, their actions undermine the very foundation of our democratic form of government.

Of course, the prosecutors knew the whole story of the Graham brothers, but somebody lied to either the judge in Texas or the judge in Louisiana.

Once the wiretaps were obtained, the prosecutors were hoping to find fraud involving a prison in Jena. That led down a dead-end street. Then there was supposed to be corruption involving a professional basketball team's going to New Orleans. This investigation also led nowhere. Finally, after going through any number of theories about what potential crimes might have taken place, the prosecutors, listening to wiretaps day after day, stumbled across the riverboat-licensing matter and, eventually, the Cascade Insurance case.

There certainly is legitimate use for <u>legal</u> wiretaps to investigate criminal activity. But there should be strong justification to invade an individual's privacy and electronically enter his home. In the Graham case, there was nothing more than second-hand information from a known con man and liar, embellished and offered as credible by prosecutors who knew the source of the information was highly questionable.

The use of wiretaps as a resource to investigate potential crime is fairly new. But protection against the unlawful invasion of one's home goes back hundreds of years, pre-dating our own Constitution. William Pitt spoke eloquently about the basic right to privacy when he told England's Parliament, "The poorest man may, in his cottage, bid defiance to all the forces of the Crown. It may be frail; its roof may shake; the wind may blow through it; the storm may enter; the rain may enter; but the King of England may not enter; all his force dares not cross the threshold of the ruined tenement."[344]

The Fourth Amendment of the United States Constitution also makes it clear that, "The right of the people to be secure

---

[344] Lessons from the Trial, Uelmen, Grald F., Andres and McMeel, 1996, Kansas City, p. 32.

in their persons, houses, papers, and effects, against unreasonable searches and seizures, shall not be violated, and no warrants shall issue, but upon <u>probable cause</u>, supported by Oath or affirmation."

And it's obvious from numerous decisions handed down by the U.S. Supreme Court that the protection of one's privacy extends to the use of the telephone. Justice Potter Stewart made this premise quite clear in his majority decision in *Katz v. U.S.* in 1967: "No less than an individual in a business office, in a friend's apartment, or in a taxicab, a person in a telephone booth may rely upon the protection of the Fourth Amendment. One who occupies it, shuts the door behind him, and pays the toll that permits him to place a call is surely entitled to assume that the words he utters into the mouthpiece will not be broadcast to the world."[345]

When it comes to wiretaps, there has to be strong evidence that a crime has been committed, and there has to be a credible source for that evidence. The Graham brothers were far from a credible source. Again, listen to the prosecutors who called the brothers "as bad as they come," "the most manipulative con men on the face of the world," and who noted that the words of the brothers, unless independently corroborated, "we believe are lies."[346]

The evidence in this case is overwhelming. The prosecutors did not tell the full truth about the Graham brothers to Shreveport judge Don Walter. They obtained their approval to wiretap Edwards' home and office by using false information. To this day, I have no argument with anything said on the tapes. But prosecutors have to follow basic rules, as laid out by the U.S. Supreme Court. In this case, they failed to get legal authorization for any of the wiretaps they obtained.

Additionally, we had to deal with "the thug element" in our case. There was absolutely no justification for prosecutor Sal Perricone to physically attack my lawyer Bill Jeffress. It was completely unprofessional, and it reflected the "gotcha"

---

[345] Ibid. 31.

[346] *Graham v. Hofheinz*, U.S. Bankuptcy Court for the Southern District of Texas, Case #96-46125-II5-13 (1997).

mentality of the prosecution team. Get Brown at any cost, even if it means physically attacking his lawyer. Bill handled the assault well, but he certainly was deeply disturbed by the attack. Perricone should have been immediately removed from the trial, sanctioned, and fully investigated by the court. This reflects poorly on Judge Clement, because such prosecutorial misconduct simply should not be allowed.

Federal prosecutors should adopt several proposals to curb misconduct. First, all states, including Louisiana, should adopt the new rule recently enacted by the Oregon State Supreme Court. Lawyers in Oregon, including prosecutors, are prohibited from engaging in any form of deceit and from encouraging others to lie.[347] One would assume that such a rule would be part of the ethics code of every state bar association. But we are seeing growing signs that federal prosecutors prefer to use covert, rather than overt, operations in their investigations. So be it. Prosecutors should use every tool available to fight crime. But federal prosecutors and FBI agents who are lawyers should not be encouraged to set up innocent victims by outright lying.

In a majority of the states, ethics rules prevent lawyers from engaging in "dishonesty, fraud, deceit, or misrepresentation."[348] Undercover officers, who are non-lawyers, should certainly be given more flexibility. But federal prosecutors and FBI agents who purposely lie should be held fully accountable.[349]

Additionally, I would urge Louisiana, as well as other states to look closely at New York Governor George Pataki's recommendation that tougher penalties be put into place for perjury in criminal cases.[350] The crime of "aggravated perjury" should be adopted, applying to testimony in criminal cases with strong penalties. When a witness goes on the stand under

---

[347] *Washington Post.* August 9, 2001 p. A-3.
[348] Louisiana State Bar Association Rules of Professional Conduct, Art. XVI, Rule 84.4. Similar rules are applicable in virtually every state.
[349] In 1998, Congress passed the McDade law, which simply requires federal prosecutors to comply with state ethics laws. Even Congress has concerns about federal prosecutors lying or misrepresenting the facts. See *U.S. News and World Report*, October 16, 2000.
[350] *New York Times,* June 13, 2001.

oath and commits perjury against a defendant, his false statements should be considered an extraordinary crime. False statements are given under oath by witnesses, including law-enforcement officers, much too often.

Judge Alex Kozinski of the United States Court of Appeals for the Ninth Circuit said it plainly: "It's an open secret long shared by prosecutors, defense lawyers and judges that perjury is widespread among law enforcement officers."[351]

I'm not sure how "widespread" such perjury is in Louisiana. But it should be a crime when an FBI agent or other law-enforcement officer commits such an act, and someone who testifies on the witness stand giving false information against a defendant should be held accountable. I applaud the efforts by the New York governor and hope other states will follow suit.

Finally, any federal prosecutor who attacks a defense lawyer should be charged with a felony. Under federal law (18 U.S.C. s 111), it is a crime for any citizen to physically attack a federal law-enforcement officer in the line of duty. But there is no such crime for a federal prosecutor who physically attacks a defense lawyer or any private citizen. What's sauce for the goose is sauce for the gander. When my lawyer was physically attacked in front of Judge Clement during my trial, the prosecutor should have been arrested on the spot. Congress should change and enlarge the existing law to protect defense lawyers and private citizens in the same way it protects federal prosecutors.

There are many decent, hard-working, competent, and law-abiding prosecutors on both the state and federal level in our country. But, as in any profession, there are a few bad eggs, which are too often tolerated by their superiors and by the courts. Strong standards that apply to prosecutors, as well as private citizens will go a long way toward restoring the belief that there is equal justice in our country.

---

[351] Stuart Taylor Jr., "For the Record," *American Lawyer* (October 1995), 72.

## II. <u>Abolish the Secrecy</u>

*Secrecy is for losers. It is time to dismantle government's secrecy.*
—Senator Daniel Patrick Moynihan[352]

You would have to look long and hard to find another trial anywhere in America over the last hundred years that can compare to the Cascade case in terms of the secrecy imposed by the two federal judges. A review of virtually every high-profile trial in this country in recent years shows that much less secrecy was imposed. The World Trade Center bombing case of 1993, the O.J. Simpson trial, the Oklahoma City bombing trial of Timothy McVeigh, Waco, Ruby Ridge—none of those trials had a veil of secrecy covering the proceedings from day one, as mine did.

## III. <u>Gag Orders</u>

*For if Men are precluded from offering their sentiments on a matter, which may involve the most serious and alarming consequences, reason is of no use to us; the freedom of speech may be taken away, and dumb and silent we may be led, like sheep to the slaughter.*[353]
—Gen. George Washington, address to the officers of the army, Newbury, New York, March 15, 1783

*But this is slavery, not to speak one's thought.*
—Euripides, *The Phoenician Women*

There certainly have been cases in our country where circumstances caused the court to legitimately impose restrictions on what information could be made public. When prosecutions involve international drug lords, terrorists, and others who pose a direct danger to the courts, the jurors, and the public at large, then it is proper to impose reasonable restrictions. But in the Cascade case there was no justification

---

[352] Daniel Patrick Moynihan, *Secrecy: The American Experience* (New Haven: Yale University Press. 1998).
[353] John C. Fitzpatrick, ed., *The Writings of George Washington* (1938), Vol. 21, p. 225.

for imposing a veil of secrecy over virtually the entire proceedings.

In federal jurisdictions throughout this country, gag orders are rarely used. The general test that most courts observe is that there must be a "clear and present danger" or a "serious and imminent threat" of prejudicing a fair trial.

In the Sixth Circuit Court of Appeals (which includes the states of Kentucky, Michigan, Ohio, and Tennessee), the "clear and present danger" test is used, but the court goes even further. It makes clear that there must be specific evidence that no reasonable person could expect a fair trial to take place unless a gag order is issued. The leading case, *United States v. Ford,* involved the criminal prosecution of a sitting member of Congress. Although the prosecutors tried their best to keep him from speaking out and defending himself, the court said strongly that such an order would be wrong. The court reasoned, "A criminal defendant awaiting trial in a controversial case has the full power of the government arrayed against him and the full spotlight of media attention focused upon him. The defendant's interest in replying to the charges and to the associated adverse publicity, thus, is at a peak. So is the public's interest in the proper functioning of the judicial machinery."[354]

The Third Circuit Court of Appeals (which includes the states of Delaware, New Jersey, Pennsylvania, and the Virgin Islands) also has upheld the right of a public official to speak out. The court stated, "A public official has a right and sometimes the duty, to address issues of public concern." The court further said that when a public official is a defendant, the fact that his public statements about the litigation "could potentially interfere with a fair trial do[es] not justify imposing restrictions on that official's speech unless there is a *clear threat* to [that] right."[355]

The Seventh Circuit (Illinois, Indiana, and Wisconsin) has stated, "Before a trial court can limit defendants' and their attorneys' exercise of first amendment rights of freedom of

---

[354] *U.S. v. Ford,* 830 F.2d 296 (1987).
[355] Dailey v. Systems Innovation, Inc., 832 F.2d 93 (1998).

speech, the record must contain sufficient specific findings by the trial court establishing that defendants' and their attorneys' conduct is a 'serious and imminent threat to the administration of justice.'"[356]

Numerous other federal and state courts have reached the same conclusion, but gag orders seem to be "in style" in Louisiana. The prosecution can file charge after charge, and motion after motion, making all types of outrageous allegations that are front-page news. This is exactly what happened in my case. Yet my hands were tied, and I could not say a word. Gag orders, like those imposed in Louisiana, are unfair to the defendant and are just plain wrong.

## IV. Anonymous Juries

*Unquestionably, the empanelment of an anonymous jury is a drastic measure, which should be undertaken only in limited and carefully delineated circumstances. An anonymous jury raises the suspicion that the defendant is a dangerous person from whom jurors must be protected, thereby implicating the defendant's constitutional right to presumption of innocence.*[357]

—Judge Maurice Mitchell Paul

Unless the defendants pose a threat to the safety or integrity of the jury, there is never justification for having any case tried before an anonymous jury.

Judge Polozola ordered an anonymous jury initially in the Edwards riverboat-licensing case. He followed this procedure by ordering another anonymous jury in the Cascade Insurance case. In both cases, Polozola issued this order without explanation and after closing all proceedings to the press. The very fact that he held "closed proceedings" fueled speculation that prosecutors might have evidence that the defendants somehow posed a risk to the safety of the jurors.

It is unprecedented for a judge to order an anonymous jury in a case that does not involve allegations of organized crime, violence, or jury tampering.

---

[356] *Chase v. Robson,* 435 F.2d 1059 (1970).
[357] *U.S. v. Ross,* 33 F.3rd 1507, 1519 (11th Cir. 1994).

If there is justification for an anonymous jury, the defendants and the public have the right to know the reasons. All filings related to the anonymous jury in both cases were placed under seal. The defendants, including me, were rightly concerned that the press and the public were misconstruing the order. Everyone charged in both the riverboat-licensing case and the Cascade case requested that the record be unsealed and that any hearings held be open to the press. Polozola denied all such requests.

As anticipated, the press assumed the worst. The *Baton Rouge Advocate* reported that anonymous juries are rarely granted and that there must be some evidence of "a pattern of violence" or of a propensity to influence jurors.[358]

Judge Polozola not only ordered an anonymous jury without giving any explanation for his action on the record, he further ordered that the issue "not be discussed publicly or in open court." This, of course, engendered further speculation that the prosecutors had proof of some present danger to the jury.[359]

There is no doubt that anonymous juries have a direct impact on a defendant's constitutional right to the presumption of innocence. "They send an unmistakable message to the jurors that the defendants are dangerous people from whom they need protection."[360]

As the Fifth Circuit Court of Appeals in New Orleans has observed, "The defendant has a right to a jury of known individuals not just because information [about the jurors] yields valuable clues for purposes of jury selection, but also because the verdict is both personalized and personified when rendered by 12 known fellow citizens."[361]

In some of the most highly publicized trials in America, where there were allegations that numerous people had been murdered, those charged were still given the names, addresses, and places of employment of potential jurors. The Unabomber

---

[358] *Baton Rouge Advocate,* September 15, 1999, p. 1B.
[359] "Some Scholars Say Anonymous Juries, Troubling, Growing," *Baton Rouge Advocate,* January 11, 2000, p. 14A.
[360] *U.S. v. Ross,* 33 F.3d 1507, 1519 (11th Cir. 1994).
[361] *United States v. Sanchez,* 74 F.3d 562, 565 (5th Cir. 1996).

trial in New York, and the Oklahoma City bombing trial of Timothy McVeigh each allowed basic information about the jurors to be given to those charged.

Again, things work differently in Louisiana. But no matter how much research you do, you won't find less justification for an anonymous jury anywhere in this country.

Anonymous juries, except in the most extreme circumstances, are wrong; the anonymous jury in the Cascade case was more than wrong. It was unconscionable.

## V.  <u>Decisions Behind Closed Doors</u>

*A trial is a public event. What transpires in the courtroom is public property.*
—Justice William O. Douglas[362]

At least in the riverboat-licensing case, Judge Polozola held a hearing "behind closed doors" before ordering an anonymous jury. In the Cascade case, he held no hearing at all.

When it came time to pick the jury in the Cascade case, all questioning of potential jurors was done in secret; the public and the press were ordered out of the courtroom. Judge Clement carried on Polozola's policy of complete secrecy.

The Sixth Amendment of the United State Constitution entitles any defendant to a "public trial."[363] The U.S. Supreme Court has always supported public trials: "The knowledge that every criminal trial is subject to a contemporaneous review in the forum of public opinion is an effective restraint on possible abuse of judicial power."[364]

There was no justification for Judge Clement to question potential jurors in secrecy and away from the public eye.

---

[362] *Craig v. Harney,* 331 U.S. 367 at 374 (1947).
[363] United States Constitution, Amendment VI.
[364] *In re Oliver*, 333 U.S. 257, 270 (1948).

## VI. Television in the Courtroom

*It is desirable that the trial of causes takes place under the public eye...because it is of the highest moment that those who administer justice should always act under the sense of public responsibility, and that every citizen should be able to satisfy himself within his own eyes as to the mode in which a public duty is performed.*
— Justice Oliver Wendell Holmes, Jr.[365]

Most federal courts in our country ban cameras in the courtroom. It's time to open them up to public scrutiny. In a democracy, the public has a right to see its court system in operation, close up.

We have a strong tradition of public trials in this country. In early colonial America, courthouses were the centers of community life, and most citizens regularly attended criminal trials. In fact, trials were scheduled on designated days and often became community events. Citizens were knowledgeable about the trials, and there was wide participation in the process. Particularly in rural America, trials were often scheduled on market day, when local farmers came to town for supplies. The courthouse was the center of activity, and courtrooms were often built to accommodate crowds of more than 300 observers.

Back then, citizens watched defendants being tried, knew when judges issued ridiculous rulings, and saw firsthand when justice was perverted. Whatever happened, the citizens were there, watching. The court system belonged to them. The televising of criminal trials would merely be an extension of this direct review by the average citizen.

Some argue that televising criminal trials would create a circus atmosphere. There is no reason to think this would be the case. In fact, many of our most dignified ceremonies, including church services and inaugurations, are televised without losing any of their dignity. Judge Burton Katz said it well: "We should bring pressure to bear on federal judges to open up their courtrooms to public scrutiny. As life appointees, they enjoy great entitlements and wield enormous

---

[365] *Cowley v. Pulsifer*, 137 Massachusetts 392, at 394 (1884).

power. They bear close watching by an informed public. I guarantee that the public would be amazed at what goes on in some federal courtrooms."[366]

As an attorney, I participated in Louisiana's first televised trial before the Louisiana Supreme Court in 1997. Senator Cleo Fields opposed my efforts to impound the cars of uninsured drivers. The proceedings were televised without a hitch. No one pandered to the cameras, and the entire procedure was straightforward and dignified. This was an important issue to many citizens in Louisiana, and they were entitled to hear the arguments and watch the trial in progress.

Virtually every federal court in America refuses to allow television cameras in the courtroom. One exception is in New Orleans where federal judge Morley Sear televises the entire proceedings. Each side has access to a tape of each day's proceedings. The cameras are concealed, and there has been no concern expressed by prosecutors or defense attorneys.

As Harvard professor Alan Dershowitz wrote in *Reasonable Doubts*:

> *Live television coverage may magnify the faults in the legal system, and show it, warts and all. But in a democracy the public has the right to see its institutions in operation, close up. Moreover, live coverage generally brings out the best, not the worst, in judges, lawyers, and other participants. If people think that what they see in televised trials is bad, I suggest they go to their local courtroom and sit quietly in the back row. They will see laziness, lack of preparation, rudeness, stupidity, posturing, and plain, ordinary nastiness—and I'm just talking about the judges! The lawyers can be even worse. The video camera helps to keep the system honest by keeping it open.*[367]

[366] Burton S. Katz, *Justice Overruled: Unmasking the Criminal Justice System* (New York: Time Warner, 1997), 238.

[367] Alan M. Dershowitz, *Reasonable Doubts* (New York: Simon & Schuster, 1996), 203. (Dershowitz and his law firm represented Governor Edwards during his appeal.)

## VII.<u>The Cost to Defend</u>

*We set our sights on the embarrassing target of mediocrity. I guess that means about halfway. And that raises a question. Are we willing to put up with halfway justice? To my way of thinking, one-half justice must mean one-half injustice, and one-half injustice is no justice at all.*[368]
—Harold Clarke, Chief Justice,
Georgia Supreme Court

The cost of defending oneself in a white-collar criminal case is staggering. Very few persons charged can afford to pay the cost of their defense. There is certainly no "level playing field" for defendants compared to the massive resources at the disposal of the prosecutors. If our system of justice in America is going to work, a defendant needs the resources to deal with the barrage of stumbling blocks thrown by the prosecutors.

In my case, I was forced to marshal my resources: all of my savings, plus substantial help from my family and my wife's family. If I had not had these financial resources, the consequences would have been much worse. Indigent defendants are particularly at the mercy of a criminal-justice system that provides few resources. There has to be a better way to see that justice is done. If, in fact, the purpose of a criminal trial is to determine the truth, then the person charged should have the resources necessary to put up an adequate defense. We will never see a level playing field. The federal government just has too many resources. During the Cascade trial, the courtroom was often half filled with prosecutors, FBI agents, and support staff. I have heard that more than 50 people worked for years on the Cascade case, at a cost of millions of dollars to the taxpayers. No defendant can match such resources. But if justice is to keep her scales in balance, a defendant must have adequate funding to challenge the prosecution.

Commenting on the cost of justice, law professor Erwin Chermerinsky says: "Most criminal defendants receive legal representation that is like the medical care provided at a public hospital—good care, but limited by all of the constraints

---

[368] Dwyer, Neufeld, and Scheck, *Actual Innocence,* p. 183.

imposed by an underfinanced, overused system. There is a double standard of justice in American society, one for the rich and one for the poor."[369]

There is something wrong with a judicial system in which persons who are well off can obtain better legal help—or better medical care—than the poor. Even if innocent defendants are eventually found not guilty, they are often financially crippled for the rest of their lives because of the high legal costs.

The *New York Times* has editorialized about the disparity of justice in our country: "It is no secret that rich and poor defendants have vastly different experiences in the criminal justice system. What continues to shock, however, is just how raw a deal the poorest defendants get. A series in *The Times* last year told of one New York lawyer who represented 1,600 poor clients at once. A defendant facing life in prison in New York State, the articles noted, could get a lawyer who is paid just $693, less than the cost of an average real estate closing."[370]

A glaring example of the disparity in the costs of criminal defense is the case of former United States Attorney General Edwin Meese, who served under Ronald Reagan. Shortly after taking office, Meese asked the federal government to pay his legal bills, which exceeded $700,000, incurred defending himself against charges of impropriety for accepting loans from people later appointed to federal jobs. The federal government reimbursed Meese, whose lawyers billed him $250 per hour. The lawyers did excellent work and certainly deserved to have their fees paid. That wasn't the problem. The real disparity, a scandal if you want to call it that, was the fact that Meese, while demanding that the government pay $250 an hour to his lawyers, was insisting that the same government be limited to paying $75 an hour, with fixed maximums, for the defense of indigents, even those charged with far more serious violations.[371]

---

[369] *Los Angeles Daily News,* July 6, 1994.
[370] *New York Times,* August 23, 2002.
[371] Alan M. Dershowitz, *Reversal of Fortune: Inside the Von Bulow Case.* New York: Random House, 1986, 258.

There is a well-known cartoon of a lawyer sitting at his desk, asking a new client a pressing question: "Well, now, just how much justice can you afford?"

The criminal-justice system should not require that an accused person bankrupt himself and his family to match the unlimited resources of the federal government in a criminal trial.

## VIII. Term Limits for Federal Judges

*There is no happiness, there is no liberty, there is no enjoyment of life, unless a man can say when he rises in the morning, he shall be subject to the decisions of no unjust judge today.*
—Daniel Webster

Federal judges are the only public officials in America who hold their positions for life. No matter how incompetent their actions on the bench or how outrageous their decisions, they are, for all practical purposes, immune from any review of what they do. Their power comes from Article III of the United States Constitution, which gives all federal judges lifetime appointments. Removal only happens through an elaborate impeachment process, in which the House of Representatives brings the charges and the Senate conducts the trial of the judge. If two-thirds of the Senate votes for removal, then and only then must the judge step down from the bench.

As Judge Burton Katz wrote in his criticism of lifetime appointments:

> In our 200-plus years as a nation, only a few federal judges have been formally impeached. The impeachment process itself, because it is unwieldy, divisive, and time consuming, is rarely invoked.
> Hence, federal judges are, frankly speaking, judges for life. No one can touch them. They are derisively called Article III Judges because their behavior is frequently autocratic, capricious and grandiose.

*Horror stories abound from the darkened chambers of the federal courts. When judges become lifetime appointees, it seems that at times they think they are in lockstep with God.* [372]

There are certainly many competent, hardworking judges on the federal bench. But when a defendant is faced with a judge who abuses his authority, there is frankly, little that can be done. The district court judge in the federal system controls the rules of the game. Although juries are supposed to decide the innocence or guilt of a defendant, they are often constrained from seeing a complete picture of the defendant's case because of the limitations set by the federal judge.

As noted criminal defense attorney Gerry Spence concludes, "In America, trial by jury has become another myth. In the trial itself, the jury is permitted to hear only the evidence the judge will allow." [373]

As I have repeatedly pointed out, the jury in my case was kept from hearing and seeing significant evidence in my favor. The jury received a distorted view of my defense, not because of their actions, but because of limitations set by the federal judge.

How can we make federal judges more accountable for their decisions? Obviously, impeachment does not work. As Thomas Jefferson commented, the impeachment provision of the Constitution "is not even a scarecrow." [374] There have to be more options.

There is growing sentiment in this country in support of term limits or reconfirmation for federal judges. California Attorney General Dan Lungren is pushing for a plan that ends lifetime tenure. He has received support from Senator Bob Smith of New Hampshire, who would impose a 10-year limit on all federal judges, including Supreme Court justices. Other members of Congress, including Congressman Henry Hyde of

---

[372] Katz, *Justice Overruled: Unmasking the Criminal Justice* System. New York: Warner Books, 1997, 175.

[373] Gerry Spence, *Give Me Liberty* (New York St. Martin's Press, 1998), 312.

[374] Merrill D. Peterson, ed., *The Portable Thomas Jefferson* (New York: Penguin Books, 1977), 562.

Illinois, have made similar proposals. Several law professors who have clerked for Supreme Court justices have suggested term limits on federal judges. And the *Washington Post* recently stated, "Only one of 50 states copies the federal government's particular brand of unelected life tenure for its highest court and no major democracy abroad does so. Most state and foreign constitutions prescribe a fixed number of years in office or a mandatory retirement age for both."[375]

I suggest a plan that would require all federal judges to submit to periodic reconfirmation by the United States Senate. Perhaps it would require a two-thirds vote to actually remove a sitting judge from office. And reconfirmation would take place every 10 years.

There has to be some requirement that judges justify the decisions they make and the procedures with which they run their courtrooms. A decent judge concerned about fairness to both sides should have no problem. Arrogant judges might have a little explaining to do. So be it.

Judges will tell you that they already have a procedure with which to police themselves. Under a law passed by Congress in 1980, each judicial circuit in the United States (there are 13) has a committee of judges; the 13 committees form a judicial council that oversees all the judges' conduct. But as Max Boot wrote in his book about incompetence on the bench, "These councils operate largely in secret and, at any rate, don't have the power to do anything beyond scolding recalcitrant judges. Even that power is exercised infrequently—which is no surprise, since this is the fox guarding the henhouse."[376]

As Americans, we assume that judges at all levels will be fair in their interpretation of the law. We assume the same thing about the referees in any pro or college football game in the country—the referees know the rules and will do the right thing. Yet when the leagues are not satisfied with the quality of the refereeing, the officials are replaced. The judge is

---

[375] *Washington Post*, August 11, 2002.
[376] Max Boot, Out of Order: Arrogance, Corruption and Incompetence on the Bench New York: Basic Books, 1998), 198.

certainly the most important component in any trial, even more than the composition of the jury.

It comes down to a question of accountability. Any well-qualified federal judge worth his salt should have no objection to a little public scrutiny every 10 years. Reviewing the performances of our federal judges will go a long way in raising the overall standards and quality of our judiciary throughout this country. As Chief Justice Warren Burger once observed: "In a country like ours, no public institution, or the people who operate it, can be above public debate."[377]

Max Boot sums it up well: "While we should always retain a high level of respect for the judiciary in principle, we shouldn't be afraid to treat individual occupants of the office with the contempt and scorn they deserve when they issue bad rulings."[378]

---

In short, we can greatly improve the present federal judicial system. It is time to open up the courtroom, abolish secrecy, televise trials so the public can watch our judges in action, and require all judges to be reconfirmed every 10 years. These few suggestions would go a long way toward silencing the criticism being leveled at our federal judiciary.

---

[377] Warren Burger, "Remarks to the Ohio Judicial Conference," September 4, 1968.
[378] Boot, Max, *Out of Order*, 22.

# Bibliography

## Books

Auden, W. H. *The Age of Anxiety.* New York: Random House, 1946.

Barth, Alan. *The Rights of Free Men: An Essential Guide to Civil Liberties.* Ed. James E. Clayton. New York: Alfred A. Knopf,, 1983.

Bass, Jack, and Jack Nelson. *The Orangeburg Massacre.* Cleveland: World, 1970.

Bock, Alan W. *Ambush At Ruby Ridge: How Government Agents Set Randy Weaver Up and Took His Family Down.* New York: Berkley Books, 1995.

Boot, Max. *Out of Order: Arrogance, Corruption and Incompetence on the Bench.* New York: Basic Books, 1998.

Bridges, Tyler. *Bad Bet on the Bayou: The Rise of Gambling in Louisiana and the Fall of Governor Edwin Edwards.* New York: Farrar, Straus and Giroux, 2001.

Cochran, Johnnie L. Jr., and Tim Rutten. *Journey to Justice.* New York: Ballantine Books, 1996.

Cohen, William S., and George J. Mitchell. *Men of Zeal: A Candid Inside Story of the Iran-Contra Hearings.* New York: Viking Penguin, 1988.

Conason, Joe, and Gene Lyons. *The Hunting of the President: The Ten-Year Campaign to Destroy Bill and Hillary Clinton.* New York: St. Martin's Press, 2000.

Connally, John, and Mickey Herskowitz. *In History's Shadow.* New York: Hyperion, 1993.

Cummings, Homer S. *Federal Justice: Chapters in the History of Justice and the Federal Executive.* Cambridge, Mass.: Da Capo Press, 1937.

Dershowitz, Alan M. *Letters to a Young Lawyer.* New York: Basic Books, 2001

Dershowitz, Alan M. *Reasonable Doubts.* New York: Simon & Schuster, 1996.

Dershowitz, Alan M. *Reversal of Fortune: Inside the Von Bulow Case.* New York: Random House, 1986.

Dwyer, Jim, Peter Neufeld, and Barry Scheck. *Actual Innocence: Five Days to Execution and Other Dispatches from the Wrongly Convicted.* New York: Doubleday, 2000.

Elffers, Joost, and Robert Greene. *The 48 Laws of Power.* New York: Penguin Putnam, 1998.

Fitzmorris, James E. Jr., and Kenneth D. Myers. *Frankly, Fitz.* Gretna, La.: Pelican, 1992.

Fitzpatrick, John C., ed. *The Writings of George Washington.* Vol. 22.1938.

Gilley, Billy H., ed. *Fragments: Wiley W. Hilburn's North Louisiana.* Ruston, La.: McGinty Publications, 1987.

Goldfarb, Ronald L. *TV or Not TV: Television, Justice and the Courts.* New York: New York University Press, 1998.

Guinther, John. *The Jury in America and the Civil Juror: A Research Project.* New York: Facts On File, 1988.

Gunn, Cathy. *Nightmare on Lime Street: Whatever Happened to Lloyd's of London?* London: Smith Gryphon, 1992.

James, Robert Rhodes, ed. *Winston S. Churchill: His Complete Speeches 1897–1963.* Broomall, Penn.: Chelsea House, 1974.

Jeffreys, Diarmuid. *The Bureau: Inside the Modern FBI.* Boston: Houghton Mifflin, 1995.

Jones, Stephen, and Peter Israel. *Others Unknown: Timothy McVeigh and the Oklahoma City Bombing Conspiracy.* New York: Public Affairs, 1998.

Katz, Burton S. *Justice Overruled: Unmasking the Criminal Justice System.* New York: Warner Books, 1997.

Kilgo, John, Sally Jenkins, and Dean Smith. *Dean Smith: A Coach's Life.* New York: Random House, 1999.

Lee, Wen Ho, and Helen Zia. *My Country versus Me: The Firsthand Account by the Los Alamos Scientist Who Was Falsely Accused of Being a Spy.* New York: Hyperion, 2001.

Luessenhop, Elizabeth, and Martin Mayer. *Risky Business: An Insider's Account of the Disaster at Lloyd's of London.* New York: Scribner, 1995.

Maginnis, John. *Cross to Bear: America's Most Dangerous Politics.* Baton Rouge, La.: Darkhorse Press, 1992.

Maginnis, John. *The Last Hayride.* Baton Rouge, La.: Gris Gris Press, 1984.

Manchester, William. *The Death of a President*. New York: Harper & Row, 1963.

Mann, Robert. *Legacy to Power: Senator Russell Long of Louisiana*. New York: Paragon House, 1992.

Mantle, Jonathan. *For Whom the Bell Tolls: The Lessons of Lloyd's of London*. London: Sinclair-Stevenson, 1992.

Messick, Hank. *The Politics of Prosecution*. Ottawa, Ill.: Caroline House Books, 1978.

Miller, Merle. *Plain Speaking: An Oral Biography of Harry S. Truman*. New York: Berkley Books, 1960.

Morris, Dick. *Behind the Oval Office: Winning the Presidency in the Nineties*. New York: Random House, 1997.

Moynihan, Daniel Patrick. *Secrecy: The American Experience*. New Haven: Yale University Press, 1998.

Peterson, Merrill D., ed. *The Portable Thomas Jefferson*. New York: Penguin Books, 1977.

Pizzi, William T. *Trials without Truth*. New York: New York University Press, 1999.

Randal, Henry Stephens. *The Life of Thomas Jefferson*. Freeport, N.Y.: Books for Libraries Press, 1970.

Raphael, Adam. *Ultimate Risk: The Inside Story of the Lloyd's Catastrophe*. London: Bantam Press, 1994.

Reeves, Richard. *President Kennedy: Profile of Power*. New York: Simon & Schuster, 1993.

Robertson, J. Logie, ed. *The Political Works of Sir Walter Scott*. London: Oxford University Press, 1904.

Safire, William. *The First Dissident: The Book of Job in Today's Politics*. New York: Random House, 1992.

Safire, William. *Full Disclosure*. Garden City, N.Y.: Doubleday , 1977.

Schmidt, Susan, and Michael Weisskopf. *Truth at Any Cost: Ken Starr and the Unmaking of Bill Clinton*. New York: HarperCollins, 2000.

Sinclair, Upton. *The Cry for Justice: An Anthology of the Literature.* New York: Barricade Books, 1915.

Sorensen, Theodore C., ed. *"Let the Word Go Forth:" The Speeches, Statements, and Writings of John F. Kennedy, 1947 to 1963.* New York: Delacorte Press, 1988.

Spence, Gerry. *Give Me Liberty! Freeing Ourselves in the Twenty-first Century.* New York: St. Martin's Press, 1998.

Spence, Gerry. *With Justice for None: Destroying an American Myth.* New York: Random House, 1989.

Taylor, Gary, and Stanley Wells, eds. *The Complete Oxford Shakespeare: I: Histories.* Oxford: Oxford University Press, 1987.

Thomas, Evan. *The Man to See: Edward Bennett Williams, Ultimate Insider, Legendary Trial Lawyer.* New York: Simon & Schuster, 1991.

Uelmen, Gerald F. *Lessons from the Trial: The People v. O. J. Simpson.* Kansas City, Mo.: Andrews and McMeel, 1996.

Uviller, H. Richard. *Virtual Justice: The Flawed Prosecution of Crime in America.* New Haven: Yale University Press, 1996.

Warren, Robert Penn. *All the King's Men.* New York: Harcourt Brace Jovanovich, 1946.

Wishman, Seymour. *Anatomy of a Jury: The System on Trial.* New York: Random House, 1986.

Woodward, Bob. *Shadow: Five Presidents and the Legacy of Watergate* New York: Simon & Schuster, 1999.

**Periodicals**

Covaleski, John M. "Stamping Out Insurer Fraud." *Best's Review* October 1994: 25, 26, 28, 30, and 31.

Lebensen, Laurie. "Criminal Law Pardon Me." *The National Law Journal* March 2001.

*Louisiana Bar Journal*, Vol. 48, No. 4: 285.*National Underwriter*, January 13, 1992.

*National Underwriter*, January 13, 1999.

Taylor, Stuart Jr. "For the Record." *American Lawyer* (October 1995): 72.

## Newspapers

*Abbeville Meridional*
*Alexandria Daily Town Talk*
*Baton Rouge Morning Advocate*
*Caldwell Watchman*
*Church Point News*
*Colfax Chronicle*
*Concordia Sentinel*
*Crowley Post Signal*
*Franklin Sun*
*Gambit Weekly* (New Orleans)
*Gueydan Journal*
*Houma Business News*
*Journal of Commerce* (New York)
*Lake Arthur Sun Times*
*Las Vegas Sun*
*London Observer*
*Los Angeles Daily News*
*Monroe News-Star*
*New England Courant* (Boston)
*New Orleans CitiBusiness*
*New Orleans Times-Picayune*
*New York Times*
*Riverside Reader* (Baton Rouge)
*Ruston Morning Paper*
*Shreveport Journal*
*Shreveport Times*
*USA Today*
*Ville Platte Gazette*
*Wall Street Journal*
*Washington Post*

## Miscellaneous Media

The Associated Press
www.Deductbox.com
Political Fax Weekly

## Other Sources

Dan Fogelberg. <u>Leader of the Band</u>. Very Best of Dan Fogelberg, Sony/Legacy, 2001.

Janis Joplin. <u>Me and Bobby McGee</u>. Pearl, words and music by Kris Kristofferson, Columbia Records, 1971.

John Elwood, William H. Jeffress Jr., and Scott Nelson. *James H. Brown Jr. v. United States of America: Petition for a Writ of Certiorari.* Washington, D.C.: Wilson-Epes Printing Co., 2001.

Tom Petty. <u>I Won't Back Down</u>. Tom Petty and the Heartbreakers Greatest Hits, MCA Records, Inc., 1993.

Tom Waits. <u>On the Nickel</u>. Heart Attack and Vine, Electra Entertainment, 1980.

# Index

# G

Gag Order, 74-75, 109-110, 112, 115-117, 148-149, 166-167, 174, 177-180, 192, 194, 196-197, 200, 205-206, 217, 221-222, 231, 272-274, 276-278, 320, 385
Gardner, Karen, 180, 237, 377
Garza, Emilio, 338
George Bush, 20, 268
Gibson, Ken, 202
Gill, James, 87, 142-143, 152, 246, 256, 274, 318, 330
Gillers, Stephen, 207
Gilley, Mickey, 290
Gonzales, Ed, 19, 29, 36-38, 43, 46, 63-64, 75, 159-160, 163-164, 204, 213, 235, 237
Gore, Al, 21, 62
Graham, Patrick, 88, 379
Grandfather Mountain, 24, 26
Gravel, Camille, 64-65, 94, 106, 120, 187, 211, 212-214, 219-220, 282, 314, 342
Gravel, Evelyn, 342
Gray, Rannah, 90, 130, 137, 144
Green, Doug, 5, 134, 202
Greenberg, Todd, 181
Guidry, Bobby, 73
Guidry, Robert, 188

# H

Haik, Ted, 147
Hainkel, John, 172
Halpin, Stan, 178
Hanna, Sam, 126, 139, 263, 289
Hansen, Robert, 296
Harriman, Averill, 216
Harriman, Pamela, 39
Havel, Vaclav, 72
Higginson, Stephen, 341, 344-345
Hilburn, Wiley, 265
Hill, Jack, 57
Hill, John, 64, 111, 127, 152, 193, 205, 276, 278-279, 288, 320-321, 331
Hill, Sam, Dr., vii
Hingle, Jiff, 21, 150, 157, 222-223, 243, 299, 305
Hingle, Madalyne, 21, 109, 150, 156-157, 299

Hudson, Tommy, 31
Humphrey, Hubert, 22-23
Hurricane Betsy, 35
Hyde, Henry, 394
Hymel, L.J., 200, 204, 213, 219

# I

Ieyoub, Richard, 5, 18, 75, 84
International Holocaust Commission, 70, 318
Irwin, Steve, 60

# J

Jackson, Robert, 379
Jefferson, Thomas, 394, 399
Jeffords, Jim, 169
Jeffress, Bill, 64, 84, 88-89, 94-95, 106, 110, 120, 128, 149, 155, 157, 166, 174-175, 178, 189, 191, 194, 198, 204, 206, 210-211, 217, 219, 222-223, 231-232, 234, 236-237, 240-241, 243-244, 247-248, 251, 254, 261, 264, 267-268, 272, 282-283, 285-286, 299, 302, 310-311, 314-315, 323, 327, 329, 340-342, 344-346, 350, 354, 357, 360-361, 368, 381
Johnson, Bobby, 73, 182
Johnson, Ernest, 181-182
Johnson, Lyndon, 22
Johnston, Bill, 291
Joplin, Janis, 314, 402
Jordan, Eddie, 86-87, 92, 127-128, 190-191, 308
Jordan, Ingasol, 23
Jordan, Michael, viii, 22, 198, 323
Justice Department, 52, 60, 83, 90, 94-95, 97, 128, 154, 167, 200, 291-293, 299, 304, 308-309, 337, 375

# K

Kadair, Roy, 191
Katz, Burton, 389, 393
Kennedy, George, 90, 137, 145, 153
Kennedy, John F., x-xi, 400
Kennedy, Ted, 22
Kennedy, Vern, 152
King, Carolyn, 204

For additional background on the entire "Brown Controversy" and current information on Jim Brown's continuing efforts to clear his name, log on to http://www.jimbrownla.com.

Additional copies of this book *Justice Denied* can be ordered through the website and are also available on compact disc.

## About the Author

Jim Brown has been one of the most enduring public officials in Louisiana over the past 32 years. He wrote many of the laws that govern Louisiana today as a state senator. He served for eight years as the Secretary of State where he was named as the most effective official in that position in the state's history. He spent 12 years as Commissioner of Insurance where he received international recognition as one of the country's top regulators. He has taught Louisiana history at both Tulane University and Louisiana State University, and has written and been published extensively about Louisiana political life. He is the father of four children, and lives in Baton Rouge, Louisiana with his wife, Gladys.